Second Language A‹ and Mixed Methods ʀᴇˢᴇᴀɾᴄʜ

For a complete list of titles please visit: www.cambridge.org/elt/silt

Second Language Assessment and Mixed Methods Research

Edited by

Aleidine J Moeller
University of Nebraska–Lincoln

John W Creswell
University of Nebraska–Lincoln

and

Nick Saville
Cambridge English Language Assessment

CAMBRIDGE
UNIVERSITY PRESS

CAMBRIDGE
UNIVERSITY PRESS

University Printing House, Cambridge CB2 8BS, United Kingdom

Cambridge University Press is part of the University of Cambridge.

It furthers the University's mission by disseminating knowledge in the pursuit of education, learning and research at the highest international levels of excellence.

www.cambridge.org
Information on this title: www.cambridge.org/9781316505038

First published 2016

A catalogue record for this publication is available from the British Library

Library of Congress Cataloguing in Publication data
Names: Moeller, Aleidine Kramer, 1948- editor. | Creswell, John W., editor. | Saville, Nick., editor.
Title: Second language assessment and mixed methods research / Edited by Aleidine Moeller, University of Nebraska-Lincoln and John W Creswell, University of Nebraska-Lincoln and Nick Saville, Cambridge English Language Assessment.
Description: Cambridge ; New York : Cambridge University Press, [2016] | Series: Studies in language testing; 43 | Includes bibliographical references and index.
Identifiers: LCCN 2015034890 | ISBN 9781316505038
Subjects: LCSH: Second language acquisition–Methodology. | Second language acquisition–Study and teaching–Research. | Language and languages–Ability testing–Research. | Language and languages–Study and teaching–Research.
Classification: LCC P118.2 .S43523 2016 | DDC 418.0028/7–dc23 LC record available at http://lccn.loc.gov/2015034890

2014037932

ISBN 978-1-316-50503-8 Paperback

Contents

Section 4
From ideas to action

Acknowledgements

The editors are grateful to all the authors for their diligence in researching and writing their contributions, and their willingness to take advice from the editors, the Series Editors and the external reviewer. The editors would also like to thank the external reviewer, Vicki Plano Clark, for her thorough feedback and refreshing perspective on an earlier draft of the manuscript, and to Sian Morgan, for her helpful notes on the revised version.

Finally, Cambridge English and Cambridge University Press are grateful to the following publishers for their permission to use copyrighted material: Sage Publications for the use of Table 1 on page 88, adapted from issue 5 of *Information Visualisation* (2006), Figure 12 on page 95, which first appeared in issue 18 of *Field Methods* (2006), and Figure 16 on page 99, which previously appeared in issue 4 of *Journal of Mixed Methods Research* (2010); Taylor & Francis for the use of Figure 17 on page 100, which first appeared in issue 18 of *Assessment in Education: Principles, Policy & Practice* (2011); and John Wiley & Sons for the use of Figure 14 on page 97, which is taken from *Journal of Advanced Nursing* issue 60 (2007). The publishers of this volume would also like to thank Dr Adel F Almutairi his kind permission to use Figure 13 on page 96, reproduced from his PhD thesis from Queensland University of Technology (2012).

Series Editors' note

'We should incorporate things of diverse nature.'
Han Yu (768-825)

This book provides a practical introduction to the use of mixed methods research in the field of language assessment.

It is intended to provide the reader with an understanding of the core concepts of mixed methods research, as well as useful guidance in designing and conducting projects that implement those concepts in validating language tests. It does so by focusing on validation as an ongoing and integrated process that is needed to account for the appropriate uses of language tests in educational and social contexts based on applications of adequate theories and supporting evidence that draw on a wide spectrum of data.

It is perhaps appropriate that the origins of the volume can be traced to an event in 2010 that embodied many of the integrative and collaborative principles that underpin the mixed methods approach.

The event in question, hosted by the Herder Institute at the University of Leipzig, brought together 45 international scholars from different educational traditions in the USA and Europe with the aim of sharing their theories and practices. Moreover, it was a multilingual event with the participants representing many different languages and diverse approaches to language teaching and learning.

The main purpose was to establish a 'crosswalk', or in other words, the possible alignment between the American Council on the Teaching of Foreign Languages (ACTFL) Guidelines and the Common European Framework of Reference for Languages (CEFR) – with several established experts representing each of the two systems in order to lead the debate. On the surface there are some similarities between the frameworks as both deal with proficiency scales that can be applied to many languages and which can be used as the basis of curriculum development, testing and certification systems. The origins and intended purposes are, however, quite different, so the bringing together of the two traditions was a challenge.

Over four days of presentations and discussion, the commonalities and differences became apparent – and it quickly became clear that comparing systems is highly complex with no straightforward alignments or easy answers (see Tschirner (Ed) 2010). However, the enthusiastic engagement between the participants from the two systems was particularly productive and the potential for new ways of thinking about old problems was highlighted. As a result, several opportunities for collaborative research emerged, one of which was an innovative idea for collaboration between the University of Nebraska–Lincoln (USA) and Cambridge English (University of Cambridge) on the use of mixed methods research.

Aleidine J Moeller and Nick Saville were both participants at the Leipzig conference, and led the subsequent collaboration and built on the inter-disciplinary thinking that was established there. On the one hand, they brought in John W Creswell – one of the leading exponents of mixed methods research – together with a talented group of graduate students in Nebraska. On the other, they brought in members of the research group based in Cambridge English, with many years of experience in implementing validation studies in 'real world' contexts and in using multiple methods to collect and analyse data to validate examinations.

This collaboration focusing on mixed methods approaches to research in language assessment flourished and grew over the following five years. A highlight in May 2012 was a 1-week seminar in Cambridge that brought together all the participants and led to the subsequent partnering of the graduate students with the Cambridge-based researchers. The interactive process over the whole period led to important learning and development on both sides and culminated in the manuscript for this volume based on joint editing and authorship.

The volume is timely, especially for the field of language assessment, where there has recently been a shift of focus towards societal concerns in establishing test validity. In the 1990s, there were calls to supplement psychometric analyses with qualitative research and the use of 'triangulation' to shed light on complex phenomena when validating tests.

For many years, there had been polarisation in research communities between qualitative and quantitative approaches, often characterised as different paradigms that were not compatible – with the supporters of each engaged in a paradigm debate - or even a 'paradigm war'. Since the 1990s, however, there has been recognition, especially in the social sciences and education, that multiple approaches can be combined to obtain useful insights and to yield rich and well-supported interpretations.

This convergence of multiple approaches into systematic research designs is where mixed methods comes in.

The volume is structured around four sections. Importantly, it takes the reader from the basic concepts to the application of the approach in practice, starting from an understanding of the core principles in Sections 1 and 2, and advancing through a number of worked examples and case studies in Section 3. In other words, the aim is to progress *from ideas to action* – as specifically highlighted in Section 4, which sets out a framework for the design and implementation of a mixed methods study.

Overall, the aim of the volume to provide useful insights and suggestions for carrying out mixed methods research in any language assessment context – whether for high-stakes international exams or for small-scale institutional tests.

Nick Saville
Cyril J Weir
November 2015

Notes on contributors

Carolina Bustamante holds a PhD in Foreign Language Education and a graduate certificate in Mixed Methods Research from the University of Nebraska–Lincoln. She is currently an Assistant Professor and Coordinator of the Secondary Spanish Education Program at the State University of New York at Old Westbury. She has taught courses in Spanish, foreign language teaching methods, instructional technology for foreign language teachers, and research methods, among others. Her research interests include second language acquisition, teacher professional development, integration of technology into language teaching, and heritage language speakers. She recently published 'The convergence of content, pedagogy, and technology in online professional development for teachers of German' (2013), at the *CALICO Journal*.

John W Creswell is an Adjunct Professor in Family Medicine at the University of Michigan. He is one of the founders of mixed methods research and is a world-renowned scholar in mixed methods. He has written extensively on mixed methods research, qualitative methodology, and general research design. His 27 books (including new editions) are used around the world and translated into more than a dozen languages. He held the Clifton Institute Endowed Professor Chair for five years at the University of Nebraska–Lincoln, served as the director of the first Mixed Methods Center in the world, co-founded the Sage publication *Journal of Mixed Methods Research*, and has served as a consultant to the health services research area for the US Department of Veterans Affairs. He has been a Senior Fulbright Scholar to South Africa (2008) and to Thailand (2012). In 2011, he served as a co-leader of a national working group at the National Institutes of Health developing 'best practices' for mixed methods research in the health sciences. In spring 2013, Dr Creswell was a visiting professor at Harvard's School of Public Health. In 2014, he was awarded an honorary doctorate from the University of Pretoria in South Africa. Recently, he has been elected president of the Mixed Methods International Research Association for 2014 to 2015. His newest book, *A Concise Introduction to Mixed Methods Research*, was published by Sage Publications in April 2014.

Coreen Docherty has been working in English language education for 20 years, having taught English, trained teachers, developed course material and managed assessment practices in a wide range of contexts. She is currently a Principal Research Manager at Cambridge English Language Assessment, responsible for investigating the impact of Cambridge English exams on stakeholders and providing research support for the Cambridge English *for Schools* exams. She is also involved in projects related to educational reform, the CEFR, learning oriented assessment and language policy development. She regularly presents at conferences and leads workshops internationally.

Mark Elliott has extensive EFL experience in the Czech Republic, UK and China, having worked as an English teacher, teacher trainer, director of studies, examiner and materials developer. He joined Cambridge English in 2008, working as an Assessment Manager on *Cambridge English: Advanced*, *Skills for Life* and provisions for candidates with special requirements. In his current role as a Senior Validation and Data Services Manager, he is responsible for pretesting and test grading and equating, and providing validation and data analysis for a range of Cambridge English and Admissions Testing Service (ATS) exams. Mark holds an MA in Mathematics from the University of Cambridge and an MA in ELT and Applied Linguistics from King's College London.

Evelina Galaczi is Principal Research Manager at Cambridge English Language Assessment. Her research focuses primarily on speaking assessment and the role of assessment to support learning. She regularly presents at international conferences and has published in academic forums, including *Applied Linguistics*, *Language Assessment Quarterly*, *Assessment in Education*, and the *Studies in Language Assessment* series (Cambridge University Press).

Tim Guetterman is an applied research methodologist and Mixed Methods Research Fellow at the University of Michigan. His teaching, research interests, and scholarship are in research methodology, namely mixed methods research and qualitative inquiry. His current methodological research and publications are focused on integrating qualitative and quantitative data. In addition, he conducts research on teaching and learning mixed methods research in his role as evaluator and faculty for the US NIH-funded Mixed Methods Research Training Program for the Health Sciences. He has extensive professional experience conducting programme evaluation with a focus on healthcare and educational programmes. Dr Guetterman provides methodological consultation on mixed methods studies across the social sciences and health sciences, and his most recent publications focus on the use of visual displays in mixed methods research.

Sheri Hurlbut is a language teacher educator at the University of Nebraska–Lincoln, where she directs the German Online Distance Education Network

(GOLDEN) and the STARTALK Chinese Teacher Institute, both graduate professional development programmes for language teachers. She is a certified 7-12 German language teacher and served in the position of German language coordinator at the university level for many years. Her current research interests include teacher professional development, intercultural competence, second language acquisition and assessment, and participatory action and mixed methods research. She specialises in curriculum development with an emphasis on online learning and Web 2.0 technology. Her most recent publication is *Leadership and its Ripple Effect on Research* in *Taking Stock of German Studies in the United States: The New Millennium* (2015).

Andrew Hustad recently completed his PhD (May 2015) in Foreign Language Education at the University of Nebraska–Lincoln. While working as a research and teaching assistant at UNL, he taught courses on linguistics, ESL teaching methods, and multicultural education. During this time, he was also involved in training institutes for Chinese teachers, as well as Chinese language academies for high-school students. As demonstrated in his dissertation work, he is interested in how phenomenology can be utilised to understand the experiences of both teachers and students of foreign language. He taught English in Beijing for several years, and also has extensive experience as both a Chinese and Spanish teacher in the United States. He is currently the chair of the world languages department at Vail Mountain School, an independent K-12 school located in Vail, Colorado, and is designing and implementing the Mandarin Chinese language programme.

Le Kang is a Ph.D student majoring in Foreign Language Education at University of Nebraska–Lincoln. She taught English at the college level in China before she came to the United States to further her study and research in language acquisition and education. Having received her teaching certification in both Chinese and ESL, she has taught Chinese and ESL in both public and private schools in the U.S. As the major instructor of several federal-funded teacher training programmes, she has also been actively involved in the professional development of language teachers. Her core competencies and research interests lie in curriculum design and development, cooperative learning, student assessment, technology integration, communicative language teaching, student centered learning and inquiry based language and culture learning. Her dissertation is on the Technological, Pedagogical, and Content Knowledge (TPACK) of Chinese Language Teachers.

Nahal Khabbazbashi holds a DPhil in Education and an MSc in Applied Linguistics and Second Language Acquisition from the University of Oxford. In her current role as Senior Research Manager at Cambridge

English Language Assessment, she works on research projects related to exams in workplace contexts, performance assessment as well as benchmarking and impact studies in Higher Education contexts. Nahal's research interests include Multi-Facet Rasch Measurement; the automated assessment of speaking; and the effects of task and test taker-related variables on performance. She has publications in journals of *Language Testing*, *Language Learning* and *Papers in Language Testing and Assessment*. Nahal has also delivered several introductory courses on language testing, speaking assessment and Rasch analysis for the Association of Language Testers in Europe (ALTE) and has presented at various conferences. She has been a reviewer for *Language Assessment Quarterly* and *Research Notes* and has experience as an ESOL teacher and an *IELTS* examiner.

Hanan Khalifa heads international education at Cambridge English Language Assessment and as such leads a cross divisional team of experts in the field of language learning, teaching and assessment working with ministries of education; and developing strategic partnerships with stakeholders in the international development field. She is the senior editor of *Research Notes* and a *Studies in Language Testing* board member. Previously, Hanan has worked as Head of Research & International Development within Cambridge English and held a ministerial role as advisor to Minister of Education; worked for international development agencies (USAID, DfID) and firms (CfBT, AMIDEAST, AIR, AED). Hanan's expertise lies in: language testing, educational assessment, monitoring and evaluation, standard setting, research (methodology, instrument design, data analysis), and institutional capacity building. Her work experience includes: teaching, curriculum and syllabus design, materials development, teacher training, planning and conducting baseline and impact studies, complex project management, internal auditing, management of large surveys (TIMMS and PISA), and leading on assessment reform. Hanan is an expert member on Council of Europe CEFR panels and EAQUALS inspection committee. She has presented worldwide, with a track record of over 60 conference presentations and 30 publications including *Examining Reading* (used as course/key reference material by ALTE and master's programmes in UK universities). She was the recipient of 1989 Hornby Award for ELT and a joint winner with Burns and Brandon of the 2013 IEAA award for Innovation in International Education.

Gad S Lim is Principal Research Manager at Cambridge English Language Assessment, where he leads research on the assessment of writing, IELTS and the Occupational English Test (OET). His research work is informed by many years of experience as an examiner, item writer, test designer, and test development manager. He has published articles and chapters on performance assessment, raters and rating scales, test validation, standard setting, and on the CEFR. He also reviews for all major language testing journals and is on the editorial board of *Assessing Writing*. Gad has taught in higher education and trained language teachers in Asia, Australia, North America, and Europe. His PhD is from the University of Michigan at Ann Arbor.

Sarah McElwee is a Principal Research Manager at Cambridge English Language Assessment, where her work focusses on selection and entrance to university, and university admissions tests. A psychologist by training, she holds a PhD in Cognitive Development from Queen's University Belfast. She has worked in a wide range of contexts in education and assessment, including as a researcher at University of Oxford and as a consultant on a number of projects in the UK and Ireland on special educational needs.

Debra R Miller recently completed a PhD degree in quantitative, qualitative and psychometric methods with a qualitative dissertation that studied the flow of mixed methods research between the global north and south. She also holds a master's degree in survey methodology with emphasis in anthropology. These degrees reflect her focal interest in the influence of tacit culture on inquiry methodology, a passion ignited through her upbringing by American parents in southern Africa. Debra consults in areas such as study design, questionnaire development and participant-friendly inquiry, encouraging clients to implement context-relevant studies through more conversational and less structured interaction. Most recently, Debra has consulted on the development of graduate methods components for a new Doctor of Education programme at a US institution. Debra has applied her methodological insight in fields as broad as education, psychology, sociology, well-being and human aspects of STEM (science, technology, engineering and mathematics). Beyond consulting, she intends to continue teaching courses in research methodology.

Aleidine J Moeller is the Edith S Greer Professor of Foreign Language Education at the University of Nebraska–Lincoln. Her areas of scholarly interest include foreign language teacher education, language assessment, online professional development, and intercultural communicative competence. She is past president of the American Association of Teachers of German and the National Federation of Modern Language Teachers Association and currently serves on the American Council on the Teaching of Foreign Languages Board of Directors. She has published widely in professional journals, has served as editor of language journals and is a frequent presenter at national and international conferences. Aleidine is an experienced public school teacher, taught language at the college level and currently is a professor of foreign language education. She serves as a consultant for school districts, universities and language projects. Her most recent publications appear in the *Modern Language Journal, Foreign Language Annals, CALICO* and *Unterrichtspraxis.*

Martin Robinson is an Assistant Director in the Assessment department of Cambridge English and is responsible for the development of new assessment products. This has included the development of *Cambridge English: Legal, Cambridge English: Financial* and the Cambridge English Placement Test. Martin is also responsible for the Cambridge English Curriculum, the Cambridge English Benchmarking service and Learning Oriented Assessment products. His work in these areas has meant leading on national projects for Ministries of Education in countries such as Malaysia, Chile and Malta. It has also included management of the language test production for the multilingual European Survey on Language Competences (SurveyLang) for the European Commission between 2008 and 2012. Before joining Cambridge English, Martin gained extensive experience in English language teaching and school management in Spain and Japan. He is qualified in PRINCE2 project management and Managing Successful Programmes (MSP) and holds a master's degree in Applied Linguistics, specialising in language testing, from the University of Reading.

Angeliki Salamoura holds a PhD in English and Applied Linguistics from the University of Cambridge. She has previously worked as a postdoctoral researcher on English language processing at Cambridge where she developed a strong background in quantitative research. As Principal Research Manager, Angeliki co-ordinates a team of Research Managers with responsibilities for the delivery of bespoke projects (e.g. benchmarking) for governmental and corporate sectors worldwide. She leads on CEFR-related issues, the English Profile Programme, second language learning and its interface with assessment. Her research interests currently include bilingualism, learner corpus analysis and test impact. Several pieces of Angeliki's work in the above fields have been published.

Nick Saville is a member of Cambridge English's Senior Management Team and is responsible for directing the work of Research and Thought Leadership. He is the elected Manager of the Association of Language Testers in Europe (ALTE), on the Board of Trustees for The International Research Foundation for English Language Education (TIRF), and is a Board member of Cambridge University's Institute for Automated Learning and Assessment (ALTA). Before joining Cambridge English he taught at the University of Cagliari (Italy) and worked in Japan. He has a PhD in Language Assessment focusing on test impact, an MA in TEFL and a BA in Linguistics. Nick publishes widely in the field and has recently completed a volume on Learning Oriented Assessment with Neil Jones. He was a founding associate editor of *Language Assessment Quarterly* and is currently joint editor of the *Studies in Language Testing* series with Professor Cyril J Weir.

Ivana Vidaković holds a PhD in Second Language Acquisition from the University of Cambridge. Previously, she worked as an EFL teacher overseas where she taught adult learners. Her role involves providing research support to *Cambridge English: Legal, Cambridge English: Financial* and *Skills for Life* examinations. She has run courses on assessment of reading comprehension and English for Specific Purposes (ESP). She has presented at international conferences and has published in the areas of language assessment and second language acquisition. Her current research interests include assessment of ESP and reading comprehension, learner corpus analysis and impact of the English language examinations on various stakeholders. She is also managing editor of *Research Notes.*

Yuchun Zhou is an Assistant Professor in the Department of Educational Studies at Ohio University, USA. She holds a PhD in research methodology from the University of Nebraska–Lincoln under the supervision of Dr John W Creswell. Her dissertation topic was the adoption of mixed methods in China using an exploratory instrument design. Her major research interests include mixed methods research designs, instrument development using mixed methods, programme evaluation, intervention research, and measurement in education. She has published a number of papers in peer-reviewed journals, including the *Journal of Mixed Methods Research*. She currently teaches courses of *Research Designs, Test Theory and Measurement* and *Qualitative Research.* She will teach programme evaluation courses and mixed methods research seminars in 2016.

Nick Ziegler is a PhD student at the University of Nebraska–Lincoln, specialising in second language acquisition and education. He is a staff developer focusing on enhancing education (PreK-12, across content areas) through technology integration at Nebraska's Educational Service Unit #5, serving 10 public school districts. He also coordinates the Southeast Nebraska World Language Cadre, providing professional development to world language educators. He was awarded a Fulbright Research Grant in the 2010-2011 academic year to study the impact of the European Language Portfolio on student capacity for self-regulated learning in Germany. He is currently President-Elect of the Nebraska International Languages Association and a board member of the Nebraska Educational Technology Association. His research interests include self-regulated learning, instructional technology, and assessment. His most recent publication is: *The Predictive Value of the Self-regulated Capacity in Vocabulary Learning Scale* (2015).

Section 1
Language assessment and mixed methods research: Fundamental considerations and symbiosis

1 The confluence of language assessment and mixed methods

Aleidine J Moeller
University of Nebraska–Lincoln

Mixed methods generates results that are both smooth and jagged, full of relative certainties alongside possibilities and even surprises, offering some stories not yet told (Greene 2008:20).

This chapter serves as an introduction to the convergence of language testing and assessment and mixed methods research. An examination of the benefits and value added of mixed methods research within the field of language testing and assessment is the primary focus.

Topics highlighted in this chapter include:

- The shift from a testing culture to an *assessment culture*
- An examination of concurrent parallel *paradigm shifts* within language teaching and learning, research approaches and testing and assessment
- The *history of language assessment* and its *connection to mixed methods*
- The fundamental principles of mixed methods research and its *application to language assessment*

Introduction

The purpose of this volume is to create a deeper understanding of the role of mixed methods in language assessment; to provide fundamental information needed to conduct mixed methods research within the context of language assessment; to provide the reader with the essentials for conducting and publishing a rigorous mixed research study; and to expand the practice of mixed methods research into the field of language testing and assessment. As noted by Hashemi and Babaii (2013:828), mixed methods research has not fully gained the 'kind of attention in applied linguistics research' that it deserves, a sentiment extended by Turner (2014:1,413) when she opined that a greater emphasis may need to be 'placed on mixed methods research in language testing venues'.

This chapter further examines the benefits and value that can be added through mixed methods research within language testing and assessment. The field of language testing and assessment is informed by linguistics, applied linguistics, language acquisition and language teaching, as well as by the disciplines of teaching, measurement and evaluation (Shohamy 2010). Language testing basically consists of two fundamental components – 'what' is being tested and 'how', or which method is used for assessing the 'what' that is being tested (Shohamy 2010). During the last 50 years the language testing field has developed from discrete-point testing focused on lexical and structural issues to a more integrative approach that utilised authentic oral and written texts, and most recently to a communicative, task-based approach where language learners perform tasks within authentic, real-life contexts. As the definition of what it means to know a language has expanded and gained in complexity, language testers have sought to develop valid language assessment tools that represent varied and different societies in different contexts. Concerns have focused on political, social, educational and ethical dimensions, the meaning of language and 'the possibilities for measuring this complex and dynamic variable' (Shohamy 2010:xv).

This chapter begins with a discussion of the movement within the language field from a testing to an assessment culture and provides general background information and context regarding the concurrent parallel paradigm shifts from language teaching to learning, and from a psychometric to a more multiplistic research approach. Next, an examination of the impact of communicative language teaching and the move towards task-based instruction on language assessment is provided, together with a history of language assessment and its connection to mixed methods. This is followed by an introduction to the fundamental principles of mixed methods research and its roots in pragmatism, and a justification for its application to language assessment research. Examples of mixed methods designs that have added insight and a broader understanding to studies on the impact of language assessment are explored.

Moving from a testing to an assessment culture

Spolsky (1977) identified three developmental stages of language testing in the 20th century: the pre-scientific, the psychometric-structuralist and the psycholinguistic-sociolinguistic. As large-scale testing gained popularity in the 20th century, statistical procedures became the primary evaluative procedures for test development and test evaluation (Kunnan 2008). Standardised norm-referenced tests were aimed at measuring a test taker's language ability compared to other students and served to rank individuals for purposes of gate keeping. Such large-scale, norm-referenced tests produced a single score without benefit of meaningful feedback that identified a test taker's strengths and weaknesses in specific language domains. These tests provided little guidance for teachers to review curricular design and instruction in order to improve language learning. This approach to testing has been described as representative of a 'testing culture' (Wolf, Bixby, Glenn and Gardner 1991).

In the 1970s the sociolinguistic view of language testing as a means of inter-personal communication that is context related became the prevailing drive towards more integrative tests. As the concept of knowledge as a universal, fixed and measurable commodity gave way to the more process-oriented approach of 'seeking and interpreting evidence for use by learners and their teachers to decide where the learners are in their learning, where they need to go and how best to get there' (Assessment Reform Group 2002), learning became viewed as context bound, with teacher feedback playing a major role in supporting and promoting student learning (Black and William 1998, Inbar-Lourie 2010, James 2001, Shepard 2005). This view of assessment reflected Vygotsky's theory, which emphasised the cultural context of individual meaning making and Piaget's cognitive development theory, which regarded learning as 'an integral and inseparable aspect of social practice' (Lave and Wenger 1991:31). With this shift in paradigm from a testing culture to an assessment culture, assessment is now regarded as a value-embedded social activity (Filer 1995) with learning and assessment viewed as being inextricably linked. This new understanding of the interactive nature of learning and the role of assessment and assessors in the instructional-learning cycle (Black and William 1998) forced a reconsideration of the psychometric paradigm, which had dominated the testing cultures (Shepard 2000).

Cambridge English advanced an ecological model of Learning Oriented Assessment (Jones and Saville 2014) in which all levels of assessment, from the classroom to large-scale testing are 'brought into a complementary relationship and coordinated to provide maximum positive impact: providing evidence to support better learning, as well as better measurement and recognition of learning outcomes' (Jones and Saville 2014:6). While responsibilities for learning remain with the teachers and students in the classroom, there is a complementary relationship between large-scale and classroom assessment.

Investigating educational and social phenomena in context required insights from multiple disciplines using diverse research designs (LeCompte 2009). Social and behavioural sciences in educational research worked together as researchers in order to pursue crucial questions about 'how schools did or didn't work, why the best intended efforts of teachers often failed, and why students were not succeeding at desired levels' (LeCompte 2009:30). Gabriel Salomon (1991) argued that educational phenomena, like classrooms, are so complex they warrant the complementary use of both 'analytic' and 'systematic' approaches and methods, perhaps most feasibly across studies. For example, speech acts and conversations are co-constructed by both interlocutors and reflect turn taking that cannot be fully captured in a discourse completion test (McNamara and Roever 2006). Given this complexity, a better understanding of the multi-faceted character of educational and other social phenomena can be obtained from the use of multiple approaches and ways of knowing. This multiple approach way of thinking yields a richer, deeper and better understanding of important facets of social and educational phenomena.

Enquiries into educational and social phenomena require exploration over time, in multiple settings and with a variety of informants. The complexity of such educational research cannot be overstated, as noted by Berliner, whose variation on the common phrase 'It's not rocket science', acknowledged the complexities of researching teaching and learning: 'Well, at least it's not educational research' (Berliner 2002).

Concurrent parallel paradigm shifts

The field of language learning and teaching experienced a similar and significant paradigm shift, moving from a focus on teaching to a focus on learning, from achievement to proficiency, from textbooks to authentic texts and digital media and most recently, from methods to measurement (Lazaraton 2002); a shift that in many ways parallels a similar movement within language assessment as the field transitioned from a testing culture to an assessment culture (Inbar-Lourie 2010). This shift from a testing to an assessment culture meant moving from:

- assessing a specific skill to assessing language more holistically
- comparing student performance with another to comparing it with established criteria
- creating assessments independent of curriculum and instruction to those aligned with curriculum and instruction, the latter being a common practice in the UK where historically assessments were aligned with curricula and instruction
- making inferences based on single, restricted evidence to those based on multiple sources
- viewing students as objects of assessment to viewing them as active participants in the process
- holding a few responsible for assessment results to making all concerned with language learning accountable for assessment results.

Assessment culture, rooted in constructivist theories, underscores how knowledge is processed and developed and encompasses broader theoretical and practical frameworks for assessing knowledge (Inbar-Lourie 2010). The emphasis lies on the link between assessment and learning, reflecting a shift towards more inclusive, multiple forms of measurement that promote learning, rather than those that merely function as an audit of learning (Gipps 1994, Stiggins 2002).

Assessment culture embraces a broadening of the assessment construct by using assessment data from different sources and multiple informants and through multiple assessment tools that include various micro and macro sources; it emphasises multiple stakeholders playing an active role, and therefore becoming integral to the assessment process (Shepard 2000). Since assessment culture views assessment as a 'context-relevant activity grounded in learning, tests are sensitive to contextual variables, to the learners' cultural and linguistic backgrounds and to the knowledge they bring with them to the assessment encounter' (Inbar-Lourie 2010:296).

Consistent with the concept of an assessment culture, Purpura (2010) described the purpose of language assessment as collecting trustworthy, score-based and descriptive information about what students *know and are able to do with language.* Key questions to emerge, therefore, are: How can score-based inferences from classroom-based assessments be used to make decisions about student readiness to benefit from instruction, about student attainment and growth or about the kind of feedback to provide learners at different points in the learning process? How can teachers use this evidence to make decisions regarding next steps related to curricular content, instructional methods and classroom materials? What impact evidence do we have about the intended consequences of our classroom-based assessments for individual learners and teachers and how do these assessments serve to promote or inhibit further learning and more effective teaching? Such questions are not easily answered through a one-size-fits-all approach when assessing complicated phenomena and multi-dimensional outcomes in applied linguistics research. A mono-method approach may very well veil contributing factors to learner performance (Upshur and Turner 1999). Solano-Flores and Trumbul (2003) argue for new paradigms for assessing language learners in light of the complexities of language knowledge and the cultural issues embedded in language acquisition. Moving to a multiplicity of research methods, or mixed methods design, can better capture the inherent complexities involved in the assessment of language classroom teaching and learning.

Communicative language teaching and language assessment

In order to fully understand the role of mixed methods in language assessment research, it is important to clarify how the shift towards communicative language teaching impacted assessment. With the move towards teaching learners how to communicate in the real world, task-based language instruction, an approach that focuses on what learners can do with language, gained considerable momentum. Task-based assessment relies on meaningful, real-world, authentic language performance that should reflect the tasks and interactions that learners are likely to encounter in real-life situations. Van Gorp and Deygers (2014:591) note that task-based language assessment 'provides a much-needed interface between theory and practice', one predominantly dependent on implementation by the classroom teacher. Interest in task-based assessment has grown among language testers as it has proven valuable in raising awareness with stakeholders about language-learning processes. The numerous variables and complexity in assessing authentic task-based communication at the classroom level in addition to the challenges such as reliability, content validity and authenticity (Bachman and Palmer 2010, Norris 2009, Wigglesworth 2008) underscore that one research method cannot fully capture the complexity of language skills.

Mixed methods research and its application to language assessment

Tashakkori and Creswell (2007) define mixed methods research as one in which 'the investigator collects and analyzes data, integrates the findings and draws inferences using both qualitative and quantitative approaches or methods in a single study or program of inquiry' (2007:4). Tashakkori and Teddlie (2008) posit that one of the strengths of mixed methods is that it brings together 'information that can result in *"meta-inferences"* about the phenomenon under study that neither the quantitative nor qualitative perspectives could do alone' (2008:101, our emphasis). They define meta-inferences as 'an overall conclusion, explanation, or understanding developed through an integration of the inferences obtained from the qualitative and quantitative strands of a mixed methods study' (2008:101). This underscores the innate connection between mixed methods research designs and the 'meta-inferences' they allow, and the 'integrative evaluative judgement' that test validity is (see Ziegler and Kang, Chapter 4, this volume).

A key feature of mixed methods research is its methodological pluralism, which provides a deeper and varied perspective versus a single research methodology. Johnson and Onwuegbuzie (2004) present mixed methods research as the 'third research paradigm', or a 'third chair, with qualitative research sitting on the left side and quantitative research sitting on the right side' (2004:15). They note: 'the goal of mixed methods research is not to replace either of these approaches but rather to draw from the strengths and minimise the weakness of both in single research studies and across studies' (2004:14–15).

When findings are corroborated across different approaches, there is greater confidence than through one approach alone; if the findings conflict, then the researcher has greater knowledge and can modify interpretations and conclusions accordingly. In many cases, the goal of mixing is not to seek corroboration, but rather to expand one's understanding (Onwuegbuzie and Leech 2004).

Khalifa and Docherty (see Chapter 11, this volume) provide an illustration of such an expansion of understanding in their test impact study, in which mixed methods extended the scope and validity of their research. The use of qualitative interviews and focus groups allowed for the inclusion of young learners as stakeholders whose voices could not be fully represented through a questionnaire. They also report how mixed methods enhanced the stakeholders' confidence in the findings as a result of the triangulation of information derived from multiple data sources. By utilising quantitative and qualitative techniques within the same enquiry question, mixed methods research can incorporate the strengths of both methodologies, providing a more defensible argument supported by richer information.

In order to investigate how language is learned and acquired in a variety of contexts, a research methodology commensurate with the research question is needed. The goal is to capture both external and internal assessments that measure knowledge, teaching, and learning in a natural setting and manner, and to analyse current practices and achievements that link assessment data in a socially interactive environment. Using a carefully chosen research methodology, a more complete picture of 'where the learners are in their learning, where they need to go and how best to get there' can be acquired (Assessment Reform Group 2002).

Mixed methods can be a challenging approach to research (Creswell and Plano Clark 2011). Guetterman and Salamoura (see Chapter 7, this volume) reviewed 10 mixed methods studies that represented a purposeful sampling of language assessment studies and examined the mixed methods features based on a checklist created by Creswell and Plano Clark (2011). They identify and describe nine methodological issues that emerged in these studies and how they negatively affected the validity of each study. They further discuss how to address each of these challenges through the addition of rigorous mixed methods and how to avoid these pitfalls when conducting language assessment studies.

Pragmatism as a lens for mixed methods

Pragmatism is an emerging research paradigm focused on practice oriented understanding (Greene 2007) that emphasises what works (Creswell 2009). Pragmatism is well suited for mixed methods research as it can shed light on how research approaches can be mixed fruitfully (Hoshmand 2003) in ways that offer the best opportunities for answering important research questions. Johnson and Onwuegbuzie (2004) argue for the use of pragmatism as the most effective mixed methods paradigm as it offers 'an immediate and useful middle position philosophically and methodologically . . . and offers a method for selecting methodological mixes that can help researchers better answer many of their research questions' (2004:17). The research question, rather than a pre-conceived worldview, is paramount and drives the choice of design. A key feature of mixed methods research is its methodological pluralism, which 'frequently results in superior research (compared to mono-method research)' (Johnson and Onwuegbuzie 2004:14). For a more detailed discussion of worldviews in mixed methods, see Ziegler and Kang, Chapter 4, this volume.

Mixed methods and the history of language assessment

In the field of language teaching and learning, assessment has taken centre stage as high-stakes tests, as well as classroom assessments, have driven instruction and curriculum. A brief history of the evolution of language assessment will provide the requisite background for better understanding parallel developments in the use of various research methodologies as researchers grapple to find ways to increase student learning, improve instruction and seek the most appropriate and effective research methods for valid and reliable assessment of both.

The field of language testing in the 1970s moved towards a sociolinguistic view of language, one that is defined by purpose and context. Language testers moved away from an analytical approach to a more integrative testing approach (Davies 2014). In the 1980s, with the rise of the language proficiency movement, the scope of language testing was broadened 'to bring it much more in line with other areas of applied linguistics' (Skehan 1998:213). Skehan (1998) noted that this could provide language testing with the positive image it lacked, and 'that tests would not always be done to people but with them' (Skehan 1998:221). The 1980s also brought additional developments that contributed significantly to language testing. These included the application of item response theory (IRT), establishment of testing boards and agencies, increase in books on language testing, and the launch of the international journal *Language Testing*.

In the 1990s and into the following decade, the issue of washback emerged as a major concern. Alderson and Banerjee (2001) define washback as 'the impact that tests have on teaching and learning. Such impact is usually seen as negative . . . however . . . a good test should or could have positive washback' (Alderson and Banerjee 2001:214). Arguments about washback and impact fostered the International Language Testing Association (ILTA) to develop a code of ethics and a code of practice. During this same timeframe the issue of validity dominated the language-testing literature, forcing a closer relationship between language testing and applied linguistics (Davies 2014).

The first decade of the 21st century has sparked research interests focused on web-based and computer-delivered tests and a growing interest in national tests. Interest in social and political issues (McNamara and Roever 2006, Shohamy 2001) and the role of language tests in immigrant and citizenship issues (Kunnan 2012) emerged, and concern for validity, washback and ethics grew. This placed increased focus on the responsibilities of test makers and developers to document the impact of tests. The impact of testing was felt at the macro level (immigration and governmental policy; education at large and society – high-stakes assessments; accountability; reform) and at the micro level (impact on test takers, teachers, schools and family). Saville (2009) has argued that the aim of an assessment provider should be to promote *positive* effects and consequences and he refers to the principle of *impact by design* (see also Saville, Chapter 2, this volume). Collection of data at both the macro and micro levels will promote a deeper understanding of how and to what extent a test/assessment influences positively or negatively policy makers, families, test takers and teaching and learning.

Language testing/assessment trends run parallel to the general trajectory of mixed methods research in the social and behavioural sciences (Turner 2014). By combining information from different sources, results can often provide valuable insight into a deeper understanding of complex phenomena under study, most especially in the areas of validity and instrument development, classroom-based assessment, large-scale assessments, construct definition, and rater effects, to name a few. Mixed methods research is growing and evolving in the language testing/assessment community because of its 'what works' orientation, and as noted previously, is most often associated with pragmatism (Turner 2014:1,406). Turner notes, however that 'there is no specific body of language testing literature that concentrates on mixed methods research development or its impact on language testing research such as is found in other fields' (e.g. in nursing, Twinn 2003). There have been few attempts to consolidate mixed methods research studies in language testing in any publication or conference presentation (Jang, Wagner and Park 2014). There is, however, in general a significant rise in the number of MA theses and PhD dissertations that use mixed methods research and include the term mixed methods research in the research study title. This forecasts and indicates that mixed methods research is expanding as a venue for investigating social phenomena.

Mixed methods research and the impact of language assessment

The impact of testing and assessment has wide and far-reaching consequences for the individual test taker (behaviour, motivation, aptitude), the teachers (curriculum, teaching to the test, textbooks), the educational system (school curriculum, funding, test preparation) and parents (home life, reinforcing learning). The social dimension of language assessment can impact immigration policy, international education, educational reform, school funding and curricula. In order to gain insight and deeper knowledge about the impact of assessments on the varied stakeholders, both quantitative and qualitative approaches are recommended for research into impact and washback (Saville 2009). Mixed methods research offers myriad data sources such as observations, interviews, questionnaires and discussions that necessarily complement each other (Alderson and Hamp-Lyons 1996) and can productively 'capitalize on merging, blending, and combining different facets of our social knowing' (Greene 2007:254). Mixed methods research requires collaboration among researchers with specialised skills. This has brought the mixed methods research community together, as their common ground lies in the 'rejection of the dichotomy between the qualitative/quantitative approaches' (Tashakkori and Teddlie 2010b).

Vidaković and Robinson (see Chapter 8, this volume) illustrate the benefits of collaboration in their community-based participatory research study focused on the development of a test of legal English – *Cambridge English: Legal*. Using an exploratory sequential mixed methods design, the researchers worked closely with a group of experts in the legal profession to create a test designed to test English skills specifically tailored to professional and academic needs in the legal field. They describe the benefits of mixed methods combining 'qualitative and quantitative research strands' as providing 'a broader and deeper understanding of an issue than either strand would on its own ... the initial qualitative needs analysis phase produced valuable information for test specifications and sample test development ... the outcomes of one phase fed into the next phase, which formed a link between qualitative and quantitative data and findings in the remaining three phases of test development research'.

Galaczi and Khabbazbashi (see Chapter 9, this volume) offer another example of how mixed methods research can contribute to good practice and positive impact in language assessment through the development of rigorous mixed methods-based assessment instruments. In this study, the authors apply an exploratory mixed methods design in the development of rating scales in the context of high-stakes speaking assessments, and illustrate how the findings and insights using complementary quantitative and qualitative methodologies and integration of findings were used in an integrated and additive manner to enhance the rating scale development process.

Elliott and Lim (see Chapter 10, this volume) describe the role of mixed methods research in the test development process of a new Reading task in the *Cambridge English: Advanced* Reading exam designed to measure language proficiency for the purpose of entry into an English-medium university environment. Using a multiphase parallel convergent design the researchers investigated validity threats in terms of the construct coverage of the reading component. The researchers noted that 'a mixed methods approach provided a robust and rigorous framework within which to conduct the research . . . facilitating the development of a task while simultaneously producing a validity argument for its intended use within the socio-cognitive framework – in other words, demonstrating its fitness for purpose'.

Khalifa and Docherty (see Chapter 11, this volume) conducted an impact study using a convergent parallel mixed methods design to investigate the impact of an international assessment introduced into the Vietnamese educational system as part of a reform effort. The authors concluded that 'quantitative approaches based in postpositivism improved the generalisability of the findings . . . the qualitative strand grounded in constructivism improved the interpretations of the overall findings because it allowed the researchers to better understand participants' realities in terms of the effect of the tests, but more importantly, allowed the researchers to collect the views from a key stakeholder group'.

Benefits and value of mixed methods research

The paramount value of mixed methods is to better understand social phenomena that are 'inherently complex and contextualized' (Greene 2007:14). The persuasive rationale for mixed methods has been to strengthen construct and conclusion validity through the triangulation of information from multiple sources. Triangulation seeks convergence, corroboration, or correspondence of results from combining information from multiple sources (Tashakkori and Teddlie (Eds) 2010a). In a mixed methods study with a triangulation intent, different methods are used to better understand the same phenomenon. If the results provide consistent or convergent information, then confidence in enquiry inferences is increased. If the results are divergent, greater insight can be gained about this phenomenon that can lead to more in-depth enquiry into a specific phenomenon. Ziegler and Kang (see Chapter 4, this volume) illustrate how triangulation can be used in language assessment research in their discussion of Rea-Dickens and Gardner's (2000) investigation of 'the nature of formative assessment in a primary language learning context' (2000:215). Participants (i.e., teachers) were asked about their perception of issues as regards assessment in the classroom (formative and summative) both qualitatively (open-ended questionnaires) and quantitatively (close-ended questionnaires). At the interpretation level, quantitative and qualitative data were reduced and organised around this parallel construct to facilitate data comparison. Using a building strategy, the combined results informed the development of the interview and observation protocols used in follow-up qualitative investigation. The quantitative component contributed to the triangulation protocol the researcher used to develop themes from the initial investigation, which built into further qualitative data collection, generating the meta-analyses presented in the findings.

There exist inherent strengths in mixed methods research that offset the weakness of a purely quantitative or qualitative language study. Data collection and analysis stages can be better integrated than in a single methodology study. According to a study conducted by Haines (2011), mixed methods studies were viewed as more valuable than single methods studies, more rigorous in investigating impact, provided a deeper understanding of impact, and provided more evidence related to the research enquiry.

Greene, Caracelli and Graham (1989) and Greene (2007) have summarised the major purposes and rationales for mixing methods:

- Multiple methods measure overlapping, but distinct facets of the same phenomena under investigation. Results from one method are intended to elaborate, enhance, illustrate or clarify results from the other generating understandings that are broader, deeper, more inclusive, and honour the complexity and contingency of human phenomena.
- Development designs use different methods sequentially in order to use the results of one method to help develop the other method or inform its implementation – as in sampling.
- Combining methods for purposes of expansion for different enquiry components extends the breadth and range of the enquiry.
- Mixed methods offers meaningful engagement with differences, intentionally seeking the discovery of paradox and contradiction, probing the contested, challenging the accepted and engaging with multiple, often discordant, perspectives and lenses.
- Focus on the political and value aspects of human phenomena promotes the discourse engagement.

The notion of divergence (or dissonance) captures the full potential of mixed methods social enquiry. Mixed methods enquiry can produce paradoxes and discordance, which, when pursued, could produce new perspectives, understandings, and insights not previously imagined. Integrating assessments that produce longitudinal and comparable data, as opposed to isolated and possibly unrelated pieces of data, may help teachers to identify linguistic breakdown or consistent misunderstandings that might be remedied through a classroom intervention.

Moeller and Theiler's (2014) study of the development of spoken language (Spanish) at the high school level over five consecutive years serves as an illustration of how a convergent data transformation mixed methods design allowed them to 'compare and contrast quantitative statistical results with qualitative findings or to validate or expand quantitative results with qualitative data' (Creswell and Plano Clark 2011:62). Proficiency speaking scores and student-produced qualitative speech samples allowed the researchers to quantitatively show the trajectory of language learning over time, while the qualitative data (speech samples) provided language samples over time. Qualitative data allowed for a deep understanding of the nature of the development of oral language production throughout the high school learning experience, while the quantitative data presented a clear and concrete trajectory of oral language development.

The findings provided a richer profile of student growth, descriptive details underlying that growth, the identification of factors related to that growth, student profiles representing annual mean growth outcome, and student profiles representing growth variation within years of Spanish language learning. The researchers noted that 'a melding, or integration of qualitative and quantitative data as illustrated in this study can enrich an understanding of the language learning process and be of value in identifying the variables that contribute to language development in the classroom' (Moeller and Theiler 2014:227).

As evidenced in the above examples, integration can appear within the research questions, within data collection, within data analysis, or in the interpretation (Creswell, Plano Clark, Gutmann and Hanson 2003). The purposeful integration of rich qualitative methods and rigorous quantitative methods informs the production of meta-inferences considered by Tashakkori and Teddlie (2008) as the true source of the value added by mixed methods.

It is noteworthy that many rigorous mixed methods research studies are conducted by researchers working in teams, or pairs. One of the challenges facing researchers is the technical knowledge and skills required to conduct rigorous mixed methods research. Typically researchers have been trained in procedures of one method or the other, but few have had detailed experience with both. This has the added benefit of helping to promote dialogue across research traditions, and potentially open up new vistas of enquiry.

Conclusion

This chapter has provided some context for the application of mixed methods research to the area of language assessment explaining the paradigm shifts to a learning and an assessment culture, and the move to a more multiplistic research approach. In addition, an introduction to the fundamental principles of mixed methods research along with a justification for its application to language assessment research was outlined, and examples of mixed methods research in the field of language assessment were provided.

As pointed out by Turner (2014) there is a greater need to pursue mixed methods research in language testing as it has much to offer researchers and the testing field. It is the hope and aim of this volume to assist researchers in better understanding the additive value of mixed methods research and ultimately bring such research into the language testing field and, generally, into the language learning and teaching research arena.

This volume provides the essential information needed to conduct mixed methods research studies as well as numerous examples of such research studies that illustrate first hand the benefits and added value of mixed methods to the language testing and assessment field. The studies in this volume reveal how issues related to language testing and assessment, ranging in topics from impact studies to rating scale development to the measurement of oral production skills, were enhanced by the incorporation of mixed methods.

2 Managing language assessment systems and mixed methods

Nick Saville

Cambridge English Language Assessment

This chapter builds on the general overview provided in Chapter 1 by considering the operational management of language assessment systems in more detail.

The aim is to orient the reader through an overview of key issues in assessment and by providing links to Sections 2 and 3 of the volume where specific applications of mixed methods to assessment research and validation are discussed.

The chapter covers the following areas:

- *Construct definition*
- Aspects of *validity, validation* and mixed methods
- The *operational cycle within assessment systems*
- Use of *data for continual improvement*
- Integrating mixed methods into the *operational cycle of test development and validation*

Introduction

In Chapter 1, Moeller considered the value that can be added by using mixed methods research in language assessment. Chapter 2 builds on this general overview by considering the operational management of language assessment systems in more detail. The focus here is on the management of the integrated processes that are needed to ensure that an assessment system meets the needs of the intended test takers and other test users, and can account for appropriate uses of language tests in educational and social contexts (Saville 2012b).

This chapter, therefore, introduces these processes and suggests the important roles that mixed methods can play in providing the supporting evidence at different stages of the assessment cycle. Two notions that are central to this discussion concern the '*what*' and the '*how*' of language assessment, namely:

a. construct definition and validation

b. the operational cycle within assessment systems.

Current thinking on validity emphasises the importance of *validation as a process* of accumulating evidence to support claims made about the underlying constructs and the appropriate inferences that can be drawn from the results. Kane (2006), for example, building on Messick's unitary concept of validity in which construct validation is central, makes the case for 'validity as argument'. He suggests that in developing a validity argument, examination providers need to prepare and present an overall evaluation of the intended interpretations and uses of the test or examination that is being validated based on evidence. Validating inferences about a construct therefore requires attention to be paid to *all aspects* of the assessment cycle, as failure in any aspect of the system may threaten validity and lead to the validity argument being undermined. Attention to the core processes in the system and how they can be monitored and improved is thus crucial.

In building and presenting a validity argument the examination provider must:

- set out claims relating to the usefulness of the test for its intended purpose and uses of results in context
- explain why each claim is appropriate by giving reasons and justifications based on relevant theories
- provide adequate evidence to support the claims and the reasoning behind them.

As a starting point the philosophical stance and 'theoretical lens' of the examination provider should be stated, as these considerations guide the way in which the validity argument is built and how the validation activities are carried out. These considerations are also important in defining and prioritising the research questions to be addressed and determining the 'theory of action' in planning and carrying out the necessary work (see Creswell (2013b), and Creswell and Zhou, Ziegler and Kang, Chapters 3 and 4 respectively, this volume, for a more in-depth discussion of the philosophical worldviews underlying mixed methods research).

The evidence to support validity claims needs to be accumulated over time. In other words, to be gathered from the outset during the design and development stages and continuing for as long as the test remains operational. The nature of the evidence itself and the methods used to collect it are central to the purpose of this volume. In considering the need for validity evidence, the methods for collecting data will be considered. It is clear that multiple methods are often needed, both quantitative and qualitative, to back up claims. A key question is how can these methods be most effectively combined and at what stages in the testing cycle can they be deployed most effectively? This is where mixed methods can play a major role. For example, not only can a mixed methods approach provide the basis for a relevant theoretical stance, but it can also be used in the following ways:

- to explain why/how data types can be used more effectively together
- to gain insights from open-ended questions to support survey data
- to use qualitative data to explain or expand on experimental outcomes
- to gain insights from a large-scale survey by conducting experimental work and seeking to explain the observations by conducting more in-depth studies (e.g. using case studies)
- to gain insights into what might be happening on a small scale and then follow up with the collection of data from a wider population to provide confirmation.

We will come back to this later in the chapter in considering the 'how' in managing assessment systems. But first we need to consider the 'what' and the nature of abilities we want to assess and report scores for.

Construct definition and validation – a socio-cognitive approach

In language education it is now widely recognised that construct definition is a necessary first step when considering the development of curricula, teaching programmes and the assessment of learning outcomes. This is a central theme throughout this volume, and simply put, it means that before we can teach or test language proficiency, we must agree on what we mean by it. In other words, we must define the specific constructs to be taught or tested based on a theory or model of what knowing a language entails.

In recent years a socio-cognitive approach has been taken by many practitioners in the field of language assessment, especially when the tests they are developing are integrated into formal educational systems. For example, the Council of Europe's Common European Framework of Reference for Languages (CEFR) provides a socio-cognitive model of language use and learning that is a useful starting point for a broad range of stakeholders in language education (Council of Europe 2001:9). It has been particularly influential in highlighting the goals of language education in terms of communicative language ability and through its action-oriented approach, which also reflects recent developments in language learning theory (e.g. social constructivism) and second language acquisition.

However, in defining constructs to support the design of test specifications and the development of test tasks covering a wide range of proficiency levels, a more highly specified model is required to serve this purpose. Since the 1980s, language testers have drawn extensively on the work of Canale and Swain (1980) and Bachman (1990) in order to define more clearly the concept of communicative language ability. More recently, building on this concept, some language testers have discussed an *interactionist perspective* that highlights the centrality of *context* in language use (e.g. Chalhoub-Deville 2003). They make the case for a model that accounts for cognition as it develops *through* social interaction – hence the need for a socio-cognitive approach.

The socio-cognitive model adopted in this volume is based on Weir (2005), represented pictorially in Figure 1. This model has been effectively deployed by a number of major examination providers in recent years and its uses have been well documented (see for example the four volumes in the Studies in Language Testing series related to the Cambridge English examinations jointly published by Cambridge University Press: Shaw and Weir 2007, Khalifa and Weir 2009, Taylor (Ed) 2011, Geranpayeh and Taylor (Eds) 2013).

The test taker/learner is prominent in this model. In designing a test for a particular context and purpose, it is important to take account of the characteristics of the intended test taker: these characteristics include demographic features (such as age, gender and language background), as well as existing knowledge, prior learning experiences and metacognitive and other psychological features (such as attitude and motivation). Collecting data about the test taker can be done both qualitatively, e.g. through a variety of qualitative means, such as interviews, focus groups and observations, and quantitatively, using questionnaires or other survey techniques.

Weir (2013a:96), in reflecting on the model, identifies three main features that he sees at the core of this approach. He comments as follows: 'In this approach each of the macro skills, reading, writing, listening and speaking, was viewed as not just the underlying trait of ability but as the constructed triangle of trait, context and score (including its interpretation).'

The *trait* in this case concerns the necessary definition of language proficiency noted above. The *cognitive,* or *theory-related,* aspect of the model is, therefore, concerned with the extent to which the cognitive processes employed by the test taker in completing test tasks are the same as those needed in carrying out tasks in 'real-world' contexts of communication. Bachman and Palmer (1996) refer to these real-world contexts as the *target language use* (TLU) domain.

Validation might include the study of the cognitive processes of test takers when engaging with test tasks and it is important to consider the extent to which the test is *interactionally authentic* (Bachman 1990:317). This may entail using both qualitative and quantitative methods. For example, verbal protocols to analyse strategies used by test takers while completing tasks, or statistical analysis of the underlying factors in responses to tasks using techniques such as structural equation modelling.

The second core feature is *context*. Context-related validity is concerned with the nature of the test tasks and the conditions under which the test is performed and which reflect the authentic use of the language in the TLU domain. It includes technical aspects related to the content of the test

Figure 1 Weir's socio-cognitive model (2005) (An example from the context of validating Listening tests)

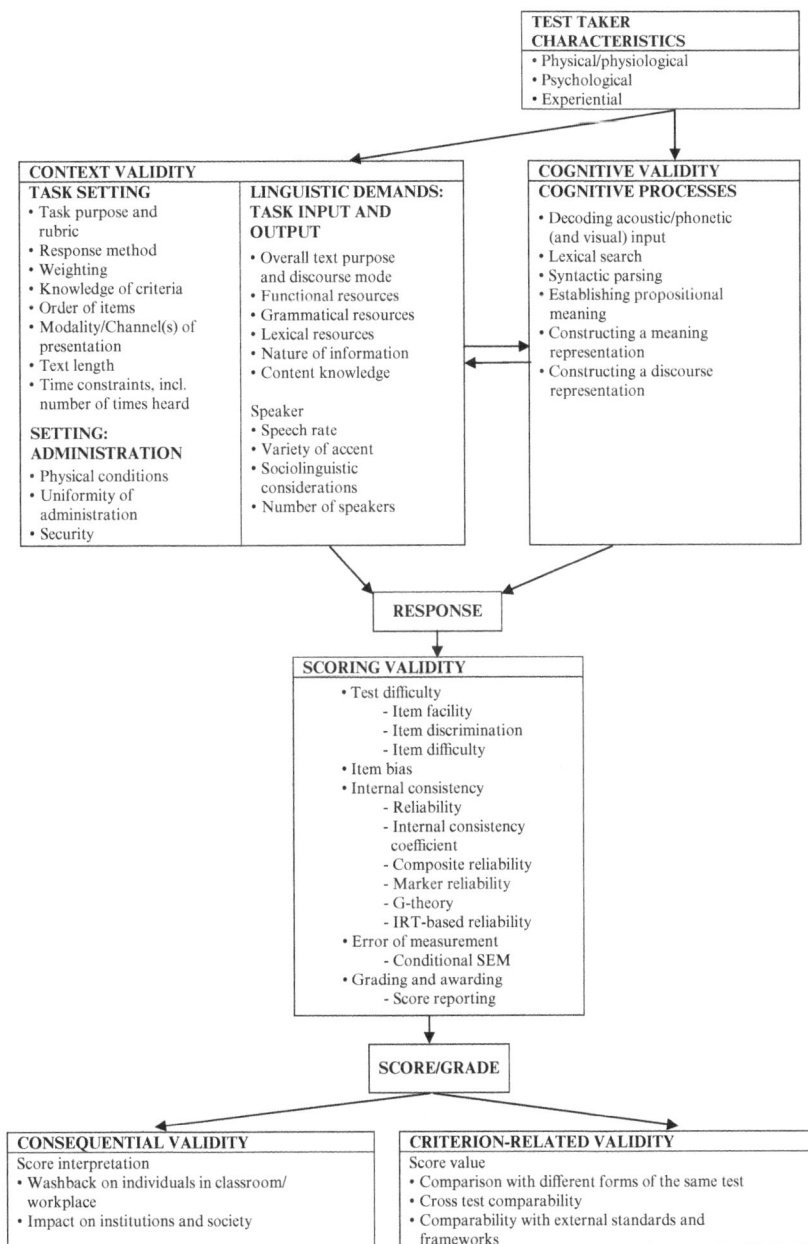

TEST TAKER CHARACTERISTICS
- Physical/physiological
- Psychological
- Experiential

CONTEXT VALIDITY

TASK SETTING
- Task purpose and rubric
- Response method
- Weighting
- Knowledge of criteria
- Order of items
- Modality/Channel(s) of presentation
- Text length
- Time constraints, incl. number of times heard

SETTING: ADMINISTRATION
- Physical conditions
- Uniformity of administration
- Security

LINGUISTIC DEMANDS: TASK INPUT AND OUTPUT
- Overall text purpose and discourse mode
- Functional resources
- Grammatical resources
- Lexical resources
- Nature of information
- Content knowledge

Speaker
- Speech rate
- Variety of accent
- Sociolinguistic considerations
- Number of speakers

COGNITIVE VALIDITY

COGNITIVE PROCESSES
- Decoding acoustic/phonetic (and visual) input
- Lexical search
- Syntactic parsing
- Establishing propositional meaning
- Constructing a meaning representation
- Constructing a discourse representation

RESPONSE

SCORING VALIDITY
- Test difficulty
  - Item facility
  - Item discrimination
  - Item difficulty
- Item bias
- Internal consistency
  - Reliability
  - Internal consistency coefficient
  - Composite reliability
  - Marker reliability
  - G-theory
  - IRT-based reliability
- Error of measurement
  - Conditional SEM
- Grading and awarding
  - Score reporting

SCORE/GRADE

CONSEQUENTIAL VALIDITY
Score interpretation
- Washback on individuals in classroom/ workplace
- Impact on institutions and society

CRITERION-RELATED VALIDITY
Score value
- Comparison with different forms of the same test
- Cross test comparability
- Comparability with external standards and frameworks

(e.g. the format of the tasks, the rubric and the topics), as well as practical features, such as the specified conditions under which the test is administered and scored.

For this aspect of the model, validation should include *a priori* investigations of the degree to which the items, tasks or questions in a language assessment are representative of the TLU domain in terms of relevance and coverage, i.e. the extent to which they are *situationally authentic* (Ellis 2003:6). Ongoing validation involves the collection of data under operational conditions in order to consider whether the test taking or scoring conditions introduce threats to validity, such as construct-irrelevant variance in the responses or inaccuracy in the scoring.

The third core feature of the model is the *scoring* of the responses leading to the outcome score and its interpretation. By creating a suitable context for eliciting evidence of the underlying trait, the test provides a valid basis for generating a meaningful and interpretable score to report to the test taker and other users. Scoring-related aspects of validity are, therefore, directly linked to both cognitive and context validity. The scoring must be accurate and the outcome scores must be adequately reliable and dependable for making decisions about the test takers.

Accuracy is clearly important in the processes used for administering and scoring tests. The aim must be to eliminate (or reduce) inaccuracies, by standardising the way test administration is carried out and by standardising the scoring, especially when human raters are used. Consistency over time is also important and tests which are administered in different locations or at different times must be equally reliable.

There are two other aspects of the validity model not discussed so far: *criterion-related aspects* and *consequential aspects*.

Criterion-related validation aims to demonstrate that test scores are systematically related to some other indicator of what is being measured. This may be to a framework of observable behaviours or to another external indicator, such as another examination measuring similar abilities. The aim is to build up an understanding of the comparability of the measure or measures.

For language learners it is particularly important for the scores on tests to be generalisable to the TLU – as noted above – or, in other words, to the real-orld tasks the test takers may be exposed to in their lives. As Weir (2013a: 99) points out: 'As a general principle in the socio-cognitive approach, language tests should, as far as is practicable, place requirements on test takers similar to those involved in communicative settings in non-test "real-life" situations.'

The effects and consequences of language assessment are therefore linked to *context* at two levels – the *micro context* of the school and the *macro context* of society at large. The important point here is the interaction between assessment, which typically takes place in formal educational settings (e.g. schools, classrooms), and the social world in wider society where the outcomes of assessment are valued and rewarded. Language learning outcomes constitute useful skills for the workplace, further education and personal development that need to be adequate for the required purpose. The test score and its interpretation must be a good indicator of what the learner can do in real-life situations and a dependable measure for making decisions.

The *consequential aspects of validity* in the model concern the positive or negative effects and consequences arising from the use of an assessment in a particular context. Test takers in particular are affected because the results of tests are used to make important decisions about them that can affect their lives. This is why a test that is biased in some way may lead to unfair decisions based on the scores, and to negative consequences for individuals who are affected.

Such effects and consequences on both individuals and systems are encompassed within the notion of *test impact* – which increasingly in recent years has become a central consideration for test providers throughout the testing cycle – not just a post-hoc form of analysis or limited to effects on teaching.

Saville (2009) has argued that the aim of an assessment provider should be to promote *positive* effects and consequences and he refers to the principle of *impact by design*. Broadly speaking, the study of impact entails the collection of data to investigate *in what ways* and to *what extent* an assessment system affects stakeholders, processes and systems in all the contexts in which it operates – both at macro societal level and at micro levels within schools and classrooms. It must take into account the influences of policymaking and social action on assessment with reference to the possible side effects and unintended consequences that can occur. It must also incorporate investigation of the effects of assessment on teaching and learning, i.e. commonly referred to as washback effects.

Anticipating impacts and finding out what actually happens in 'real-life' contexts provides the basis for making necessary improvements to the operational assessment cycle. The ability to engage in well-managed interaction with stakeholder groups and to implement changes in order to improve educational outcomes or mitigate negative consequences associated with tests is key to achieving the desired impact.

These considerations are integral to the concept of *impact by design*: it depends on well-defined constructs (with a coherent validity argument and supporting evidence), and an *ex ante* approach to anticipating the possible consequences of a given policy in the contexts where the assessments are to be used. Furthermore it requires operational systems to include routine validation procedures to collect, store and access the necessary data and to have a capability to change the system when necessary.

Validation and mixed methods

In Section 2 of this volume, mixed methods designs are discussed with general guidance on the steps that need to be taken in designing mixed methods projects in the context of test validation.

Ziegler and Kang (Chapter 4) outline five mixed methods designs and provide 'heuristic illustrations' based on published papers in the field of language assessment. For example, they illustrate how a mixed methods design might be employed within a validation programme to investigate the washback effect of a test in a particular educational context, as noted above. They suggest that, by conducting both a quantitative survey and qualitative interviews with relevant participants, and by drawing upon inferences made from the comparison between data sets, the mixed methods researcher would produce a more comprehensive understanding of the effects being studied than if only one method had been used.

Altogether they include three illustrations of mixed methods projects focusing on washback:

- washback effects related to the National Matriculation English Test (NMET) in China
- the washback effect of an assessment tool on instructional planning
- the washback of introducing a test of spoken language ability for international teaching assistants.

Other illustrative projects include: an investigation of native and non-native teachers' judgements of spoken English; the motivation of secondary school students to learn a foreign language in schools; and formative assessment of language in elementary school contexts.

In a similar way, Miller and Bustamante (Chapter 5) introduce the reader to procedural diagrams in mixed methods research and illustrate their discussion with relevant examples (for example, in developing and validating rating scales for the assessment of speaking).

In Section 3 of this volume, Guetterman and Salamoura (Chapter 7) focus specifically on test validation processes and how they can be enhanced through the application of rigorous mixed methods components. In so doing, they develop the general concepts of validity and validation introduced in this chapter. Following their chapter, four examples have been chosen to illustrate how the different mixed method designs have been used in validation projects. These examples also illustrate the following specific aspects of validity taken from the socio-cognitive approach discussed above:

- Chapter 8, context aspects of validity
- Chapter 9, scoring aspects of validity

- Chapter 10, cognitive and context aspects of validity
- Chapter 11, consequential aspects of validity (impact).

Taken as a whole, they are useful testimonials to the applicability of mixed methods in addressing a wide range of assessment questions and issues.

The operational cycle within assessment systems

In the next section of this chapter, we move on to consider ways in which the socio-cognitive approach (the '*what*') interacts with the *core processes* of an integrated assessment system (the '*how*') – what we have referred to as the operational cycle within an assessment system. The aim here is to highlight the areas of the cycle where information may need to be collected using a variety of research methods, and to raise awareness of the potential benefit of using a mixed methods approach.

As in the previous section, the focus will be on the types of information which can be collected and used in order to:

a) contribute to the evidence supporting the validity argument and as a requirement for ongoing validation

b) identify where operational processes within the cycle need to be improved or updated.

The operational cycle within assessment systems can be conceptualised as a series of logical steps, starting with the test design, progressing to administration, reporting of results, and ending with evaluation. Versions of this cycle are typically found in the main handbooks on language test development, although the names and number of the stages in the cycle may vary (see for example, Alderson, Clapham and Wall 1995, Bachman and Palmer 1996, 2010, Hughes 2003, Weir 2005).

Figure 2, based on the *Manual for Test Development and Examining* (Association of Language Testers in Europe/Council of Europe 2012), shows a typical operational assessment cycle.

This version of the operational assessment cycle starts with the decision to produce an assessment, followed by an initial developmental phase and then the implementation of the operational system based on recurrent processes with specific aims. This cycle is consistent with Bachman and Palmer (1996) who outline a three-stage model: *design, operationalisation and test administration*.

Consultation with stakeholders is important throughout the assessment cycle, not only to address technical issues, such as appropriacy of the test content, but also to address practical aspects which affect the practicability of the test and which might also impact validity. For example, longer tests increase reliability because they capture more responses, but may be impractical to administer or can impact negatively on learners due to fatigue or

Figure 2 Operational assessment cycle

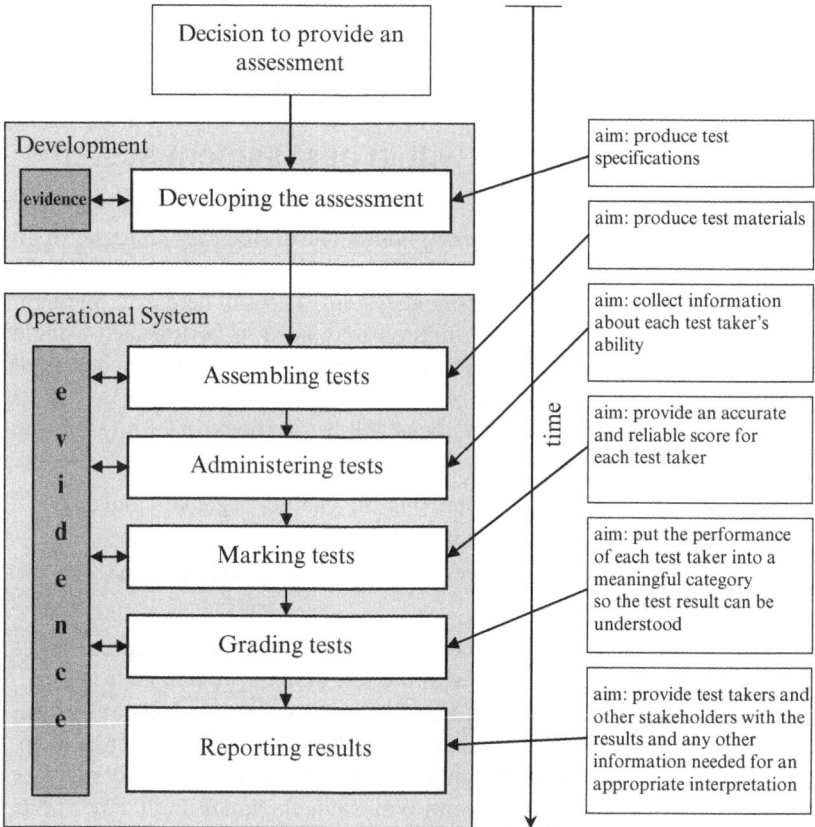

loss of concentration. An example of the importance of consultation with stakeholders is provided by Vidaković and Robinson (see Chapter 8, this volume) in their discussion of the development of a test of English for legal professionals.

Threats to validity, and so to the consistency and dependability of outcomes, can be introduced at many stages of the operational assessment cycle. This means that this area requires particular attention when designing and implementing a validation programme. Apart from minor mistakes or inaccuracies in carrying out an assessment, variability in test scores may also be systematically introduced by factors other than variations in the trait being assessed. This kind of unplanned variation is called *error* and needs to be identified and estimated as part of the validation programme and is a key feature of the operational analysis that must be carried out as a routine feature of the assessment cycle. For example, construct irrelevant variance that is a threat to the overall meaning of test scores and the reliability of decisions made on the basis of them may be caused by a range of factors. These include: variability in test administration conditions; variations in the test takers' own behaviours; variability in the behaviour of scorers; and unexpected variations in the functioning of test tasks. An illustration of the importance of considering threats to validity is given by Elliott and Lim (see Chapter 10, this volume), who provide a detailed description and discussion of the steps taken to minimise the potential effects of threats to validity in the development of a new task for a test of academic English.

By linking test taker data to their test responses, the assessment provider can estimate the reliability and fairness of the test: the overall reliability; the reliability of the sub-group scores; potential sources of unfairness and potential bias. Where threats to validity can be identified, changes to the test design or the operational system can be implemented to mitigate the problems.

As part of the routine validation process, data must be collected to make sure that the test remains fit for its intended purpose and appropriate for the intended test takers. In this approach the capture and accrual of evidence in the form of many kinds of information and data take place at *all stages in the cycle*. This is consistent with the socio-cognitive approach to validation that was presented earlier.

From an operational point of view, the assessment cycle is a series of core processes of the kind that are central to a quality management system, as illustrated in Figure 3.

The literature on educational and psychological measurement has recently turned its attention to the concept of quality (Saville 2012b). For example, Wild and Ramaswamy (Eds) (2008) describe a *'quality triangle'*, the three sides of which are: *planning and design*; *monitoring and improvement*; and *implementing standards*.

The aim of a quality management system is not only to maintain and support error-free operations, but also to enhance the system by implementing continual improvements – in the case of language assessment, improvements to both the test design and the processes (see Saville 2012b). So defining

Figure 3 Continual improvement cycle

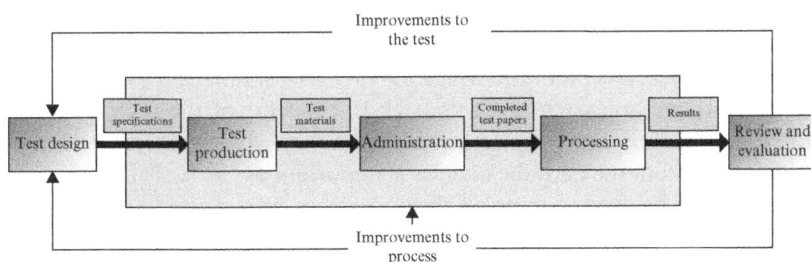

and implementing the processes effectively is crucial. When processes are defined and agreed, quality control and quality assurance procedures can be carried out to ensure that they are not only being followed, but are also effective and efficient. The link between quality management principles and the assessment cycle should be apparent here – the aim in both cases is to eliminate inaccuracies and to avoid error or inconsistencies in the core processes. This supports the validity argument in that key aspects of the operational cycle could introduce threats to validity (e.g. construct-irrelevant variance) if quality control is not exercised effectively.

The operational cycle begins when there is a perceived need for a new or revised test, and the process can be broken down into three stages: planning, design and development. The first task in the planning stages is to define the intended context and use of the prospective test by identifying stakeholders and their needs (as shown in the projects discussed by Vidaković and Robinson, Chapter 8, this volume, and Elliott and Lim, Chapter 10, this volume). Attention must be paid to both theoretical and practical considerations. The key output of the product development stage is a set of test specifications. Most developments include extensive trialling of materials which are analysed and reviewed before the final specifications are produced. This is a document or documents defining the test, an *a priori* validity argument and its operational requirements. The specifications act as a 'blueprint' for the operational production of tests.

When a test is administered for the first time it moves into the operational phase; an iterative process that is repeated for each test version or session involving routine production of test versions; administration; and post-exam processing. The main stages of post-exam processing include scoring, analysis and the reporting of results. Data on the test takers, test materials, scoring and grading procedures must be captured and analysed routinely for all sessions and used for quality assurance purposes.

All assessments and related services must be reviewed and evaluated regularly. Ongoing reviews should take place during the routine monitoring of operational processes, and also periodically to ensure that the assessment system remains fit for purpose. In some cases this kind of review may lead to a decision to withdraw the test or to re-start the cycle from the beginning. It is axiomatic that improvements can always be made and are fundamental in both quality management and validation – an iterative cycle, following the Plan, Do, Check, Act model on which the ISO 9001 standard is based.

The iterative approach takes us back to the start of the cycle as illustrated in Figure 3. The use of relevant data collected from the operational systems and from the periodic reviews is important as the basis for action – what needs to be done to improve the assessment system and to ensure that the needs of the stakeholders are being met effectively and that any negative impacts can be mitigated. Galaczi and Khabbazbashi (see Chapter 9, this volume) provide us with an illustration of the considerations involved in revising a test or a key feature of a test, in their discussion of the development of a revised set of assessment scales for a test of speaking ability.

The methods and approaches to finding out what is happening in context in the operational phase must include an ability to carry out macro-analyses of large-scale aggregated data, as well as micro-analyses of views, attitudes and behaviours in local settings such as schools and classrooms. Both quantitative and qualitative data can be collected throughout the assessment cycle, and mixed method research designs can be particularly suitable for investigating socio-cultural and socio-political contexts surrounding the use of assessments at a regional or national level. Quantitative analysis captures the overall patterns, trends and growth, while qualitative analysis enables researchers to monitor variability in local settings and to work with the 'ecological' features of context (Jones and Saville forthcoming 2016). The project reported by Khalifa and Docherty (see Chapter 11, this volume) on the investigation of the impact of a Cambridge English test provides an example of this macro–micro link in the collection and consideration of macro-level test performance data and socio-contextual factors, alongside micro-level data on stakeholder attitudes.

The *timeline* is particularly relevant for validation within the operational assessment cycle, and in particular for impact-related research of the kind described above. The timing of concurrent or sequential phases in a research design in order to combine qualitative and quantitative methods fits well with the notion of validation as an ongoing process. Increasingly we would expect to see *longitudinal designs* which have a number of anticipated phases over an extended period being used in validation programmes so that insights gained in one research phase can be followed up in a subsequent phase, e.g. a quantitative survey followed up by interviews with participants, and so on.

Integrating mixed methods into the operational and continual improvement cycles

In the previous section, the procedural dimension of assessment was illustrated showing how a well-managed operational cycle is necessary to develop and deliver high-quality language tests and to implement continual improvements over time. The link is therefore made between administrative aspects of test management and theoretical concerns related to validity and validation. The importance of collecting many types of data to support the validity argument and to drive improvements has also been highlighted and it should be clear that the systematic and rigorous use of mixed methods designs can help achieve these twin aims.

From an assessment point of view, the types of evidence required to build a validity argument and to improve the tests depend on the phase of the operational cycle and whether there are opportunities for data collection within routine procedures or whether research projects need to be set up to address specific validation questions which cannot otherwise be addressed (e.g. in designing new test formats or rating procedures). From the mixed methods point of view, there are three main considerations: the *type* of design (basic or advanced); the *purpose* of integrating the methods; and the *timing* of the strands and *sequencing* of the data collection. For example:

- qualitative and quantitative data collected independently then compared and contrasted
- quantitative findings followed up and explained using qualitative data
- qualitative findings followed up and generalised using quantitative data
- mixed methodology employed to collect data over time in multiple phases.

These approaches vary from the basic integration of independent data at any moment in time, to the complex integration of mixed methods data collected repeatedly in various ways over an extended period. Methodological explanations and illustrations of these designs are provided in Section 2 (as noted above) and case studies of the integration of mixed methods in language assessment projects can be found in Section 3. As the reader becomes more familiar with the terminology and procedural features, it is hoped that the opportunities for implementing mixed methods approaches within the operational assessment cycle (as shown in Figure 2) will become clearer.

Conclusion

In light of this discussion, it is suggested that assessment providers would benefit from a fully fledged validation 'toolkit' that enables mixed method research designs to be used effectively in the ongoing management of assessment systems and in the integration of validation programmes within operational processes. This presents significant challenges – including the development of the necessary skills to carry out such a programme and the allocation of the necessary time and resources for implementation under operational conditions. A tall order?

This challenge is addressed in the following chapters whereby the intersection between assessment systems, validation and the use of mixed methods will be explored in greater depth with a dual focus – one lens on the philosophical and theoretical dimensions and the other on practical guidance and suggestions for practice.

In the next chapter (Chapter 3), Creswell and Zhou return to the historical and philosophical roots of mixed methods and describe how it has expanded into 'the third methodological revolution'. They conclude with five concrete recommendations in designing mixed methods research in the context of language assessment. These are then explored in the rest of the volume, through a focus on methodology in Section 2, a look at case studies in Section 3, and a practical framework for the design and implementation of mixed methods studies in Section 4. The aim is to guide the reader 'from ideas to action' and to provide useful suggestions for carrying out mixed methods studies – whether for the management of high-stakes, international exams or for conducting small-scale classroom-based assessments.

Section 2
Conducting mixed methods research: Key elements, steps and considerations

3 What is mixed methods research?

John W Creswell
University of Nebraska–Lincoln

Yuchun Zhou
Ohio University

This chapter provides an overview of mixed methods and links the discussion into the testing and language assessment area. Topics covered include:

- A *definition* of mixed methods
- The *historical development of* this methodology and the expansion of mixed methods across different disciplines and across countries around the world
- The *value* of using mixed methods
- *Philosophical stances* used in this mode of enquiry
- The *skills* required using this approach and types of research designs available
- *Validity* approaches and criteria to evaluate a high-quality mixed methods study
- Recommendations *for using mixed methods in language assessment*

Introduction

The testing and assessment in second language learning literature extends into topics about individual test takers, teachers in school classrooms, educational systems of schools, policy makers, government bodies, test developers and designers, and the impact of tests on parents, stakeholders and communities. This literature spans both developed and underdeveloped countries around the world. Moreover, it portrays the importance of gathering evidence of language learning from many sources, including sources that provide both the numeric, statistical information as well as the textual, personal experiences of individuals and stakeholders. Each source of data is insightful in its own right, but when the data is combined or 'mixed', an added value follows for language learning and assessment, as discussed in

Moeller, Chapter 1, this volume (see also Jang, Wagner and Park 2014). This 'mixing' is the key idea in a new popular approach to social, behavioural, and health research called mixed methods research.

In the last couple of years, my colleagues at Nebraska and I have worked closely with Cambridge English to encourage mixed methods as a more central feature of testing and language assessment. We have provided workshops and advised them on projects. What is reported in this chapter is a summary of the major features of mixed methods research that we have introduced. Having this summary will provide essential background information for understanding the basics of this methodology and its potential for applications and the broad methodological context underlying the rest of the book. Testing and assessment in language learning is simply the new frontier for using mixed methods.

Defining mixed methods

Mixed methods research in the field of language assessment involves the collection and combination of quantitative (numbers oriented) data and qualitative (text and stories oriented) data in the test development and assessment process. This combination has applicability in several testing arenas, such as gathering both forms of data when developing a test, examining how test takers and stakeholders view the utility of a test, revising the rating scales for a test, and assessing the appropriate level for a test based on an individual's language ability. Mixed methods research is not simply collecting both quantitative and qualitative data. It goes beyond this to bring together, combining, or integrating both forms of data. It involves the combination (or integration) of the two databases (Bryman 2006a) to provide something larger than either database by itself. This combination of two databases will add value to our understanding of research problems and potential solutions (Haines 2011). Mixed methods is not simply collecting qualitative data and analysing it quantitatively. There is a name for this approach: content analysis (Krippendorff 2013). Mixed methods research involves collecting *both* quantitative and qualitative data – and we believe that each form will yield a different picture of the problem we are studying. Mixed methods is not collecting *multiple* forms of qualitative data, such as observations and interviews, or *multiple* forms of quantitative data, such as surveys and experimental data. Arguing that quantitative and qualitative data provide different pictures of our problems, then distinct advantages accrue from collecting both forms of data. Mixed methods is not mixed models. Mixed models is a quantitative technique to thinking about different levels of numeric data in a study. Mixed methods is not simply formative and summative evaluation. It has more components, such as mixed methods questions, mixed methods designs, and other features that make it a systematic methodology for research.

Those applying mixed methods to language assessment also need to recognise the difference between qualitative and quantitative data. Qualitative data consists of open-ended responses where individuals provide their own individual perspectives and ratings to questions. Quantitative data consists of closed-ended quantitative responses where the enquirer sets the questions and the response categories in advance, and then records information based on these categories. Combining, then, means that open-ended responses and closed-ended responses are brought together. They are sometimes merged, where they come together as one overall result or sometimes they are connected where one builds on the other. At times, one database may play a supporting role to a larger database, as when qualitative data is added to experiments. This is called embedding the qualitative data within an experiment. Thus, the way we combine the two databases is through merging, connecting, or embedding, and these three forms of integration are well established in the mixed methods literature (Creswell and Plano Clark 2011).

Thus, mixed methods involves at least four major components:

- the collection and analysis of both quantitative and qualitative data in response to research questions
- the integration or combination of both forms of data within these procedures
- the use of a specific design for conducting this integration
- the framing of the design within philosophical assumptions (to be discussed later).

Historical roots of mixed methods

These four elements of mixed methods have developed in scope and sophistication during the last 30 years. The field of mixed methods began during the mid-1980s and early 1990s in the subject areas of sociology, evaluation, education, and the health sciences. During this period, nine groups of writers all came to mixed methods at about the same time (Brewer and Hunter 1989, Bryman 1988, Crabtree and Miller 1992, Creswell 1994, Fielding and Fielding 1986, Greene, Caracelli and Graham 1989, Morse 1991). They represented different countries, different disciplines, and different positions on the philosophy-to-practice continuum. They worked largely independently from each other but operated, we believe, from a common logic. This logic was that qualitative research was coming of age as a legitimate approach in the social, behavioural, and health sciences, that there was value in bridging the two approaches to research rather than keeping them separate, that the methodological tools that we use needed to be expansive rather than limited in scope, and that enquiry ought to be practical and useful.

This logic formed over time from a number of ideas. Beginning in the

1970s, researchers, especially individuals in sociology and evaluation, were collecting both quantitative survey data as well as qualitative interview data (Sieber 1973). Then during the mid-1980s to the early 1990s, the writers (who we might call the 'founders') of mixed methods began writing about how to combine both quantitative and qualitative data in a systematic way. By the late 1990s, Tashakkori and Teddlie (1998) began describing this approach to research as a distinct 'methodology', a set of procedures that enquirers might employ. They then formalised the field by editing in 2003 the *Handbook of Mixed Methods in Social and Behavioral Research* (Tashakkori and Teddlie (Eds) 2003) that mapped the many dimensions of the field from philosophy to practice. By 2007, the *Journal of Mixed Methods Research* was published by Sage Publications, and it hosted an international and interdisciplinary set of editorial members. Mixed methods, meanwhile, was growing within the health sciences, and the entire field received wide encouragement when the US National Institute of Health funded a project to develop a set of guidelines for reviewers and for applicants, called *Best Practices for Mixed Methods Research in the Health Sciences* (Creswell, Klassen, Plano Clark and Smith 2011). Within a couple of years, individuals from several countries, including the US and Great Britain, organised the Mixed Methods International Research Association (MMIRA) (mmira.org) that began sponsoring international and regional conferences in 2014 and 2015 respectively. Through these years, the field of mixed methods has expanded through philosophical perspectives and through procedures to advance a methodology useful in many fields, and especially in testing and assessment.

The expansion of mixed methods

In light of these developments, mixed methods today is referred to as the 'third methodological movement', a tacit acknowledgement that mixed methods has followed the development of both quantitative and qualitative research (Tashakkori and Teddlie 2010b). This is the first methodological development in research to take advantage of the digital age to promote its growth. This is a methodology being picked up by the most prestigious institutions in the world, through courses at Harvard University, through workshops at Johns Hopkins, and through this book being published by Cambridge English, in collaboration with Cambridge University Press. It is an approach to research that is being increasingly defined and clarified, especially for the novice researcher (see Creswell 2014a). Its appeal lies in its intuitive nature, since people often draw together both the numeric data and the stories in everyday life, such as when television newscasters present the news, attorneys argue in courtrooms, and doctors discuss the test results and take a personal history with patients. Mixed methods is a practical, useful approach to thinking about research, which is larger than the quantitative communities of investigators, larger than the qualitative communities of enquirers, and reaching out to a worldwide movement that both scholars and practitioners in language assessment need to know (Onwuegbuzie 2012). Its prevalence is seen in the large number of books on the subject – estimated to be 29 authored or edited books – coming from international authors (Onwuegbuzie 2012). It has expanded across the social and behavioural sciences through both empirical and conceptual articles about mixed methods into fields such as psychology (Mayring 2007); family science (Plano Clark, Huddleston-Casas, Churchill, Green and Garrett 2008); education (Johnson, Onwuegbuzie and Turner 2007); counselling psychology (Ponterotto, Mathew and Raughley 2013); and journalism (Creswell and McCoy 2011). It is now travelling around the world through workshops, conferences, and publications in countries as diverse as South Africa (Creswell and Garrett 2008), England (O'Cathain, Murphy and Nicholl 2008), Bosnia (Jones and Kafetsios 2005), Mozambique (Igreja, Kleijn and Richters 2006) and Jordan (Clark, Shahrouri, Halasa, Khalaf, Spencer and Everson-Rose 2012). That it would apply now to the field of language testing and assessment (see Jang et al 2014, Turner 2014) is a recent application.

The value of using mixed methods

As mixed methods emerges in testing and language learning, a natural question to ask is: 'Is mixed methods better than using either quantitative or qualitative research?' This question implies a 'value-added' element which is necessary to understand (and perhaps use) mixed methods (Haines 2011). Mixed methods researchers operate under the assumption that the combination of both quantitative and qualitative research provides added value to the use of each approach by itself. This assumption is not easy to prove. What is the rationale for using mixed methods? We can simply look at mixed methods studies today and see that they offer more evidence when both forms of data are collected, and they provide new insights when both forms are involved.

For example, we can conduct a survey and report results. These results may be expected, or, more likely, be surprising or even contradictory to the literature. Why not follow up the survey with qualitative data collection – such as one-on-one interviews – to help explain the results? This is mixed methods research. As another example we could administer an instrument to a sample, say a sample of individuals in Uganda. Because the instrument likely comes from the US and the Western world, it may or may not be a good instrument to collect data. Instead of administering a non-culturally specific instrument, we might first conduct some exploratory interviews with individuals, learn how they are thinking culturally about the topics, then design or find an instrument that might fit their context and their views, and then administer the instrument. In this process we have effectively combined the initial qualitative data with later quantitative instrument data, or, used mixed methods research. In a final example, we might have an instrument that we will administer to a sample of individuals, say an instrument measuring motivation to learn a new language. We are, however, administering this instrument in a setting we may not know, such as Brunei, the small country just above Malaysia. We really do not know whether our assessment of motivation will be a good one. We could conduct some interviews at the same time we are administering the instrument and ask individuals how they learn a new language. We could then compare our results from the instrument and from our interviews to see if we get consistent results or reinforcing results. We have effectively used quantitative and qualitative data collection in tandem in mixed methods research.

The philosophical underpinnings of mixed methods

Another concern often voiced is the philosophical basis for conducting mixed methods research (Creswell and Plano Clark 2011). We must first admit that we all bring a worldview (or paradigm) to our research, whether we make it explicit or not. This worldview is a set of beliefs or values that inform how we undertake a study (Lincoln and Guba 1985). These beliefs may relate to what type of evidence we use to make claims for knowledge (epistemology), to characterise the nature of reality in the world (ontology), to express values and biases in a project (axiology), and to identify the methods used in the study (methodology). These philosophical assumptions have been largely introduced by qualitative researchers and announced (and often changed) in each new edition of the *SAGE Handbook of Qualitative Research* (Lincoln, Lynham and Guba 2011). The different belief systems (or alternative paradigms) can be discussed as postpositivist, constructivist, transformative, critical theory, and pragmatism. As shown in Table 1, any of these five belief systems could provide the foundation for a mixed methods study. They differ in terms of how researchers view reality, how claims are made for what constitutes knowledge, the use of values and biases, and in the methods or methodology used.

In mixed methods writers from the earliest days were concerned about what philosophical tenets provided a foundation for this method of enquiry (Creswell and Plano Clark 2011). People often associated methods with philosophy, and when researchers, for example, collected qualitative focus group data, it was often associated with more of a constructivist worldview of understanding multiple meanings. When researchers gathered data on instruments it reflected a reductionistic perspective associated with postpositivism (Creswell 2014b). How can two different worldviews co-exist, as is being suggested in mixed methods?

Table 1   Alternative belief systems (or paradigms) used in mixed methods

Philosophical assumptions	Postpositivist	Constructivist	Critical theory	Transformative	Pragmatism
Nature of reality	External reality	Individual reality	Social, political reality	Society-changing reality	Both external and individual reality (pluralistic)
Claims for knowledge	Objective claims	Subjective claims	Value-based claims	Power and justice claims	Problem-centred
Values/biases	Not expressed	Expressed	Negotiated	Based on needs	Real-world based
Methodology	Chiefly quantitative	Chiefly qualitative	Dialogue-based	Change oriented	Mixed methods

Sources: Creswell (2014b); Creswell and Plano Clark (2011); Lincoln, Lynham and Guba (2011)

The answer some mixed methods researchers have given to this question is to look for one underlying philosophy that informs both quantitative and qualitative data collection. Thus, some mixed methods writers adhere to pragmatism (i.e. focused on 'what works' and practice) as a philosophy (Tashakkori and Teddlie 2010b), to critical realism (Maxwell 2012), to transformative approaches (Mertens 2009) and to dialectic pluralism (Johnson 2012).

The philosophical stances being taken by mixed methods researchers range from adopting a single philosophy as the underlying underpinning, using multiple philosophical stances, or to choosing a philosophy based on the type of mixed methods design in the project (e.g. as seen in Creswell and Plano Clark 2011). In this last case, the philosophy may shift from an initial postpositivist philosophy during the survey segment of the study to more of a constructivist philosophy during the open-ended interviewing. The choice depends on how much a researcher knows about these different philosophies and which ones seem to resonate with a particular mixed methods project. A companion issue is whether to be explicit about worldview in the report of a mixed methods study. In the health sciences, we do not see much philosophy explicitly stated; in the social and behavioural sciences, it is commonplace. When it is inserted in a mixed methods plan, the responsibility falls to the researcher to explain it and to provide ample references so that readers can follow up on its use. Further, the researcher needs to be explicit about how it informs the mixed methods project (Creswell 2014a, also see Chapter 4, this volume).

The skills needed to conduct mixed methods

Philosophy introduces the need for a specific skill set of understanding to undertake mixed methods research. Unquestionably, to gather data in any of these scenarios requires time, resources, knowledge of mixed methods procedures, and skills. Individuals sometimes look at mixed methods with scepticism because they feel that it requires a large repertoire of research skills. It is true that mixed methods researchers need to have a working knowledge of both quantitative and qualitative data collection and analysis (Creswell 2014a). Coursework in statistics and experiments, as well as in qualitative interviewing and observations are required. At the University of Nebraska–Lincoln we ask students to complete both quantitative courses and qualitative courses *before* they enter the mixed methods course. This all suggests that mixed methods might be considered an advanced methodology for the most sophisticated researcher.

People say that these expanded skill sets are not present in a single researcher (Creswell 2014a). This may be true, but as our research methods become more sophisticated, the researcher of the future will have a wide range of skills to study problems. At present, one option for the new researcher is to collaborate with individuals who hold diverse methodological skills – form a mixed methods academic team (Creswell et al 2011). An example of such inter-disciplinary collaboration can be seen in the projects described by Vidaković and Robinson (Chapter 8, this volume) and Galaczi and Khabbazbashi (Chapter 9, this volume). The measurement specialist can collaborate with the community stakeholder specialist in a mixed methods language assessment project. There are ways to bring together teams of individuals for a research project that assembles different approaches to research, and this explains why mixed methods writers have begun an extensive dialogue about how to conduct mixed methods teamwork (O'Cathain et al 2008). Regardless of working in a mixed methods team, or conducting research as the 'lone' investigator, the skills need to be put in place for conducting this form of research, and it involves understanding the methods of both quantitative and qualitative research as well as the basics of mixed methods research.

The emerging designs to use

Another skill is to understand what mixed methods designs exist and which one is best suited for a particular problem in testing and assessment. No topic has been discussed more thoroughly than the types of designs available to the mixed methods researcher (see the numerous typologies of designs as discussed in Creswell and Plano Clark 2011). As a methodology, mixed methods research is not alone with this idea. In the early days of experimental research, attention was given to the types of experiments and the threats to validity in each type of design (Campbell and Fiske 1959). In the early days of qualitative research in the social sciences, the classifications of types of qualitative approaches were discussed and debated (Jacob 1987). In mixed methods, we have seen many classifications of types of designs and even discussions about whether designs should be a central feature of planning a mixed methods study. The book by Creswell and Plano Clark (2011) identified 13 different classifications of designs from different authors and different disciplines. With the many classifications and types of designs has come rather substantial confusion about how to develop procedures, how to name these designs, even how to draw a picture of the design. We feel that designs are not that complex in mixed methods research.

Recently we have sorted the types of designs into two categories: basic designs and advanced designs (see Ziegler and Kang, Chapter 4, this volume, for a more complete discussion of the types of designs, and the chapters in Section 3 for case studies of practical applications of a range of mixed methods designs). Within these types, researchers can innovate with variations, but knowing the basic designs, we believe, is essential to clearly presenting the procedures in a study. Further, we believe that within each mixed methods study is a basic design that the investigator hopes to accomplish. Then the basic designs can be expanded into more advanced designs that still include the basic design, but add on certain features to make the design more complicated.

The place to start in designing a mixed methods project is to ask yourself, 'What is my intent for the procedures of combining the quantitative and qualitative data?' Three implementation decisions are available to a researcher: either the intent is to combine the two databases by merging them to see if they converge (or are consistent); to have one database precede the other, and connect the two databases; or to embed one smaller database within a larger database or design (see Ziegler and Kang, Chapter 4, this volume). Going through this simple logic of intent will lead to the basic design for a study.

The approach in testing and language learning that we would advocate would be to consider several possible designs (Creswell and Plano Clark 2011). One type of basic design is called the *convergent design*. In this design, the intent of the research procedures is to combine the two databases so that an enquirer can see if the results are similar from quantitative and qualitative research to the same question or problem. In research language, it may be to demonstrate convergent validity. It may be to simply compare the results to see if they are consistent, inconsistent, or even contradictory. When inconsistent or contradictory results follow in a project, they need to be resolved. Because of these challenges, the convergent design is not easy to implement. An easier design, and one that graduate students often gravitate to, is the *explanatory sequential design*. The intent of this design procedure is to use follow-up qualitative findings to help explain initial quantitative results. So, the two databases are phased in – first quantitative, such as a survey, followed by qualitative, such as focus groups. We can reverse the two phases in the explanatory sequential design and emerge with an *exploratory sequential design*. The intent of this design procedure is more complicated than the explanatory design. Its intent is to see if exploratory qualitative results can be generalised to a large sample. The procedure is to explore first in order to develop a good measurement instrument or good intervention procedures that might work with a specific sample of a population. For example, in global health, this design is popular because instruments (and interventions) cannot be simply administered to a cultural group in an undeveloped country (Betancourt, Meyers-Ohki, Stevenson, Ingabire, Kanyanganzi, Munyana, Mushashi, Teta, Fayida, Cyamatare, Stulac and Beardslee 2011).

If we look closely at a published mixed methods study, we can find a basic design in operation, whether it is made explicit or not. At a more advanced level, we can surround these basic designs with another feature. We might include the basic design within a pre- and post-test experiment, called an *intervention design*. This type of mixed methods design might be used in language assessment to determine if a classroom intervention improves students' ability to learning language reading skills. Another type of advance design would be a *social justice design* in which one of the basic designs is framed by a need to bring about change. For example, in an underdeveloped nation, a survey would first be administered to test takers in a rural area to assess their willingness to learn the English language followed by interviews to explain their survey results. The entire project would be aimed at a social justice goal of raising the language level of people in the rural village. Another advanced design would be to conduct a mixed methods evaluation project of the success of a Cambridge English test in an underdeveloped country. An example of this design is given by Khalifa and Docherty (Chapter 11, this volume) in their study of the impact of an examination for young learners in Viet Nam. This mixed methods evaluation would have data collected concurrently and sequentially to establish whether the use of a test impacted the views of stakeholders in the community about the value of testing. It would consist of a number of steps, such as an initial needs assessment, the identification of a theory, the design of a programme on testing, and an evaluation of the success of the programme. Specific quantitative and qualitative projects would be connected in a *multistage evaluation mixed methods design*. (see Nastasi, Hitchcock, Sarkar, Burkholder, Varjas and Jayasena (2007) for an example of this in Sri Lanka). In a final type of advanced design, the researcher may develop case profiles of different types of cases illustrating a problem and gather both quantitative and qualitative data and integrate it within each case. This *case study* advanced mixed methods approach would be useful in identifying cases of different stakeholders in a community and conducting an impact study of the use of English language tests on different groups of people, such as community leaders, teachers, and administrators of schools. For each case, qualitative interview data would be combined with questionnaire data to help build the profiles.

With these basic and advanced designs, how is one to choose which design best fits a plan for a mixed methods study? The place to start would be with the intent of the design: to merge databases (convergent design), to have one follow the other (explanatory sequential or exploratory sequential design), or to embed mixed methods research within an experiment, a social justice agenda, a programme evaluation, or a case analysis (see Ziegler and Kang, Chapter 4, this volume). Building on this would then be to assess what mixed methods designs are popular in an investigator's particular field, whether the researcher is more comfortable starting with quantitative or qualitative research, the ease of using the design, since the designs vary in their phases and complexity, and the relationship of the design to the research questions being addressed.

Other aspects of design to use

Consider now that the type of design becomes a centrepiece for developing many other aspects of a good mixed methods study. Once the project director or researcher/research team have a reason for using mixed methods, and a question that is best answered through mixed methods, then it is time to focus on the type of design. Let's take a simple illustration from the language assessment area to illustrate these points. Assume that we are interested in learning how the school administration uses test results of students in the school to improve the teacher's instruction in the classroom. Assume further this issue will lead to a convergent mixed methods design. The design can be foreshadowed by the *title* of a mixed methods study and provide a useful interplay among the various parts of a project. We can now title the project that leans in the direction of the convergent design. In this project we might assess how the test results (quantitative data) compare with interviews with teachers about their teaching practices (qualitative data). Thus, we might title our project: 'The Confluence of Test Results and Perceptions of Teaching Practices in the School Classroom'. The design can also relate closely to the *mixed methods research question*. This is a new type of question not found in our standard research methods books, but one that has emerged in the mixed methods literature (Tashakkori and Creswell 2007). An example of a convergent design mixed methods question would be: 'Are the results of student test scores reflected in practices mentioned by the teachers in the classroom?' Further, it is important in mixed methods research to state quantitative, qualitative, and mixed methods questions. The design can also help us order the *sequence* of these questions. Since, in our hypothetical project, we are merging the results from the quantitative student scores with the qualitative interview data, we could start with either the quantitative or qualitative research questions, and then follow them with the mixed methods question (see Creswell et al 2011). If our project began with a survey (quantitative) followed by qualitative data (an explanatory sequential design), we would order our questions in a way consistent with quantitative first, followed by qualitative, and then mixed methods. Thus, the design can assist in deciding how to order these questions (e.g. in a project where surveys precede the interviews, we might order the questions as quantitative, qualitative, and then mixed methods). The design can be portrayed in a *diagram* of the procedures (see Miller and Bustamante, Chapter 5, this volume, and examples of procedural diagrams in the chapters in Section 3). Diagrams are used in projects to picture the theory operating in the mixed methods study (see Classen, Lopez, Winter, Awadzi, Ferree and Garvan 2007); they are also used in visualising the process of selecting participants in experimental designs (see the CONSORT guidelines in Schulz, Altman and Moher 2010). Thus, we can use them in mixed methods research to present procedures that are often complicated because of collecting and analysing both quantitative and qualitative data. This diagram would show that we are collecting both student performance scores and themes from teachers about how the scores impact their classroom teaching. These two databases would then be compared to see if there is convergence (low-performing students are given special instruction) or divergence (low-performing students are not given any special attention in the classroom). The design also helps us think about how to *represent* the results in a *joint display* (see Ziegler and Kang, Chapter 4, this volume) so that we can easily compare the student scores with the teacher perceptions. As shown in Table 2, we can integrate the two databases in a single table by arraying the student scores (e.g. classrooms with high, medium, and

Table 2 Joint display of a convergent design with hypothetical data

Quantitative test score classes	Qualitative interviews with teachers about using test data results in classroom teaching	Divergence or convergence of views
High-performing student classes	• Test results used in lesson plans • Introduced regularly • Used for forming groups	Convergence: in classrooms with high student test scores, the quantitative information from test results is used extensively
Average-performing student classes	• Some activities based on test results • Irregular review of test scores	Some convergence: in classrooms with average student scores only a modest number of activities are based on test information
Low-performing student classes	• Test results not used • Brought in at the end of the year • Minimal attention in activities	Convergence: in classrooms with low test scores, little emphasis placed on the importance of test results

low student performance scores) in one column and the classroom teacher perceptions of use of the scores (e.g. specific activities implemented versus no specific activities implemented) in another column. We can look across these columns to determine whether student scores seem to impact classroom teaching, and we can provide an additional column in which we discuss why the quantitative results and the qualitative results converge or diverge.

The validity strategies in mixed methods

The strategies used to examine validity in a mixed methods study should also reflect the specific design (Creswell and Plano Clark 2011). Discussions to date in the mixed methods literature have emphasised the importance of establishing validity for both the quantitative and qualitative strands of a project (see, for example, Tashakkori and Teddlie 1998; and more recently Onwuegbuzie and Johnson 2006). Also recent discussions have arrayed traditional quantitative, traditional qualitative, and mixed methods types of validation under a general framework of construct validation and they have incorporated several discussions of mixed methods validity under this common rubric (Dellinger and Leech 2007). In addition, authors have discussed how it relates to the research design and data collection, data analysis, and interpretation of findings (Onwuegbuzie and Johnson 2006, Teddlie and Tashakkori 2009). For example, Teddlie and Tashakkori (2009) addressed validity in mixed methods as it relates to the design and the interpretation stages of research. They discuss design quality (suitability given the questions, fidelity of the quality and rigour of procedures, consistency across all aspects of the study, and analytic implementation of procedures) and interpretive rigour (consistency with findings, consistency with theory, interpretations given participants and scholars, and distinctiveness in terms of credible or plausible conclusions). Onwuegbuzie and Johnson (2006), on the other hand, focused on data analysis, calling validity 'legitimization' (2006:57) and they specified a typology. They conceptualised legitimisation (e.g. the design, the data analysis, or the interpretation), and specific procedures that mixed methods researchers employed in the data analysis phase of their research.

Although these are useful models for thinking about validity in mixed methods, we feel that it cannot be adequately addressed (or made specific) as a procedure unless the researcher conceptualises it within a research design. The act of combining qualitative and quantitative approaches raises potential validity issues that extend beyond the validity concerns that arise in the separate quantitative or qualitative methods procedures. For example, in a convergent design, validity is compromised if the questions are not parallel between the quantitative and qualitative strands of the design. In an explanatory sequential design, validity suffers if the results from the initial quantitative phase are not followed up in the qualitative second phase. We have called these 'validity threats' to the design and they are mentioned in Creswell's book (Creswell 2014a). In sum, this sensitivity to linking validity threats to designs provides a useful way to think about validity in mixed methods projects (see Ziegler and Kang, Chapter 4, this volume, for a useful taxonomy of validity consideration in mixed methods studies and an illustration of applying this taxonomy in the study described by Galaczi and Khabbazbashi, Chapter 9, this volume).

Emerging evaluation standards

Finally, any discussion about mixed methods needs to address the emerging standards of evaluation for a high-quality mixed methods project. We should be cautious about a definite set of standards in any field, although the testing and assessment area seems quite comfortable with standards that apply across countries and the use of language. In mixed methods, for example, the National Science Foundation issued *The 2002 User-Friendly Handbook for Project Evaluation* that contained a section on mixed methods evaluations (www.nsf.gov/pubs/2002/nsf02057/start.htm). The Robert Wood Johnson website for the *Qualitative Research Guidelines Project* (www.qualres.org) in 2008 provided a practical set of guidelines useful for the qualitative component in a mixed methods project. In 2010, the United States Agency for International Development (USAID) issued a discussion about tips for conducting mixed method evaluations, and articles have been written about basic guidelines for research in mixed methods research in medical education (Schifferdecker and Reed 2009). Workshops, in a way, advance how mixed methods is being and perhaps should be conducted, such as the 2012 National Institutes of Health (NIH) workshop on 'Using Mixed Methods to Optimize Dissemination and Implementation of Health Interventions'. As mentioned earlier, in 2011, the NIH in the US issued recommendations for mixed methods on their website (obssr.od.nih.gov/mixed_methods_research).

In addition, mixed methods writers have advanced their own criteria for elements that should be in a good mixed methods project. One comes from Great Britain (O'Cathain et al 2008) and the second from the United States (Creswell and Plano Clark 2011). O'Cathain et al (2008) offered guidance for Good Reporting of a Mixed Methods Study (GRAMMS):

- describe the justification for using a mixed methods approach to the research question
- describe the design in terms of the purpose, priority, and sequence of methods
- describe each method in terms of sampling, data collection and analysis

- describe where integration has occurred, how it has occurred, and who has participated in it
- describe any limitation of one method associated with the presence of the other method
- describe any insights gained from mixing or integrating methods.

This is a helpful list because it focuses on key points raised by mixed methods researchers over the years and it would add rigour and systematic procedures for those engaged in mixed methods language assessment projects. It calls for a justification or reason for mixed methods, a specification of the type of design and its purpose or intent, the rigorous methods of data collection and analysis, the centrality of integration in a study, the limitations or validity threats that may arise, and the value of using mixed methods. It parallels, too, many of the points raised by Creswell and Plano Clark (2011) in their list of aspects central to a good mixed methods project. The researcher should:

- collect both quantitative and qualitative data
- employ rigorous procedures in the methods of data collection and analysis
- integrate or mix (merge, connect, or embed) the two sources of data so that their combined use provides better understanding of the research problem than one source or the other
- use a mixed methods research design and integrate all features of the study with the design
- convey research terms consistent with those being used in the mixed method field.

In retrospect, we might add to this list to encourage those conducting mixed methods in testing and assessment to cite the literature both in mixed methods and in the studies that have incorporated these methods, as documented in the following Section 2 applications and the Section 3 specific projects undertaken by Cambridge English.

Recommendations

How, then, might we think about designing and conducting a mixed methods project in the field of testing and language assessment?:

1. It is first of all important in mixed methods to *gather both quantitative and qualitative data* whether the topic relates to specific tests or the assessment process of evaluating the impact of the test (see Moeller, Chapter 1, and Saville, Chapter 2, this volume). Furthermore, mixed methods is more than simply collecting both forms of data – it also involves combining (or linking or mixing) the two types of data so that

their value, in combination, becomes greater than either the quantitative or qualitative data alone.

2. The use of mixed methods in language testing and assessment will provide a model for the field of measurement worldwide to expand its approach beyond traditional quantitative applications to include qualitative approaches and to begin to see the value of *integrating both quantitative and qualitative data and results*.

3. It is helpful to *convey to audiences the philosophy* behind a mixed methods project. Testing and language assessment personnel have several philosophies from which to choose, and there are options from which to select depending on the orientation of the researcher, the topic and goals of the study, and the audience for a project.

4. To conduct a mixed methods project requires *three sets of skills*: skill in quantitative research, skill in qualitative research, and skill in mixed methods research. This latter skill can be obtained from reading the general mixed methods literature as well as specific applications in testing and assessment.

5. At the heart of mixed methods research lies *the research design* (see Ziegler and Kang, Chapter 4, this volume, for an in-depth discussion of mixed methods research designs). The design informs many aspects of a mixed methods project. Testing and assessment scholars and practitioners need to have a reason for choosing a design, provide a diagram of it, and interrelate the design to other important procedures, such as the title, the mixed methods research question, the visual portrayal of the procedures, the ways to represent integration across databases, and the validity considerations as well as the evaluation criteria.

The remaining chapters in this volume provide in-depth discussion and illustration of all of these key aspects of mixed methods research.

4 Mixed methods designs

Nick Ziegler
Le Kang
University of Nebraska–Lincoln

This chapter provides a comprehensive framework for understanding the processes involved in mixing quantitative and qualitative methods to generate high-quality meta-inferences, the source of the value added in conducting mixed methods research.

Topics highlighted in this chapter include:

- The *components* of the mixed methods study required of producing *synergy* between quantitative and qualitative strands

- Strategies for generating *meta-inferences* at the *design level, methods level, and interpretation level* of mixed methods studies

- *Heuristic illustrations* of the mixed methods designs in second language assessment
- The evaluation of *mixed method validity concerns* specific to generating *high-quality meta-inferences* when conducting mixed methods research

The purpose of combining both quantitative and qualitative methods is to produce a synergetic effect, whereby the whole is greater than the sum of its parts (Nastasi, Hitchcock and Brown 2010). The mixture allows for complementary methodological strengths and non-overlapping weaknesses (Johnson and Onwuegbuzie 2004) and can result in superior research findings and outcomes (Johnson, Onwuegbuzie and Turner 2007) through the production of meta-inferences (Tashakkori and Teddlie 2008). This chapter builds on the general overview of mixed methods presented by Creswell and Zhou (Chapter 3, this volume), and introduces a comprehensive framework for understanding how to accomplish this synergetic effect within the context of second language assessment. This will be accomplished in three sections: the components of a mixed methods study, heuristic illustrations of the mixed methods designs in second language assessment, and validity concerns specific to generating high-quality meta-inferences when conducting mixed methods research.

Components of the mixed methods study

Mixed methods research is defined as 'research in which the investigator collects and analyses data, integrates the findings, and draws inferences using both quantitative and qualitative approaches in a single programme of inquiry' (Tashakkori and Creswell 2007:4). The purposeful integration of findings from both data sets enables the researcher to draw inferences, producing a synergetic effect whereby the 'combined effect of mixing methods approaches results in both a research process and outcomes (findings) that are greater than those produced by the application of either the qualitative or quantitative approach alone' (Nastasi et al 2010:321). To accomplish the synergetic effect, mixed methods studies involve more than the use of both quantitative and qualitative approaches (see Creswell and Zhou, Chapter 3, this volume). Figure 1 illustrates how the use of mixed methods bridges the quantitative vs qualitative divide to produce a synergetic effect.

Traditionally, the quantitative approach (see Figure 1) adopts the postpositivist worldview which attempts to predict, control and generalise findings (Merriam 2009). The ontological assumption made is that reality is objective, and therefore singular. Generalisable theories are produced and tested to explain reality. The researcher engages in deductive reasoning, a top-down approach starting from the theory moving down to the data. Quantitative surveys are developed and/or administered. The results of rigorous investigation are used to evaluate the theory, assessing generalisability.

On the other side of the Venn diagram, traditionally, the qualitative study involves a constructivist, or interpretive, worldview, which attempts to describe, understand and interpret the phenomenon of interest. The ontological assumption is that reality is subjective, and therefore multiple realities are produced from the multiple perspectives individuals have (Creswell 2013b). The purpose of study is to develop a rich description of the specific context investigated. This inductive, bottom-up approach uses the data to develop

Figure 1 Comparison of quantitative, mixed and qualitative methods

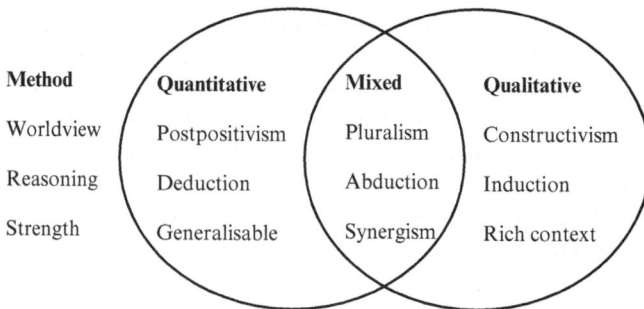

Method	Quantitative	Mixed	Qualitative
Worldview	Postpositivism	Pluralism	Constructivism
Reasoning	Deduction	Abduction	Induction
Strength	Generalisable	Synergism	Rich context

the understanding of the context. Due to the epistemological assumption that reality is socially constructed and multiple in nature, generalising from one context to another is not useful and, by its nature, impossible (Denzin and Lincoln 2011).

There has been much debate investigating whether the mixed methods approach can bridge the divide between quantitative and qualitative methodologies. This has centred on the incompatibility thesis: 'compatibility between quantitative and qualitative methods is impossible due to incompatibility of the paradigms that underline the methods' (Teddlie and Tashakkori 2003:14–15). While this debate continues (see Denzin and Lincoln 2011), mixed methods research continues to gain momentum as a third methodology generally (Hall and Howard 2008), within applied linguistics generally (Hashemi and Babaii 2013), and within language testing and assessment specifically (Jang, Wagner and Park 2014, Turner 2014).

In response to the incompatibility thesis, mixed methods studies embrace paradigm pluralism, 'the belief that a variety of paradigms may serve as the underlying philosophy for the use of mixed methods' (Teddlie and Tashakkori 2012:779). Remaining flexible with underlying philosophical assumptions allows the researcher to focus on the purpose of the study at hand, to most adequately answer the research questions. Mixed methods research recognises the strengths and limitations of quantitative and qualitative methods, seeking to combine the two to come to a more complete understanding of real-world phenomena (Creswell 2011).

Throughout a mixed methods study, the researcher engages in both inductive (pattern discovery) and deductive (theory or hypothesis testing) logic to uncover the best set of explanations for understanding one's results (Johnson and Onwuegbuzie 2004). Creatively generating insights and making inferences based on the quantitative and qualitative data involves a third form of reasoning, termed abduction (Teddlie and Tashakkori 2012). Abduction is a 'kind of reasoning that moves back and forth between induction and deduction' (Morgan 2007:71). The use of abductive logic is the basis for the claim that mixed methods produces a synergetic effect.

The strength of the mixed methods study lies in synergism between quantitative and qualitative methods, whereby the 'combined effect (mixing methods) is greater than the sum of individual effects (qualitative or quantitative alone)' (Hall and Howard 2008:251). Purposefully integrating rich qualitative methods and rigorous quantitative methods informs the production of meta-inferences that otherwise would not be possible. A meta-inference is 'an overall conclusion, explanation, or understanding developed through an integration of the inferences obtained from the qualitative and quantitative strands' (Teddlie and Tashakkori 2009:101). Meta-inferences are the true source of the value added by mixed methods.

Fetters, Curry and Creswell (2013) identify three possible outcomes for meta-inferences generated from integrating quantitative and qualitative strands: confirmation, expansion, and/or discordance. Confirmation occurs when findings are mutually corroborated. The two data sources produce similar findings, enhancing the overall credibility, or validity, of the study (Bryman 2006b). To facilitate this comparison, it is recommended that the quantitative and qualitative strands address similar, or parallel, constructs (Greene 2008). Expansion occurs when the findings from two strands diverge, with one expanding on, or explaining, the other (Fetters et al 2013). Generally, expansion occurs when the qualitative and quantitative strands are conducted sequentially. The initial analysis of the first strand (quantitative or qualitative) informs the investigation (research questions, data collection and analysis) of the second, thereby enhancing the study (Bryman 2006b). Finally, it is also possible that discordance emerges between the quantitative and qualitative strands. Discordance occurs when 'qualitative and quantitative findings are inconsistent, incongruous, contradict, conflict, or disagree with each other' (Fetters et al 2013:2,144). When confronted with discordance between data strands it is important to investigate the source of the contradictions, as they may lead to the development of new understandings about the nature of the phenomenon of interest (Venkatesh, Brown and Bala 2013). This investigation may also lead to sources of bias within the quantitative and qualitative strands requiring a re-examination of the data, further data collection, or recommendations for follow-up studies (Fetters et al 2013).

Producing meta-inferences is the purpose of mixed methods studies (Venkatesh et al 2013). They stem from the inclusion of points of interface, where the two data sets mix or connect in some way, throughout the programme of study (Guest 2013). Fetters et al (2013) provide a framework for understanding where and how these points of interface can occur: design level, methods level, and interpretation level.

Design level

The two fundamental considerations when designing a mixed methods study are the purpose and the timing of quantitative and qualitative integration (Guest 2013). Creswell and Plano Clark (2011) provide a parsimonious set of three basic designs and two advanced designs to help conceptualise the multitude of possibilities (see Table 1). These designs will be explored heuristically in the next section; however, an overview here will serve to complete this framework for understanding how mixed methods research accomplishes its synergetic effect.

The two typical features of the three basic designs are: 1) the use of a pragmatic worldview, and 2) one iteration of quantitative and qualitative strands. First, the pragmatic worldview is described as a middle position

Table 1 Mixed methods designs

	Name	Purpose of integration	Timing of strands
Basic	Convergent	Quantitative results and qualitative findings are compared and contrasted	Quantitative and qualitative strands are conducted independently
	Explanatory	Qualitative methods are used to explain quantitative results	Quantitative data is collected and analysed prior to the qualitative strand
	Exploratory	Quantitative methods are used to generalise qualitative findings	Qualitative data is collected and analysed prior to the quantitative strand
Advanced	Embedded	Mixed methodology is employed in a programme of study utilising a specific theoretical lens, paradigm, or methodology	Timing of qualitative and quantitative strands depends on the theoretical lens, paradigm, or methodology utilised
	Multistage	Mixed methodology is employed in a programme of study involving multiple phases	Multiple iterations of quantitative and qualitative data collection and analysis are involved

philosophically (Johnson and Onwuegbuzie 2004), that 'emphasises the importance of the research questions, the value of experiences, and practical consequences, actions, and understanding of real world phenomena' (Creswell 2011:276). The adoption of a different worldview, paradigm, or methodology is the key distinction between the use of a basic design and the use of an embedded design, the first advanced design. Second, the three basic designs involve only one iteration of qualitative and quantitative data collection and analysis, as seen, for example in the impact project described by Khalifa and Docherty in Chapter 11, this volume. Multiple iterations of quantitative and/or qualitative strands constitute the use of a multistage design, the second advanced design, an illustration of which can be seen in the scale development project discussed by Galaczi and Khabbazbashi, Chapter 9, this volume. The differences between the three basic designs lie in the purpose and the timing of integration between the quantitative and qualitative strands.

Investigating confirmation, the purpose of the *convergent design* is to compare and contrast quantitative results and qualitative findings. The procedures are rather straightforward – to collect both quantitative and qualitative data at separate times, to analyse both databases separately, to integrate the results, and then to explain why they are similar, different, or perhaps contradictory. Thus meta-inferences are generated through merging the two data sets during the interpretation phase of the study, after both the quantitative and qualitative strands have been independently conducted and analysed (for an illustration, see Khalifa and Docherty, Chapter 11, this volume).

There are two chief difficulties in conducting this design. First, the researcher needs to anticipate bringing the two database results together, which requires asking the same, or parallel, questions on both the quantitative and qualitative data collection procedures. This is referred to as 'merging', a methods level strategy for generating meta-inferences. A second difficulty is how to actually compare (or integrate) the two databases when one is numeric (quantitative) and the other is text (qualitative). Researchers are not accustomed to thinking about this comparison. Mixed methods researchers have developed various interpretation level strategies to accomplish this, such as transforming one database so that it can be merged directly with the other database, referred to as 'data transformation' (Onwuegbuzie and Teddlie 2003), or through creating tables or graphs that array both quantitative and qualitative results together, referred to as 'joint displays' (Creswell and Plano Clark (2011), see also Guetterman and Salamoura, Chapter 7, this volume).

In the end, the interpretation from the convergent design is based on whether the findings from the two databases converge or diverge. For example, a researcher interested in the washback effect of a test (as illustrated in the project reported by Khalifa and Docherty, Chapter 11, this volume) may conduct both a quantitative survey and qualitative interviews investigating parallel constructs with a set of participants. After the data was independently analysed, the researcher would compare and contrast the findings from both strands. Drawing upon the meta-inferences made from merging the data sets would produce a more comprehensive understanding of the washback effect than having included either the qualitative or the quantitative strands alone.

Investigating expansion, the purpose of the *explanatory design* is to use qualitative methods to establish a rich explanation of the quantitative results from the participants' perspectives. This is a sequential design involving first the collection and analysis of the quantitative strand followed by the qualitative strand. As such, the explanatory design facilitates two points of interface between the quantitative and qualitative strands: during the building, or transition, from the quantitative to the qualitative, and at the interpretation level when integrating the qualitative findings with the initial quantitative results.

There are two crucial challenges associated with the explanatory design. First is deciding which quantitative results require further investigation (termed 'building', a methods level strategy). This will depend on the project, but often qualitative follow-up data helps explain the major quantitative results (e.g. significant results, effect sizes) or findings that are surprising and not easily explained in the literature or in theory (Creswell 2015). The second challenge is selecting an appropriate sample of participants with whom to follow up. Generally, it is best to select a purposeful sub-sample from participants who had participated in the quantitative phase of the study. This allows the researcher to supplement the understanding built from the quantitative methods with qualitative methods without needing to first establish that the quantitative measures are generalisable to a new sample. The sampling strategy will depend on the purpose of the study as well. Using the quantitative results to inform the sampling procedure selected is termed 'connecting', a methods level strategy. This is most commonly done by identifying cases characteristic of the normal, or average, quantitative responses (i.e. typical case) or selecting cases characteristic of the extreme quantitative responses (i.e. maximum variation).

Meta-inferences are generated in the interpretation phase, after the qualitative findings have been analysed. To follow our washback example, a researcher interested in the washback effect of a test may decide to first conduct and analyse a survey given to a large number of test takers. The quantitative results may identify areas for further investigation which could be investigated qualitatively with a purposefully selected subsample of the original participants. As such, the qualitative findings would build on the quantitative results, providing an explanation of the areas identified for further investigation.

Reversing the order of the quantitative and qualitative strands is a defining component of our next basic mixed methods design: the *exploratory design*. The intent is to see if, or to what extent, exploratory qualitative results can be generalised to a larger sample. This typically involves using the qualitative results to develop a good measurement instrument or good intervention procedures that might work with a specific sample of a population (as seen, for example in Galaczi and Khabbazbashi, Chapter 9, this volume). Distinct from the explanatory sequential design (which has two phases – first quantitative, and then qualitative), the exploratory sequential design actually has three phases. The first phase would be exploratory and qualitative, the second phase would be the development of an instrument or an intervention, and the third phase would be to test out the instrument or intervention. Thus the three phases make for a more rigorous design than two phases involved in the explanatory design.

The challenge in this design lies not only in the use of more phases, but also at two distinct points in conducting the study. First, the researcher needs to determine from the initial qualitative exploration what information from the findings to use in the design of the instrument or the intervention activities. So the quotes, codes, and themes from the qualitative phase need to be transformed into questions for an instrument or into specific activities that might go into an intervention trial. A second challenge lies in creating the quantitative instrument or intervention. Rigorous scale and instrument development can be challenging, requiring many steps. This too applies to the creation of activities for an intervention.

Integration typically occurs at both the methods and the interpretation levels. Following our example, a researcher interested in the washback effect of a test may decide to first conduct qualitative interviews with a small set of participants. If the researcher is interested in establishing the degree to which their qualitative findings can be extrapolated to a larger population, the emerging themes could inform the development of a quantitative survey to be administered with a larger sample. The results from the quantitative data collection and analysis would serve to generalise the qualitative findings.

While these three basic designs account for the overwhelming majority (89%) of mixed methods research published in the field of applied linguistics between 1995 and 2008 (Hashemi and Babaii 2013), the range of potential combinations of quantitative and qualitative enquiry in mixed methods designs is limitless (Maxwell and Loomis 2003, Tashakkori and Teddlie (Eds) 2003). For this reason, the two advanced designs included in Table 1 are more general umbrella terms without prescriptive steps, as is the case with the basic designs. These are included for the purpose of conceptualising the multitude of other possibilities. Examples of other designs which combine qualitative and quantitative enquiry can be seen in the chapters in Section 3.

In accordance with paradigm pluralism, *embedded designs* (the first advanced design in Table 1) involve the use of mixed methods to enhance a programme of study utilising a specific theoretical lens, paradigm, or methodology (Creswell and Plano Clark 2011). Embedded designs could entail a single basic design, or multiple iterations of quantitative and/or qualitative strands embedded into a specific theoretical lens. The purpose and timing of data integration will depend on the selected paradigm and the overall purpose of the study, potentially occurring at all three levels (design, methods and interpretation).

An example of an embedded design stemming from a more quantitative perspective is the mixed methods *intervention design*. The intervention design involves the integration of qualitative components into a randomised controlled experimental design. A useful way to think about this adaptation is to consider bringing qualitative data collection into the trial before the trial begins, during the trial, or after the trial concludes. In some mixed methods intervention design studies, the qualitative data flows into the trial at multiple points in conducting the experiment. The argument for using qualitative data is that it helps to contextualise the quantitative results.

The challenge in this design is that the quantitative experimental researcher needs to know and understand how to use qualitative research, or, alternatively, seek out team members who can bring qualitative skills into the study. This design is also subject to the challenges that arise in the basic designs, and the type of basic design being used in the intervention trial will introduce its own set of issues that need to be addressed. A further challenge lies in how to visualise this type of design. We encourage visualising this design by advancing the flow of activities in an experiment, and then adding in the qualitative data collection and analysis where it occurs in the experiment.

Overall, the intervention mixed methods design seems to be gathering interest and momentum (Lewin, Glenton and Oxman 2009). Continuing with our hypothetical example, a researcher interested in the washback effect of a test may decide to establish randomised experimental and control groups of participants who either take the test or do not take the test. Before the test is administered, the researcher could use a convergent design to establish baseline data. Sometime after the test, the researcher could then conduct another convergent design to measure change attributed to the intervention. In this case, the use of mixed methods to investigate the test's impact effect would significantly enhance the intervention study's ability to attribute differences between the control and experimental groups to the use of the test due to a more complete understanding generated by the multiple iterations of quantitative and qualitative strands.

A further example of embedded designs stemming from a more qualitative perspective is the mixed methods *social justice design*. Social justice designs employ a critical worldview, seeking to 'change, emancipate, [and/or] empower' (Merriam 2009:11). Other frameworks could be used as well, such as feminist, racial or ethnic, a community-based participatory framework, or a lifestyle orientation or disability framework. The key idea is that a basic mixed methods design is framed by a larger orientation to help address social justice.

Challenges in using this design include identifying how the framework will actually flow into the mixed methods study, and describing the framework in some detail at the outset of a study so that the reader clearly understands its use in the project.

In the context of second language assessment, community-based participatory research is a collaborative effort between research institutions and community members designed for the explicit purpose of benefiting the participating community (Sandoval, Lucero, Oetzel, Avila, Belone, Mau and Wallerstein 2012). An example of this research approach is provided by Vidaković and Robinson, Chapter 8, this volume. A difficulty in the development of second language assessments is ensuring that a test produces its intended impact (i.e. consequential validity). This is especially difficult when considering the diversity of cultures, societies, and communities to which the test takers belong. If confronted with evidence challenging the consequential validity of a test within a specific population of test takers, the use of a mixed methods community-based participatory research programme could be employed. Potentially an exploratory sequential design could be used to qualitatively ascertain the perception of the test's impact with a small group of stakeholders that leads to a survey administered to a larger sample of stakeholders to generalise the findings from the qualitative phase. Community members could then be involved in refining the test, which would need to be quantitatively validated. A final exploratory design could be used to establish the consequential validity of the refined test. In this example, the use of mixed methods facilitates the involvement of community members for the purpose of improving the impact, or washback, the test has in the community.

The second advanced mixed methods design is the *multistage design*. The multistage design is a programme of study that involves multiple iterations of quantitative and qualitative strands, but it relies on the pragmatic paradigm. It is not embedded into a separate paradigm or methodology. The inclusion of multiple phases emphasises the characterisation of mixed methods as an 'iterative, cyclical approach' (Teddlie and Tashakkori 2012:781) to conduct-ing research. As with the embedded design, the starting point (convergent, exploratory, explanatory – or a traditional qualitative/quantitative phase) will depend on the specific purpose of the programme of study. Consistent with all mixed methods designs, the synergetic effect of including both quan-titative and qualitative methods stems from the points of interface between the two (Guest 2013). Because the multistage design involves more than one full cycle of research, it is possible to incorporate the results from one mixed methods phase at multiple points throughout the course of the study (termed 'embedding', a methods level strategy). Following our hypothetical washback example once more, a multistage design could be used to investi-gate the longitudinal effect of a test in a given community. Potentially, the same convergent design could be used on an annual basis to investigate the changes in washback over time. A further example can be seen in Galaczi and Khabbazbashi, Chapter 9, this volume.

Together, the three basic designs and the two advanced designs provide a conceptual framework for understanding mixed methods at the design level. One fundamental difference between the basic and advanced designs is that the steps involved in conducting one of the basic designs are purpose-fully more prescriptive. Heuristic illustrations from language assessment will further elucidate those steps in the next section of this volume. However, now we turn to methods level points of interface to provide a better understanding of the range of possibilities involved in mixed methods research.

Methods level

Points of interface occurring at the methods level involve integrating the quantitative and qualitative strands during data collection and initial analy-sis phases of a programme of study. Fetters et al (2013) present four strate-gies for accomplishing this (see Table 2).

Connecting quantitative and qualitative strands is most common when using sequential designs. It entails using the analysis of one to inform the purposeful sampling strategy of the other. Following our washback example from the explanatory design, the researcher may decide to use the results of

Table 2 Methods level: Strategies

Strategy	Definition
Connecting	Analysis of one strand informs the sampling strategy of the other
Building	Analysis of one strand informs the data collection of the other
Merging	Investigating parallel constructs in both strands to facilitate comparison
Embedding	Linking data collection and analysis at multiple points

the survey conducted with a larger sample of stakeholders to help identify the subsample of participants to follow up with qualitatively. Connecting could also occur in the course of an exploratory study, if, for example, the participants in the qualitative strand were asked to identify stakeholders to be included in the quantitative strand. Regardless of the purposeful sampling strategy selected (maximum variation, typical case, referral, etc.), using the results from one strand to inform sampling strategy of the other enhances the overall programme of study, producing a synergetic effect (see Onwuegbuzie and Johnson 2006 and Onwuegbuzie and Collins 2007, for an extensive typology of mixed methods sampling designs).

Building between strands is also common in sequential designs. It involves using the analysis of one strand to inform the data collection and analysis of the other. For example, researchers using an explanatory design may use their quantitative analysis to inform their interview protocol, to produce an illustration, or explanation of the quantitative findings (Bryman 2006b). Conversely, qualitative findings in an exploratory design could help generate hypotheses and/or develop instruments to be used during the quantitative strand (O'Cathain, Murphy and Nicholl 2008).

Merging involves investigating parallel constructs in both the quantitative and qualitative strands for the purpose of comparison. This is a tenet of the convergent design. It requires that data be collected both quantitatively and qualitatively using similar or parallel questions (Fetters et al 2013). For example, researchers conducting a convergent mixed methods study investigating the washback effect of a specific test may ask participants to fill out a survey with Likert-scale questions. These questions would ask a large group of participants to what degree they agree or disagree with statements assessing different dimensions of the test's washback effect (e.g. the test has significantly impacted how I teach my students). The researcher could also include a qualitative component asking participants to assess the same dimensions of the test's washback effect (e.g. please explain how the test has impacted how you teach your students). Consolidating the quantitative survey results and the emergent qualitative themes facilitates a comparison between the two strands, significantly enhancing the study by generating a more comprehensive understanding of the phenomenon of interest, as can be seen in the study presented by Khalifa and Docherty, Chapter 11, this volume.

Embedding is a fourth strategy for generating points of interface at the methods level. It is important to note that here the term 'embedding' is different from the design level strategy 'embedded'. Embedding at the methods level refers to linking the data collection and analysis of one strand (through connecting, building, and/or merging) to the data collection and analysis of the other at multiple points (Fetters et al 2013). Embedding is more typical of advanced designs involving multiple phases, but could also occur in one of the basic sequential designs (i.e. explanatory or exploratory). For example, a researcher conducting a multiphase mixed methods design investigating the longitudinal washback effect of a test may begin with an exploratory study. The qualitative strand could establish a rich description of how stakeholders view the test, which could inform the creation of a quantitative questionnaire (i.e. building) to establish the generalisability of the qualitative findings. To establish a longitudinal perspective, the next academic year the researcher may conduct an explanatory design using first the same quantitative questionnaire (i.e. merging) to compare results, followed by a qualitative phase informed by both the results from the comparison (i.e. building) and also designed to facilitate a comparison (i.e. asking parallel questions) with the initial qualitative strand (i.e. merging). In this way the methods level strategy of embedding has been used to link the initial qualitative strand throughout the data collection and analysis of the entire study at multiple points.

Connecting, building, merging, and embedding are four strategies mixed methods researchers can use to facilitate points of interface between quantitative and qualitative strands at the methods level of a programme of study. The synergetic effect mixed methods produces increases as the points of interface increase (Guest 2013). While these methods can be used with any of the basic designs, some combinations are more frequent. For example, the sequential designs are more partial to connecting strategies, as they entail the collection and analysis of one strand of data before the collection and analysis of the other. It is important to reiterate that the source of the value added through mixed methods lies in the meta-inferences generated through the purposeful combination of quantitative and qualitative strands. We now turn to the interpretation level strategies for producing those meta-inferences.

Interpretation level

The decisions made at the design and method level enable researchers to integrate findings from both strands and inform the creation of meta-inferences, the true source of the value added in mixed methods investigations. Integrated mixed methods data analysis involves 'the joint and interactive analysis of data represented in different forms' (Greene 2008:14). Table 3 presents the steps and strategies for integrated analysis.

The first step of integrated analysis is to facilitate the integration of

Table 3 Interpretation level – integrated analysis steps and strategies

Steps	Strategies
Data preparation	Reduction, transformation, consolidation
Data analysis	Correlation, comparison, importation
Data integration	Results synthesis, warranted assertion analysis, joint display

qualitative and quantitative results. Data preparation strategies include reduction, transformation and consolidation. While possible, it is not expected that each strategy will be utilised within one programme of study.

The goal of data reduction is to reduce the qualitative findings and the quantitative results into manageable chunks of information. This can be accomplished through crossover analysis or non-crossover analysis strategies. Whereas non-crossover analysis involves using the analysis methods associated with one tradition to reduce the data from that tradition e.g. thematic analysis of qualitative data (Onwuegbuzie and Teddlie 2003), crossover analysis involves the use of analysis methods associated with one tradition (e.g. quantitative analysis) with data from the other tradition (e.g. exploratory factor analysis of qualitative findings) (Onwuegbuzie and Combs 2010).

Data transformation entails converting one data set into the other (Onwuegbuzie and Teddlie 2003). This requires either quantitising qualitative data or qualitising quantitative data. It is done for multiple purposes: to enable pattern recognition in qualitative themes, facilitate the fusion of quantitative and qualitative data sets, and evaluate relationships between independent and dependent variables (see Sandelowski, Voils and Knafl 2009). Of the two, quantitising qualitative data is the most prevalent in mixed methods studies (Creswell and Plano Clark 2011). The process generally entails counting the frequency of emergent codes from qualitative data sets, but can also involve the use of rubrics to assess the quality of responses (see Moeller, Theiler and Wu 2012). The major benefit of quantitising is that, using statistical methods, quantitised data can be compared directly to quantitative data collected separately (Driscoll, Appiah-Yeboah, Salib and Rupert 2007).

Data consolidation is another preparation strategy. It involves 'combining or merging multiple data sets to create new or consolidated codes, variables, or data sets' (Onwuegbuzie and Combs 2010:422). This can entail the combination of two or more quantitative data sets, two or more qualitative data sets, or both quantitative and qualitative data sets. The resulting data set can then be analysed in the next step of mixed methods integrated analysis.

Data analysis is the second phase of mixed methods integrated analysis. The purpose of this phase is to look for patterns emerging from the quantitative and qualitative data (Greene 2007). Three strategies for accomplishing this goal include: data comparison, data correlation and data importation.

Data comparison involves directly comparing quantitative results and qualitative findings. To that end, both strands are organised around common constructs, research questions, or research purposes (Greene 2008). After this initial reduction and organisation of the data, data comparison requires that the researcher compare and contrast both strands, an example of which can be seen in Elliott and Lim, Chapter 10, this volume. One strategy for facilitating the investigation of the patterns that emerge from various data sets is generating a mixed methods matrix (O'Cathain et al 2008). For example, along the vertical axis, the researcher could enter the constructs of interest, and along the horizontal axis, the researcher could include the reduced findings from the various data sources.

Data correlation is an analytic process which may occur after data transformation. The researcher may correlate quantitative data with quantitised data from qualitative sources, or potentially correlate qualitative data with qualitised data from quantitative sources (Onwuegbuzie and Combs 2011).

Data importation, also referred to as typology development, is a final method of mixed methods data analysis. Similar to the building strategy used at the methods level, data importation involves using the findings from one strand to inform the analysis of the findings from the other (Onwuegbuzie and Combs 2010). One example of data importation is the use of extreme case analysis, whereby the extreme cases are identified through the analysis of one data type and followed up using the other data type (Caracelli and Greene 1993). Data importation may also lead to an additional iteration of data collection, potentially necessitating the return to design level strategies in order to more comprehensively address the research question. O'Cathain et al (2008) refer to this as following a thread. This underscores the flexibility inherent to the iterative nature of mixed methods research.

The final phase of mixed methods integrated analysis is to generate meta-inferences, the conclusions produced from integrating quantitative results and qualitative findings. It is important to reiterate the three possible outcomes that meta-inferences produce: confirmation, expansion, and/or discordance (Fetters et al 2013). In some cases, the quantitative results and the qualitative findings will produce mutually confirming outcomes. In others, one strand may build upon the other, providing a more in-depth expansion or explanation. Finally, it is possible that the two strands produce contradictory outcomes, rendering it difficult to produce meta-inferences. In these cases, it is important to further investigate the source of the discordance, either through analytic strategies such as data importation, or potentially another iteration of data collection. Three approaches for attaining meta-inferences include: results synthesis, warranted assertion analysis and joint display.

Results synthesis (see McConney, Rudd and Ayres 2002) involves a systematic, five-step assessment of each 'line of evidence' producing the mixed methods equivalent to statistical significance (see Table 4). A line of evidence

Table 4 Results synthesis procedures

Steps	Procedures
Step 1	Reduce and organise data sources around programme goals, or research questions
Step 2	Assess the direction and magnitude of each data source
Step 3	Determine the criteria of worth for each data source
Step 4	Calculate the synthesis equation
Step 5	For studies involving more than one research question, conduct steps 1–3 for each and average the results from the synthesis equations to assess the overall effect

refers to data stemming from one specific source (e.g. surveys). Data from each line of evidence is first reduced and organised around programme goals, or research questions. Next, the direction and magnitude of each of the lines of evidence is assessed using the following rubric: large negative effect = −2, small negative effect = −1, no discernible effect = 0, small positive effect = 1, and large positive effect = 2. After this, the criteria of worth is determined by assessing each line of evidence, assigning a 1 (low), 2 (medium) or 3 (high) for each of the following criteria: accuracy, closeness to those impacted, relevance, representativeness, and the quality of data collection. It should be noted that both assessing the direction and magnitude and the criteria of worth is up to the researcher's discretion. Next, to calculate the synthesis equation, the products of steps 1 and 2 (assessments for direction and magnitude and criteria of worth) for each line of evidence are summed up. This produces the mixed methods equivalent to statistical significance, whereby a value larger than 50 (either positive or negative) produces a significant effect. The final step for studies involving multiple research questions or programme goals is to average each of the synthesis equations for the individual research questions, producing an overall evaluation of the phenomenon of interest. The results synthesis approach is most appropriate when conducting a convergent mixed methods design, assessing the confirmation or discordance of multiple data sources.

Warranted assertion analysis (see Smith 1997) is an analysis strategy better suited to investigating expansion between data sets (see Table 5). A fundamental difference between the more deductive results synthesis and the more inductive warranted assertion analysis is that the researcher does not engage in data reduction before beginning integrated analysis. The first step in warranted assertion analysis is to organise the data in raw form. Next, the researcher repeatedly combs through the data sources, searching for claims, or 'warranted assertions'. For example, descriptive analysis of quantitative data may inform investigation of qualitative sources which may then inform the basis for further quantitative analysis. In this way, evidence supporting the claims is then collected. Finally, the data is revisited onces more searching for disconfirming evidence in order to refine the claims.

Table 5 Warranted assertion analysis procedures

Steps	Procedures
Step 1	Organise data in raw form
Step 2	Generate warranted assertions by repeatedly reading data sets as a whole
Step 3	Collect evidence for each claim
Step 4	Iteratively refine claims through searches for disconfirming evidence

The use of joint displays is another approach for integrated data interpretation that organises findings from both strands into a single visual representation (Creswell 2013b, see also Guetterman and Salamoura, Chapter 7, this volume, and the case study illustrations in Section 3). This enables the researcher to investigate the relationships between the quantitative and qualitative strands and develop a more comprehensive understanding of the phenomenon of interest (Lee and Greene 2007). The mixed methods matrix discussed during data comparison at the analysis phase is an example of a joint display; however these visual representations can take many forms, depending on the nature of the programme of studies (see Onwuegbuzie and Dickinson 2008). Beyond generating meta-inferences, an additional benefit of the joint display is its usefulness when reporting them (Fetters et al 2013).

Generating meta-inferences from the quantitative and qualitative strands is the most vital step of a mixed methods study. Results synthesis, warranted assertion analysis and joint displays are three strategies for accomplishing this. This is not, however, an exhaustive list of approaches used by researchers. Others include bracketing and bridging (Venkatesh et al 2013), pattern matching (Greene 2008), side-by-side comparison (Creswell 2013b), Frederick Ericson's modified method of analytic induction (cited in Greene 2007), and triangulation protocol (O'Cathain et al 2008). This is also not an exhaustive list. It is plausible that as mixed methods matures as a third methodology, a more parsimonious set of strategies for producing meta-inferences will be agreed upon and validated by theorists; however, currently it is the researchers who are driving our understanding, experimenting with novel ways for accomplishing this task within a programme of study (Greene 2008).

This concludes our discussion of the components of a mixed methods study. It is through these design, methods and interpretation level strategies for producing points of interface that researchers seek to generate meta-inferences. It should be noted that while producing meta-inferences is the source of the value added in conducting mixed methods research, many researchers in the social sciences, and specifically in the field of applied linguistics, either do not report or do not engage in the interpretation level strategies necessary to do so (Hashemi and Babaii 2013, Jang et al 2014).

We now turn to heuristic illustrations of mixed methods designs in second language assessment. These examples will further explain the relations between the design, methods and interpretation level points of interface, providing a more prescriptive account of the basic designs and a clearer understanding of the advanced designs.

Heuristic illustrations of mixed methods designs in second language assessment

The purpose of this section is to develop a clearer understanding of how to combine the design, methods, and analysis level strategies for conducting mixed methods studies in the field of second language assessment. This is accomplished through heuristic illustrations from the literature and organised by design: convergent parallel, explanatory sequential, exploratory sequential, embedded, and multistage. The illustrations here are further discussed and expanded by the four case studies in Section 3.

Convergent parallel design

A review of the literature suggests that the convergent parallel design is the most commonly used design, accounting for 72% of mixed methods research published in the field of applied linguistics between 1995 and 2008 (Hashemi and Babaii 2013), and 91% of the studies in the field of language testing and assessment between 2007 and 2013 (Jang et al 2014). The convergent design involves two relatively independent strands: one quantitative and the other qualitative. Inferences made on the basis of the results from each strand are merged to form integrated interpretations, or meta-inferences, at the end of the study (Creswell and Plano Clark 2011).

Table 6 presents a study illustrating the use of convergent parallel design in language assessment. Kim (2009) conducted an investigation into native and non-native teachers' judgements of oral English performance. To get a better understanding of native (NS) and non-native (NNS) teachers'

Table 6 Convergent mixed methods studies in second language assessment: Example

Citation	Kim (2009)
Purpose	Explore native and non-native teachers' judgements of oral English performance
Design level strategies	Convergent parallel design
Methods level strategies	Merging
Interpretation level strategies	Data reduction, Typology development, Data transformation, Data comparison
Mixed methods value added	The qualitative component was used to corroborate the quantitative findings

judgements of oral English performance, Kim developed her quantitative research questions as: 1) 'Do NS and NNS teachers exhibit similar levels of internal consistency when they assess students' oral English performance?', and 2) 'Do NS and NNS teachers exhibit interchangeable severity across different tasks when they assess students' oral English performance? Kim's qualitative research question was: 'How do NS and NNS teachers differ in drawing on evaluation criteria when they comment on students' oral English performance?' (Kim 2009:188).

Kim (2009) carried out the quantitative and qualitative strands simultaneously. Study participants from both the NS and the NNS groups rated the responses from a semi-direct oral English test conducted individually with 10 student participants. Each teacher rated every student's performance on each task, so that the data matrix was fully crossed. The quantitative strand was informed by the rater's use of a four-point rating scale, and the qualitative strand consisted of written comments justifying their ratings. This constitutes the methods level merging strategy as data from both the quantitative and qualitative strands was used to compare how NS and NNS teachers assess students' oral proficiency.

The quantitative data consisted of 1,727 valid ratings, awarded by 24 teachers to 80 sample responses by 10 students on eight tasks. The data was analysed using the FACETS computer program. Three different types of statistical analysis were carried out to investigate teachers' internal consistency, based on: 1) fit statistics; 2) proportions of large standard residuals; 3) the single rater/rest of the raters (SR/ROR) correlation. The qualitative data included 3,295 written comments. Typology development and data transformation guided the analysis of qualitative written comments. First, the written comments were analysed based on evaluation criteria with each written comment constituting one criterion. Research assistants independently open-coded the comments, resulting in 19 recurring evaluation criteria with a 95% inter-rater agreement. Next, the 19 evaluative criteria were compared across the two teacher groups through a frequency analysis, informed by counting the number of times each criterion was mentioned by the NS and NNS teacher raters.

After collecting and analysing two independent strands of qualitative and quantitative data, results were merged to look for convergence, divergence, contradictions, or relationships between the two databases (i.e. data comparison). The researcher reported the meta-inferences produced using side-by-side comparison in the discussion section of her article. Side-by-side comparison entails discussing the results from one strand, directly followed by the discussion of the results from the other (Creswell and Plano Clark 2011). Kim (2009) first presented and discussed the results from the quantitative statistical analysis. Next, the qualitative results were presented. Assessing the fit of the data from both strands, the researcher concluded that the qualitative data confirmed the quantitative data, producing a better understanding of the phenomenon of interest than either quantitative or qualitative data alone.

This is a heuristic illustration of how convergent parallel designs can be applied in the field of language assessment. Other examples include Barkaoui's (2007) investigation into the effects of two different rating scales on English as a foreign language (EFL) essay scores, rating processes, and raters' perceptions; Baker's (2012) study on the individual differences of decision-making style (DMS); Busse and Williams' (2010) exploration into the motivation of students studying German at English universities; Lee and Greene's (2007) study on the predictive validity of an English as a second language (ESL) placement test; Moeller and Theiler's (2014) investigation into the development of spoken Spanish language at the high school level; and Khalifa and Docherty's (see Chapter 11, this volume) investigation on the impact of international assessments. The convergent parallel design is an intuitive choice for many researchers, because it is the type of design that was first discussed in the literature and has become increasingly popular across research domains (Teddlie and Tashakkori 2006). Since both types of data are collected and analysed at the same stage of the research, the design lends itself to researchers looking for efficiency.

Explanatory mixed methods design

The purpose of the explanatory design is to explain quantitative results with qualitative findings to provide a clearer understanding of a phenomenon of interest. It is carried out in two distinct phases starting with the collection and analysis of the quantitative data, followed by the collection and analysis of the qualitative data. Results from the initial quantitative phase may guide the sample selection (i.e. connecting) and/or the data collection (i.e. building) of the qualitative phase. While the research may favour either the quantitative or the qualitative strand in the explanatory sequential design, an emphasis is typically placed on the initial, quantitative strand.

In the context of second language assessment, the explanatory sequential design is most useful when the researcher wants to not only examine the trends, the impacts, or the relationships with the quantitative data of the assessments, but also to explain the causes or mechanisms behind them. Therefore, the design enhances the explanatory power of the quantitative measurement by supplementing it with detailed qualitative descriptions and analysis. Isaacs and Trofimovich's (2012) article on developing guidelines for rating comprehensibility is a good example of the explanatory sequential design (see Table 7).

The problem Isaacs and Trofimovich (2012) addressed was that little is known about the underlying factors raters use when assessing comprehensibility, a holistic evaluation of a second language learner's communicative

Table 7 Explanatory sequential design in second language assessment: Example

Citation	Isaacs and Trofimovich (2012)
Purpose	Develop L2 comprehensibility scale guidelines
Design level strategies	Explanatory sequential design
Methods level strategies	Merging, embedding
Interpretation level strategies	Data reduction, Data transformation, Data importation, Data comparison, Joint display
Mixed methods value added	The meta-inferences derived informed the development of new comprehensibility scale guidelines

success. Consistent with explanatory sequential designs, Isaacs and Trofimovich (2012) began by deductively assessing how the linguistic factors associated with comprehensibility in theory relate to holistic evaluations of comprehensibility. Speech samples were first collected from 40 French learners of English with varying English ability levels, in which learners independently created a story from eight sequenced images. These speech samples were transcribed and analysed according to 19 speech measures which Isaacs and Trofimovich (2012) derived from literature on comprehensibility. Next, 60 novice raters (defined as individuals who had neither received specialised language training nor had second language teaching experience) independently assigned comprehensibility scores to each of the 40 speech samples. Comprehensibility scores were holistic assessments on a 9-point Likert scale (1 = extremely poor, 9 = extremely proficient). The correlations between the holistic evaluations of comprehensibility and each individual speech measure revealed the degree to which each individual speech measure reflected the overall evaluation of comprehensibility, establishing a rank order.

In the second phase of their study, Isaacs and Trofimovich (2012) sought to expand their investigation into the construct of comprehensibility inductively through qualitative analysis. Investigating parallel constructs both quantitatively and qualitatively is an example of the methods level strategy merging. Three experienced raters (defined as individuals who had both received specialised language training and had second language teaching experience) were interviewed to explore factors they perceived as important when holistically assessing comprehensibility. Second, the experienced raters each rated the 40 speech samples included in the first phase using the same Likert scale. Finally, after having assessed each of the 40 speech samples, the experienced raters were asked to complete an open-ended questionnaire investigating the rationale behind their holistic rating. Using the methods level strategy of embedding, the results from the novice raters' assessments of the 40 samples were integrated into both the construction of a 10-category coding scheme describing the most salient underlying factors of comprehensibility, and the development of the final guidelines for assessing comprehensibility.

Multiple mixed methods interpretation level strategies informed the development of the final guidelines for assessing comprehensibility. An example of data transformation and data importation, the holistic quantitative evaluations of the 40 speech samples categorised the speech samples into three qualitative comprehensibility levels (low, intermediate, and high) to inform a joint display. In another example of data transformation and data importation, Isaacs and Trofimovich (2012) calculated the frequency of counts for each of the 10 coded categories (i.e. underlying factors of comprehensibility) also included in a joint display. The resulting joint display illustrated the frequency of coded categories into a matrix allowing for meta-inferences to be drawn as to which coded categories more frequently were used to describe each of the comprehensibility levels. The final guidelines for assessing comprehensibility were informed by meta-inferences generated from data comparison assessing which constructs were most salient for each of the comprehensibility levels.

Isaacs and Trofimovich (2012) adeptly employed the explanatory sequential design to generate a user-friendly guide for developing second language comprehensibility scales. Other examples of the explanatory sequential design include Williams, Burden and Lanvers' (2002) investigation into student perceptions of issues related to motivation in learning a foreign language, Magid's (2009) study on second language learners' motivational self system from a Chinese perspective and Wesely's (2013) investigation into language-learning motivation in early adolescents. Compared with concurrent mixed designs, the explanatory sequential design is easier for the single researcher, because it is more straightforward to conduct the two strands in separate phases and collect only one type of data at a time. In addition, the studies typically unfold slower and in a more predictable manner (Teddlie and Tashakkori 2006). Nevertheless, challenges exist in conducting research with the explanatory sequential design, since it requires more time to implement the two phases and researchers need to be careful with choices of results to be followed up and purposeful sampling in the second phase (Creswell and Plano Clark 2011).

Exploratory mixed methods design

The primary purpose of the exploratory sequential design is to use quantitative results to generalise qualitative findings (Creswell and Plano Clark 2011). It is characterised by an initial phase of qualitative data collection and analysis followed by a phase of quantitative data collection and analysis. Typically, the methods level building strategy is employed, with the qualitative strand informing the subsequent quantitative data collection and analysis. Since the intent of the exploratory design is to expand the scope of the qualitative phase and further to investigate the problem quantitatively by using a larger sample, it is particularly useful to develop and validate measurement instruments like questionnaires, tests, rating scales, inventories; to identify new variables for further study in the quantitative phase; to develop a contextualised taxonomy or typology; to test an emergent theory or classification; or to determine if contextualised factors can be generalised to different groups (Creswell and Plano Clark 2011, Teddlie and Tashakkori 2006).

Qi's (2005) article on the causes of the undermined washback effects of the National Matriculation English Test (NMET) in China is an example of the exploratory sequential design with instrument development (see Table 8). The aim of the paper was to examine the factors that played a role in shaping the intended washback of NMET. The study began with a qualitative phase consisting of: unstructured, individual interviews in Chinese with the six English inspectors; in-depth semi-structured individual interviews with the eight test constructors, 10 teachers, and 10 students; and a group interview. Axial coding, the process of assessing how codes relate to each other through both inductive and deductive thinking, was used to analyse the qualitative data.

Based on the qualitative findings, the methods level buildings strategy was used to develop two versions of a questionnaire (one for the teachers and one for the students) in order to investigate to what degree the qualitative findings could be applied to a larger number of participants. Questionnaires from 378 teachers and 976 students were used for the data analysis in the quantitative phase. The quantitative questionnaire data was analysed to extract frequencies and means (i.e. data reduction) as a cross check (i.e. data comparison) on the generalisability, or transferability, of the findings from the qualitative strand.

While the exploratory sequential design has numerous applications in the field of second language assessment, it has not been widely employed.

Table 8 Exploratory sequential design in second language assessment: Example

Citation	Qi (2005)
Purpose	Explore the causes of the undermined washback effects of the National Matriculation English Test (NMET) in China
Design level strategies	Exploratory sequential design with instrument development and testing
Methods level strategies	Building
Interpretation level strategies	Data reduction, Data comparison
Mixed methods value added	The quantitative component generalises the results from the qualitative phase to a population

According to Hashemi and Babaii (2013), only 7% of the mixed methods research published in the field of applied linguistics between 1995 and 2008 adopted exploratory sequential designs. When using the exploratory sequential design, researchers must be cautious of the challenges concerning conducting an exploratory mixed methods study, because it requires more time to implement the two phases. Moreover, researchers also need to be careful about sampling in the different phases, using qualitative data and analysis to generate quantitative measures, as well as ensuring the validity and reliability of the newly developed instrument (see Guetterman and Salamoura, Chapter 7, this volume, for a further a discussion of this issue).

Embedded mixed methods design

The embedded mixed methods design applies a specific theoretical lens (e.g. qualitative case study or quantitative experimental study) to address the purpose of the study. The researcher's application of mixed methods is informed by that theoretical lens, but is flexible to the pragmatic need to best answer the research questions. As such, the range of potential combinations of mixed methods designs and theoretical lenses is infinite, resulting in the inability to prescribe the specific steps involved in embedded mixed methods designs. Instead, we turn to two illustrations (see Table 9).

Stemming from a more quantitative lens, Myers and Tucker (2011) conducted a mixed methods intervention study to examine the impact that training teacher candidates in using a language assessment tool designed to identify students' needs had on their instructional planning. Quantitatively,

Table 9 Embedded mixed methods studies in second language assessment: Examples

Citation	Myers and Tucker (2011)	Rea-Dickens and Gardner (2000)
Purpose	Examine the washback effect of the ADEPT language assessment tool on teacher candidates' instructional planning	Explore 'the nature of formative assessment in a primary (elementary) language learning context' (2000:215)
Design level strategies	Explanatory sequential design embedded into an intervention study	Convergent design embedded into a case study with follow-up qualitative phases
Methods level strategies	Merging	Merging, Building
Interpretation level strategies	Data reduction, Data comparison	Data reduction, Data comparison
Mixed methods value added	The qualitative component provided a further explanation of the quantitative results	The quantitative component was used to corroborate the qualitative findings

pre- and post-training questionnaires measuring teacher candidates' knowledge of teaching practice were administered. Using the methods level strategy of merging, the questionnaires were followed up with a qualitative phase (i.e. interviews) to 'provide further information on the effectiveness of the ADEPT [assessment of interest] training as it applied to actual teaching practices' (Myers and Tucker 2011:65). Results from both strands were reduced to parallel constructs and presented separately before engaging in the analysis strategy of data comparison in their discussion section. In lieu of a control group to establish the training's effectiveness, the qualitative component significantly enhanced this study by investigating teachers' attribution of changes in their knowledge of best practices to the training they had received.

Utilising a qualitative lens, Rea-Dickens and Gardner embedded a convergent design into a case study to investigate 'the nature of formative assessment in a primary (elementary) language learning context' (Rea-Dickens and Gardner 2000:215). The convergent design used the methods level strategy of merging to ask participants (i.e. teachers) their perception of issues with assessment in the classroom (formative and summative) both qualitatively (open-ended questionnaires) and quantitatively (closed-ended questionnaires). At the interpretation level, quantitative and qualitative data was reduced and organised around this parallel construct to facilitate data comparison. This application of mixed methods to inform the triangulation protocol used in a qualitative study is fairly common (Creswell and Plano Clark 2011). Using a building strategy, the combined results then informed the creation of the interview and observation protocols employed in follow-up qualitative investigation. In a process similar to warranted assertion analysis (however this was not identified), data from all sources was reassessed to establish themes. True to a case study approach, the results are presented holistically as a narrative organised by theme, instead of separated into phases. The use of mixed methods significantly enhanced this study. The quantitative component contributed to the triangulation protocol the researcher used to develop themes from the initial investigation, which built into further qualitative data collection, generating the meta-analyses presented in the findings.

These two heuristic illustrations serve to show how embedded mixed methods designs are being applied in the field of second language assessment. Other examples include Bateman's (2002) use of an embedded convergent design into an ethnography on promoting and assessing cultural learning; Fox's (2004) use of an embedded exploratory mixed methods design into a grounded theory investigation into tracking validity; Fulcher's (1997) use of an embedded explanatory mixed methods design into a quantitative evaluation of a test's validity and reliability; and Vidaković and Robinson's (Chapter 8, this volume) use of community-based participatory research in test development. The embedded design significantly enhances a study employing a specific theoretical lens through the inclusion of data strands not typical to that theoretical lens and the mixed methods analysis level strategies used to produce meta-inferences. We now turn to multistage mixed methods designs.

Multistage mixed methods design

Multistage mixed methods designs involve more than one complete iteration of data collection and analysis, each relying on quantitative, qualitative or mixed methods. Through these multiple iterations, the multistage mixed methods design is able to address a larger research purpose by breaking it into multiple smaller, semiautonomous, studies. In accordance with pragmatism, the order and creative combination of these smaller quantitative, qualitative and/or mixed methods studies depends entirely on how the researcher chooses to answer the larger research purpose and results in an infinite range of possibilities. Therefore, it is not possible to prescribe how to conduct a multistage mixed methods study.

The most common application of multistage mixed methods designs in second language assessment is the development and validation of an assessment. Table 10 illustrates two similarly designed studies, both comprised of three phases: a needs evaluation phase (either of an existing assessment or for a new assessment), a phase to develop (or revise) an assessment informed by the findings from phase 1, and a phase evaluating (or validating) the new (or revised) assessment. While similar in purpose, and even general layout, the two studies vary greatly in methodology.

Table 10 Multistage mixed methods studies in second language assessment

Citation	Saif (2006)	Zhao (2013)
Purpose	Create 'positive washback through the introduction of a test of spoken language ability specifically designed for international teaching assistants' (2006:1)	Develop 'and validate an analytic rubric that can be used to capture voice in written texts' (2013:202)
Design level strategies	Multiple phases: convergent needs assessment -> test development -> mixed methods intervention study on the test's washback effect	Multiple phases: convergent rubric evaluation -> rubric revision -> quantitative rubric validation
Methods level strategies	Building, Merging	Building, Merging
Interpretation level strategies	Data reduction, Data comparison	Data reduction, Data comparison
Mixed methods value added	Mixed methods significantly enhanced to all three phases of this study: needs assessment, test development and intervention study on washback	The qualitative strand included in the convergent design significantly enhanced the rubric evaluation and informed the revision of the rubric

First, Saif conducted a study designed to 'create positive washback through the introduction of a test of spoken language ability specifically designed for international teaching assistants' (Saif 2006:1). Before creating the test, the researcher decided to conduct a needs analysis with three stakeholder groups (graduate advisors/administrators, undergraduate students, and the international teaching assistants) using a convergent mixed methods design. The methods level strategy of merging was used to assess parallel constructs (e.g. the need for a new test and the communicative tasks required of international teaching assistants) both quantitatively (questionnaire) and qualitatively (interviews and document analysis). The mixed methods analysis level strategy of data reduction facilitated data comparison between the quantitative and qualitative strands, organised around the parallel constructs. The results of this first phase indicated the need for a new test to ensure that international teaching assistants were capable of the communicative tasks involved in teaching undergraduates.

Using the methods level strategy of building, the communicative tasks identified in phase 1 were operationalised into test items during the second phase of test development. The final phase utilised an intervention mixed methods design (an embedded design) constructed to both validate the test and measure its washback effect. A group of international teaching assistants were randomly assigned to two different 4-week training programmes: a control group (not using the new test) and an experimental group (using the new test). Quantitative (questionnaires and pre–post test results) and qualitative data gathering (interviews and observations) was conducted before, during and after the training programme. Once again, data reduction facilitated data comparison of parallel constructs across strands. The results showed that not only was the test valid and reliable, but it also produced its desired washback effect of increasing international students' ability to accomplish the desired communicative tasks as a result of the additional emphasis ESL teachers placed on these tasks during the training programme.

The use of mixed methods significantly contributed to each phase of this multistage design. The researcher pragmatically engaged in abductive logic, moving back and forth between deduction and induction, to construct, validate, and evaluate a test designed for positive washback.

In the second example study, Zhao sought to 'develop and validate an analytic rubric that can be used to capture voice [i.e. an author's unique style] in written texts' (Zhao 2013:202). In the first phase, the researcher conducted a convergent mixed methods study investigating a preliminary voice rubric based on a theoretical model. The methods level strategy of merging was used to investigate the raters' perception of the rubric's ability to capture voice in the written texts. Using a building strategy, the results from quantitative (principal component analysis of raters' assessment of 200 writing samples) and qualitative (raters engaged in think-out-loud protocols during and interviews after assessing the writing samples) strands were reduced and compared to inform the revision of the rubric in the second phase. The third phase entailed a quantitative validation study of the revised rubric. The use of mixed methods significantly enhanced this study by including the raters' voices in the revision of the rubric.

In Chapter 2, this volume, Saville depicts the test development process as an iterative cycle of continuous improvement concerning multiple facets of validity. Inherent to multistage studies is an infinite range of possibilities for the application of mixed methods well suited to meet the complexities of test development. Other examples from the field of second language assessment include Sasaki's (2004) 4-phase longitudinal investigation into students' writing proficiency; Jianda's (2007) 4 phase development and validation of a pragmatics test; Uiterwijk and Vallen's (2005) 3-phase investigation into linguistic sources of item bias; Galaczi and Khabbazbashi's (Chapter 9, this volume) multistage exploratory sequential rating scale development; and Elliott and Lim's (Chapter 10, this volume) multistage development and validation of a new Reading task in the *Cambridge English: Advanced* test. The value of mixed methods in multistage designs lies in the use of meta-inferences generated within (or between) stages to inform the direction of the following stages, as well as generating meta-inferences from all strands across stages.

In this section we provided a more prescriptive account for integrating the design, methods and analysis level strategies into the basic mixed methods designs. In regard to the advanced designs, the goal has been to illustrate the application of the mixed methods components to the infinite range of possibilities inherent to the flexible and iterative nature of mixed methods designs. While we feel that the studies included are good examples of mixed methods research in second language assessment, it should be noted that few of these studies explicitly address the interpretation level strategies used to produce the meta-inferences made between the quantitative and qualitative strands. Echoing Jang et al's (2014) findings from an investigation into the application of mixed methods in the field of language testing and assessment, as the field moves towards adopting mixed methods designs, researchers must focus more on the interpretation level steps and strategies required for producing high-quality meta-inferences.

Producing quality meta-inferences in mixed methods research

Throughout this chapter we have referred to meta-inferences generated through combining quantitative and qualitative strands as the true source of the value added when conducting mixed methods research. In the first section we explored the methodological considerations (i.e. design, method, and interpretation level strategies) for producing these meta-inferences. Next, the heuristic illustrations in the second section served to further develop the reader's understanding of the various mixed methods designs within the context of second language assessment. However, the conclusion was drawn that a more explicit emphasis needs to be placed on ensuring high-quality meta-inferences (Hashemi and Babaii 2013, Jang et al 2014).

Apart from conducting rigorous qualitative and quantitative strands, generating high-quality meta-inferences requires that the researcher address a separate set of validity concerns specific to mixed methods. Two sets of theorists have independently investigated this topic: Tashakkori and Teddlie (2008) and Onwuegbuzie and Johnson (2006). The purpose of this section is to synthesise these two sets of constructs into a single table (see Table 11) of mixed methods validity concerns to be addressed in order to guide researchers towards producing high-quality meta-inferences, the source of the synergetic effect in conducting mixed methods research. We begin with Tashakkori and Teddlie's (2008) comprehensive framework for conceptualising validity concerns specific to mixed methods research.

Similar to quantitative and qualitative methods, validity concerns in mixed methods address both internal and external validity. Tashakkori and Teddlie (2008) divide internal validity concerns into design quality, standards for the evaluation of methodological rigour, and interpretive rigour, standards for evaluating the quality of the meta-inferences generated. According to their framework, design quality is further differentiated in terms of design suitability (i.e. the extent to which the design selected matches the research purpose and questions), design adequacy/fidelity (i.e. the extent to which the researcher adequately implements each component of the design selected), analytic adequacy (i.e. the match between the research purpose/questions and the analytical techniques used to generate meta-inferences), and within design consistency (i.e. the consistency of design procedures implemented to produce the meta-inferences).

Interpretive rigour is also divided into subcomponents: interpretive consistency (i.e. the consistency between meta-inferences), theoretical consistency (i.e. the consistency between the meta-inferences generated and the current theoretical understanding of the phenomenon of interest), interpretive agreement (i.e. the degree to which both participants and other scholars agree with the meta-inferences generated), interpretive distinctiveness (i.e. the degree to which the researcher has eliminated other meta-inferences that potentially could be made from the data), and integrative efficacy (i.e. the degree to which the inferences generated from the individual quantitative and qualitative strands are effectively integrated to form meta-inferences).

External validity concerns (i.e. inference transferability) relate to the degree to which the meta-inferences generated are generalisable to other individuals/groups/entities (i.e. population transferability), to other contexts/settings (i.e. ecological transferability), to other time periods (i.e. temporal

Table 11 Mixed methods validity concerns: Terms and definitions

Internal validity concerns

Design quality	Standards for evaluating methodological rigour
Paradigmatic mixing	Extent to which the researcher effectively combines or blends the underlying beliefs inherent to quantitative and qualitative approaches
Design suitability	Match between research questions/purpose and design used
Weakness minimisation	Extent to which the weaknesses from one approach are compensated with the other
Design adequacy/fidelity	Adequately implementing each component of the design used
Analytic adequacy	Match between research questions/purpose and integrated data analysis techniques used
Within design consistency	Consistency of procedures from which meta-inferences emerge

Interpretive rigour	Standards for evaluating meta-inference quality
Commensurability legitimisation	Extent to which abduction is used to effectively switch between quantitative and qualitative logic, or lenses
Interpretive consistency	Consistency between inferences resulting from data analysis
Theoretical consistency	Consistency between resulting meta-inferences and current theories
Interpretive agreement	Consistency of meta-inferences across scholars and participants
Interpretive distinctiveness	Degree to which the researcher has eliminated other possible interpretations
Integrative efficacy	Degree to which inferences from each strand are effectively integrated to form meta-inferences

External validity concerns

Inference transferability	Standards for evaluating the generalisability of meta-inferences
Political legitimisation	Extent to which consumers value the meta-inferences stemming from the mixed methods study
Population transferability	Generalisability to other individuals, groups or entities
Ecological transferability	Generalisability to other contexts and settings
Temporal transferability	Generalisability to other time periods
Operational transferability	Generalisability to other methods of measuring the phenomenon of interest

transferability), and to other methods of measuring the phenomenon of interest (i.e. operational transferability).

Tashakkori and Teddlie's framework (2008) provides a succinct set of constructs for assessing validity concerns in mixed methods studies. Onwuegbuzie and Johnson (2006) offer a separate set of nine measures for assessing validity issues (termed legitimation) in mixed methodology. It is important to note that these two frameworks do not oppose each other; they complement each other to provide a more comprehensive understanding of validity in mixed methods research (Ihantola and Kihn 2011). To facilitate the integration of these two frameworks, Onwuegbuzie and Johnson's (2006) framework is discussed according to how we feel their new concepts fit into Tashakkori and Teddlie's (2008) organisation of mixed methods validity concerns: design quality, interpretive rigour, and inference transferability.

Design quality

The majority of Onwuegbuzie and Johnson's (2006) constructs fit into Tashakkori and Teddlie's concept of design quality (i.e. standards for the evaluation of methodological rigour). According to our analysis, Onwuegbuzie and Johnson (2006) add two new constructs, three sub-constructs and one parallel construct. The two new constructs are pragmatic mixing legitimisation and weakness minimisation legitimisation. First, pragmatic mixing legitimisation (i.e. the extent to which the approach effectively combines and blends the underlying beliefs inherent to quantitative and qualitative approaches) is a top-level construct that refers to the pragmatic worldview central to mixed methods research. Second, weakness minimisation legitimisation (i.e. the extent to which the weaknesses from one approach are compensated with the other) represents the fundamental goal of mixed methods research to produce a more comprehensive understanding of a phenomenon of interest than would be possible through quantitative or qualitative methods alone.

The three sub-constructs we identify are sample integration legitimisation, sequential legitimisation, and conversion legitimisation. Because all three of these refer to strategies for producing meta-inferences, we feel they fall under Tashakkori and Teddlie's (2008) broader construct of within design consistency (i.e. the consistency of procedures from which meta-inferences emerge). Sample integration legitimisation (i.e. the extent to which the sampling strategy used in both strands yields high-quality meta-inferences) requires that researchers have a rationale for the sampling strategy, or strategies, used in both strands that relates to the analysis strategies the researcher plans to use to produce meta-inferences. Sequential legitimisation (i.e. the extent to which the researcher minimises issues relating to the potential problem wherein the meta-inferences are a product of the sequencing of strands) requires the researcher to have a rationale for the order in which the strands are conducted and to take into account how that order may affect the results. Finally, conversion legitimisation (i.e. the extent to which data transformation yields high-quality meta-inferences) refers to having a rationale for the use of the mixed methods analysis level strategy (i.e. data transformation) for producing meta-inferences, which may or may not be used in a programme of study. Identifying these as sub-constructs does not reduce the importance for considering these components of the more broadly defined construct of within design consistency.

A final construct that Onwuegbuzie and Johnson (2006) include is multiple validities legitimisation (i.e. the extent to which the researchers address the validity concerns with the quantitative, qualitative, and mixed methods components of their studies). This is a parallel construct to Tashakkori and Teddlie's (2008) design adequacy/fidelity (i.e. adequately implementing each component of the design used) with the added emphasis on the validity concerns related to those components. For the purpose of parsimony, our integrated table (see Table 11) includes Tashakkori and Teddlie's (2008) term, design adequacy/fidelity, with the understanding that this refers the general fidelity of the researcher to best practices in quantitative, qualitative and mixed methodologies.

Interpretive rigour

Two of Onwuegbuzie and Johnson's (2006) nine validity concerns for conducting mixed methods research fall under Tashakkori and Teddlie's (2008) umbrella term of Interpretive rigour (i.e. standards for the evaluation of inference quality): commensurability legitimisation and inside–outside legitimisation. Commensurability legitimisation is a new construct which refers to the extent to which abduction is used to effectively make Gestalt switches between deductive (quantitative lens) and inductive (qualitative lens) logic throughout the course of study to inform the production of high-quality meta-inferences.

Inside–outside legitimisation (i.e. the extent to which the researcher effectively integrates both the researcher's theoretical perspective and the participants' practical perspectives) is a parallel construct with Tashakkori and Teddlie's (2008) interpretive agreement (i.e. consistency of meta-inferences across scholars and participants). Our integrated checklist uses interpretive agreement to refer to this shared construct.

Inference transferability

Onwuegbuzie and Johnson (2006) add a new concept to inference transferability (i.e. the degree to which meta-inferences are generalisable): political legitimisation. Political legitimisation refers to the extent to which consumers value the meta-inferences stemming from the mixed methods study. While mixed methods research continues to gain acceptance as a third methodology, there are still those who reject it (i.e. proponents of the incompatibility thesis). Political legitimisation addresses the concern that some consumers may reject the meta-inferences produced by mixed methods studies on philosophical grounds.

As a third methodology, mixed methods has its own set of validity concerns specific to producing high-quality meta-inferences, the source of the value added. The purpose of this section was to integrate two independent frameworks, culminating in the creation of the table of concerns for researchers to address mixed methods validity (see Table 11 for terms and definitions, and the Appendix for a fillable form). This table is designed to act as a guide for mixed methods researchers through the design, methods and interpretation level decisions for generating meta-inferences, presented in our first section. An illustration of its use can be seen in Galaczi and Khabbazbashi (Chapter 9, this volume). We feel the use of this table will significantly enhance the quality of meta-inferences researchers produce, both in the field of second language assessment specifically and across fields of studies generally. Moreover, this table could also be used by editors of peer-reviewed journals to assess the quality of articles entailing mixed methodology.

Conclusion

The source of the value added in conducting mixed methods research is the quality of the meta-inferences generated from the integration of quantitative and qualitative data sets. However, the validity of those meta-inferences depends on the purposeful implementation of mixed methods procedures at the design level, methods level, and interpretation level of a study. Investigation into the application of mixed methods in second language assessment and applied linguistics has shown that researchers tend to either not engage in or not report the use of sufficiently rigorous interpretation level strategies (Hashemi and Babaii 2013, Jang et al 2014). The purpose of this chapter has been to provide readers with a comprehensive framework of mixed methods designs to address this deficiency.

Appendix

Validity concerns for mixed methods researchers to address

Validity concern	How I have addressed this concern:
Internal validity concerns	
Design quality	
Paradigmatic mixing	
Design suitability	
Weakness minimisation	
Design adequacy/fidelity	
Analytic adequacy	
Within design consistency	
Interpretive rigour	
Commensurability legitimisation	
Interpretive consistency	
Theoretical consistency	
Interpretive agreement	
Interpretive distinctiveness	
Integrative efficacy	
External validity concerns	
Inference transferability	
Political legitimisation	
Population transferability	
Ecological transferability	
Temporal transferability	
Operational transferability	

5 Drawing mixed methods procedural diagrams

Debra R Miller

University of Nebraska–Lincoln

Carolina Bustamante

State University of New York at Old Westbury

This chapter introduces mixed methods procedural diagrams and provides examples for both convergent and sequential designs, outside and within the language assessment area. Topics in this chapter include:

- An *introduction* to visual displays and procedural diagrams
- *Notation* in procedural diagrams
- A *checklist* with the elements that a procedural diagram should contain
- Published *examples* of various styles for procedural diagrams
- A *tutorial* for drawing a mixed methods procedural diagram using basic software

Introduction

Reports of mixed methods studies often include a procedural diagram or graphic that conveys research procedures in visual form. Such diagrams often include information about collecting and analysing data, as well as interpreting findings and results of the study (Creswell 2015). A procedural diagram helps to make the components of a mixed methods study comprehensible and cohesive. Diagrams provide an overview of procedures that may be useful for readers or, in the case of a presentation, for listeners.

Mixed methods studies in language assessment typically consist of multiple stages of data collection and analysis, and are complex and elaborate in nature (see for example, Hurlbut, Chapter 6, Guetterman and Salamoura, Chapter 7, this volume). Simplifying the complexity of these procedures requires visual or graphic representation that communicates key aspects of complex data clearly. Procedural diagrams are especially effective in making quantitative and qualitative aspects of a mixed methods research study accessible and transparent to stakeholders.

Drawing on mixed methods literature, this section introduces visual displays in general and procedural diagrams in particular. The discussion of mixed methods procedural diagrams includes notation and the role of visual displays in mixed methods research. A checklist for quality of procedural diagrams serves as the basis for introducing examples of diagrams published in language assessment articles. Lastly, examples of diagrams for basic (explanatory sequential, exploratory sequential, and convergent) and advanced mixed methods designs (see Ziegler and Kang, Chapter 4, this volume) are provided.

Visual displays

Visualising research involves 'techniques, processes, and tools' by which researchers 'understand, present, and frame research' (Wheeldon and Åhlberg 2012:1). Accordingly, visual displays are diagrams, maps, or graphs that clarify complex processes (see Dickinson 2010). They can assist with stages of research such as eliciting data (e.g. Prosser 2007), depicting a study's design (e.g. Yin 2014), or displaying results or findings (e.g. Erwin, Brotherson and Summers 2011). Visual displays can also assist researchers and readers with collecting data, visualising or reporting data, and understanding the design of a mixed methods study (Onwuegbuzie and Dickinson 2008, Wheeldon and Åhlberg 2012). As adjuncts to texts, visual displays can facilitate 'communication, thinking, and learning' (Schnotz 2002:101). More specifically, by 'combining words, numbers, and pictures', graphic displays make complexity accessible (Tufte 2001:180).

Examples of visual displays

In quantitatively focused research, visual displays often include concept maps (which provide visual representations of theories). A concept map is a top-down graphical device that organises and represents knowledge (Eppler 2006, Novak and Cañas 2008). Figure 1 shows an example of a concept map representing mixed methods research as described by Creswell (2015). Concept maps involve a textual concept (a semiotic signifier) such as words or other symbols inside a shape such as a circle or a rectangle. They generally show relationships between concepts by using arrows. Concept maps may move from general to more specific aspects and represent a series of events (Wheeldon and Åhlberg 2012).

In qualitatively focused research, concept maps can help organise analysis (Kinchin, Streatfield and Hay 2010). More often, visual displays in qualitative research include mind maps in a radial shape (Eppler 2006, Wheeldon and Åhlberg 2012) (e.g. Figure 2). In addition to data collection purposes, mind maps help researchers reflect on and organise their research. The overall approach to mind maps allows for the inherent ambiguity and flexibility of qualitative research.

Figure 1 Concept map of mixed methods studies

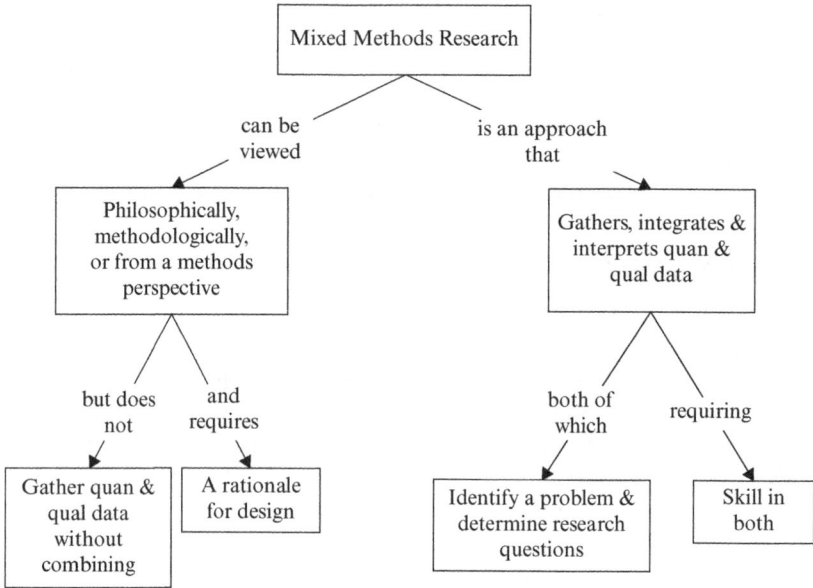

Figure 2 Mind map of mixed methods studies

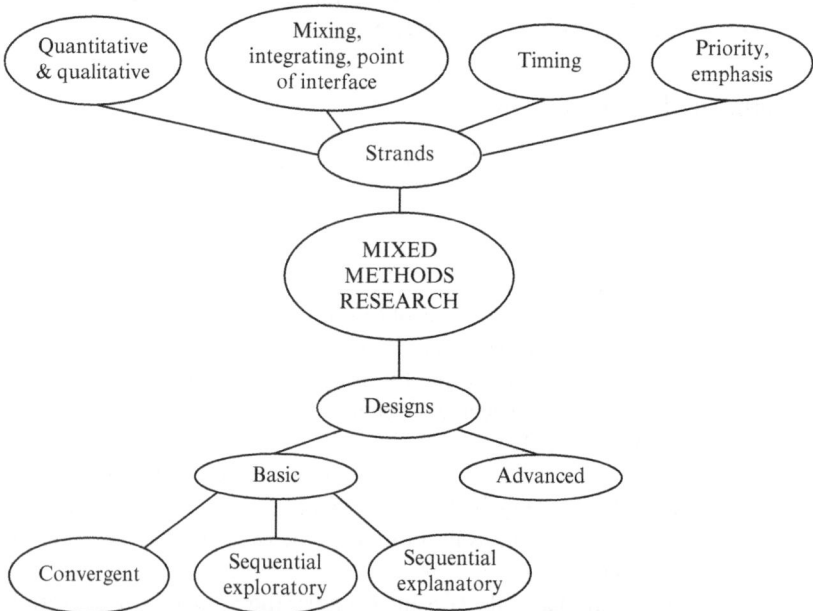

Eppler (2006) compares a variety of visual displays that may be used to represent research, such as concept maps, mind maps, conceptual diagrams, and visual metaphors (see Table 1; adapted from Eppler 2006, Table 1 includes new content for the thumbnails and condenses characteristics).

Procedural diagrams

A subset of visual displays, diagrams convey context-specific concepts through schematic figures (Tversky, Zacks, Lee and Heiser 2000) and help to structure and simplify 'potentially complex reasoning' (Gurr and Tourlas 2000:483). The dimensions of a diagram must be considered to allow viewers to appropriately interpret the meaning intended (Tversky et al 2000). A diagram's dimensions include its syntactic elements (e.g. shapes and lines) contextualised by the media of space (Tversky et al 2000) and colour (Bresciani and Eppler 2007). Closed shape elements such as circles and ovals represent landmark points in a process and sort or organise process components. For arrays of shapes, proximity is key to perceived meaning (Tversky 2001). Lines represent a straight and systematic path, and spatial elements are a metaphor for time (Freeman 2004, Gurr and Tourlas 2000, Tversky et al 2000). Arrows show functional direction, provide temporal sequence, and help to link relationships (Gurr and Tourlas 2000, Tversky et al 2000). Based on regularity and pattern of cultural use, colour schemes may provide different symbolic value (Machin 2007). Colours can group elements of a diagram. The subtleness, or intensity of colours, influences their potential meaning. The 'purity' and 'hybridity' of colours may also affect meaning, as we shall see when the use of colour to show a mix of qualitative and quantitative data is discussed later in this chapter.

Mixed methods procedural diagrams

Mixed methods procedural diagrams are one-page visual displays that guide the viewer through stages of data collection, analysis and mixing (see Creswell and Plano Clark 2011). The diagram represents an assessment or research project, helping viewers to understand what happens at each step, as well as the sequence of those steps. More specifically, a diagram conveys the complexity of a mixed methods design, clarifies the design in the researcher's mind, clarifies the design for readers, or viewers (useful when presenting a research programme to stakeholders) and bridges different audience perspectives.

Morse (1991) first discussed the use of notational symbols in mixed methods procedural diagrams. Creswell and Plano Clark (2011) provided an expanded notation list:

- the shortened terms *quan* and *qual* indicate quantitative and qualitative strands respectively

Table 1 Comparison of concept maps, mind maps, conceptual diagrams and visual metaphors (Adapted from Eppler 2006)

	Concept map	Mind map	Conceptual diagram	Visual metaphor
Thumbnail				
Definition	A top-down diagram showing relationships between concepts	A radial diagram with connections between hierarchies	A depiction of an abstract concept, systematically specifying relationships between categories	A graphic structure using familiar shapes to organise content
Benefit	Shows systemic relationships	Seamlessly shows sub-topics	Analyses a topic	Meaningfully conveys message
Guidelines	Summarise topics or clarify abstract elements	Hierarchically structure main aspects of material	Label boxes with arrows	Place key elements of a method or concept in a graphic metaphor
Graphic elements	Boxes and bubbles with text and arrows	Central bubble with coloured branches and text above	Left to right or top to bottom	Text in visual structure, sometimes with arrows
Orientation	Top-down	Centre-out	Left to right or top to bottom	Bottom-up, top-down, in-out, or out-in
Design rules	Start with main concept on top; add boxes for related concepts; use arrows for relationship	Start with main topic in centre; add branches for sub-topics	Label boxes and add corresponding text	Provide a clear message relating to a conceptual domain
Adaptability	Flexible, branching out	Somewhat flexible but always radial	Fixed diagram shape	Fixed metaphor shape
Memorability	Low	Medium to high	Low to medium	High
Understandability	High	Low	Medium	High

- *UPPERCASE* indicates a project strand with higher priority, implying lowercase for a strand with lower priority, e.g. *QUAL and quan*
- an arrow (→) indicates the relationship between sequential strands where one of the strands is more dominant than the other, e.g. *QUAL→quan*
- a plus sign (+) indicates the relationship between simultaneous strands, e.g. *QUAL+QUAN*
- (parentheses) indicate a strand 'embedded in a larger design or . . . theoretical framework' (Creswell and Plano Clark (2011:109) citing Plano Clark 2005), e.g. *QUAN(qual)*
- double arrows (→←)indicate recurring qualitative and/or quantitative strands (Nastasi, Hitchcock and Brown 2010), e.g. *(qual→←quan)* indicating for example *qual→quan→qual→quan*
- [brackets with smaller font] indicate a series of projects with a mixed methods project as one of those projects, e.g. *QUAL[QUAN→qual]→QUAN*
- an equal sign (=) indicates the purpose for mixing (Creswell and Plano Clark 2011), e.g. *QUAN→qual=explaining results.*

Table 2 lists recommended steps for drawing mixed methods procedural diagrams, adapted from Ivankova, Creswell and Stick's 'rules for drawing visual models for mixed-methods designs' (2006:15) and more recently from Creswell and Plano Clark (2011). The adaptations include several reworded and resequenced statements, and an added mention of a timeline (see also Guetterman and Salamoura, Chapter 7, this volume for a list of mixed methods components in mixed methods diagrams, and the case studies in Section 3 for examples of procedural diagrams used).

Table 2 Recommended steps for drawing mixed methods procedural diagrams

✔	Recommended steps
☐	Create a descriptive title.
☐	Choose a horizontal or vertical orientation.
☐	Show higher emphasis or priority with UPPER CASE and lower priority with lower case.
☐	Show stages of data collection or analysis with boxes (see Figure 3).
☐	Show mixing or the point of interface of quantitative and qualitative strands with circles or ovals (see Figure 3).
☐	Show integrated interpretation of quantitative and qualitative results with circles or ovals (see Figure 3).
☐	Show flow of procedures with arrows (→).
☐	List procedures of each stage and mixing component.
☐	Use concise language.
☐	Embrace simplicity.
☐	Fit diagram to a single page.
☐	Add a timeline delineating each portion of the study (Kubanyiova 2007).

Figure 3 Example of boxes and ovals distinguishing strands and mixing

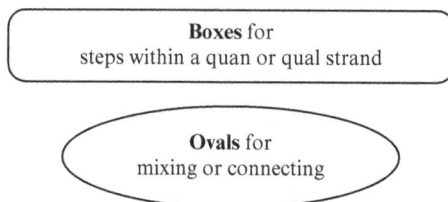

Boxes for
steps within a quan or qual strand

Ovals for
mixing or connecting

Examples of procedural diagrams

Basic mixed methods designs

In line with the checklist in Table 2, we propose the following diagrams for basic mixed methods designs including exploratory sequential, explanatory sequential, and convergent designs.

Exploratory sequential designs begin with a qualitative phase that builds to a quantitative phase (Creswell (2015); see also Creswell and Zhou, Chapter 3, this volume and Ziegler and Kang, Chapter 4, this volume). An exploratory sequential diagram starts with a rectangle that represents the qualitative phase, includes an oval that indicates building to a rectangle for the quantitative phase, and ends with an oval for interpretation. Notation includes an arrow moving from the qualitative to the quantitative phase. When the emphasis is on the quantitative phase, 'QUAN' is uppercase (Figure 4) whereas when the emphasis is on the qualitative phase, 'QUAL' is uppercase (Figure 5), a distinction that Creswell and Plano Clark (2011) make. In Figures 4 to 8, procedures are shown generically. Diagrams of actual studies would specify relevant procedures of data collection and analysis, as illustrated in the procedural diagrams in the chapters in Section 3.

Explanatory sequential designs begin with a quantitative phase followed by a qualitative phase (Creswell 2015; see also Ziegler and Kang, Chapter 4, this volume). An explanatory sequential diagram starts with a rectangle for the quantitative phase, includes an oval that indicates following up with a rectangle for the qualitative phase, and ends with an oval for interpretation. Notation includes an arrow moving from the quantitative to the qualitative phase. Figure 6 shows emphasis on the quantitative phase and Figure 7 on the qualitative phase.

Convergent designs collect quantitative and qualitative data and then merge the results for purposes of comparison (Creswell 2015; see also Ziegler and Kang, Chapter 4, this volume). A convergent diagram starts with adjacent rectangles for qualitative and quantitative components, continues to an oval to indicate comparison or relationship of results from both components, and ends with an oval for interpretation (see Figure 8). Notation includes a plus sign between QUAL and QUAN.

Figure 4 Basic diagram and notation: Exploratory sequential with quantitative priority

An exploratory mixed methods study to generalise findings

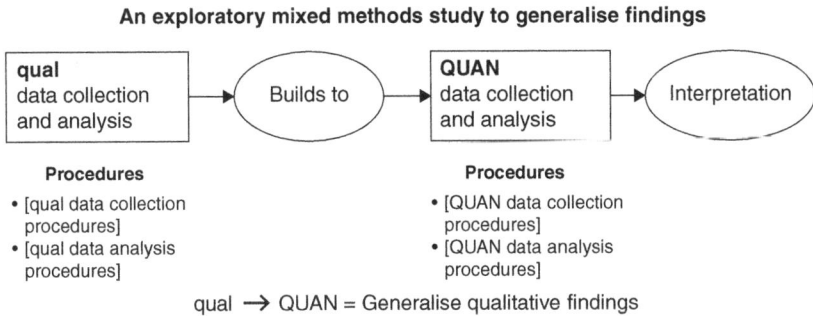

| qual data collection and analysis | → | Builds to | → | QUAN data collection and analysis | → | Interpretation |

Procedures
• [qual data collection procedures]
• [qual data analysis procedures]

Procedures
• [QUAN data collection procedures]
• [QUAN data analysis procedures]

qual → QUAN = Generalise qualitative findings

Figure 5 Basic diagram and notation: Exploratory sequential with qualitative priority

An exploratory mixed methods study to develop a taxonomy

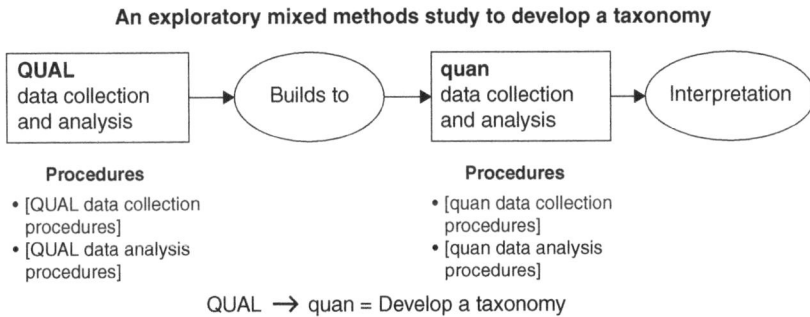

| QUAL data collection and analysis | → | Builds to | → | quan data collection and analysis | → | Interpretation |

Procedures
• [QUAL data collection procedures]
• [QUAL data analysis procedures]

Procedures
• [quan data collection procedures]
• [quan data analysis procedures]

QUAL → quan = Develop a taxonomy

Figure 6 Basic diagram and notation: Explanatory sequential design with quantitative priority

An explanatory mixed methods study to explain quantitative results

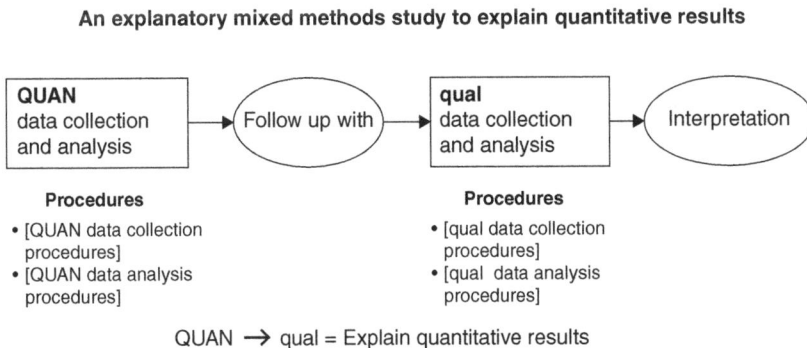

| QUAN data collection and analysis | → | Follow up with | → | qual data collection and analysis | → | Interpretation |

Procedures
• [QUAN data collection procedures]
• [QUAN data analysis procedures]

Procedures
• [qual data collection procedures]
• [qual data analysis procedures]

QUAN → qual = Explain quantitative results

Figure 7 Basic diagram and notation: Explanatory sequential design with qualitative priority

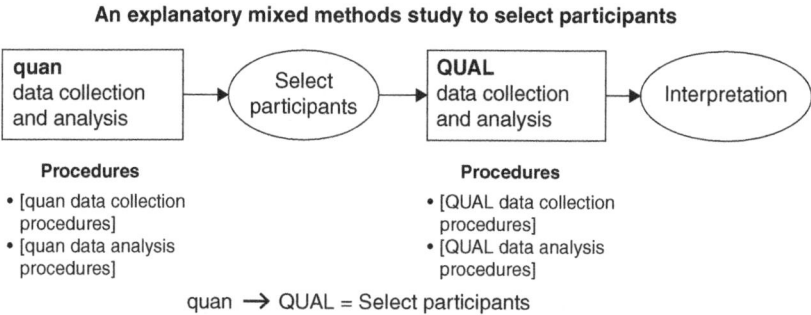

An explanatory mixed methods study to select participants

| quan data collection and analysis | → | Select participants | → | QUAL data collection and analysis | → | Interpretation |

Procedures
- [quan data collection procedures]
- [quan data analysis procedures]

Procedures
- [QUAL data collection procedures]
- [QUAL data analysis procedures]

quan → QUAL = Select participants

Figure 8 Basic diagram and notation: Convergent design

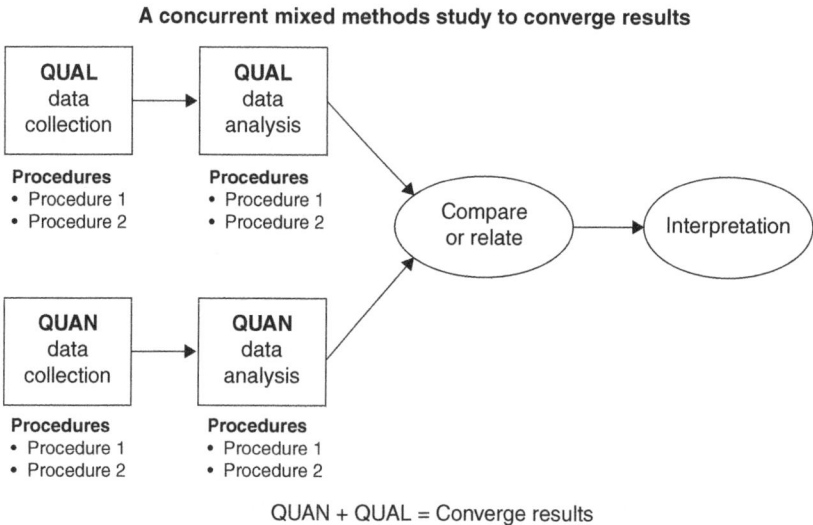

A concurrent mixed methods study to converge results

| QUAL data collection | → | QUAL data analysis |

Procedures
- Procedure 1
- Procedure 2

Procedures
- Procedure 1
- Procedure 2

Compare or relate → Interpretation

| QUAN data collection | → | QUAN data analysis |

Procedures
- Procedure 1
- Procedure 2

Procedures
- Procedure 1
- Procedure 2

QUAN + QUAL = Converge results

Advanced mixed methods designs

As examples of advanced mixed methods designs, Figure 9 shows an intervention design, Figure 10 shows a social justice design, and Figure 11 shows a multi-phase evaluation design as Creswell (2015) describes them.

Published mixed methods procedural diagrams

This section discusses published diagrams from the mixed methods literature across all fields of study chosen to represent a wide array of examples.

Procedural diagrams outside language assessment

Examples in this section include procedural diagrams for sequential explanatory and embedded mixed methods case study designs. The first example, taken from Ivankova et al (2006) provides a visual display model for sequential explanatory design procedures. The authors provided a clear title and a

Figure 9 Advanced: Intervention design (adapted from Creswell 2014a:52)

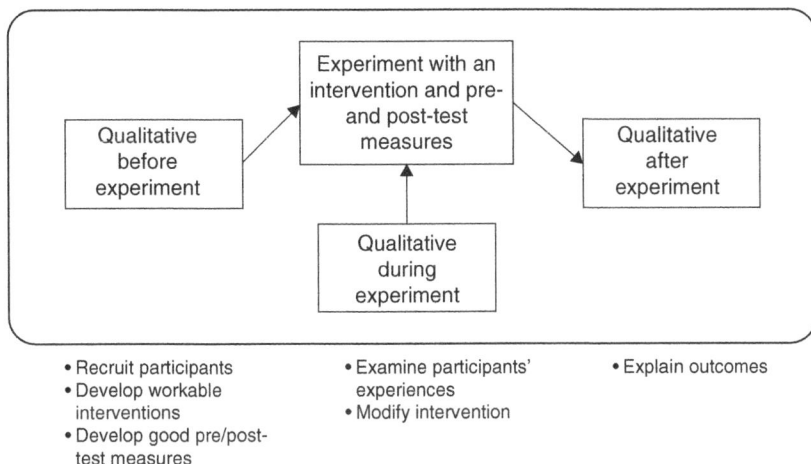

- Recruit participants
- Develop workable interventions
- Develop good pre/post-test measures

- Examine participants' experiences
- Modify intervention

- Explain outcomes

Figure 10 Advanced: Social justice design (adapted from Creswell 2014a:53)

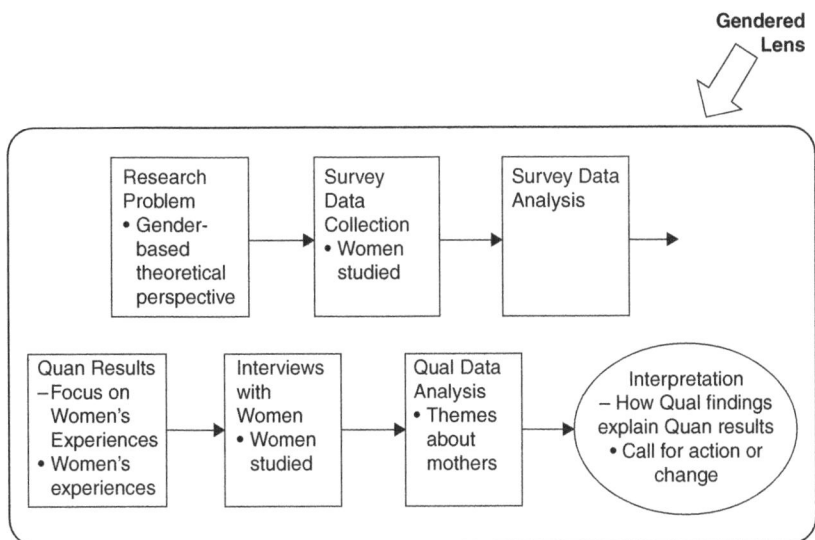

Figure 11 Advanced: Multistage evaluation design (adapted from Creswell 2014a:54)

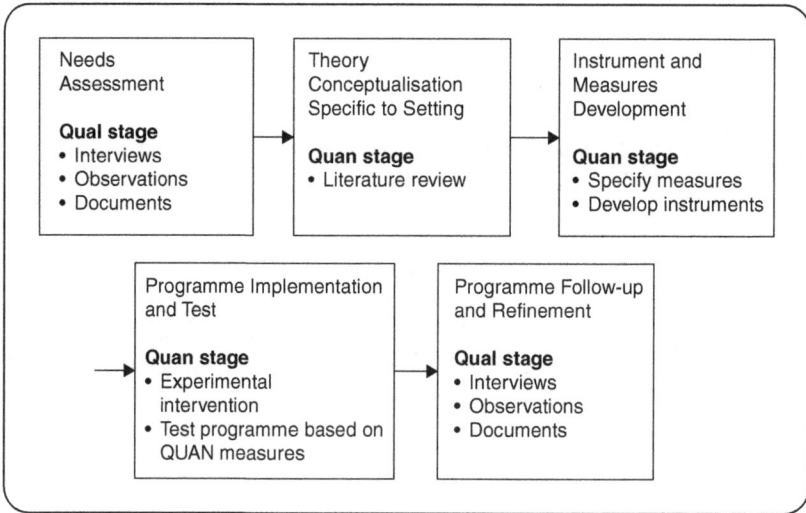

consistent vertical orientation (see Figure 12). They indicated the priority of the qualitative phase using uppercase letters. Boxes indicate stages of data collection and analysis, ovals indicate connecting and integration as forms of mixing, and arrows indicate the flow of procedures. This diagram lists products separately from procedures (an appropriate but not necessary distinction), using concise language within a single page. Although there is no timeline on the diagram, in all, it clearly provides study details.

In the second example, illustrating a convergent case study, Almutairi (2012) studied the impact of diversity in a nursing workforce. His diagram added detail such as the case, aim, context, and units of analysis of a concurrent mixed methods study (see Figure 13). This one-page diagram includes a descriptive title. The overall orientation is vertical, with sub-units of analysis horizontal. Boxes indicate qualitative and quantitative approaches, as well as data collection and analysis, and the oval indicates mixing. Arrows indicate the specified flow of procedures and language is concise. The diagram indicates the complexity of the study with simple text.

In the third example, Rosenberg and Yates (2007) demonstrated ways in which schematics can clarify procedures for and increase the rigour of case studies through including methodological procedures and content information (see Figure 14). By combining procedures and themes, they presented schematic representations as visual maps that 'relate[d] elements of a whole and [gave] structure to the audit trail' (Rosenberg and Yates 2007:448). Their schematic representation of a mixed methods case study includes a title

Figure 12 Sequential explanatory design (adapted from Ivankova et al 2006)

Visual Model for Mixed Methods
Sequential Explanatory Design Procedures

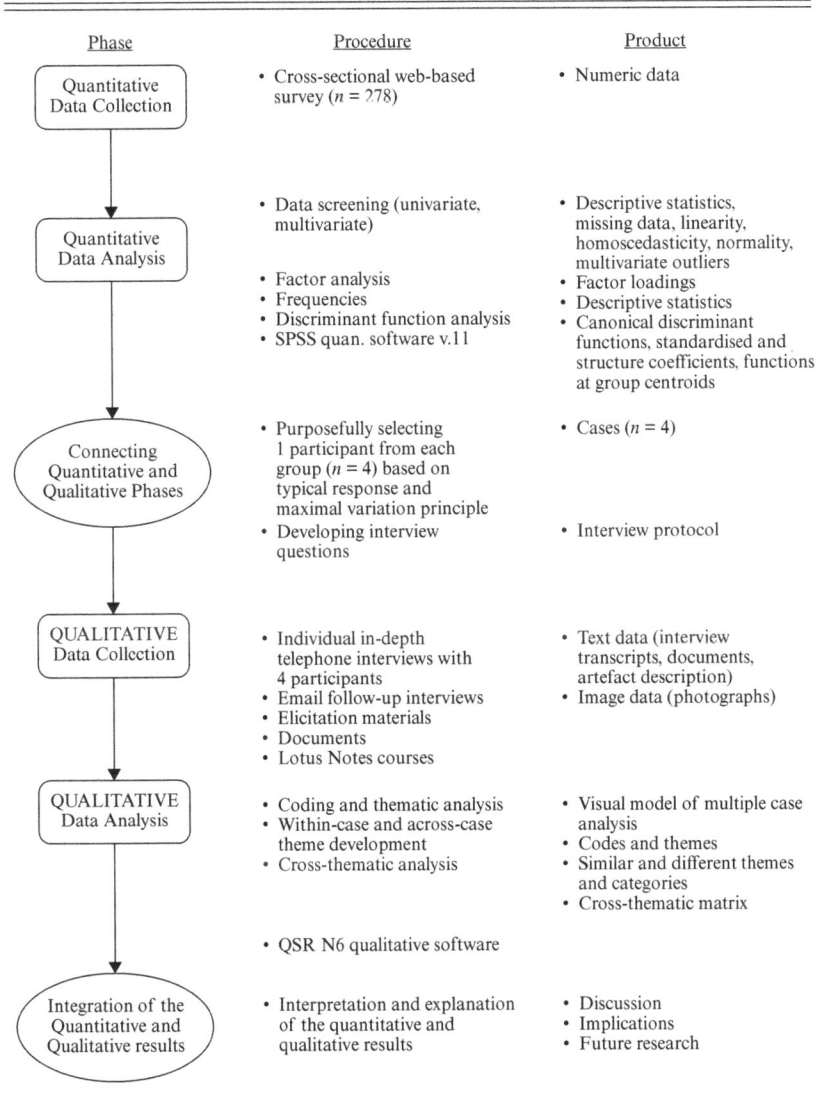

Phase	Procedure	Product
Quantitative Data Collection	• Cross-sectional web-based survey ($n = 278$)	• Numeric data
Quantitative Data Analysis	• Data screening (univariate, multivariate) • Factor analysis • Frequencies • Discriminant function analysis • SPSS quan. software v.11	• Descriptive statistics, missing data, linearity, homoscedasticity, normality, multivariate outliers • Factor loadings • Descriptive statistics • Canonical discriminant functions, standardised and structure coefficients, functions at group centroids
Connecting Quantitative and Qualitative Phases	• Purposefully selecting 1 participant from each group ($n = 4$) based on typical response and maximal variation principle • Developing interview questions	• Cases ($n = 4$) • Interview protocol
QUALITATIVE Data Collection	• Individual in-depth telephone interviews with 4 participants • Email follow-up interviews • Elicitation materials • Documents • Lotus Notes courses	• Text data (interview transcripts, documents, artefact description) • Image data (photographs)
QUALITATIVE Data Analysis	• Coding and thematic analysis • Within-case and across-case theme development • Cross-thematic analysis • QSR N6 qualitative software	• Visual model of multiple case analysis • Codes and themes • Similar and different themes and categories • Cross-thematic matrix
Integration of the Quantitative and Qualitative results	• Interpretation and explanation of the quantitative and qualitative results	• Discussion • Implications • Future research

Figure 13 Mixed methods convergent design embedded in a case study (adapted from Almutairi 2012)

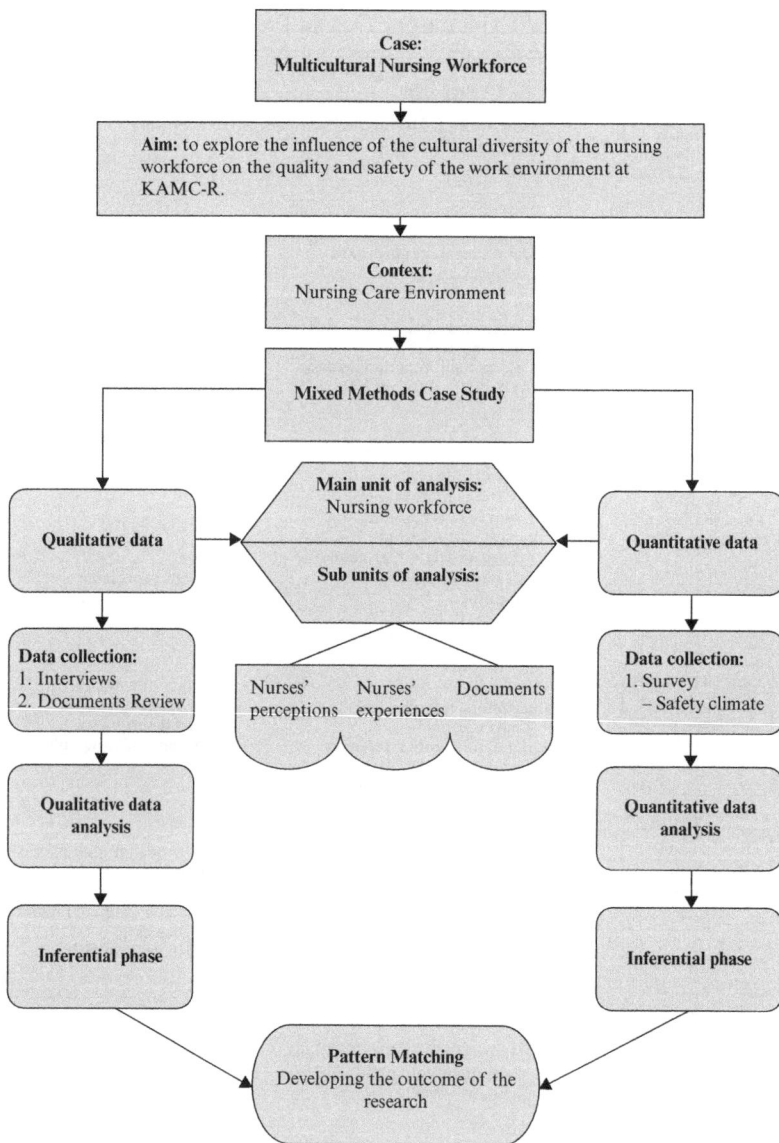

Figure 14 Methodology plus content: Mixed methods case study (Rosenberg and Yates 2007)

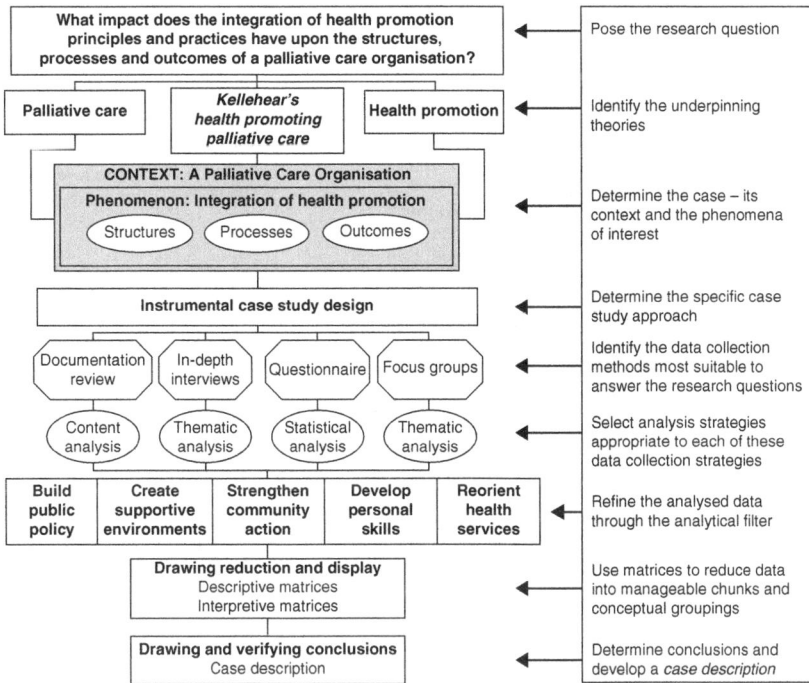

(omitted from this reprinted version), and it does not indicate priority of a particular strand. The figure uses octagons for data collection, ovals for data analysis, and rectangles for resulting themes and mixing. The lines indicate flow of schematic components without arrowheads for direction. The language is concise and the diagram fits on a single page.

A further example is taken from Bustamante (2014:1), who studied professional development on Web 2.0 for teachers of Spanish using an embedded convergent mixed methods design (see Ziegler and Kang, Chapter 4, this volume), in which qualitative and quantitative data was embedded within a case study. Her diagram (see Figure 15) shows that a more sophisticated yet clear display may use colour (in this case greyscale) to distinguish qualitative and quantitative strands, and mixing. In the original diagram, Bustamante (2014) used the primary colours of blue for the rectangles on the left and yellow for the rectangles on the right to represent distinct qualitative and quantitative strands, and the secondary colour of green for the ovals to represent mixing strands.

Figure 15 Convergent: Vertical with timeline (Bustamante 2014)

EMBEDDED CONVERGENT MIXED METHODS CASE STUDY

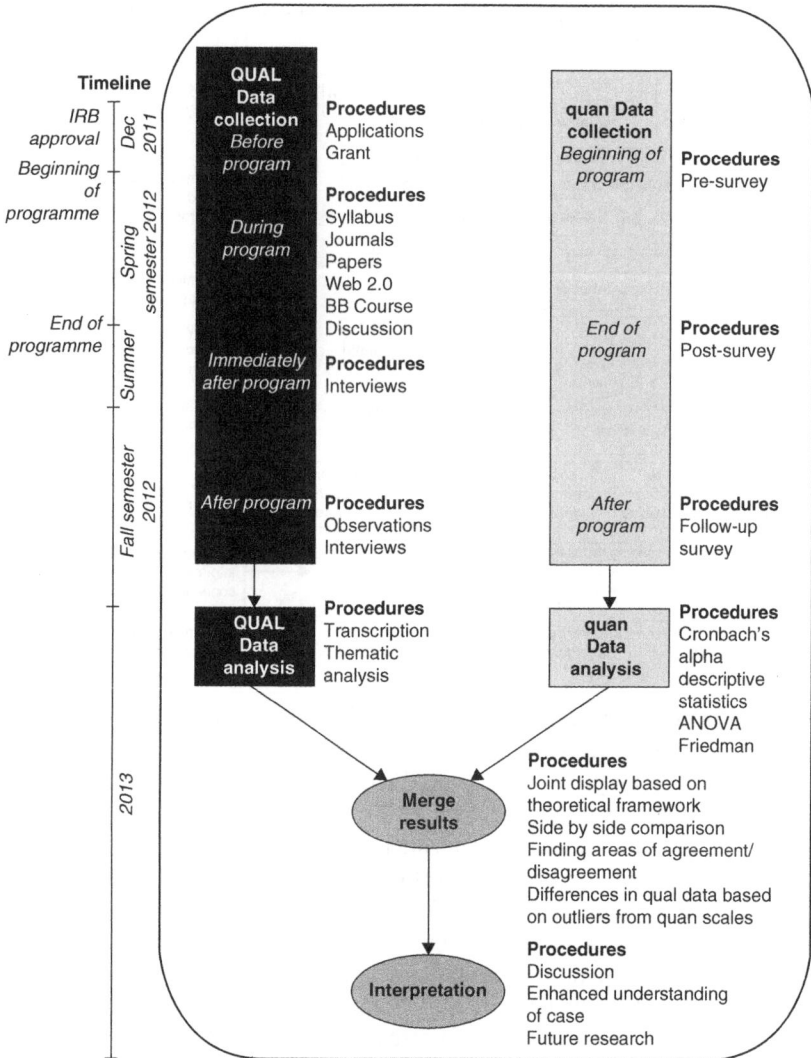

Timeline

IRB approval — *Dec 2011*

Beginning of programme — *Spring semester 2012*

End of programme — *Summer*

Fall semester 2012

2013

QUAL Data collection

Before program — **Procedures** Applications Grant

During program — **Procedures** Syllabus Journals Papers Web 2.0 BB Course Discussion

Immediately after program — **Procedures** Interviews

After program — **Procedures** Observations Interviews

QUAL Data analysis — **Procedures** Transcription Thematic analysis

quan Data collection

Beginning of program — **Procedures** Pre-survey

End of program — **Procedures** Post-survey

After program — **Procedures** Follow-up survey

quan Data analysis — **Procedures** Cronbach's alpha descriptive statistics ANOVA Friedman

Merge results — **Procedures** Joint display based on theoretical framework Side by side comparison Finding areas of agreement/ disagreement Differences in qual data based on outliers from quan scales

Interpretation — **Procedures** Discussion Enhanced understanding of case Future research

Procedural diagrams in language learning and assessment

This section discusses diagrams from two interesting mixed methods studies related to language learning or language assessment. See Guetterman and Salamoura (Chapter 7, this volume) for a discussion on how language assessment literature as a whole depicts mixed methods diagrams.

In the first example, a study of language learning motivation in early adolescents, Wesely (2010) includes a generic title that represents analysis phases (see Figure 16). The intended orientation is horizontal. However, the vertical arrows associating data type with phase may give a mixed impression of horizontal and vertical orientations. The diagram concisely indicates data collection and analysis procedures, and easily fits on one page.

In the second example, a study on assessment scales for large-scale speaking tests, a more complex diagram is presented. Galaczi, ffrench, Hubbard and Green (2011) include a title that describes the purpose of the study (see Figure 17). The diagram is based on consultation, development, and research tasks rather than on quantitative and qualitative phases. The orientation is primarily vertical, and the diagram uses flow chart symbols in place of rectangles and ovals, so priority is not indicated. This single-page diagram conveys the complexity of the study design using concise language.

Figure 16 Procedural diagram (Wesely 2010)

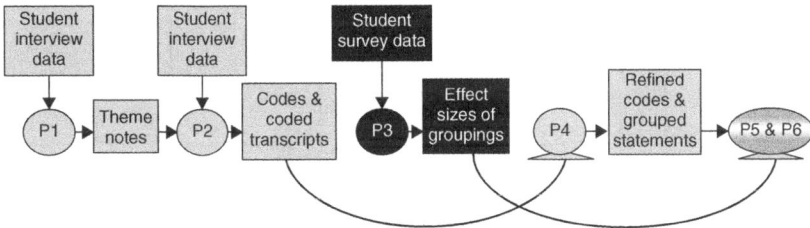

How to draw mixed methods procedural diagrams

Procedural diagrams can be drawn using a variety of software. Programs specialising in graphic design, like CorelDRAW® (www.coreldraw.com) or Adobe Illustrator® (http://www.adobe.com), may be used. IHMC Cmap Tools (cmap.ihmc.us) is free software designed specifically for research diagrams such as concept maps. However, software as simple as PowerPoint® (office.microsoft.com) works very well for this task. As the latter is one of the most widely available programs for both Windows® and Mac OS® operating systems, this chapter uses the PowerPoint® presentation graphics program to explain step by step how to draw a mixed methods procedural diagram, including all the elements from the checklist for procedural diagrams (Table 2) presented in the literature review.

Figure 17 Procedural diagram (Figure 1 from Galaczi et al 2011)

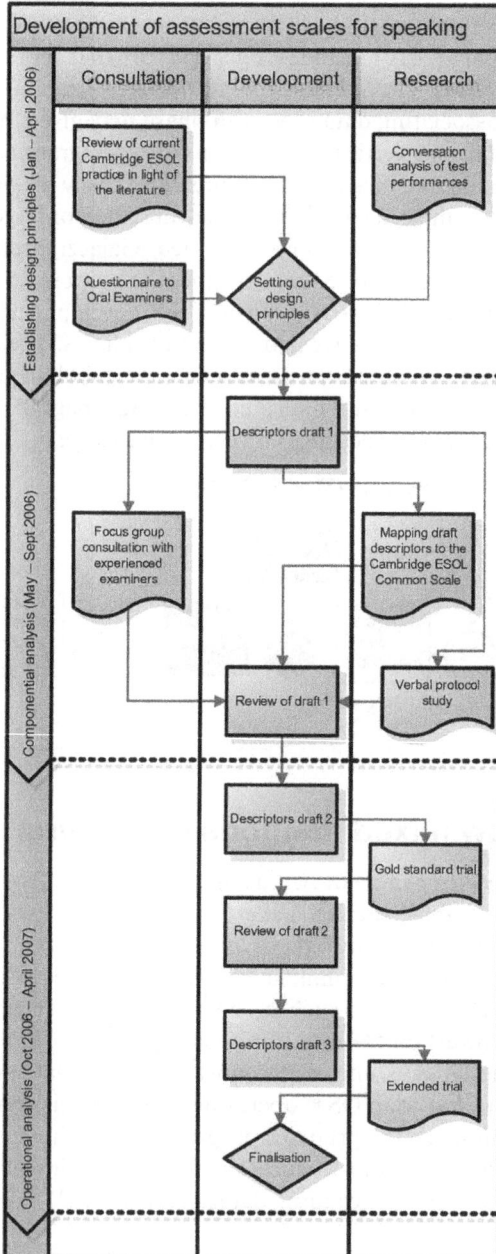

1) Display orientation

From a technical perspective, the first step when drawing a procedural diagram is deciding the orientation (conceptually, providing a title is the first step; however, for technical purposes this tutorial will guide you to add a title after the diagram is complete). Your diagram, including all components, should follow either a horizontal (e.g. left to right) or vertical (e.g. top to bottom) orientation (see Figure 18). When mixed methods studies are conducted in distinctive phases, conveying the chronology of your project clearly is an important aspect of an effective diagram. This is difficult to represent in procedural diagrams that engage both horizontal and vertical orientations.

Figure 18 Horizontal or vertical orientation in a procedural diagram

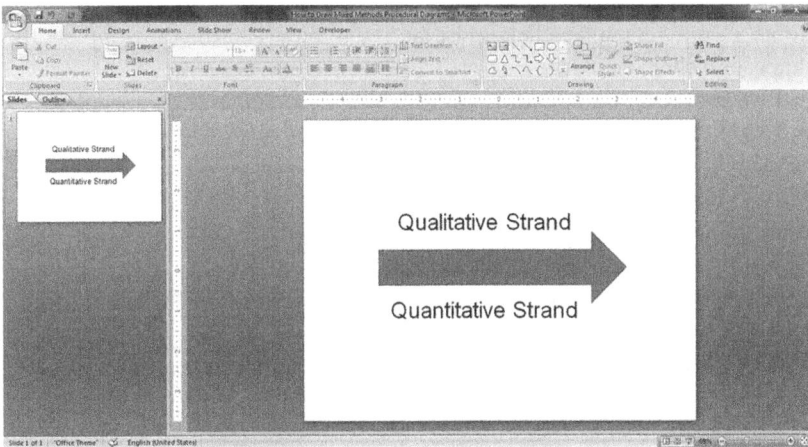

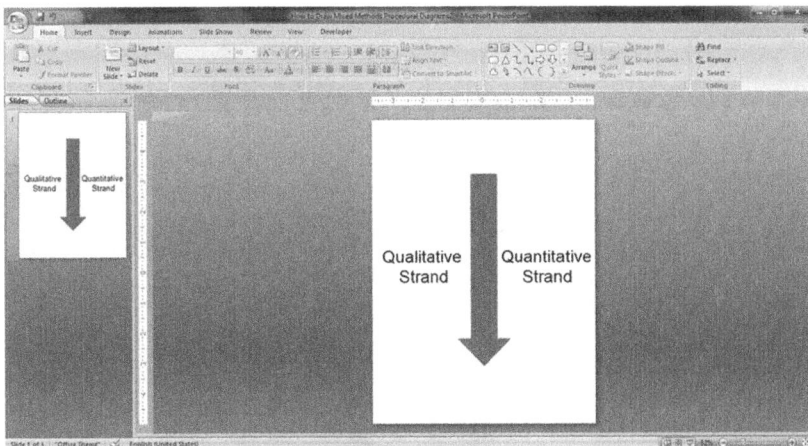

2) Basic shapes

Procedural diagrams involve two basic shapes: rectangles or boxes for the stages of data collection and analysis in the qualitative and quantitative strands, and circles or ovals for the stages of data mixing and interpretation. The example presented here is for a convergent parallel mixed methods design displayed with a horizontal orientation (drawn in PowerPoint® for PC. Although the software version for the Apple Mac has a slightly different interface, the menu options are basically the same, so this tutorial is useful for Mac users as well).

Open a new document in PowerPoint®. Go to *Insert*, click on *Shapes*, and click on one of the rectangles from the pop-up menu (see Figure 19).

Once you click on the rectangle, a cursor in the shape of a plus sign (+) will appear. Place the cursor anywhere in the document window where you want to place your rectangle, click and drag it diagonally until you complete the shape, and click again (see Figure 20).

For this procedural diagram we will draw four rectangles (data collection and data analysis for the qualitative strand, and data collection and data analysis for the quantitative strand). Therefore, repeat the same steps three more times. Arrange the rectangles in parallel with each other, because the

Figure 19 Inserting basic shapes in a procedural diagram

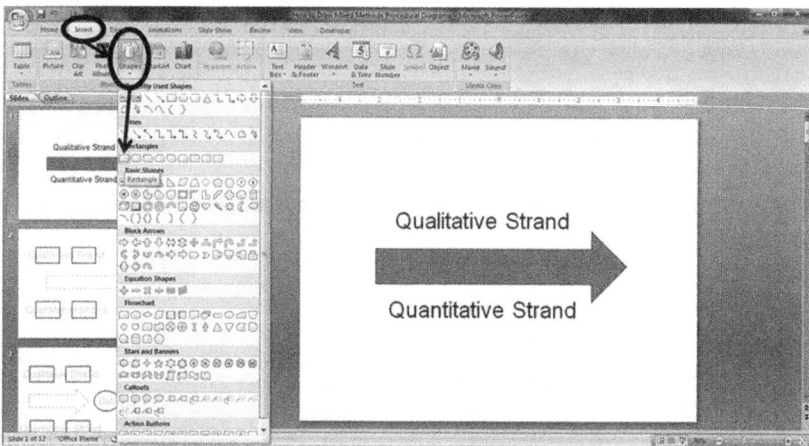

Figure 20 Drawing a rectangle

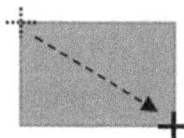

orientation of this diagram is horizontal (left to right) and in a convergent parallel study the phases for data collection and analysis may occur at about the same time (see Figure 21).

If you are considering including your diagram in a printed publication, it is a good idea to change the fill colour of your shapes to white and the colour of the lines to black. In the last step of this section the use of other colours will be discussed. To change the colour of your shapes, select the shape by clicking on it and use the *Shape Fill* and *Shape Outline* tools in the *Home* tab (see Figure 22).

Repeat the same steps you followed to create the rectangles, this time selecting an oval instead. Create two ovals and place them in the middle of

Figure 21 Placing boxes for data collection and analysis for qualitative and quantitative strands

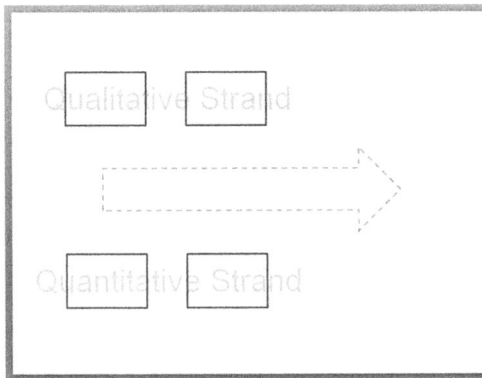

Figure 22 Shape Fill and Shape Outline tools

the two strands, because this is the point where the qualitative and quantitative data will be connected and interpreted (see Figure 23).

3) Notation in shapes

The literature review section described the notation used in procedural diagrams. Each rectangle, or box, should indicate the strand (quan vs. qual), the priority (caps vs. low caps), and the phase (data collection or data analysis). The ovals should indicate the merging/mixing of data or interpretation of merged/mixed data.

To add text to a PowerPoint® shape, simply click on the shape and start typing. In this example the qualitative strand has the priority (see Figure 24).

In this example, the notation text for the strands is bold to differentiate it from the data collection and analysis text. To change the colour, font, or size of the text, select the text by placing the cursor at its beginning and drag it till the end. Once the text is highlighted, a pop-up menu with text options will appear. Select the colour, font, and size of your choice. These same options are also located in the *Home* tab, *Font* tools (see Figure 25).

4) Procedural diagram flow

To indicate the chronological order of the different phases in your mixed methods study, use arrows to connect the shapes. Following the same instructions from step 2 (basic shapes), insert arrows between the boxes and ovals indicating the flow of the study. Go to *Insert*, click on *Shapes*, and click on the one-head straight arrow from the pop-up menu (see Figure 26).

Figure 23 Rectangles and ovals in a convergent parallel design

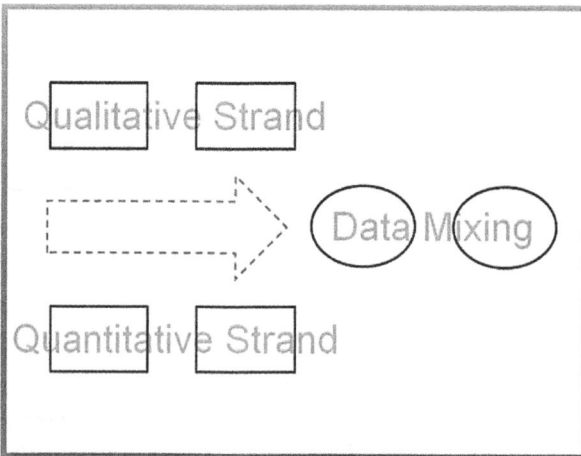

Figure 24 Notation within shapes in a procedural diagram

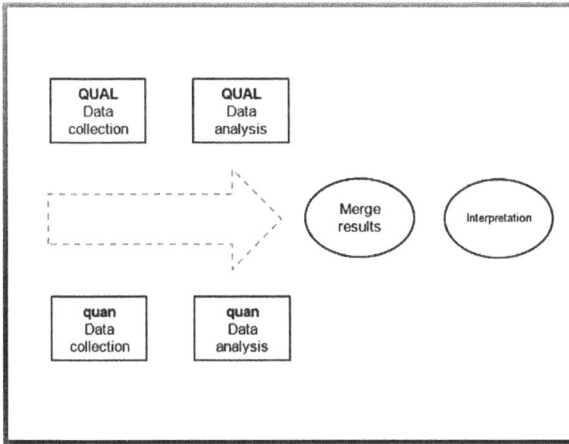

Figure 25 Changing the properties of text

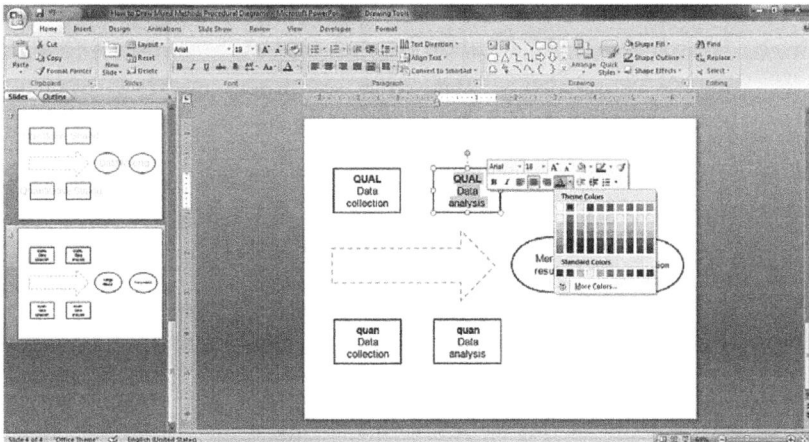

Once you click on the arrow, the cursor in the shape of a plus sign (+) will appear again. Place the cursor on the first box in the upper left and you will notice that four small squared indicators of the middle points of each side of the box will become visible. These indicators act as snap points for the tail and head of your arrow. Click on the middle point in the right side of the first box and drag your arrow to the middle point in the left side of the second box. When you approach the second box, the indicators will become visible in that box (see Figure 27).

Repeat the same steps to connect the rest of the boxes and ovals. Note that

Figure 26 Inserting arrows in a procedural diagram

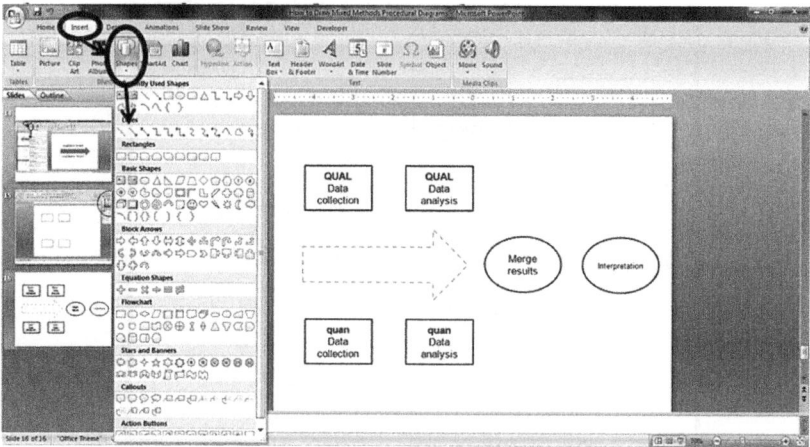

Figure 27 Drawing an arrow

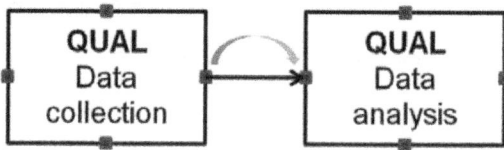

the two boxes to the right should be connected to the first oval to indicate the flow of procedures from data collection to analysis (see Figure 28).

To change the colour or weight of an arrow, select the arrow by clicking on it. Go to *Shape Outline* in the *Home* tab and select the colour and weight of your choice. Make sure your arrows are visible and the arrowheads large enough (see Figure 29).

5) Procedures

It is important to indicate the procedures of each phase of the study. For example, list methods of data collection (i.e. interviews, journals, observations, essay responses, test scores, surveys, etc.) that pertain to each strand under the corresponding box. These procedures should be expressed using concise language, ideally in a list format, and consistently placed on the same side of each box or oval. This will result in a clear and well-organised procedural diagram. In this example, the procedures are located under each shape.

To insert a text box in PowerPoint®, go to *Insert*, click on *Text Box*, and click on *Horizontal Text Box* (see Figure 30).

Figure 28 Shapes connected by arrows in a procedural diagram

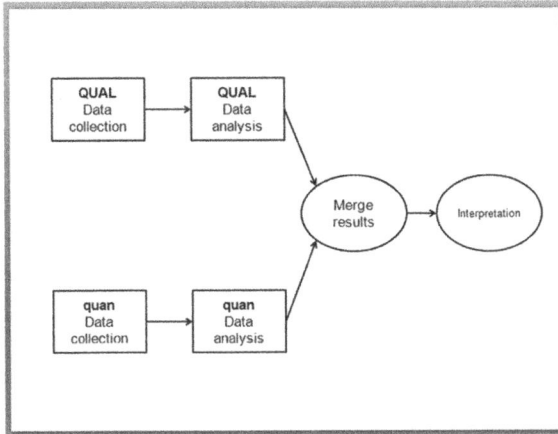

Figure 29 Changing the properties of arrows and lines

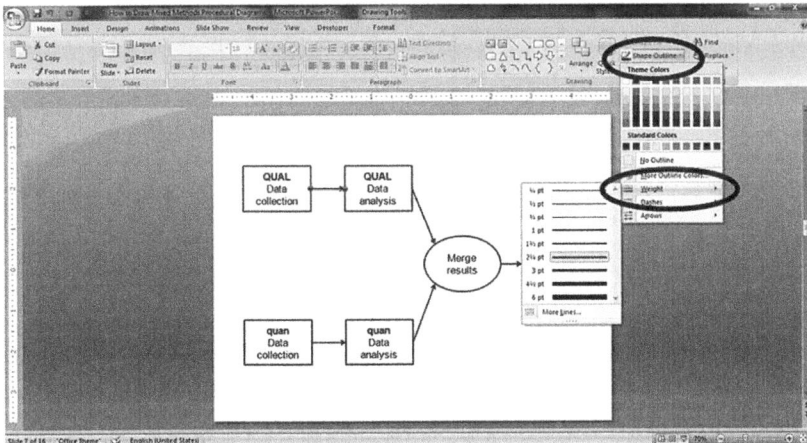

Place the cursor under the first box and simply start typing. Again, to change the colour, font, or size of the text, select the text by placing the cursor at the beginning of the text and dragging the cursor to the end of the text. Then follow the instructions from step 3 (notation in shapes). Make sure that your text is of adequate size and font, and that it is readable at first glance, both in print and on a screen (see Figure 31).

Repeat the same steps to insert a text box for each phase of the study. Place all your procedures under the corresponding shapes (see Figure 32).

Figure 30 Inserting a text box

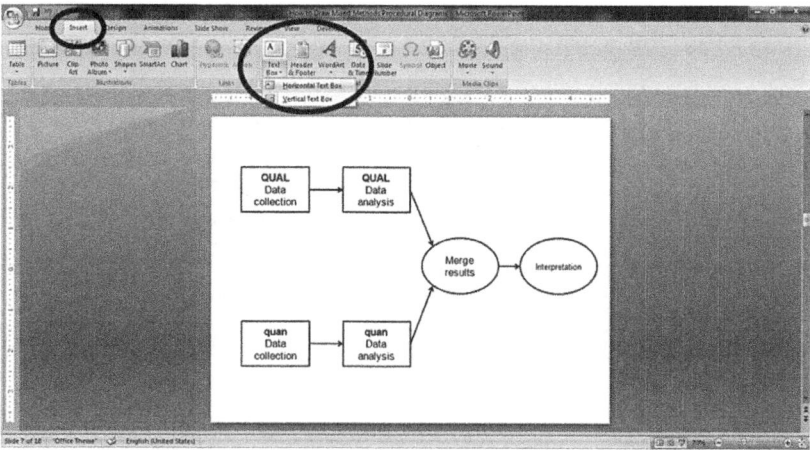

Figure 31 Writing in a text box

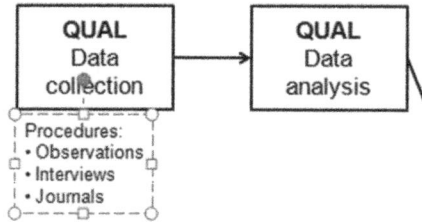

6) Timeline

Adding the timeline is the last step in developing the procedural diagrams. A timeline in a procedural diagram conveys when the different phases in the project occur and how long each is expected to take. The timeline may give the number of months or years each phase will take or, if known, the approximate dates (e.g. month and year).

Arrange the timeline according to the same orientation in which you arranged the procedural diagram. For example, if the diagram is horizontal, arrange the timeline horizontally as well. Differentiate each phase in the timeline, using simple short perpendicular lines. In this example, the timeline is located at the bottom of the diagram.

To insert a line in PowerPoint®, follow the instructions for inserting an arrow in step 4 but select a straight line instead. Begin by drawing a line from left (first phase or box) to right (last shape or oval) along your whole procedural diagram, placing it at the bottom of the document. To make the

Figure 32 Procedures in a procedural diagram

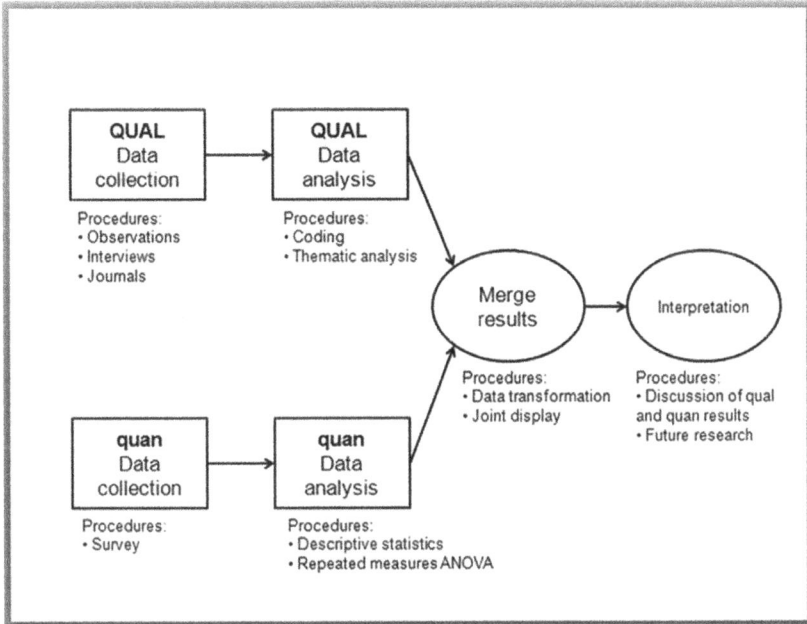

line perfectly horizontal or vertical, hold the *Shift* key while drawing (see Figure 33).

To differentiate each phase in the timeline, repeat the steps to insert a line, draw short vertical lines this time, and locate them in the corresponding place on the horizontal line (see Figure 34).

Lastly, add the text with the dates or number of months or years for each phase in a location corresponding with the timeline. Follow the same instructions for inserting a text box from step 5 (Procedures) (see Figure 35).

7) Title

It is important to add a title identifying the design of your study. The purpose of a mixed methods procedural diagram is to clarify the flow of the qualitative and quantitative strands and how these will be merged or mixed, so the title of your diagram should refer to the research design, rather than to the name of the project, or title of your article. As with the procedures, the title should be simple and concise. Ideally, it should be placed at the top of your diagram. Again, follow the same instructions for inserting a text box from step 5 (Procedures) (see Figure 36).

Figure 33 Inserting a line for a timeline

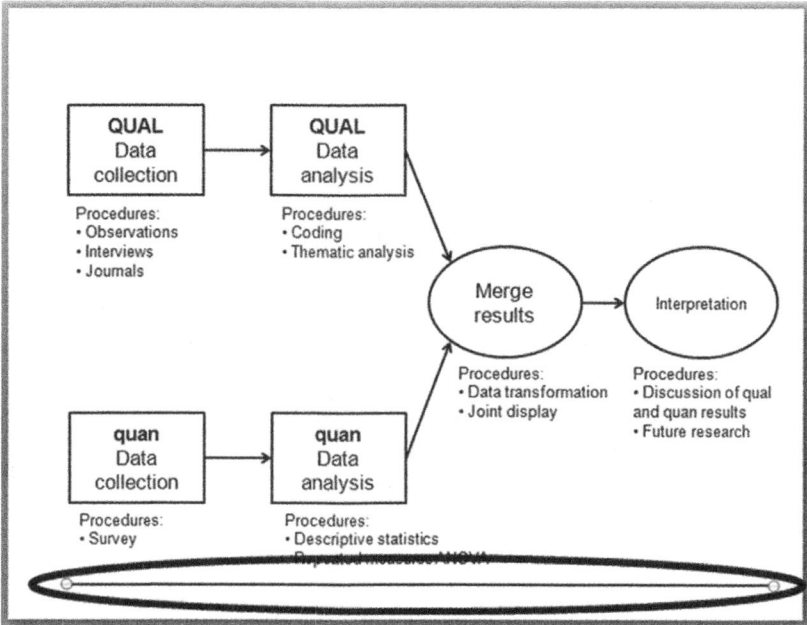

Figure 34 Differentiating phases in a timeline

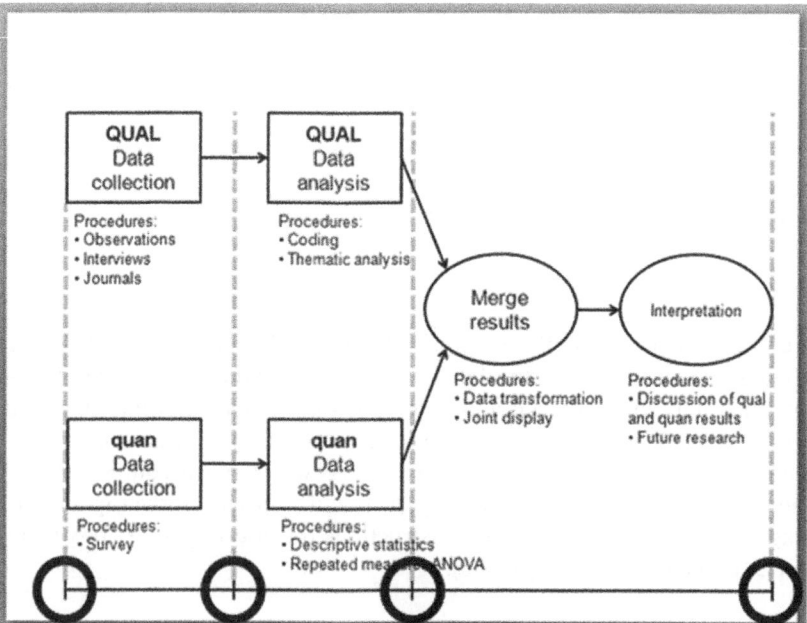

Figure 35 Adding time frames in a timeline

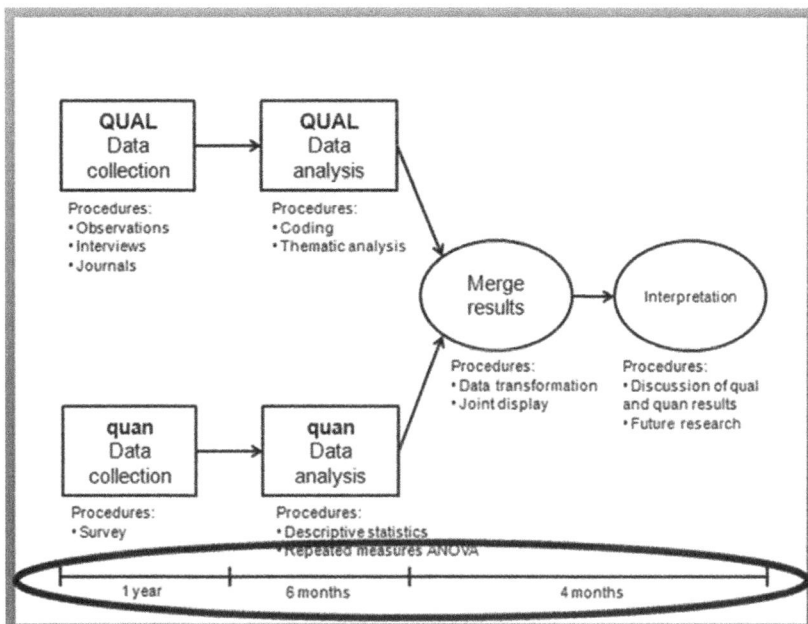

Figure 36 Adding a title to a procedural diagram

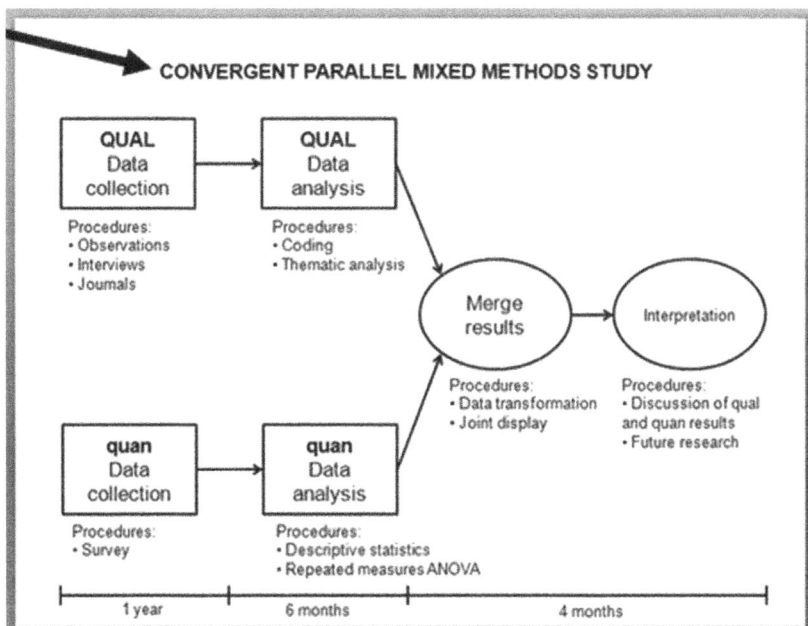

Figure 37 Colour in a convergent procedural diagram

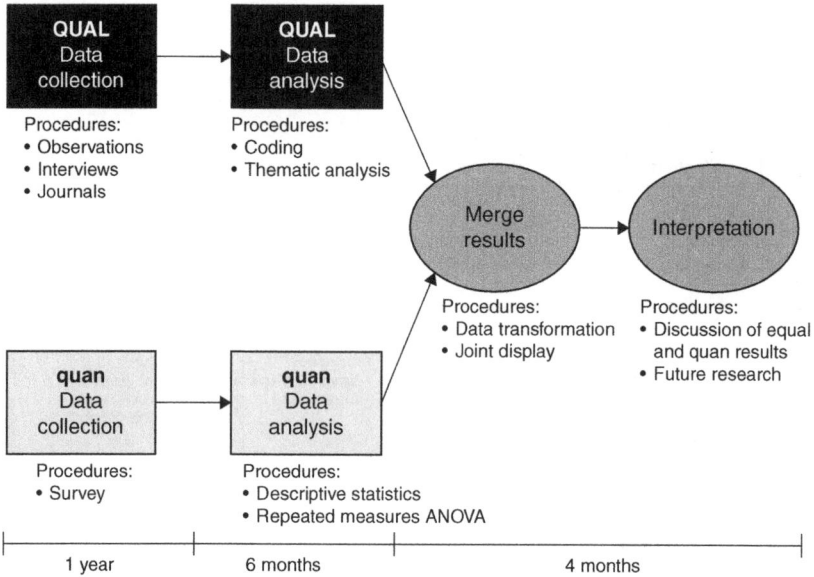

8) Use of colour

We previously suggested selecting black and white (or gray tones) in procedural diagrams intended for printed publication; however, when publishing online or presenting a procedural diagram at a conference, or for stakeholders in a project, the use of colour can help to visually differentiate the qualitative and quantitative strands and to clearly convey the mixing of the two. Consider adopting the additive aspect of colour theory by mixing complementary colours for this purpose (Hashimioto and Clayton 2009) by means of colours that can be seen clearly against the background of the page. For example, the diagram shown in grayscale in Figure 37 could represent qualitative data collection and analysis through yellow-shaded boxes, and quantitative data collection and analysis boxes through blue-shaded boxes. The figure would then represent merging and interpretation phases through green-shaded ovals.

To summarise, a mixed methods procedural diagram should be as simple as possible and all elements should fit on a single page. Too much text would make the information contained in the diagram challenging to access and a diagram spread over more than one page would interrupt the flow of the information.

Examples of procedural diagrams created using these steps

The following two examples portray mixed methods procedural diagrams suggested for mixed methods studies in the language learning and assessment field, created using the steps for drawing a procedural diagram above.

The first example describes an explanatory sequential study (see Figure 38). Williams, Burden, and Lanvers, in their study '"French is the language of love and stuff": Student perceptions of issues related to motivation in learning a foreign language' (2002), developed a matrix of external and internal factors to motivation, which subsequently developed into a Language Learning Motivation Questionnaire (LLMQ). The investigation was carried out in three schools in the south-west of England. The LLMQ was first used in order to obtain an overview of the strength of different motivational factors and to examine differences between gender, age and language studied. The questionnaire was administered to 228 pupils during class time by the researchers. Mean scores for groups or subgroups of students across areas of motivation were compared using an independent samples t-test. Internal consistency for each subscale was measured using Cronbach's alpha. In addition, the teachers of each class were asked to rate every student's *language proficiency* as A (high), B (middle), or C (low). The differences between each group of students were investigated by means of ANOVA with regard to their attitudes towards language learning and their sense of agency.

Results from the questionnaires enabled the researchers to identify areas for further in-depth investigation. Twenty-four pupils were subsequently interviewed to follow up such aspects of interest. The data arising from these interviews was coded and content analysed. Based on the findings, implications for teachers of languages were proposed. It was also suggested that expanding studies of motivation into other subjects could be useful in enhancing understanding of students' motivation across the curriculum.

The second example (see Figure 39) describes a convergent parallel study. 'An investigation into native and non-native teachers' judgments of oral English performance: A mixed methods approach' (Kim 2009) depicts how native English-speaking (NS) and non-native English-speaking (NNS) teachers evaluate students' oral English performance in a classroom setting. This study aimed to offer a comprehensive and diverse illustration of rating behaviour, examining both the *product* that the teachers generate (i.e. the numeric scores awarded to students) and the *process* that they go through (i.e. evaluative comments) in their assessment of students' oral English performance. The same weight was given to both quantitative and qualitative methods, with neither method dominating the other.

Ten Korean students were selected from a Canadian college-level language institute. Twelve NS Canadian teachers of English and 12 NNS Korean

Figure 38 Suggested procedural diagram for Williams, Burden, and Lanvers' explanatory sequential design (2002)

Motivation to Learn a Foreign Language:
An Explanatory Sequential Diagram
Willams, Burden & Lanvers (2002)

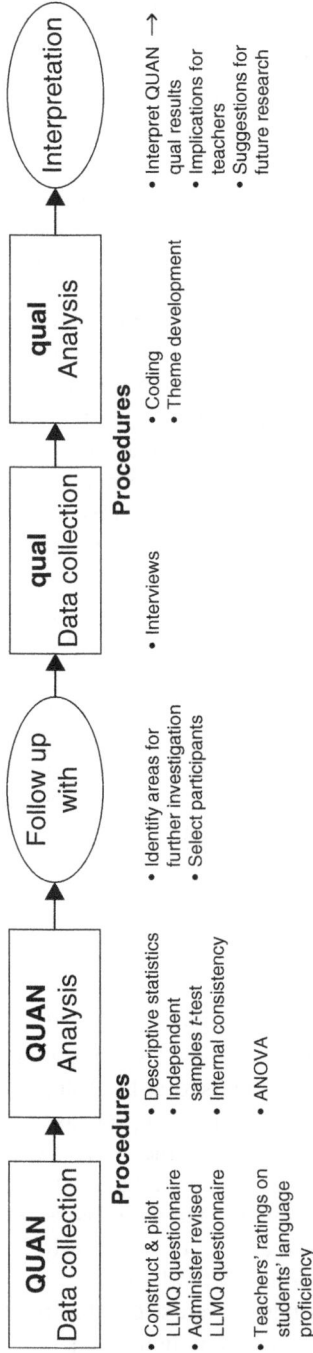

QUAN
Data collection

QUAN
Analysis

Follow up
with

qual
Data collection

qual
Analysis

Interpretation

Procedures

- Construct & pilot LLMQ questionnaire
- Administer revised LLMQ questionnaire
- Teachers' ratings on students' language proficiency

- Descriptive statistics
- Independent samples *t*-test
- Internal consistency
- ANOVA

- Identify areas for further investigation
- Select participants

- Interviews

Procedures

- Coding
- Theme development

- Interpret QUAN → qual results
- Implications for teachers
- Suggestions for future research

teachers of English constituted the NS and NNS teacher groups, respectively. A semi-direct oral English test was developed for the study. The purpose of the test was to assess the overall oral communicative language ability of non-native English speakers within an academic context. A 4-point rating scale was developed for rating. The test was administered individually to each of 10 Korean students, and their speech responses were simultaneously recorded as digital sound files. Test response sets were distributed to both groups of teachers. Teachers rated the students' test responses according to the 4-point rating scale first and then justified those ratings by providing written comments either in English or in Korean. A total of 1,727 valid ratings were awarded by the teachers. A Multi-Faceted Rasch Measurement was used to analyse the ratings. Four facets were specified: student, teacher, teacher group, and task. Three different types of statistical analysis were carried out to investigate teachers' internal consistency, based on: 1) fit statistics; 2) proportions of large standard residuals between observed and expected scores; and 3) a single rater–rest of the raters correlation. Teachers' severity measures were also examined in three different ways based on: 1) task difficulty measures, 2) a bias analysis between teacher groups and tasks, and 3) a bias analysis between individual teachers and tasks.

A total of 3,295 comments justifying ratings written by the teachers were analysed via typology development and data transformation. Comments were open-coded and 19 recurring evaluation criteria were identified. A second coder conducted an independent examination of the original uncoded comments of 10 teachers (five NS and five NNS teachers); results reached approximately 95% agreement. The 19 evaluative criteria were compared across the two teacher groups through a frequency analysis.

The comparable internal consistency and severity patterns that the NS and NNS teachers exhibited appear to support the assertion that NNS teachers can function as assessors as reliably as NS teachers can. The study's results offer no indication that NNS teachers should be denied positions as assessors simply because they are not native speakers of English.

Future recommendations

As mixed methods diagrams evolve, it is recommended that they include more conceptual or substantive aspects of a study. Vee diagrams could serve this function. Consistent with their name, Vee diagrams are shaped like a 'V' (see Figure 40) (Åhlberg, Åänismaa and Dillon 2005, Wheeldon and Åhlberg 2012). One side of the diagram could represent conceptual aspects of a study, while the other side could represent methodological and process-related aspects. Relating methodological to conceptual aspects of studies would further connect diagrams to the substantive purposes they represent, and could further engage more of an argument-based approach to validity.

Figure 39 Suggested procedural diagram for Kim's convergent parallel design (2009)

A Comparison of Native and Non-Native Teachers: A Convergent Parallel Diagram

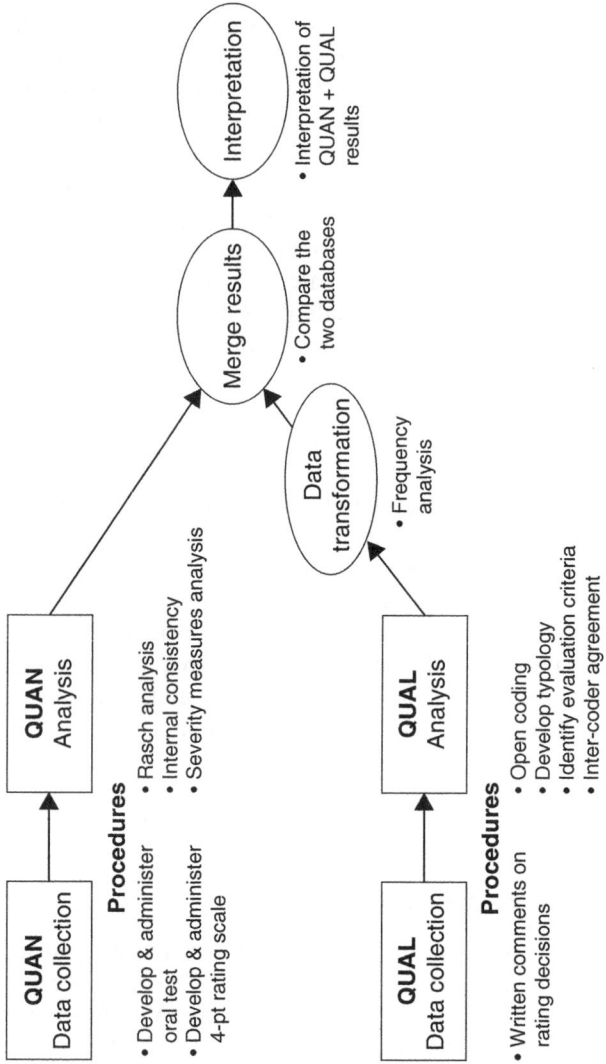

Kim (2009)

QUAN
Data collection

Procedures
- Develop & administer oral test
- Develop & administer 4-pt rating scale

QUAN
Analysis

- Rasch analysis
- Internal consistency
- Severity measures analysis

QUAL
Data collection

Procedures
- Written comments on rating decisions

QUAL
Analysis

- Open coding
- Develop typology
- Identify evaluation criteria
- Inter-coder agreement

Data transformation

- Frequency analysis

Merge results

- Compare the two databases

Interpretation

- Interpretation of QUAN + QUAL results

Figure 40 Vee heuristic possible representation of Wesely (2010)

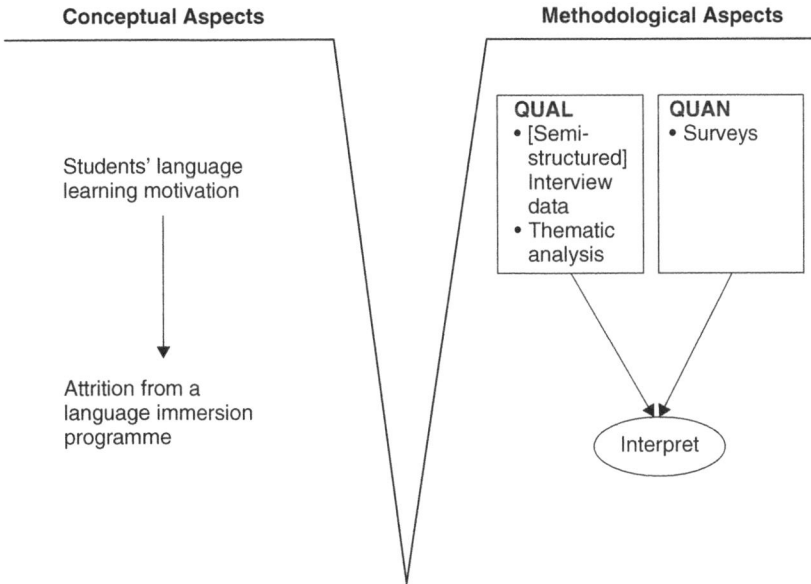

Limitations of diagrams in the social sciences

A key issue in attempting to visually communicate the design of a language-related study to researchers and stakeholders from a broad range of backgrounds is that different communities and individuals may regard '*cognitive* and *emotive* aspects' of some concepts very differently (Wheeldon and Åhlberg 2012:176, italics original). Visual representations may serve some groups of people better than others. For example, visual components may provide more meaning for some cultural groups and verbal components for other cultural groups (Molyneaux 1997). The amount of detail needed may also vary by culture, and across contexts (James 1997). However, visual representations may also help to move beyond language limitations across various kinds of human experience (Wheeldon 2010).

To what extent does absence of a component in a display indicate absence of the component from the represented study or intended study (Wheeldon and Åhlberg 2012)? The complexity of a display influences its interpretation. Consequently, as a reader it is important to not solely rely on the information conveyed by the diagram to understand the details of a mixed methods study.

Conclusion

Visual diagrams and displays involve asynchronistic communication between designers and readers, meaning that designers and readers do not communicate at the same time). As designers, we bring our cultural assumptions, our understanding of our study and intentions towards it. Readers bring their life experiences with no previous understanding of a study. Designers carefully think through the design of the diagram, whereas readers process a diagram largely based on first impression. Designers consciously, but readers subconsciously organise diagrams (see Stafford 2007 on subconscious organisation and conscious focusing relative to images and media). Therefore, as research study and diagram designers, it is imperative to construct visual displays with sufficient details to communicate to readers what they need to know, using concise language. It is important to be intentional about the details of a procedural diagram, so that readers can comprehend the series of steps involved in a mixed methods study.

Acknowledgements

The images in this chapter that are Microsoft product screen shots are used with permission from Microsoft.

6 Writing and publishing mixed methods studies in second language learning and assessment: Ten essential elements

Sheri Hurlbut
University of Nebraska–Lincoln

This chapter outlines 10 essential elements to include when writing up a mixed methods research study for publication. The highlights include:

- *Unique challenges* mixed methods studies pose to authors
- *Step-by-step* instructions for writing mixed methods articles
- *Practical tips* for improving the chances of publication
- *Checklists* for finalising articles for submission

Introduction

Second language learning and assessment research may incorporate a variety of qualitative, quantitative, and mixed methods research methodologies and may be reported in a variety of ways, in dissertations, reports, and articles in peer-reviewed journals. When second language acquisition and assessment research involves a mixed methods methodology, there are a number of unique challenges to be considered. Unlike more traditional single-method studies, in a mixed methods study there are *both* quantitative and qualitative data collection and analysis procedures to describe and results to present. The mixing or integration of that data must also be explained, as well as the conclusions drawn based upon that integrated data. There are issues related to the proper crafting of the title, introduction, purpose statement, and research questions that are unique to mixed methods studies, and the researchers' worldview and theoretical approach must be consistent with a mixed methods research philosophy. In this chapter, these topics will be explored in the context of writing a mixed methods study for publication. The information is presented in step-by-step fashion in the form of 10 essential elements to consider. These elements are arranged in the order they would typically appear in a mixed methods journal article or dissertation: title, introduction, purpose statement, research questions, foundations, methods, results, discussion, references, and appendices.

It is not enough just to know how to write a good mixed methods article, dissertation, or thesis, however. If the research goal is to have meaning beyond the clinical or academic setting, you will need to make it available to as many readers as possible. The last section of this chapter presents information related to the publication of mixed methods studies that will help increase a manuscript's odds of being accepted for publication. Practical tips on how to select the appropriate journal for submission, hints on what editors look for when evaluating manuscripts, and strategies to reduce an article to fit tight page constraints are all included. Also given is a checklist of elements to include in an empirical mixed methods study that can be used as you are finalising your article for submission. In addition, the Appendix contains questions and practical examples related to the essential elements presented.

Our discussion begins with a consideration of the first essential element of a good mixed methods article: the title.

Essential element 1: Title

Mixed Methods Title
• short and succinct
• mention major topic
• participants and site
• include 'mixed methods'
• neutral form
• foreshadow mixed methods design

(Adapted from Creswell and Plano Clark 2011:145–146)

Choosing an appropriate title under which to publish a mixed methods study is one of the most important steps in the writing process. When trying to attract the attention of readers and other researchers perusing journal listings and databases for potentially useful articles, the title of the study is often the only device to pique their curiosity enough to read further. For this reason, a study's title can be even more important than its abstract. Many readers will judge the worthiness and applicability of the research based on the title alone before deciding to invest additional time in reading the abstract or article for further information.

The title chosen for final publication may have little resemblance to the provisional one with which you began. Developing a good title starts early in the research design process and continues throughout all stages of the project, including data collection and analysis. The working title chosen is a first step to provide 'focus' and forces the researcher to 'take a stand' (Creswell 2014a:25). It will likely be modified multiple times as the research problems become clearer and the methods employed to investigate those problems become more refined.

The format of a study's title is determined in large part by the research methodology itself, but all good titles, regardless of whether they are for quantitative, qualitative or mixed methods studies, contain key elements that provide the reader with certain fundamental information. These elements include:

- the research topic
- the participants and, if possible, the site
- the name of the research approach; and
- the characteristic language associated with that particular approach.

For example, a good *quantitative* title mentions the topic, names the dependent and independent variables, includes the participants and site, and also contains such quantitative verbs as 'compare', 'relate', 'predict', 'explain' or 'correlate'. It may indicate that a theory is being tested or a relationship is being investigated. It might also contain directional language such as 'positive', 'negative', 'less than' or 'exceeds'. An example of a well-crafted quantitative title would be 'Subject-Specific Factors that Positively Influence the Use of iPads in the Foreign Language Classroom'.

A good *qualitative* title includes the participants and site as well, and mentions the central phenomenon, but avoids positive or negative terminology, opting instead for more neutral terms such as 'discover', 'explore', or 'understand in depth'. A qualitative title will often mention the specific approach used, such as case study, grounded theory or phenomenology, and the verbs will be in their '-ing' form, i.e. 'discovering', 'exploring', or 'understanding'. For example, 'Exploring the Adventures and Calamities of Studying Abroad: A Multiple Case Analysis' contains all of the hallmarks of a well-phrased qualitative title.

A good mixed methods title will mention the major topic, the participants and site, include the words 'mixed methods' or their equivalent, and foreshadow the specific mixed methods design used, i.e. exploratory, explanatory or convergent. The most effective mixed methods titles are usually short (ideally less than 10 words) and use neutral language, i.e. they are neither overtly quantitative nor overtly qualitative in nature. Two-part titles separated by a colon can be quite effective, such as 'Language Learning Motivation in Early Adolescents: Using Mixed Methods Research to Explore Contradiction'. This title meets most of the criteria outlined above for a good mixed methods title in that it is relatively short (13 words), mentions the major topic (language learning motivation), names the participants (adolescents), includes a neutral verb in its '-ing' form (using), specifically mentions mixed methods research methodology, and foreshadows the research design (exploratory) with the word 'explore'.

Essential element 2: Introduction

Introduction
• topic under study
• problem: real life or 'gap'
• justification of importance
• explanation: how it fills 'gap'
• justification for use of mixed methods
• audience that will benefit

Adapted from Creswell and Plano Clark (2011:148–150)

The second essential element to include in writing a mixed methods study is the introduction. The introduction can be thought of as the *argument* for your study, and as is true with all arguments, its ultimate goal is to set forth a series of logical reasons why readers should believe in the merits of the research claims. The initial step in writing an effective introduction is to capture the reader's attention in the first few lines. One way to do this is to introduce the research topic using what is known as a narrative hook: a literary device employed at the beginning of a story to arouse curiosity in the reader. Statements that elicit emotion, questions that provoke further thought, and key statistics that provide context, are all types of narrative hooks that can be effective in stimulating reader interest. Other strategies include appealing to a broad readership, situating the research topic within a larger context, or providing a frame of reference for the study. The opening sentence for a research study about non-native speakers of English in US schools might read, 'While English is the official language of the United States, according to the US Census Bureau, in 2011 over 21% of people in the US spoke a language other than English in the home' (Ryan 2013).

Once the introduction has captured the readers' attention, the research problem should be clearly stated next. It may be a real-life, practical problem, such as the shortage of qualified Chinese teachers in the United States, or a research-based problem represented by a gap in the literature, such as a scarcity of rigorous, well-designed mixed methods studies in the area of foreign language assessment. Ideally, the problem will be a combination of these two types: real-life and research-based. The research problem should be briefly stated in one or two sentences that begin with a phrase such as 'an issue faced by . . .' or 'a current problem is . . .'. Good examples would include: a) an issue faced by foreign language teachers is access to up-to-date computer technology available to every learner, and b) a current problem in the field of second language acquisition is the lack of valid, time-efficient instruments to assess foreign language (FL) speaking proficiency.

After you have stated the research problem, the importance of the study as a whole needs to be justified. The justification will be based on prior literature and will explain how the current study intends to fill the gaps or deficiencies that exist. The justification section will typically be one to several paragraphs long, and may include such elements as broad trends pertinent to the problem, summaries of groups of studies with similar findings, quotes from experts calling for further research in the area, or even observations based on your own or others' personal experiences. If a gap in the literature is being addressed, the nature of that gap should be described. Perhaps the circumstances surrounding the problem are unique in some way, or the current study offers a new way of looking at the problem in a different light. Maybe there are flaws in prior studies you would like to address, or you are simply replicating a study done elsewhere in order to add to the knowledge base.

In addition to justifying the study as a whole, if there is a methodological deficiency in the current literature, your justification for employing mixed methods to address that methodological deficiency needs to be stated. The phrasing of the justification statement should foreshadow the basic or advanced design you have chosen. For example, if an exploratory design is used, the justification might be: the existing literature has not produced an adequate instrument thus far. For a convergent design, the following may be noted: prior studies focusing on only one method (quantitative or qualitative) have not provided a complete understanding of the problem. The justification for an explanatory study might state: prior studies have focused on intervention outcomes, but have not examined why those outcomes may have occurred based on the intervention itself.

Finally, a good introduction should also mention the individuals, groups and/or institutions that stand to benefit from the results of the study. This will often include the participants and researchers themselves, but may also involve employers, colleagues, community members, policy makers, or even the research community at large due to unique or unusual research methods employed.

Essential element 3: Purpose statement

Mixed Methods Purpose Statement
• overall intent of project • mixed methods design and definition • quan purpose statement • qual purpose statement • rationale for design

The purpose statement has been described as the single most important statement in an entire research study (Creswell 2013a, Creswell and Plano Clark 2011). It describes the overall intention of the project and is usually placed at the end of the introduction, right before the research questions. 'Clear purpose statements are important in all types of research, but the need for clarity is especially important in a mixed methods project in which many elements of qualitative and quantitative research need to come together' (Creswell and Plano Clark 2011:153). A complete mixed methods purpose statement should include: a) the intention of the project, b) the specific mixed methods design used and its definition, c) separate qualitative and quantitative purpose statements, and d) a rationale for the mixed methods design.

Because the purpose statement is such a crucial element, it is important to have a direct, explicitly worded statement, which includes words such as 'purpose', 'aim', or 'intent' in its formulation. It is possible to condense the purpose statement of a purely qualitative or quantitative study into a single sentence, such as, 'The purpose of this case study is to explore the unexpected consequences of an online Web 2.0 professional development course for high school German teachers'. However, because a mixed methods study is much more complex than this, its purpose statement will often be up to a paragraph in length. Researchers may choose to restate all or part of a study's title in the purpose statement, which is acceptable practice.

The full name of the mixed methods design being used, such as exploratory sequential or convergent parallel, is part of the mixed methods purpose statement. Because not all readers are equally familiar with mixed methods research methodology, incorporating a short (one sentence) definition of the design is a good idea. It gives you an opportunity to educate the uninformed and remind readers of the design's key components. For example, Creswell and Plano Clark (2011:154) recommend including the following definition as part of a purpose statement for a convergent design: 'A convergent parallel mixed methods design will be used, and it is a type of design in which qualitative and quantitative data are collected in parallel, analysed separately, and then merged.'

Every mixed methods purpose statement contains two sub-statements representing separate purpose statements for each of the two strands of data, one qualitative and one quantitative. The *quantitative* purpose statement lists the variables (independent on left, dependent on right), participants, site, and type of data collected. It may also contain directional language, such as 'negative' or 'positive', 'greater than' or 'less than'. The *qualitative* purpose statement will state the central phenomenon, participants, site, and methodology. The language will include action verbs such as describe, understand or explore.

Finally, the purpose statement should conclude with the reason why a particular mixed methods design was chosen. The reason for collecting two forms of data and the rationale for how that data is mixed must be clearly stated. For more information about rationales associated with each of the basic mixed methods designs see Ziegler and Kang, Chapter 4, this volume.

The sample mixed methods purpose statement below, taken from a convergent parallel mixed methods study about majoring in German (Hurlbut 2013:1), illustrates how the component parts mentioned fit together into a cohesive whole. The aim of the study, name and definition of the design, qualitative and quantitative data collected, and rationale for mixing are all identified for you by underlining.

> This mixed methods study will explore the process of becoming a German major (aim of study), with the primary intent of developing a merged theory grounded in the critical incidences and experiences of the participants and enhanced by L2 motivation questionnaire results. The main objective of the research will be to gain a deeper understanding of the changes German majors experience over time, so that university German departments can better serve them at all levels. A convergent parallel mixed methods design (name of design) will be used, in which qualitative and quantitative data are collected in parallel, analysed separately, and then merged during interpretation (definition of design). In this study, a grounded theory approach has been chosen to address the qualitative strand because it is the ideal tool when looking for meaning in a situated social context. Through in-depth interviews (qualitative data) with German graduates, and majors at all levels of German study, a more complete picture of the process will emerge. Quantitative data will be collected simultaneously alongside qualitative data through the administration of an L2 motivation questionnaire (quantitative data), which will also include demographic information. A correlational design will be used for the quantitative strand, in which relationships between and among variables such as type of motivation, level of study, participation in study abroad, and major will be sought. Although motivation is not the only factor in determining major fields of study, it is considered an important piece of the puzzle. The primary reason for collecting both qualitative and quantitative data in this study is complementarity (rationale for mixing). By comparing and contrasting the two forms of data and synthesizing

them to form a merged theory, greater insight into understanding the process of becoming a German major will be gained than would otherwise be obtained by considering either type of data separately.

Essential element 4: Research questions

Research Questions
• include three types of questions
– Quan
– Qual
– mixed methods
• order depends on design

After communicating the intent of the research in a clearly worded purpose statement, it is important to list the research questions. It depends on the type of publication being prepared, but typically, research questions appear at the very end of the introduction section. This would certainly be the case in graduate theses and dissertations, but may not always be possible in journal articles (Creswell 2014a), as space is often limited and researchers must pick and choose what to include and what to leave out to maximise the use of their allotted word count.

Research questions are the specific questions posed at the beginning of a study to focus and guide the enquiry process. In a mixed methods study, because both quantitative and qualitative methods are employed, the researcher should prepare separate quantitative, qualitative, and mixed methods questions. The order in which these questions are presented depends upon the research design (see Ziegler and Kang, Chapter 4, this volume). For example, if an exploratory mixed methods design is followed, in which qualitative data is collected and analysed before quantitative data, then the qualitative research question(s) will be listed first, followed by the quantitative question(s), and then the mixed methods question(s).

Quantitative research questions may be stated either in the form of a hypothesis or a question. The hypothesis form, traditionally used in experiments, can be written either as a *null statement* (e.g. 'There is no significant difference between writing proficiency in heritage and non-heritage speakers of Spanish') or as a *directional statement* (e.g. 'Study abroad experiences lead to higher retention rates in foreign language programmes'). These two hypothesis forms can be restated in question form as follows: 'Is there a significant difference between writing proficiency in heritage and non-heritage speakers of Spanish?' and 'Do study abroad experiences lead to higher retention rates in foreign language programmes?' The question form is quite typical in mixed methods studies, but either form is acceptable, as long as it is used consistently throughout.

A quantitative research question, whether stated as a hypothesis or as an actual question, should identify all of the variables being measured, with independent variables appearing first, followed by dependent variables, and then by mediating and covariate variables. Characteristic quantitative questions might compare groups, relate variables, describe trends, measure outcomes or test theories.

Qualitative questions are more open ended than quantitative questions (e.g. 'What does it mean to be proficient in a language?') and they use neutral, non-directional language rather than words with positive or negative connotations (i.e. How do beginning Chinese students experience learning Chinese characters?). The qualitative portion of a study is customarily guided by one central overarching question followed by a small number of sub-questions to further refine the enquiry process. These central overarching questions often begin with the words 'how' or 'what' rather than 'why', 'when' or 'how much', which are more quantitative in nature. Through careful word choice, questions can be tailored to specifically indicate the type of qualitative methodology being used. For example, in a grounded theory study, the qualitative question might read: 'What explanation can be given for foreign language students' higher American College Test (ACT) scores?' In a case study, the question might refer to the group of participants being investigated, such as, 'How do high school Italian teachers work together in professional learning communities to create common assessments?'

Well-written qualitative questions focus on *one* single phenomenon. Compare the following two qualitative research questions: 1) How do middle level students describe the experience of learning French through Teaching Proficiency through Reading and Storytelling (TPRS)? 2) How do FL teacher preparation programmes assess the speaking proficiency of their graduates and what are the implications of teachers' varying proficiency levels on student achievement in the FL classroom?

In the first question, it is clear that just one central phenomenon is being investigated: the experience of learning French through TPRS. In the second question, there are two phenomena mentioned: a) different ways of evaluating FL speaking proficiency and b) implications of teacher proficiency levels on student achievement. It would be better if the second example were broken into two separate questions: one central question (e.g. 'What are the implications of teachers' speaking proficiency on student achievement in the FL classroom?') and one sub-question (e.g. 'How do FL teacher preparation programmes assess the speaking proficiency of their graduates?').

The third type of research question, the mixed methods research question, should be expressed in such a way that the reason or intention for mixing the quantitative and qualitative data is readily apparent. The mixed methods question will relate to the specific mixed methods design being used and can be stated in three different ways: a) as a methods-focused question, b) as a content-focused question, or c) as a combination of the two. Creswell (2014a:74) gives examples of typical *methods-focused questions* for each of the six basic and advanced mixed methods designs:

Convergent – To what extent do the qualitative results confirm the quantitative results?

Explanatory – How does the qualitative data explain the quantitative results?

Exploratory – To what extent do the qualitative findings generalise to a specified population?

Intervention – How do the qualitative findings enhance the interpretation of the experimental outcomes?

Social Justice – How do the qualitative findings enhance the understanding of the quantitative results in order to identify inequalities?

Multistage – Combine the previous questions for the different phases in the project to address the overall research goal.

Content-focused versions of some of these questions might look like this:

- Convergent – How do the attitudes and beliefs of FL teachers support their classroom-based assessment practices?
- Explanatory – How can immigrant students' circumstances at home explain their variable performance on summative ESL assessments?
- Exploratory – Are students' experiences with language proficiency testing in small primary schools similar to those in larger schools in the same district?

If possible, it is best to combine both a methods focus and a content focus when writing mixed methods questions. The resulting form is called a *hybrid* mixed methods question (Creswell and Plano Clark 2011:163; see also Guetterman and Salamoura, Chapter 7, this volume). There are different ways to construct hybrid questions depending on the type of design being used. For example, a hybrid question for an exploratory study might read: What results emerge from comparing the qualitative language motivation and attitude data from exploratory focus groups with the quantitative data measured by the language-motivation instrument? Some of the language used in this question emphasises the methods (focus groups, outcome based, instrument) and some emphasises the content (language motivation, attitude).

Searching for well-written questions in the literature and modelling their wording and construction is a legitimate way to build your own question-writing skills.

Essential element 5: Foundations

Foundations
• philosophical/worldview assumptions • theoretical framework • literature review depends on design

The foundations upon which the research is built inform all aspects of the study, from the initial assumptions made, to the research methods chosen, to the ways data is collected and interpreted, to the conclusions drawn from those interpretations. Three key pillars make up the foundations of any research study: the researcher's philosophical worldview (see Creswell and Zhou, Chapter 3, this volume), the theoretical lens or framework being applied (if any), and the review of pertinent literature from the field.

Sharing the researcher's worldview with the reader, either implicitly or explicitly, is common practice in mixed methods studies. It is important to be able to articulate the paradigms that guide the researcher's thinking, not only so that the researcher can gain personal insight regarding various decisions made about the study, but also so that others can better understand the methodological choices made and more accurately evaluate the conclusions drawn based on those choices (see Guetterman and Salamoura, Chapter 7, this volume). There are several components that combine together to make up your worldview as a researcher: ontology, or how you view the nature of reality (Is it singular or multiple?), epistemology, or what you consider knowledge (Is it absolute or ever changing?), axiology, or the role of researcher and participant values (Do they impact results?), methodology, or how studies are conducted (Is there just one best way?), and rhetoric, or how research is written (Is it necessary to follow prescribed guidelines?) (Creswell 2013a:19–22). Not all components of a researcher's worldview will be explicitly stated in writing, especially in journal articles, but a close read of the article will reveal subtle clues as to its nature, found, for example, in the type of research problem chosen, the questions posed, the design used, the types of data collected, the data analysis techniques employed, and the conclusions drawn. All research methods have advantages and disadvantages, and there is rarely only one way to tackle a research problem, but the worldview of the researcher will heavily influence how they choose to go about it. For example, a researcher who espouses postpositivist philosophies will preference quantitative experimental methods, whereas constructivists will be more interested in listening to the voices of participants by using qualitative techniques.

Because mixed methods researchers combine a variety of quantitative and qualitative methods together into one study, reconciling the underlying conflicting paradigms into one cohesive research philosophy may pose a challenge. In response to this dilemma, some researchers have chosen to embrace pragmatism (i.e. 'what works', what is practical), others adhere to the tenets of critical realism (humans are capable of learning objectively about the world), and still others embrace dialectic pluralism (tensions between competing stances are presented in a symbolic 'dialogue').

The inclusion of theory into a mixed methods research design is not absolutely required, but theories, such as Krashen's Monitor Model (1982) or Long's Theory of Interaction (1983), are very commonly incorporated into second language learning studies. Theories can be integrated into mixed methods studies in a variety of ways. A theory may inform just the quantitative phase, for example, by predicting, explaining, or generalising results, or it may serve as a context on the qualitative side for developing protocols and interpreting participant behaviour. Transformative theories, such as feminist or queer theories, may serve a more overarching purpose and be used as a lens through which to view all aspects of a research project to ensure that outcomes are advanced that bring about change. Another type of theory, Participatory Action Research, has gained in popularity in educational studies as 'one of the best possible ways to improve school and individual practices' (James, Milenkiewicz and Bucknam 2008:1). Participatory Action Research involves participants collaboratively in all phases of the research process, enables participants to solve problems of interest to them, and improves participants' involvement, expertise, and sense of professionalism. If a theory is to be incorporated into a mixed methods study, it is important to explicitly name the theory and its authors, describe its tenets in detail, and explain how it will be applied in the particular situation. Transparency is the best way to ensure clarity when including theories in mixed methods research studies.

The last element to make up the foundations section is the literature review. The literature review gives meaning, motivation, and direction to the research and can vary considerably in length and placement depending upon the purpose of the publication. In a journal article, for example, there is normally only room to include a brief summary of the most significant works in order to establish the importance of the current study within the context of the field as a whole. For theses or dissertations, however, researchers will have completed an extensive review of the literature and should present their analysis and synthesis of it in a thorough, logical fashion. This will demonstrate their deep understanding of the subject matter and provide a firm foundation for the research design. The literature review will frame the research problem, provide a rationale for the research questions, give readers the necessary background knowledge, report results of previous studies to serve as a comparison, give examples of pertinent theoretical applications, and lend support to the research methodology.

In order to organise the literature logically for the reader, it is helpful to divide it into subtopics. In a dissertation or dissertation proposal, the author may even want to go so far as to create a literature map for the dissertation committee to show them what has already been studied and how the new research fits in. This map could be in the form of an inverted pyramid with the broad topics on the top branching to narrower ones on the bottom. Included in the map will be studies written by major national and/or international experts in the field organised into three to five subcategories. Sometimes authors will even include literature maps as appendices in journal articles.

In addition to reviewing the relevant literature, it is also important to cite quantitative, qualitative, and mixed methods studies that have been conducted under similar circumstances using the methodology you have chosen. If there are no mixed methods articles available in the enquiry of interest, studies that are as close as possible and that use similar methodology can be reviewed.

There are many places to incorporate worldviews and theoretical lenses into a mixed methods study. They make an appearance in virtually all sections of the mixed methods write-up, from introduction to conclusion. In the following example, the authors explicitly state both their worldview and theoretical lens in their introduction (keywords are underlined):

> Taking a critical realist perspective (worldview) informed by Rosenbaum's (1990, 2000) model of self-control (theoretical lens), we combine a quantitative measure of learned resourcefulness with a qualitative text-based analysis to characterize the processes that come into play in the self-management of pain for high- and low-resourceful clients following a multimodal treatment-based pain programme (Kennett, O'Hagan and Cezer 2008:318).

Essential element 6: Methods

Methods
- information about mixed methods research
- information about mixed methods design
- challenges of design
- diagram of procedures
- data collection (quan and qual)
- mixed methods data analysis
- validity considerations
- ethical issues
- reflexivity

Readers and reviewers of a mixed methods study may not be as knowledgeable about mixed methods research as they are about older, more established methodologies, so it is important to define terms that may be new or unfamiliar, cite well-known experts from the mixed methods field in order to acquaint readers with key concepts, and integrate currently accepted mixed methods terms into the writing so readers are repeatedly exposed to the latest terminology. Incorporating these suggestions when writing the methods section will also serve to establish the writer's credibility as a legitimate mixed methods researcher.

In addition to providing information about mixed methods in general, it is necessary to provide a thorough explanation of the specific research design you have chosen (see Ziegler and Kang, Chapter 4, this volume). This will include defining the design itself and explaining its associated procedures in detail. Important topics to mention are the independence or interactivity of the qualitative and quantitative strands, the priority of these strands, the timing of the quantitative and qualitative data collection and analysis phases, and the point of interface where quantitative and qualitative data is integrated. Incorporating a diagram of research procedures is advisable, as it can help clarify methods and procedures in complex studies in a way that words alone cannot express (see Ziegler and Kang, Chapter 4, this volume).

Each mixed methods design has its own special challenges (see Miller and Bustamante, Chapter 5, this volume). These challenges should be disclosed in the methods section and a discussion of how each challenge was overcome (or not) should be provided. For example, sequential designs take an extended period of time to complete, exploratory designs require two different samples, and data in convergent designs does not always converge as expected if qualitative and quantitative data have nothing in common. If you encountered characteristic problems such as these, how did you get around them? Did everything go as planned? What compromises did you have to make in order to complete your study? The methods section is the place to address these issues.

In addition to describing the research design, one of the principal purposes of the methods section is to provide details of the data collection and analysis procedures. Important aspects of data collection, such as sample size, participant selection criteria, types of data collected, and safety procedures followed (i.e. proper institutional approval obtained), should be outlined for both the qualitative and quantitative strands. A detailed description of how and when both types of data were analysed is essential, as well as an explanation of how and when the different types of data were merged, connected or converged. This merging or connecting of the quantitative and qualitative data is at the heart of what it means to be a mixed methods study, so it is crucial that this connection be explicitly and thoroughly explained.

Threats to mixed methods validity, defined as potential problems during data collection, data analysis, and interpretation that 'might compromise the merging or connecting of the quantitative and qualitative strands of the study and the conclusions drawn from the combination' (Creswell and

Plano Clark 2011:239), should also be addressed in the methods section (see Chapters 3 and 4, this volume). Validity threats vary depending on the mixed methods design being used. For example, in an explanatory design, individuals should be chosen for the qualitative follow-up from the pool that participated in the quantitative first phase, whereas in an exploratory design, the individuals in one strand should not be duplicated in the other. A common pitfall some researchers face in convergent studies is to collect two different types of data that do not address the same topic and can therefore not be merged. See Creswell and Plano Clark (2011) for a comprehensive listing of potential validity threats when merging or connecting data and strategies for minimising those threats.

Issues related to research ethics, such as disclosing the purpose of the study, treating participants with respect during data collection, providing reciprocity for participation, gaining informed consent when necessary, and treating confidential information appropriately should be addressed. If an Institutional Review Board (IRB) was involved, you may want to mention this in the methods section.

As is customary with qualitative research, many mixed methods researchers also opt to disclose the role they play in contributing to the construction of meaning in a study. They prefer to acknowledge the difficulty of remaining completely objective during the research process. This disclosure may range from implicitly suggesting the possibility of bias by writing in the first person, to explicitly including a formal reflexivity passage or statement in the methods section. Common items to be found in such statements include the researcher's background and training in the field, their skills as a researcher, personal biases or experiences that may influence data analysis, physical and human resources available for the research, and a timeline for the project.

Essential element 7: Results

Results
• order results to match design
• address quan, qual and mixed methods questions
• mix data consistent with design
• include tables, figures, joint displays
• consider reporting by theme with quotes

The results section is where study data is presented and findings are described. In a mixed methods study, because both quantitative and qualitative data are collected and analysed separately, the results and analyses of that data are usually also reported separately. The order in which the quantitative and qualitative results and findings appear in the write-up depends upon the type of design used. For example, in an explanatory sequential design, the quantitative results from an experiment or survey would be reported first, followed by the findings from the qualitative data gathered to explain those quantitative results. In an exploratory instrument development design, on the other hand, the order would be reversed with qualitative findings preceding quantitative results.

Because space is often limited when writing up a mixed methods study, it is worthwhile to think about how results can be reported most efficiently. Some writers choose to use their research questions as a scaffold upon which to build the results section. They briefly restate or refer to each research question individually (in the proper order corresponding to the research design), and systematically report the quantitative, qualitative and mixed methods results relating to each question. Other researchers choose to report their results in a narrative style organised in sections corresponding to the research design. In a convergent design, for example, they would first provide a narrative description of all of the results from one strand (the strand with highest priority), and then present all of the results from the other strand in a parallel fashion. This would be followed by a narrative comparing the two. If there is plenty of room, some researchers prefer to include tables and graphs for quantitative and qualitative results separately, but it is often more efficient and effective to display these results together in joint displays (discussed in depth later in this section).

In addition to separate quantitative and qualitative data reporting and analysis, the results section must also address how the two strands of data are brought together (see Ziegler and Kang, Chapter 4, this volume). This constitutes the 'mixing' portion of a mixed methods study, also known as integration or the point of interface (Morse and Niehaus 2009). Without the integration of data, a study cannot technically be considered a mixed methods study.

When data is integrated or mixed it is highly variable and dependent on the design employed; it can happen at any point during the research process (see Ziegler and Kang, Chapter 4, this volume). Mixing can occur:

- during data collection, i.e. if students are asked to answer both open- and closed-ended questions on a language learning motivation survey
- during data analysis, i.e. if qualitative interview findings about language learning strategy use are transformed into frequencies, combined with quantitative survey data, and analysed together; or
- during discussion, i.e. if quantitative high-stakes test scores and qualitative think-aloud journals are compared to look for complementarity.

No matter when and where the mixing occurs, it is critical to report the circumstances of that mixing in detail. Integration may be reported in a narrative passage about data collection, which would appear in the methods section, data analysis, which would appear in the results section, or post-analysis integration, which would appear in the discussion/conclusion section. In order to make the point of integration explicit, it is recommended that it be clearly marked on a procedural diagram (in the methods section) using an arrow, a label, highlighting or some other highly visible method that attracts the attention of the reader.

How the researcher chooses to integrate the data depends on the research design as well, and also on the purpose for integration. There are four basic types of mixed methods data integration (Creswell 2014a; see also Ziegler and Kang, Chapter 4, this volume):

- merging – analysing quantitative and qualitative strands separately and then comparing them (i.e. convergent)
- explaining – qualitative data is used to explain quantitative data (i.e. explanatory sequential)
- building – qualitative results are used to build the quantitative phase, such as in creating a new instrument or designing a new intervention (i.e. exploratory sequential)
- embedding – qualitative results are used to augment or support quantitative results (i.e. qualitative data augments an experiment) or vice versa (i.e. small amount of quantitative data embedded in case study).

In a mixed methods study, clearly explaining the data integration process is one of the most important functions of the results section. As mentioned above, it is possible to create one common graphic (table, chart or graph), called a joint display, which organises qualitative and quantitative results alongside one another, and includes information about how the two types of results are integrated (see Guetterman and Salamoura, Chapter 7, this volume). Reporting mixed methods research results using a joint display is highly recommended because it is space-efficient and emphasises the mixing aspect of the research study visually. There are different types of joint displays, each with its own advantages and specific purposes. Some of the most common are (Creswell 2014a):

- Side-by-side – quantitative and qualitative results presented in adjacent columns with similarities and differences displayed in the third column. Good for highlighting convergence/divergence in convergent parallel studies.
- Theme by statistics – qualitative themes arrayed on horizontal axis, quantitative results on vertical. Cells contain quotes or frequency counts or both. These displays highlight convergence/divergence.

- Follow-up results – quantitative results in first column, qualitative follow-up results in second column, explanation of how qualitative explains quantitative in third column. Used in explanatory sequential studies.
- Building an instrument – qualitative quotes/codes/themes in first column(s), corresponding items/variables/scales derived from those elements in second column.

Essential element 8: Discussion

Discussion
- order to match design
- interpret results in light of literature
- summarise major quan, qual and mixed methods results
- discuss limitations
- discuss implications for practice
- suggest further research

The eighth essential element to include in writing a mixed methods study is the discussion section. Some researchers divide this section down even further into two parts: a discussion, in which research results are discussed in the context of the study itself, and a conclusion, where the results are placed within a broader context. For our purposes, we will combine these two functions into one all-inclusive discussion section.

Generally, the discussion section begins with a summary of the study's major quantitative, qualitative and mixed methods findings. As usual, and consistent with the rest of the document being written, the order of reporting of these findings in the discussion section will be commensurate with the research design being used. For example, if the study uses an explanatory design, the major quantitative findings will be summarised first, followed by the major qualitative findings, and then the integrated findings. This beginning 'summary portion' of the discussion section gives researchers a chance to once more reiterate the major concepts examined in the study and to provide a broad overview of the results for the reader. When writing this section, key guiding questions are: 'What major findings do I want readers to remember from this study? What are the key understandings I want to leave them with?'

Once the major findings have been summarised, they need to be interpreted in relation to the study itself. How do the results relate to the original research questions? Did the methods chosen yield results sufficient to answer all of the questions originally posed? Were any of the results inconsistent or unexpected? What about the research purpose? Was the original intent of the study fulfilled? If not, why not? A discussion of the findings with respect to the theoretical lens used should also be included here. The discussion section is the writer's chance to elaborate on key observations, offer conclusions based on those observations, and postulate on their implications for future practice.

Next, the results of the study should be placed within a broader context by showing how they relate to current literature in the field. How can the obtained results be interpreted in light of what others have previously reported? Did the study confirm or disprove any prior research? Were the gaps identified in the literature review partially or totally filled? Has the research added to the knowledge base in any unexpected ways? In addition to the scholarship presented in the original literature review, additional studies may need to be brought in at this point to help further explain the findings or support the conclusions. These new studies can serve as a basis for comparison or provide an alternative perspective from which to interpret the data.

Any research limitations should be mentioned now, such as insufficient sample size, problems finding qualified participants, timing issues, etc., as well as potential weaknesses identified during the course of the study in either the research design or implementation. Ethical considerations and problems should also be addressed. The discussion section is a common place to find a reflexivity passage that situates the researcher in the context of the research (Berg and Lune 2012), if it has not already been included elsewhere in the paper.

It is clear that the discussion section provides the researcher a forum to elaborate upon knowledge acquired, lessons learned, and insights gained, but it also provides an opportunity to bring attention to issues we still do not fully understand. It is helpful to readers if researchers take a moment at the end of a paper to outline topics they feel are worthy of future research. These suggestions may be either general or specific and may include topics related to the subject matter of the study or to the research methodology itself. Researchers and other scholars, such as doctoral students, will often look for research ideas in the discussion sections of articles in their area of interest.

Essential element 9: References

References
• follow journal's formatting guidelines, e.g. – APA – MLA – Chicago – Harvard Reference Style

The ninth essential element that must be included in any scholarly publication is the reference section, sometimes called Works Cited. This section is simply a listing of all sources cited in the text. One important purpose of the reference section is to provide readers with enough information so that they can locate original sources, if necessary or desired. There are myriad types of resources authors may cite, including such diverse items as books, journal articles, conference presentations, government publications, speeches, websites, unpublished dissertations, and even personal conversations, so the specific information necessary to track down any one particular type of resource may be quite different from that required to find another, and there would be multiple ways of presenting this necessary 'tracking' information in a references list.

Over the years, various institutions have developed their own guidelines regarding how references should appear in their publications. Guidelines developed by the American Psychological Association (APA), Modern Language Association (MLA), and University of Chicago Press (Chicago Manual of Style) are examples of such systems that have been widely adopted by publishers of academic books and journals, particularly in the United States. *The Modern Language Journal*, *Foreign Language Annals*, and journals published by the American Educational Research Association (AERA), for example, all follow APA guidelines, and some international journals, such as *Language Testing*, published in the UK, use APA style as well. Another common style used in many European journals is the Harvard Reference Style. Some publishers even create their own proprietary style sheets, which must be followed when writing articles for their journals, such as De Gruyter Mouton, publisher of *The European Journal of Applied Linguistics*. It is crucial, therefore, to consult the publisher's/journal's website for submission guidelines before presenting a manuscript for consideration. Editors may refuse to accept manuscripts that do not meet formatting guidelines, regardless of their content.

In addition to giving readers the appropriate tracking information, a second purpose for providing a detailed reference list is to acknowledge other authors' ideas and contributions to your work. Most research is built on a foundation created by others, and it is important to recognise this by giving other researchers credit where credit is due. Each academic discipline has its own set of conventions when it comes to citation, but when in doubt, it is better to err on the side of over-citing in order to avoid any suspicion of plagiarism.

A third important purpose of the references section is to indicate to readers the scope and breadth of the reported research. Before reading a single word of text, an informed reader will be able to scan the works cited and make a snap judgement about the rigour of the project based solely on the sources listed. This holds true for references related to content as well as methodology. If you were conducting a study about motivation in second language learning, you probably wouldn't omit seminal works by Dörnyei. Similarly, if you were developing a grounded theory and failed to reference Glaser and Strauss or Charmaz, most knowledgeable readers would question the soundness of your conclusions. It is essential, therefore, to include references to well respected mixed methods researchers when conducting a mixed methods study. Including references to ground-breaking texts and pioneering authors in the field establishes the credibility of a mixed methods researcher. As mentioned previously, it is also important to include references to studies in the field that have employed the same or similar mixed methodology. These types of references fulfil two purposes: they demonstrate a thorough background in the content area and also indicate the researcher's familiarity with the mixed methods design chosen.

One last note about the reference section: space is often a problem when submitting mixed methods journal articles for publication, particularly when the methodology is especially complex. Most journals have strict page limits for submissions, but it is helpful to know that in some instances these page limits do not include the reference section. This is worth checking before resorting to cutting content in an attempt to shorten a manuscript.

Essential element 10: Appendices

Appendices
• interview/observation protocols
• coding schemes
• quan instruments
• participant quotes
• photos and images
• procedural diagrams
• move items to online appendix if over page limit

The final essential element to consider when writing a mixed methods article is the appendices. A key question to consider is whether an appendix/

appendices should be included in the first place. According to the Purdue University Online Writing Lab, also known as the Purdue OWL (a useful website containing writing resources such as the MLA and APA style sheets), 'appendices allow you to include detailed information in your paper that would be distracting in the main body' of the work (Driscoll and Kasztalska 2013). This definition pertains to many of the items that might be included in an appendix for a mixed methods study, such as interview protocols or complex statistical tables. The detailed nature of these items could interrupt the flow in the main body of the text. However, there is an additional reason that mixed methods researchers often choose to take advantage of appendices. As mentioned previously, journals enforce strict page limits on authors and with the extensive amount of information to be reported in a mixed methods study, it is often impossible to include everything relevant in the body of the text. Creating an appendix for supplementary material can be an attractive alternative, because it is possible that appendices may not be included in the total page count. Some publishers offer authors the option of publishing supplementary materials online as a way to make additional information available to readers. The size limitations for items published online are often much less restrictive.

More traditional studies often contain lists, specifications, charts, tables, and graphs in appendices, because they are either too large to include in the main text or are not allowed in the main body by the publisher. This is certainly true for mixed methods studies as well. However, there might be other types of items you had not considered incorporating into your mixed methods write-up because you thought them too bulky that would be ideal candidates for appendices. Examples of such large items include interview and observation protocols, qualitative coding schemas, quantitative survey instruments, participant quotes, and photos and images. Mixed methods procedural diagrams and joint data displays are two more examples of large graphical items that could be suitably displayed in an appendix. Consider including all of these larger items as supplementary materials in an appendix, as they will give readers a more complete picture of the research process and study results.

Issues related to publication of mixed methods articles

Components of design	Rigorous mixed methods include
• mixed methods title • abstract including mixed methods design • rationale for use of mixed methods • mixed methods purpose statement/study aim • quan, qual and mixed methods research questions • stated worldview and theory • results presented consistently with design • quan and qual results integrated/merged/connected • challenges that limit findings identified • unique contribution to mixed methods literature • recent mixed methods books and articles cited	• mixed methods advantages • mixed methods design • diagram of procedures • methodological challenges • quan and qual data collection and analysis • ethical issues • validity

Now that we have discussed the essential elements to consider when writing a mixed methods study, it is time to turn to several issues related to the publication of the work, including tips for selecting an appropriate journal for submission, items editors look for when evaluating manuscripts, strategies to reduce the length of mixed methods articles, and components to include in a mixed methods empirical study.

One of the most satisfying rewards for the hard work of designing and implementing any research study is seeing the results of that study appear in print. In order to maximise the likelihood an article will be published, it is important to approach the manuscript submission process in a strategic way and submit only to those journals that are most likely to consider the work.

An important first step in choosing the appropriate journal to contact is to assess the journal's openness to mixed methods research in the first place. You can do this by studying past issues to see what types of articles they typically tend to publish, by researching the editorial board's interests and expertise, and by carefully reading through the submission guidelines posted on the journal's website. If the submission guidelines do not mention mixed methods, or are focused solely on either quantitative or qualitative methodology alone, that journal may not be the most suitable choice.

The following quote taken from the submission guidelines of the *Modern Language Journal* would indicate this journal is at least open to the idea of mixed methods research. In order to determine how open, however, you would still need to examine past issues to evaluate actual practice: 'Studies increasingly use both quantitative and qualitative data in order to be able to capture the complexity of language use, teaching, and learning. Therefore, authors of so called mixed methods studies are encouraged to observe the quality expectations associated with both research approaches' (John Wiley and Sons 2013).

There are different types of outlets for publishing mixed methods studies. Creswell (2014a) categorises journals that publish mixed methods articles into three types:

- those specialising exclusively in mixed methods research,
- those friendly to mixed methods research, and
- those in specific fields of discipline open to mixed methods research.

He identified four journals in the first category that specialise exclusively in mixed methods research: *Journal of Mixed Methods Research, International Journal of Multiple Research Approaches* (online), *Field Methods*, and *Quality and Quantity*. Among the journals friendly to mixed methods research were *International Journal of Social Research Methodology, Qualitative Inquiry*, and *Qualitative Research*. The following journals are members of a growing list in the field of second language acquisition and assessment that have a track record of publishing mixed methods studies: *Foreign Language Annals, Modern Language Journal, Language Learning Journal, Language Testing, Language Assessment Quarterly, Assessing Writing* and *CALICO Journal* (online).

Journals falling into any one of the three categories mentioned could be potential candidates for submission of a mixed methods study, but the best choice for submission will depend in large part on the type of article. Is it a purely methodological article, in which the goal is to emphasise the research methods over the findings because they are particularly interesting or noteworthy for some reason? Or is it an article about an empirical study conducted using mixed methods research methodology whose main goal is to report on important findings in the field? If the emphasis is on the methods alone, a journal in the first (or possibly second) category above would be more suitable, whereas if it is an empirical study employing mixed methods, submitting to journals of all three types could be considered.

The next step after deciding which journal(s) to approach is to start thinking like an editor. Different journals have different audiences, and it is important to keep the target audience in mind when fine-tuning the work for publication. If a journal is not targeted to a mixed methods audience, you may need to spend extra time educating them and would need to include visual aids such as procedural diagrams (see Miller and Bustamante, Chapter 5, this volume) and joint displays to help readers organise and understand the methodology. John Creswell, co-founder of the *Journal of Mixed Methods Research*, has reviewed hundreds of mixed methods submissions and shared the following list of characteristics he looks for in evaluating a mixed methods manuscript (2014a:89):

- both quantitative and qualitative data in the methods section
- evidence of integration (without integration, it is just a multiple methods study, not a mixed methods study)
- recent mixed methods publications in the list of references
- characteristics unique to mixed methods ('mixed methods' in the title, rationale for gathering both quantitative and qualitative data, mixed methods questions, joint display, etc.).

One of the biggest challenges in writing a mixed methods article is trying to condense a large amount of information into a small amount of space to conform to the restrictive length requirements of most journals. As mentioned already, mixed methods articles can be shortened by reporting results compactly in charts and tables and by including supplementary information in appendices or on publisher websites, but another way to approach the problem is to break empirical studies up into three articles: a quantitative article, a qualitative article, and a mixed methods article. The articles can be published as a set concurrently or sequentially in the same journal, or in separate journals and cross-referenced (Stange, Crabtree and Miller 2006). A further option is to publish longer articles online.

In closing, two practical tools for mixed methods researchers are given below, which were mentioned in Creswell and Zhou, Chapter 3, this volume. The first is a set of six guidelines created by O'Cathain, Murphy, and Nicholl (2008) that offer helpful guidance on Good Reporting of a Mixed Methods Study (GRAMMS). The second is Creswell's (2014a:94) checklist of elements to include in an empirical mixed methods manuscript. Each of these tools should prove useful to researchers as reminders of the key points to keep in mind when writing and publishing effective, informative, and well-crafted mixed methods articles.

Good Reporting of a Mixed Methods Study (GRAMMS)

- Describe the justification for using the mixed methods approach to the research question.
- Describe the design in terms of the purpose, priority, and sequence of methods.

- Describe each method in terms of sampling, data collection and analysis.
- Describe where integration has occurred, how it has occurred, and who has participated in it.
- Describe any limitation of one method associated with the presence of the other method.
- Describe any insights gained from mixing or integrating methods (O'Cathain et al 2008:97).

A checklist for mixed methods elements in a manuscript for submission

1. Include a mixed methods title.
2. Add an abstract that conveys the type of mixed methods design.
3. Convey how the problem merits a mixed methods study (rationale).
4. Create a mixed methods study aim or purpose statement.
5. Create quantitative, qualitative, and mixed methods research questions.
6. Consider stating the worldview underlining research and use of theory.
   a. Include rigorous mixed methods:
      i. Discuss advantages of using mixed methods
      ii. Identify type of mixed methods design
      iii. Present diagram of procedures
      iv. Identify methodological challenges
   b. Describe quantitative and qualitative data collection and analysis:
      i. Include ethical issues
      ii. Discuss validity
7. Report the results in a manner consistent with the mixed methods design.
8. Discuss the integration of quantitative and qualitative data (Creswell 2014a:94).

Acknowledgements

I would like to acknowledge the contributions that Dr Aleidine J Moeller, Dr John Creswell, and Dr Vicki Plano Clark have made to this work. Without their expert teaching, mentorship, and generosity of spirit, the writing of this chapter would not have been possible. For that I thank them.

Appendix
Applying what you have learned

Essential element 1: Title

What type of study (quantitative, qualitative or mixed methods) is most likely represented by each of the following titles?

1. How College Freshmen Choose a Major: A Grounded Theory Study
2. Gap in Presentational Writing Ability Between Heritage and Non-Heritage Foreign Language Students
3. A Narrative and Graphical Depiction of Classroom-Based Assessment Trends in US Foreign Language Classrooms
4. The Interactions Between the Effects of Implicit and Explicit Feedback and Individual Differences in Language Analytic Ability and Working Memory
5. An Investigation into Native and Non-Native Teachers' Judgments of Oral English Performance: A _____ Approach.

Essential element 2: Introduction

A. What type of study (explanatory, exploratory or convergent) is represented by each of the following problem statements (Creswell and Plano Clark 2011)?

> A need exists in the literature . . .
> 1. . . . not only to explore a topic because variables are unknown, but to assess the extent that these results can be generalised.
> 2. . . . not only to obtain quantitative results, but to explain such results in more detail.
> 3. . . . to obtain different, but complementary data on the same topic.

B. In the following introduction taken from Busse and Williams' (2010:67) article 'Why German? Motivation of Students Studying German at English Universities', identify the:

> 1. topic, 2. research problem, 3. justification, 4. gap, and 5. audience.

> In recent years, falling student numbers in modern foreign languages such as French and German at GCSE and A-level in the UK have generated much debate. The fall in numbers comes as little surprise to language teachers. Enthusiasm for modern foreign languages in secondary schools is all too often short lived. Researchers have been aware of this motivational decline for some time (Chambers 1999), and differing views on the root of the problem have been put forward, situated both on the macro, i.e. societal (Coleman, Galaczi, and Astruc 2007), as well

as the micro, i.e. school and classroom (Macaro 2008), levels of language learning. While previous studies tended to focus on the factors that cause students to turn away from language learning, this paper will consider those that contribute to their sustained involvement. It will look at students who are setting out to study German as a foreign language at university level. This is an avenue worth exploring, as much insight can be gained from students who actually manage to sustain their motivation all the way through school to university level. The findings presented are part of a larger longitudinal study on motivational processes of students studying for modern language degrees in German at two high-profile universities in the UK.

Essential Element 3: Purpose statement

Please see pages 124–126 for an example of a purpose statement.

Essential Element 4: Research questions

A. Identify whether the following research questions are quantitative, qualitative or mixed methods.

1. What process describes the acquisition of irregular past tense forms in unrehearsed interpersonal communication?
2. Fourth grade students perform better on spelling tests when they receive verbal instructions than when they receive rewards or no reinforcement.
3. How do the motivation questionnaire results provide an enhanced understanding of the process of becoming a German major as described in interviews and focus groups?
4. What happens to learner engagement when a Reading Recovery programme is implemented?
5. How do the convergence of the qualitative findings from the interviews, journals, discussions, and observations, and the concurrent survey data, enhance the description and interpretation of the case?
6. Are there significant differences in participants' technology, pedagogy, and content knowledge from pre to post to follow-up measures?

B. Identify the mixed methods design associated with the following questions.

1. In what ways do the survey results generalise the themes that emerged from the interviews?
2. To what extent do personality profile ratings agree with teachers' impressions of their own teaching styles?
3. In what ways do the think-aloud journals help to clarify the standardised test results?

Essential Element 5: Foundations

Identify the worldview and/or theoretical lens in the following passage. Are they implicit or explicit? What is the evidence supporting your conclusion?

> The aim of this article is to demonstrate how quantitative and qualitative methods can be used together in feminist research. Despite an increasing number of texts and journal articles detailing mixed methods research, there are relatively few published reports of its use in feminist study. This article draws on a study conducted in regional Australia, exploring gender and social capital. Through the analysis and interpretation of data derived from a large survey and in-depth interviewing, the author will demonstrate the power of the mixed methods approach to highlight gender inequality. Despite past reluctance of feminists to embrace quantitative methods, the big picture accompanied by the personal story can bring both depth and texture to a study (Hodgkin 2008).

Worldview: _____

Implicit or explicit? _____

Evidence: _____

Theoretical lens: _____

Implicit or explicit? _____

Evidence: _____

Essential Element 6: Methods

Which of the following items would *not* typically appear in the methods section?

1. Joint display showing merging of results
2. Description of interview procedures
3. Mention of gift cards given to participants
4. Raw data scores from survey instruments
5. Professional background of the researcher
6. Procedural diagram
7. References to mixed methods research
8. Purpose of the study
9. Definition of the research design
10. Central research question

Essential Element 7: Results

Refer to the following joint display created for a mixed methods study of preschool inclusion (Li, Marquart and Zercher 2000) and answer the following questions.

1. What type of joint display is this?
2. What type of results are reported in column A? Column B?
3. How is the data integrated in this joint display?
4. Which design was probably used in this study?

	Column A	Column B
	Comparison of Information from Interview and Questionnaire Data: Examples of Four of the Six Themes	
Theme	**Face-to-face Interviews**	**Online Questionnaire**

1. How assessment looks in today's FL classroom.	Depends on whether formative or summative. Formative assessment examples include:
	• informal comprehension checks
	• creative writing tasks
	• written and oral quizzes
	Summative assessment examples include:
	• traditional paper & pencil tests
	• performance-based assessments
	   ○ oral interviews
	   ○ presentations
	   ○ Web 2.0 projects
		• 39% of teachers use commercial publisher tests as primary source of assessments
		• Only 20% use performance-based summative assessments, although 80% feel performance-based assessments are preferable to traditional tests. Reasons for not using:
		   ○ lack of time to administer
		   ○ difficult to grade
		   ○ difficult/time consuming to create

2. How FL classroom assessment decisions are made.	Factors affecting assessment decisions fall into three categories related to: 1. educational community, 2. individual teacher, or 3. student considerations. Factors mentioned in choosing assessments: • purpose/how results used • classroom realities such as diverse student population/ absenteeism • availability of technology • district requirements • assessments available from publisher	Top three factors listed that determine what assessments are chosen: • curricular requirements • time • purpose of assessment (formative vs. summative)

Major Topics (row label spanning the left side of the table)

3. How teachers learn about FL assessment methods.	Teachers have little formal training in assessment, yet often write their own assessments based on: • on the job training • trial and error • suggestions from peers • skills refined over time/with experience	The most helpful supports were: • other teachers • methods courses • publisher resources Only 5% of teachers had had formal professional development in classroom assessment
4. How professional development influences FL classroom assessment practices.	Reported changes in assessment practices include: • increased collaboration among peers/development of common assessments • improved ability to accurately assess student learning • expanded repertoire of assessments • improved ability to interpret test data for the purpose of improving teaching and learning	• 90% of teachers used common assessments at least once in the semester following the FL assessment professional development workshop • 85% of teachers felt grades more accurately reflected student learning based on modifications made to assessments previously used • 60% of teachers are more confident in the accuracy of their assessments

Essential Element 8: Discussion

Match elements commonly associated with the discussion section (left-hand column) with their purposes/characteristics (right-hand column). Note: There are three extra answers.

1.	summary of major findings	a.	mention problems encountered during research
2.	recommendations for future research	b.	results situated in a broader context
3.	limitations and weaknesses	c.	researcher situated in context of study
4.	incorporation of current literature	d.	questions left unanswered
5.	integration of research questions/purpose	e.	quantitative, qualitative and integrated results restated
		f.	joint display of results included
		g.	results situated in context of study
		h.	discussion of integration procedures

Answers

Essential Element 1: Title

1. qualitative, 2. quantitative, 3. mixed methods, 4. quantitative, 5. mixed methods

Essential Element 2: Introduction

A: 1. exploratory, 2. explanatory, 3. convergent
B: 1. motivational decline, 2. falling student numbers, 3. gain insight into problem, 4. no studies look at students with high levels of motivation, 5. all individuals associated with the school system in UK – implied

Essential Element 4: Research questions

A: 1. qualitative, 2. quantitative, 3. mixed methods, 4. qualitative, 5. mixed methods, 6. quantitative
B: 1. exploratory, 2. convergent, 3. explanatory

Essential Element 5: Foundations

1. worldview = critical realism, explicitly stated, 2. theoretical lens = Rosenbaum's model of self-control, explicitly stated.

Essential Element 6: Methods

Answer: 1, 4, 8, and 10 would *not* be included in the methods section.

Essential Element 7: Results

1. side-by-side, 2. column A = qualitative results, column B = quantitative results, 3. qualitative themes from interviews are compared to quantitative results on the major topics in the survey, 4. convergent

Essential Element 8: Discussion

Answers: 1. e, 2. d, 3. a, 4. b, 5. g

Section 3
Mixed methods research in language assessment: Case studies

7 Enhancing test validation through rigorous mixed methods components

Timothy C Guetterman
University of Michigan

Angeliki Salamoura
Cambridge English Language Assessment

This chapter discusses the procedural issues relating to the essential components of mixed methods test studies in language assessment. Topics covered include:

- *Issues* that may arise when conducting mixed methods studies in language assessment
- How to address the issues through eight *rigorous mixed methods components*
- An overview of the *nature of the test validity argument and how* the proposed mixed methods components enhance its methodological rigour
- An *illustration* of each mixed methods component using a language assessment study
- Mixed methods components in the *test validation process*

Introduction

Conducting a mixed methods study in language assessment can be a challenging task. In this chapter, we describe the methodological/procedural issues that commonly arise when conducting mixed methods research in language assessment and we propose a list of essential components of mixed methods studies in this area. We claim that these are the components that language assessment researchers should incorporate in their studies to produce a mixed methods study that is consistent with current mixed methods quality standards for publication. We demonstrate critically how conducting a rigorous mixed methods study can strengthen the investigation of test validity and the building of a validation argument in language assessment. Language assessment researchers conducting, writing and reviewing mixed methods studies can use this information to identify issues and ways to improve their research study.

The chapter is organised as follows: We first outline the nature of the validity argument that language testers need to provide to support the interpretation of test results, and how a mixed methods approach has been used in these types of studies. In doing so, we describe the methodological issues that commonly arise in such studies. These problems tend to impede impeccable methodological reporting. In the chapter, we describe each of these issues and how they negatively affect the validity of the study. For each, we present how to address the issues through rigorous mixed methods components when conducting the study. Finally, we present what these components will add to the investigation of test validity and the development of a test validation argument.

Test validity

Building a test validity argument has long been viewed as an essential part of any test development or revision project in the field of language assessment. It is concerned with the overarching question of whether a test is appropriate for its purpose and contexts of use (the 'fitness for purpose' argument, see Cambridge English 2013). Language testers conduct studies to accumulate evidence to support the interpretation of test scores for a particular use and context (Kane 2006).

We will argue that there are three dimensions in test validity that are particularly relevant in our discussion of how mixed methods components add value, strengthening the building of a validity argument. Test validity:

- is a *multi-componential* (albeit unitary) concept
- is built by *integrating evidence* from its different components in a systematic way, and
- is an ongoing, *continuous* process.

After outlining these three dimensions of test validity here and following the presentation of the issues that arise when conducting mixed methods studies, we will pick up this thread again at the end to discuss how the proposed features can contribute to and enhance these aspects of validity and the construction of a test validity argument.

In contemporary theories of test validity and validation and in Messick's (1989:13) seminal paper, in particular, validity is defined as 'an integrated evaluative judgement of the degree to which empirical evidence and theoretical rationales support the adequacy and appropriateness of inferences and actions based on test scores and other forms of assessment'. Implicit in the use of the adjective '*integrated*' above is that there are different aspects or components to test validity, and a number of models and frameworks have been proposed to capture and account for these different aspects.

The Cambridge English approach to test validation, for example, is based on five fundamental considerations for test development: Validity, Reliability, Impact, Practicality and Quality (VRIPQ; Saville 2003, Cambridge English 2013, see also Saville, Chapter 2, this volume). Test development and revision should aim at delivering assessments which are valid for their context of use, have adequate reliability (internal consistency), are designed to deliver a positive impact, are practical to administer, and follow comprehensive quality control and quality assurance processes. The Cambridge English approach is also informed by a socio-cognitive framework for test validation (developed by Weir 2005 and further elaborated in Shaw and Weir 2007, Khalifa and Weir 2009, Taylor (Ed) 2011, Geranpayeh and Taylor (Eds) 2013). This framework identifies five aspects of validity to account for during test development: cognitive-related, context-related, scoring-related, criterion-related and consequential aspects of validity. The Cambridge English approach to test validation combines the five VRIPQ test qualities and the five validity aspects/components of the socio-cognitive model in a complementary way under one framework which illustrates the complexity and multi-componential nature of test validity and validation (Figure 1).

Test validity is also an '*integrated evaluative judgement*' as its different aspects should be considered in tandem when making the evaluation.

Figure 1 The multiple components of the Cambridge English approach to test validation (Cambridge English 2013)

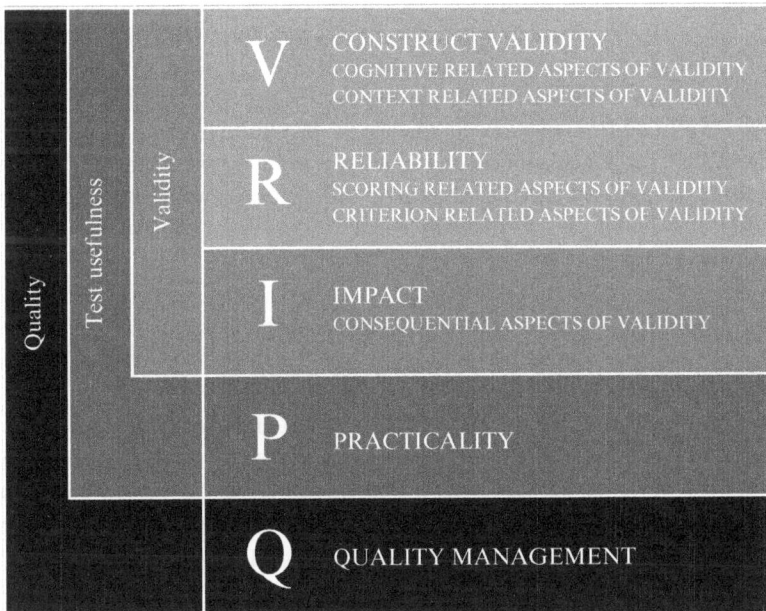

Evidence pertaining to the different components of validity influence each other in the building of the validity argument. The socio-cognitive framework, for example, acknowledges the close interrelationship between the cognitive and contextual aspects of validity, whereas the Cambridge English approach to validation judgements regarding test reliability is informed by both scoring-related and criterion-related aspects of validity, while test usefulness takes into account both validity and practicality considerations, and so on (see Figure 1). In their discussion of mixed methods, Tashakkori and Teddlie (2008) claim that one of its strengths is that it brings together 'information that can result in *"meta-inferences"* about the phenomenon under study that neither the quantitative nor qualitative perspectives could do alone' (2008:101, our emphasis). They go on to define meta-inferences as 'an overall conclusion, explanation, or understanding developed through an integration of the inferences obtained from the qualitative and quantitative strands of a mixed methods study' (2008:101). In this respect, there is a natural affiliation between mixed methods research designs and the 'meta-inferences' (see Ziegler and Kang, Chapter 4, this volume) they allow, and the 'integrative evaluative judgement' that test validity is.

Drawing on Messick's (1989) theory of validity, later definitions profile yet another, third dimension of the concept: the continuous nature of test validation. Bachman and Palmer (1996:22) define test validation as the 'ongoing process of demonstrating that a particular interpretation of test scores is justified. . .'. Test validity is not a singular project that takes place during the initial test development only. Test development and operationalisation is, by necessity, a cyclical and iterative process (Saville 2003) that takes place over a period of time and is best mediated and monitored by quality management systems (Saville 2012b, see also Saville, Chapter 2, this volume) to ensure that the test always meets the necessary requirements and standards. In addition, some test aspects can only be validated over time such as, for example, the consequential aspects (impact) of test use and implementation (see the socio-cognitive framework, Weir 2005). As a result, test validation should also be seen as an ongoing, continuing process.

What issues arise when conducting mixed methods studies in language assessment?

A rigorous mixed methods study will assist researchers constructing a language test validity argument. Specifically, the mixed methods approach supports both the multi-componential and integrated aspects of the ongoing test validation process. Mixed methods research has many potential ways to add value to the investigation of essential test qualities, such as validity, reliability, impact, practicality, and quality. This potential value of mixed methods research resides in the notion that it yields a better understanding of the aspect under investigation. However, this value does not come without a cost. Specifically, mixed methods can be a challenging approach to research (Creswell and Plano Clark 2011). For the field of language assessment, which is relatively new to mixed methods, the challenges are apparent. To support this assertion, we reviewed a small body (n=10) of reports and drafts of mixed methods studies in language assessment over the last 10 years. The studies represent a purposeful sample of studies in diverse publication outlets. The small number of studies allowed us to achieve sufficient depth in our analysis of mixed methods features. We conducted a search using terms 'mixed methods', 'qualitative and quantitative' to screen mixed methods studies in addition to the 'AND' operator with terms 'language assessment', 'language testing', 'test impact', 'washback', 'backwash'. We searched all possible combinations of these terms in the Academic Search Premier and Google Scholar databases. For inclusion in the review, the studies had to meet three criteria: 1) addressed a language assessment purpose, 2) described a mixed methods approach, defined as the collection, analysis, and integration of both qualitative and quantitative data (Creswell and Plano Clark 2011), and 3) contained a complete description of methods adequate for our analysis. The search yielded 10 studies that met the criteria (Baker 2012, Barkaoui 2007, Cheng 1997, Elder, Knoch, Barkhuizen and von Randow 2005, Erfani 2012, Fox 2009, Khalifa, Nguyen and Walker 2012, Perrone 2011, Ross 2005, Wesely 2010).

To review the studies, we used a checklist advanced by Creswell and Plano Clark (2011) to examine the features of mixed methods studies. Through the review, we have identified nine issues that arose in this body of mixed methods language assessment studies. These issues may provide insights and cautions for researchers undertaking mixed methods studies in language assessment. These problems are: 1) the form and wording of research questions, 2) the discussion of the philosophy undergirding the project, 3) specification of the rationale for collecting both quantitative and qualitative data, 4) the level of detail in mixed methods procedural diagrams, 5) the description of mixed methods integration procedures (i.e. connecting, building, and providing more complete understanding), 6) the rigour of qualitative data collection and other qualitative procedures, 7) the rigour of quantitative instrument development, 8) effective use of joint displays, and 9) the incorporation of how mixed methods added value to the study into the conclusion. In the following section, we describe each of these issues and discuss how they negatively affect the validity of the study. We discuss how to address each issue through the addition of rigorous mixed methods components (given in the sections to follow in italics) when conducting validation studies. We provide an explanation of each component with a particular focus on what it will add to the language assessment study. The ordering of the issues reflects the typical order of procedures in conducting research (Creswell 2014b). It is important for researchers to be familiar with these issues in order to avoid pitfalls when conducting their own studies. In addition, this section will assist those who review mixed methods studies as a journal reviewer, mentor, or supervisor of graduate students.

Form and wording of research questions

In our review, we found that the form and wording of research questions was an area in need of improvement. The research questions did not match the mixed methods approach. They may have been solely quantitative or solely qualitative and lacked the recommended mixed methods question (see Creswell (2015) and Creswell and Zhou, Chapter 3, this volume). When the research questions do not match the design, the reader is left without this important guidepost for the study. Furthermore, when studies do not include a mixed methods question, the researcher is not taking full advantage of the mixed methods approach whereby the qualitative strand and quantitative strand are rigorous but together yield better, richer information. The research questions should reflect this premise.

How to address the issue through rigorous mixed methods components

Ideally, the mixed methods study will include qualitative, quantitative, and *mixed methods research questions* (see Hurlbut, Chapter 6, this volume). The research question is important because it provides the reader with signposts to understand the central ideas in the language assessment study (Creswell 2012) and links the study's purpose to how it was conducted (Plano Clark and Badiee 2010). The study needs to have a quantitative and qualitative research question guiding those strands, respectively (Teddlie and Tashakkori 2009), in addition to a mixed methods question that aligns with the integration strategy used (Plano Clark and Badiee 2010).

Language assessment researchers have three types of mixed methods research questions available: issue-focused, procedural/mixing methods focused, and hybrid research questions (Creswell and Plano Clark 2011, Plano Clark and Badiee 2010). Conducting a study comparing the washback of the *International English Language Testing System (IELTS)* with the TOEFL iBT® on test preparation in Iran, Erfani (2012) wrote a research question focused on the issues: 'Is there any significant difference between teaching activities in *IELTS* and TOEFL iBT® preparation courses?' (2012:186). From a procedural/mixing focus, the question might be rewritten as: 'How do the qualitative findings confirm or contradict the quantitative results concerning significant differences between teaching activities in the *IELTS* and TOEFL iBT® preparation courses?' Finally, an example of a hybrid question might be: 'What results emerge when comparing the qualitative findings of classroom observations and teacher interviews with the quantitative results of a teaching activities questionnaire to examine differences in teaching activities between the *IELTS* and TOEFL iBT® preparation courses?' The procedural and hybrid examples reflect the convergent design with the words 'confirm', 'contradict', and 'comparing'. Of course, the choice of question should fit the community of practice for the target audience (Plano Clark and Badiee 2010).

Discussion of philosophical worldviews or framework

The next issue that arises when using mixed methods to conduct language assessment studies is the need to discuss the philosophy that undergirds the project. In our review, philosophy was not often mentioned. An explanation of the philosophical principles of the project grounds the study for the reader and gives a context for both the content and methods used. This explanation is important because the use of mixed methods may differ depending on the researcher's philosophical foundations. To take an example, consider a mixed methods exploratory sequential design whereby a qualitative interview phase is followed by an instrument design quantitative phase, as discussed in Ziegler and Kang, Chapter 4, this volume. Mentioning the philosophy of each phase (e.g. constructivism for the qualitative interview phase and post-positivity for instrument design) is important because it shares the worldview the researcher employed when conducting the study. It provides a more cohesive representation of the research and gives the reader a particular stance to read the study and follow the logic. Furthermore, including a statement on the philosophy used places research in better alignment within research communities that emphasise the particular philosophy guiding the research, such as specifying a realist approach.

How to address the issue through rigorous mixed methods components

Incorporating philosophical and theoretical orientations while conducting the study will assist individuals involved in the research. An example of an explicitly stated philosophical foundation is the *Principles of Good Practice* (Cambridge English 2013) adopted by Cambridge English. Clarifying the adopted worldview from the start of the study provides guidance to the researcher in other procedural issues that arise.

Mixed methods scholars have brought philosophy and theories into publications in two ways: (a) presenting it at the beginning as an overall framework for the study or (b) threading it throughout the paper to inform many aspects of the study (Creswell (2015) and Creswell and Zhou, Chapter 3, this volume). Writing it into the study explicitly helps the reader to understand the worldview of the researcher. Bachman, Davidson, Ryan and Choi (1995) used a theoretical framework for the test content analysis of the *First Certificate in English* and the TOEFL. However, a researcher might also thread a philosophy throughout a study. In this manner, the philosophy will inform qualitative interview questions, quantitative instrument development, and interpretation of findings within the chosen framework. The researcher can then include discussion of the framework throughout the study to explain how it informed the procedures.

Description of the rationale for a mixed methods design

Another common issue is a missing rationale or reason for applying a mixed methods design. Because mixed methods designs are not suited to all research problems, it is important to justify a mixed methods approach. When the rationale is missing, it raises methodological concerns among mixed methods experts (e.g. Bryman 2006a, Greene 2007). Furthermore, mixed methods approaches tend to use more resources, including labour, costs, and the duration of involvement – particularly in the sequential designs. Thus, the rationale or reason for using mixed methods is often needed to justify the cost.

How to address the issue through rigorous mixed methods components

Several papers (e.g. Bryman 2006a, Collins, Onwuegbuzie and Sutton 2006, Greene, Caracelli and Graham 1989) have advanced lists of the *rationale or reasons for selecting a mixed methods design* (also see Moeller, Chapter 1, this volume). While it is particularly important in proposals for research or funding, specifying the reason for using the design will help the researcher team make procedural decisions. When writing a study, it helps the reader understand the researcher's choices, making for a clearer paper and perhaps opening the idea of mixed methods to others studying similar research problems in language assessment. When writing about the mixed methods design, advancing both the name of the design (e.g. convergent design) and the rationale for the design (e.g. to qualitatively explain the quantitative results) communicates this more clearly to the reader (see also Ziegler and Kang, Chapter 4, this volume). For example, when studying rater decision-making style, Baker (2012) cited the intent of the design writing: '. . . the patterns of qualitative data (in the write-aloud comments) are compared to sources of quantitative data (the deferred scores and use of score levels) . . .' (2012:229). She also labelled the design as convergent and cited her source. Writing the intent strengthened the description of the design for the reader by including all the intent with specific examples (e.g. 'write-aloud comments').

Level of detail in procedural diagrams

The level of detail in procedural diagrams is another issue that arises in mixed methods studies in language assessment. As noted in Miller and Bustamante, Chapter 5, this volume, procedural diagrams are a way to visually depict the progression through the steps of a mixed methods study. While our examination of the literature noted an increasing use of procedural diagrams, the diagrams did not have the optimal level of detail to inform the reader of the exact process followed in the study. The diagrams tended to indicate the major steps involved in the study, for example quantitative data collection following qualitative analysis in an exploratory sequential study. The diagrams did not, however, have details to describe the procedures or products at each step of the study. Finally, and perhaps most important for a mixed methods study, the diagrams did not identify the integration by giving a clear and detailed description of the integration approach. The lack of detail in procedural diagrams has an effect on the overall reporting of the study, presenting a less than complete picture. The reader needs to see the procedures clearly through this concise visual display. When that is missing, the reader will struggle to match the specific procedures with the larger process.

How to address the issue through rigorous mixed methods components

Miller and Bustamante, Chapter 5, this volume, provide a thorough discussion of how to *create procedural diagrams*. It is an important mixed methods component when planning, proposing, or disseminating a study. Furthermore, sharing it with team members conducting a study will provide an easily digestible visual for understanding the process of conducting the study.

Description of integration procedures

As we mentioned in the previous section in our chapter, mixed methods studies in language assessment need to describe mixed methods integration procedures in more detail. While the procedural diagrams present a depiction of the process, the reports in language assessment need to identify the method of integration. For example, consider an explanatory sequential study in which the researchers first administer a survey and then follow up with interviews. There is a need to describe mixed methods integration procedures that *connect* the survey results to the particular sample of interview participants. Studies of language assessment might also use integration procedures that lead from qualitative interview findings to an instrument design. An exploratory sequential study may begin with qualitative interviews of key stakeholders of a language test in order to develop a questionnaire about the test. In this example, the researchers need to describe specifically how interview findings are *building* to the questionnaire. They should discuss, for example, how the stakeholders' perspectives informed the questionnaire. Did codes become variables? Did themes become scales? Did participant quotes inform items? Without this explanation, it may appear the interview findings did not systematically build to the questionnaire. Finally, in other cases, the integration might involve data transformation of qualitative data to quantitative data (Barkaoui 2007). Studies in language assessment might involve the use of a think-aloud procedure during test validation. Researchers then code these comments numerically and conduct further statistical analysis of the underlying constructs of the test. From a mixed methods perspective, these types of studies may be vague in describing the coding or content analysis (Galaczi 2014, Krippendorff 2013) that lead to the numeric data. Because researchers could use a variety of procedures to transform data (e.g. using frequency counts of codes, weighting codes based on perceived importance), it is important to explain the specific procedures transforming qualitative data to numbers.

Integration is critical to the conduct of mixed methods research, as it is its defining procedure (Creswell and Plano Clark 2011). Bryman (2006a) reviewed mixed methods studies and found that integration procedures were lacking in general. Thus, this issue is not specific to language assessment and remains widespread. To a critical eye, however, the lack of integration causes a mixed methods study to appear unsophisticated and will likely raise further methodological questions. More importantly, the study will not fulfil the potential of its methodology for addressing the mixed methods research questions.

How to address the issue through rigorous mixed methods components

Two primary ways to address the lack of apparent integration are to 1) *use appropriate integration procedures* and 2) *use joint displays* to present quantitative and qualitative results together. First, when conducting a mixed methods study, it is critical to apply appropriate procedures to integrate the qualitative and quantitative strands. Researchers select from four approaches to integration: connecting, merging, building, and embedding (see Fetters, Curry and Creswell 2013, Plano Clark, Garrett and Leslie-Pelecky 2009, and Ziegler and Kang, Chapter 4, this volume). For example, consider a study of a test's washback on teaching (e.g. Cheng 1997) that begins with interviews and classroom observations followed by the development and administration of a survey. We now have a label, *building*, for this type of integration where the researcher uses qualitative findings to develop survey items. Regardless of the approach, integrating appropriately will distinguish a rigorous mixed methods study. Second, joint displays, as discussed in the subsequent section in this chapter and illustrated in Section 3 in this volume, can provide a method of integration for the researcher.

Effective use of joint displays

Our review revealed the need to consider how tables can be constructed to portray quantitative and qualitative data together as both a method of integration and a way to represent mixed methods analysis. These tables, known as joint displays (Creswell and Plano Clark 2011), were typically not provided in the language studies reviewed. Rather, qualitative findings and quantitative findings appeared, often with a visual display, separately. When the joint display is missing, the study's overall interpretations and conclusions are weakened. Using a joint display, however, is valuable to demonstrate the researcher's use of integration procedures. As noted, integration is the distinguishing characteristic of a mixed method versus multimethod study. Researchers describe integration through a clear procedural diagram, a description of integration, and a joint display that visually depicts integration. When one or all of those components are missing, the entire premise of the mixed methods design is questionable.

How to address the issue through rigorous mixed methods components

Integrating qualitative and quantitative strands is a cognitive process. The *use of joint displays* is a particularly key component of mixed methods studies in language assessment that can assist the researcher in this cognitive process. As already noted, joint displays provide a method of integration for the researcher and visually demonstrate that integration method for the reader. Joint displays are a procedure to present the qualitative findings and the quantitative results in a single table or figure to help compare the two sources of data (Creswell 2015). The type of joint display depends on the particular mixed methods design. For example, a convergent design of the impact of a language test might include a table that arrays the quantitative scale results as rows against the qualitative themes or representative quotes in columns. A common variation of the convergent design in language assessment is the data transformation of qualitative codes into numeric data. For example, Bachman, Davidson, Ryan and Choi (1995) examined test content and presented the content codes as rows with descriptive statistics in columns. Presenting the results in a single table demonstrated the data transformation procedure, method of integration (i.e. merging), and integrated results in a single display. Joint displays will also assist the language assessment researcher using other mixed methods designs. For example, in a single display, a researcher using an exploratory sequential design for instrument development can align qualitative codes to the eventual items on the instrument. Khalifa and Docherty (Chapter 11, this volume) provide a further illustration of using a joint display to align quantitative and qualitative data from a convergent design. Furthermore, computer software, such as MAXQDA (VERBI GmbH 2014), can assist language assessment researchers in developing joint displays of quantitative and qualitative results.

Rigour of qualitative procedures

Another common issue in our review of language assessment studies is a lack of rigour of qualitative procedures. Although mixed methods takes advantage of the strengths of both quantitative and qualitative approaches, each strand must be able to stand up to critique independently. Two types of qualitative issues arose in our review of language assessment studies. First, interview design was mentioned but in a general sense. The studies did not go into detail about the interview selection, procedures related to the interview, or include the full set of interview questions. Second, the studies did not mention qualitative validity or accuracy of data. From a qualitative perspective, validation is a systematic process to assess the accuracy of findings from the perspectives of both the researchers and participants (Creswell 2013a). Failing to include these details presents a serious limitation of the published study.

How to address the issue through rigorous mixed methods components

The rigour of the qualitative strand can be enhanced by *incorporating rigorous qualitative procedures* when designing a study, adhering to the procedures when conducting the study, and specifying those procedures when disseminating the study (see Hurlbut, Chapter 6, this volume). For example, using interview and observational protocol are recommended practices in qualitative data collection (Creswell 2013a). Including the protocols in a written report then allows the reader to act as co-researcher by following the flow of the research procedures. In addition, qualitative validation strategies are necessary to ensure the accuracy or trustworthiness of the qualitative findings (Creswell 2013a). The validation strategies include member-checking, use of multiple data sources, agreement among multiple coders, and use of rich data (Maxwell 2013). A qualitative study should include two or more strategies (Creswell 2013a) and describe the steps to ensure validity. Adding this component to the procedures enhances the credibility of the qualitative findings. Because these findings are in some way integrated with quantitative data in a mixed methods study, the reader must be assured that qualitative findings are robust.

Rigour of quantitative instrument development

As with the qualitative strand, quantitative procedures also need attention to rigour. Rigour was an issue that was particularly noteworthy in reviewing language assessment studies that use an exploratory sequential mixed methods design for the purpose of the development of an instrument to administer to a large group. A problem with these studies is the need to improve the rigour of the quantitative research instrument development. While the section on issues with integration focused on the integration, the concern here relates to the steps in instrument development. The language assessment studies often did not mention a pilot test of the instrument. A pilot test is an important procedure in instrument design to assess whether individuals in the sample understand the question and can complete the survey (Creswell 2012, Dillman 2000). Next, the language assessment studies tended to be vague about the psychometric properties of the instrument. Issues such as the reliability of scores and construct validity evidence for the instrument were not specified. This issue is important to enhance the rigour of instrument development. Addressing the issue improves the validity of the overall study by adding credibility to questionnaires used and increases confidence in its results.

How to address the issue through rigorous mixed methods components

The issue of the rigour of instrument development is related to a broader issue of consistency between the qualitative and quantitative approaches used in the mixed methods study. This consistency, or lack thereof, is where threats to validity arise in mixed methods research. Simply, the qualitative and quantitative data should work together, through appropriate integration, to address common research questions. As with the rigour of the qualitative approach (discussed in the previous section), the quantitative approach must also employ rigorous procedures that can stand alone. Although the issue of validity arose when examining exploratory sequential mixed methods designs, here we address *recognising and acknowledging threats to mixed methods validity* more generally as it applies to other mixed methods designs.

Researchers can mitigate problems, such as lacking rigour in instrument development, when conducting mixed methods research by *recognising and acknowledging threats to validity*. As with quantitative and qualitative research, scholars are now considering the threats to validity in the mixed methods designs. Creswell (2015) presents potential threats for six mixed methods designs (see also Ziegler and Kang, Chapter 4, this volume). Here we discuss threats in the basic designs (explanatory sequential, exploratory sequential, and convergent) that are relevant for the language assessment researcher. In the explanatory sequential design, threats include the decision of what quantitative results need follow-up, the sampling of the follow-up participants, relevant interview questions, and ensuring that the qualitative data indeed explains the quantitative results. Next, validity threats in the exploratory design involve how the qualitative findings build to the instrument and the use of good psychometric procedures in instrument development. Finally, the potential threats to validity in convergent designs relate to parallel qualitative phenomena and quantitative constructs or variables, decisions to use equal or unequal sample sizes between strands, parallel units of analysis, integration approaches, and explanation of divergent results (e.g. teachers describe impact differently in interviews than reflected in surveys).

Recognising these threats will assist the language assessment researcher in planning a study, and acknowledging the threats as limitations in the report will add credibility to the publication.

Discussion of value added by mixed methods

Finally, another component often missing from language assessment studies is the discussion of the *value added* by mixed methods. The studies we reviewed included no mention of value added (see Chapters 1 and 2, this volume, for a discussion of the value of mixed methods). Although similar to the rationale, the value added by mixed methods is a different concept. Both rely on the assumption that combining qualitative and quantitative methods maximises their strengths and leads to an even better study. The *rationale* for using mixed methods is a reason for mixing. It is a design decision made prior to conducting the study, communicating why the researcher selected a mixed methods approach instead of a mono-method approach, such as a correlational design. On the other hand, the contemplation of *value added* occurs after the study. Because mixed methods does involve more time and resources, it is important to return to the initial assertion (i.e. rationale or reason) at the end of the study to examine whether the extra resources added value to the study.

Returning to the value added by mixed methods is important for several reasons. For example, a validation study in language assessment is a complex topic and applying mixed methods is likely to yield more evidence. As we build an argument for validity, evidence is what we need. Thus, a discussion of value added supports the validity argument and the decision to use a mixed methods design initially. In another illustration, consider a study of the impact of language assessment whereby the researchers conducted qualitative interviews with stakeholders and then developed an instrument to assess impact in the community. Readers are likely to perceive the mixed methods study as more rigorous, and by extension, more credible. Nevertheless, it is important to discuss the value added to highlight the importance of mixed methods. A simple solution for this example is to include a section that discusses how an improved instrument resulted from, first, conducted interviews, and then systematically developing an instrument that fits the population being studied. If the impact is complex and involves socio-cultural issues, integrating qualitative and quantitative methods may be the best way to uncover unknown types of influence, to define the types of influence, and to understand mechanisms for impact. However, the researcher must be explicit both for the reader and the language assessment research community by detailing how mixed methods yielded a better understanding of the impact.

How to address the issue through rigorous mixed methods components

Discussing the value added by mixed methods is central to its legitimation (Creswell in press, and see Moeller, Chapter 1, this volume). Haines (2011) defined mixed methods value as the ability of the methodology 1) to help readers better understand the study and findings, 2) increase confidence in findings, 3) provide more evidence and completeness, and 4) inform and contribute to overall validity. As previously discussed, at the end of the study the researcher should revisit whether and how mixed methods added additional insight. Haines (2011) conducted a study on value added by mixed methods. In the study, participants read studies using mixed methods, qualitative, and quantitative approaches and then rated their impression on a survey and discussed their impressions during interviews. Haines (2011) found a number of ways that readers perceive added value from mixed methods, and suggested that they:

- lead to an increased understanding of the topic studied
- yielded more evidence
- were viewed as more rigorous; and
- can address complex phenomena research questions.

For a language assessment researcher, discussing value added might include a discussion of how converging interviews with test results led to a better understanding of how test impact occurred. Or, it might involve discussing how beginning with a qualitative exploration led to an instrument with stronger construct validity evidence. Adding that discussion of value added, in whatever way it occurs, will strengthen the paper with a final justification of the use of mixed methods design. Furthermore, that discussion advances mixed methods as a field and serves as a reference for other language assessment researchers considering what design will best address their research problem.

Table 1 presents a short checklist, which could be used to review a mixed methods study for rigorous components. The list provides a quick self-critique for researchers and other users such as those evaluating papers in language assessment that use mixed methods designs. We argued that ensuring rigorous mixed methods components when conducting research will address these potential problems. The components represent recent scientific developments (Creswell in press) in mixed methods research. A mixed methods study that incorporates these components can strengthen the building of a validation argument in language assessment by offering a balanced and complementary approach of investigating essential test qualities, such as validity, reliability, impact, practicality, and quality.

Table 1 Mixed methods components to include in language assessment studies

✔	Component of a rigorous mixed methods study
☐	Identifying the rationale or reasons for selecting a mixed methods design
☐	Writing a mixed methods research question
☐	Incorporating philosophies and theories into mixed methods studies
☐	Integrating the qualitative and quantitative strands using a specific procedure
☐	Using joint displays to present the quantitative and qualitative results together
☐	Recognising and acknowledging threats to validity in the mixed methods design
☐	Conducting both strands using rigorous methods of data collection and analysis
☐	Discussing value added by mixed methods relative to a single method approach

Mixed methods components and test validity

In the previous section we put forward nine rigorous mixed methods components and discussed what each will add to a mixed methods study. In this section we turn our attention to how a rigorously conducted mixed methods study can strengthen the investigation of test validity and the building of a validity argument. We argue that, if applied consistently, the components enhance the methodological rigour of a test development or revision project and by extension the validity of the evidence presented in support of the test validity argument. In doing so, mixed methods and the proposed components can also support three key dimensions of test validity, which we identified at the beginning of this chapter. We will start by exemplifying how these components can be implemented when conducting a monomethod test validity study before we turn to the discussion of the links between rigorous mixed methods components and test validation.

Applying the rigorous mixed methods components in a language assessment study

We will take the rating scale development study described by Galaczi and Khabbazbashi, Chapter 9, this volume, as an example to illustrate how the aforementioned rigorous mixed methods components can be applied in practice, strengthening the methodological rigour of the study and by extension enhancing the robustness of the evidence supporting the validity argument of the scale under development. Galaczi and Khabbazbashi report a large-scale multistage project which aimed to develop and validate a set of revised rating scales for a suite of high-stakes L2 speaking tests. (Note that only a schematic presentation of the project will be provided here for the purposes of illustrating the components in practice. For a more detailed exposition of the study and the scale development process see Galaczi and Khabbazbashi, Chapter 9, this volume, and Galaczi, ffrench, Hubbard and Green (2011).) The project comprised four stages as follows:

- Planning stage where issues with the current scale were identified and the scope of the revision project was laid out.
- Stage 1 (Qual) where an analysis of test taker speaking performances and open-ended examiner feedback on the 'old' scales guided the drafting of the first version of the revised scales.
- Stage 2 (Quan + Qual) where scaling of the revised descriptors against the Cambridge English and CEFR speaking scales, and examiner feedback while using the revised scales were used to evaluate the first draft and produce a second version.
- Stage 3 (Quan) where ratings using the revised scales with a big group of examiners and test takers were used to finalise the scales.

At the Planning stage of the study the following components were applied:

- *Identify the rationale or reasons for selecting a mixed methods design*

To gain a richer insight into scale development issues and a broader coverage of the speaking construct, the researchers decided to use two complementary approaches to scale construction, 'expert judgement' and 'empirically informed' methods. These, in turn, would yield both qualitative and quantitative data, as outlined in the project stages above. The rationale for selecting the particular mixed methods design was based on the main purpose of the study, which was to develop a quantitative instrument – a rating scale – using qualitative and quantitative evidence (hence, an exploratory sequential basic design) and on the fact that scale development often requires an iterative process of planning, piloting, revising and further piloting before finalising the instrument (hence, a multistage design that adds to the basic exploratory sequential design).

- *Writing a mixed methods research question*

The researchers identified the overall research goal for the study as '[e]mpirically-supported development of a set of assessment scales for second/ foreign language speaking tests'. Based on this goal, the researchers might write a broad mixed methods research question such as: How does the qualitative data support the development of a set of assessment scales for second language speaking tests? The question is consistent with the identified purpose yet general enough to span the three-stage study. A mixed methods question maintains a research focus on integration throughout the complex scale development.

- *Conducting both strands using rigorous methods of data collection and analysis*

The researchers acknowledged the importance of methodological rigour at the planning stage and built requirements into the various studies to ensure methodological quality. In the qualitative strand, for instance, Conversational Analysis procedures (Atkinson and Heritage (Eds) 1984) were used when analysing learner language, whereas recommendations for conducting

Verbal Protocol investigations (Green 1998) were closely followed in the data collection and analysis of raters' verbalised thoughts when using the scales. In the quantitative strand, the data set requirements for data connectivity when carrying out Multi-Facet Rasch Measurement were observed.

During the three stages of the project, the following procedures were identified:

• *Incorporating rigorous qualitative procedures*

The authors delineated their qualitative data sources as the learner speaking test performance and examiner survey comments. They then provided the procedures for analysis of each. For example, they discussed test performance analysis, beginning with transcription using Conversation Analysis and followed by iterative 'data exploration strategy' as their method of analysis. A critical point was their mention of independent analysis by two researchers, which lends credibility to the findings. Furthermore, the authors addressed qualitative validation strategies generally, mentioning credibility, transferability, dependability, and confirmability (Lincoln and Guba 1985).

• *Incorporating philosophies and theories into mixed method studies*

The authors acknowledge that the initial qualitative stage is informed by the constructivist paradigm, which allows for an inductive exploration and interpretation of complex phenomena/realities, such as test takers' speaking performances. The following quantitative stages, where the revised scale is drafted and piloted, are embedded within a post-positivist paradigm which will allow them 'to distill the richness and complexity of learner language to a finite set of discrete descriptors and subsequently to a single score or set of scores'.

• *Using appropriate integration procedures*

In addition to labelling the design (multistage exploratory sequential) and its intent (to develop a quantitative instrument, a rating scale, using both qualitative and quantitative evidence), the integration procedures within each stage and from one stage to the next were specified. The researchers presented their overarching 'iterative approach to revising and finalising the assessment scales based on all recommendations from QUAL and QUAN phases'. When reporting the results of the study, it will then be important to specify the integration procedures at each stage. For example, in the study researchers would describe how they used the initial qualitative phase to *build* to the subsequent revised version of the scales in Stage 2.

During the different stages of the study, the following methodological components were implemented:

• *Using joint displays of qualitative and quantitative findings*

When writing up the study, a joint display is particularly useful to represent integration in the study and illustrate how the stages link to one another. Using a joint display matrix to map how the stage 1 qualitative findings informed each specific alteration could serve to connect the qualitative phase to the instrument. Rows could contain each qualitative theme. Columns could contain each category of revision: changes to assessment categories, the weighting for each category and the number of scale points. Cells would then provide the specific revision. Another example of joint displays is evident in stage 2 of the study in which the authors represent data transformation and integrated results. Discussing data transformation, the researchers noted 'verbal protocols were also converted to quantitative codes in order to examine the extent to which different assessment categories from the scales were used'. The final joint display then represented the integrated findings in a pie chart. (See also Khalifa and Docherty, Chapter 11, this volume, for an example of a joint display.)

• *Recognising and acknowledging threats to validity*

In Stage 1 of the study, which was qualitative and focused on the initial development of the draft scale descriptors, the research team acknowledged the methodological issue of balancing two competing trends in scale construction: 'on the one hand, the need to develop scales which have construct coverage, accurately and comprehensively capture the constructs of interest and are therefore relatively long and detailed, and on the other hand, the need to consider usability and produce scales which can be used by examiners in real time and are therefore relatively short and succinct.'

In Stage 2 of the study, which involved a nested convergent design with collection of both quantitative and qualitative data from examiners (scaling of draft descriptors against Cambridge English and CEFR scales; and verbal protocols of using the draft descriptors in rating performances), the researchers considered the methodological issue of using equal or unequal sample sizes between the two strands. Following Creswell's (2014b) recommendation that the qualitative sample would typically be much smaller than the quantitative sample needed to generalise results to the overall population, the researchers opted 'to draw samples from the same population of examiners and test takers' performances, but to use different individuals [and sizes] for both samples'.

Discussing such issues helps explain decisions taken in terms of methods (e.g. sampling) and instrument development (e.g. length of scale) and adds to the methodological validity of the whole study. It also contributes to the discussion of balancing out test qualities, such as Validity (adequate construct coverage) on the one hand and Practicality (optimal scale length) on the other.

• *Discussing value added*

In their conclusion, the authors acknowledge that by using a mixed methods approach they were able to capitalise on complementary strengths and counterbalance methodological weaknesses of the different methods used in the study. In turn, this advantage allowed them to build a strong validity argument about the robustness of the final product of the project – the revised set of assessment scales.

Enhancing test validity through rigorous mixed methods components

At the beginning of this chapter we identified three dimensions of test validity, which we argue can be strengthened by a mixed methods research design and the proposed components discussed above (see Table 1). First, test validity is a unitary but *multi-componential concept*; it entails different aspects (see Figure 1), all of which should be investigated when constructing a validity argument. Some aspects of test validity lend themselves better to quantitative investigations; others to qualitative investigations. For example, scoring-related aspects of validity (e.g. reliability) typically require quantitative evidence whereas consequential aspects of validity (e.g. investigating stakeholders' perceptions of certain test aspects) often call for qualitative evidence. More often than not, however, the investigation of aspects of test validity involves both types of evidence. For example, the development and revision of language proficiency or rating scales frequently requires a combination of intuitive, qualitative and quantitative data, as we saw in the previous section (see also Council of Europe 2001:207–216). In time, evidence pertaining to different aspects of validity need to be brought together to build an overall test validity argument.

Table 2 summarises how rigorous mixed methods components assist the process of test validation. Mixed methods components (e.g. identifying the best design for combining the strands, ensuring the use of rigorous methods within each strand, and incorporating the philosophical and theoretical foundations of the research) can help link and structure the different investigative strands in a principled way, while at the same time provide an overview of the whole project for both researchers and readers. For example, as illustrated in the previous section, the development of a rating scale requires insights from multiple types of evidence, ranging from expert judgement to qualitative and quantitative data, raising the question of how to combine and weigh them when it comes to interpretation. Likewise, when constructing an overall test validity argument, the researcher's challenge is to connect multiple forms and sources of evidence for the argument. Following a mixed methods design and deciding on the philosophy/theory endorsed in each design stage guides the researcher when planning the purpose, priority and sequence of methods (data collection and analysis). Taking again the example of the rating scale development, we see that the purpose of the study – developing a quantitative instrument by exploring primarily qualitative but also quantitative

Table 2 Mixed methods components in the test validation process

Test validity/validation	Component
• A unitary but *multi-componential* concept that requires the collection and combination of multiple sources of evidence	• Identifying the rationale or reasons for selecting a mixed methods design • Incorporating philosophies and theories into mixed methods studies • Incorporating rigorous procedures for both strands
• Built by *integrating evidence* from its different components in a systematic way	• Writing a mixed methods research question • Using appropriate integration procedures • Using joint displays to present the quantitative and qualitative results together • Recognising and acknowledging threats to validity in the mixed methods design
• An *ongoing, continuous* process that requires collection of evidence over time	• Discussing value added by mixed methods relative to a single method approach

data – guided the choice of the design (multistage exploratory sequential). The choice of the design, in turn, informed the structure of the project and how the various investigative strands linked to each other – the analysis of learner performances and initial feedback from examiners comprised the first (qualitative) stage which led to the first draft of the revised scale; the mapping exercise with the draft scale and verbal protocols with speaking examiners comprised the second (quantitative and qualitative) stage which led to the second draft of the scale, and so on. Finally, identifying the theoretical paradigms guiding the stages helped elucidate the nature of the analysis implemented – e.g. constructivism underpinned an inductive exploration of speaking performances using Conversation Analysis in the initial qualitative stage.

Second, the test validity argument is built not by merely aggregating or putting together different types of data but by *integrating* the different strands of evidence in a systematic way to reach an evaluative judgement. And in this respect, mixed methods have much to offer in terms of signposting the type of and reason for data integration. We advocate for the use of consistent terminology when it comes to naming the rationale for the design chosen, as well as the *integration procedures* used in the study (e.g. connecting, merging, building or embedding). When working with multiple types of evidence, as was for example the case in the scale development project, consistent terminology helps explain how each set of data/evidence integrates with the others and how each contributes to the development of the scale. In addition, when working with a team of validation researchers, consistent terminology will facilitate collaboration. Each of the members of the team can more clearly articulate their particular contribution.

Understanding of the common threads among the different investigative strands and the analysis procedures can be further enhanced by providing *appropriately worded mixed methods research questions*, by presenting *a joint display of the quantitative and qualitative results* for comparison purposes, and by *acknowledging methodological issues or threats to the validity of the mixed methods research design*. For example, the validity argument supporting the use of a rating scale does not consist of multiple independent strands of evidence. A cohesive understanding of how well the scale measures speaking performance is needed. The same holds for the overall test validity argument, which requires a comprehensive integration of evidence from all aspects of test validity. These mixed methods components allow for a cohesive argument by providing methods to integrate various strands and to discuss methodological issues (e.g. competing demands in scale construction). This integration then leads to inferences about a test's qualities that are most useful in its ongoing development (e.g. Validity, Reliability, Impact, Practicality, and Quality; does the scale cover adequately the speaking construct under investigation (Validity) and does it support reliable ratings (Reliability) without being overly long (Practicality)?).

Third, test validity is an *ongoing*, iterative process that takes place over time. According to the Cambridge English approach to test validation (Cambridge English 2013, see also Saville, Chapter 2, this volume), evidence for test validation is collected and accumulated over time. We begin to gather evidence at the design and development stages and continue to do so as long as the test remains operational. The 'multistage evaluation' mixed methods design is particularly fitting in keeping with this temporal, cyclical dimension of test validation. The scale development study, for example, adopted this design precisely to accommodate a series of sequential smaller-scale studies and trials where subsequent stages drew on previous stages' findings. For instance, examiner feedback on the 'old' scales fed into the draft descriptors of the revised scale; and similarly, data from scaling and examiner use of the draft descriptors fed into a second version of the revised scale, and so on, until the final set of descriptors was in place. Once a scale becomes operational, evidence for its validity continues to be collected by monitoring, for example, the reliability of the ratings made by speaking examiners who use the scale, whereas the scale itself is subject to revision at regular intervals, a mechanism which, in turn, ensures test quality.

Finally, *discussing the value added* by mixed methods is a component that will strengthen the methodological validity of any test validation study by offering an added justification of the methods chosen as well as a reference for future design choices. Moreover, discussing value added provides a reflection on how well the mixed methods approach met the original rationale for its use. The researcher can suggest potential improvements for future studies. In this manner, other language assessment researchers can learn from the study, applying it to their validation efforts. Although this justification is bound to vary depending on the nature and context of the study and test, a common theme emerging from the validity studies of Section 3 in this volume appears to be the complementarity of methods that ultimately yields richer, more robust evidence of test validity.

Summary

In this chapter, we described the methodological issues that commonly arise when conducting mixed methods research in language assessment and the essential components of rigorous mixed methods studies in this field in order to addresses these issues. The key methodological issues are:

- the form and wording of research questions
- the discussion of the philosophy undergirding the project
- specification of the rationale for collecting both quantitative and qualitative data
- the level of detail in mixed methods procedural diagrams
- the description of mixed methods integration procedures (i.e. connecting, building, and providing more complete understanding)
- the rigour of qualitative data collection and other qualitative procedures
- the rigour of quantitative instrument development
- using tables and graphics effectively to present quantitative and qualitative data together, and
- the incorporation of how mixed methods added value to the study into the conclusion.

Then, we presented eight rigorous mixed methods components for language assessment studies, with the following components:

- identifying the rationale or reasons for selecting a mixed methods design
- writing a mixed methods research question
- incorporating philosophies and theories into mixed methods studies
- using appropriate integration procedures
- using joint displays to present the quantitative and qualitative results together
- recognising and acknowledging threats to validity in the mixed methods design
- incorporating rigorous quantitative and qualitative procedures, and
- discussing value added by mixed methods relative to a single method approach.

Applying these components will assist the researcher in conducting a rigorous mixed methods study that is consistent with current mixed methods methodological procedures. At the same time, attending to these components when conducting mixed methods research will also enhance the investigation of test validity and strengthen the development of a test validation argument. Table 2 provides a link between these components and the process of a test validation study.

8 A community-based participatory approach to test development: The International Legal English Certificate

Ivana Vidaković

Martin Robinson

Cambridge English Language Assessment

This chapter exemplifies the integration of a community-based participatory approach to research (CBPR) and a mixed methods design in the
development of a test of English for Specific Purposes (ESP). There are
three key focuses:

- The *features of CBPR* in general and in this study, including the
  roles of research partners from project conception onwards and the
  usefulness of this approach in ESP test development
- The use of the *exploratory mixed methods design* for test development
- The different *phases of the test development process: needs analysis*,
  which resulted in a sample test design; *viability study*, which resulted
  in further modifications to the test; *trial study*, which led to further
  refinements to the test and test launch

Introduction

In 2004, a partnership was formed between Cambridge English Language
Assessment and TransLegal, a firm of lawyers who are linguists, to develop a
test of legal English – *Cambridge English: Legal* (aka *the International Legal
English Certificate (ILEC)*). This partnership is an example of a community-
based participatory research approach (CBPR) to test development, which is
still rather novel in language assessment. Within this approach, legal content
specialists had an active role in the development of the *ILEC* test, as research
partners to language assessment specialists, rather than just research subjects.
TransLegal was the (legal) community research partner, whilst the community,
defined by professional background and the interests of its members, consisted
of lawyers, law students and lecturers in law. While the ultimate goal of the
mainstream public health and social science CBPR studies is to initiate social

change (Strand, Marullo, Cutforth, Stoecker and Donohue 2003), the goal of this test development project is to impact future test users (e.g. test takers, employers, universities) positively by providing a test of English tailored to their specific professional and academic needs. This goal is related to the concept of impact by design in language assessment, which starts from the 'premise that assessment systems should be designed from the outset with the potential to achieve positive impacts and takes an ex ante approach to anticipating the possible consequences of using the test in a particular context' (Saville 2012a:5). The outcome of this collaboration was a test of English for Specific Purposes (ESP) for law students and practising lawyers seeking employment in an international legal setting. The exam is set at B2 and C1 levels on the Common European Framework of Reference for Languages (CEFR, Council of Europe 2001), while a test certificate at C1 level on the CEFR is evidence of the ability to use English in a university or a legal workplace setting.

A CBPR approach joins partners with diverse skills, knowledge, expertise and sensitivities: non-academic researchers who belong to a community and academic researchers who are external to the community. In this way, the insiders' and the outsiders' perspectives on the investigated issue are brought together. As such, a CBPR approach enhances the relevance and usefulness of the findings and improves the quality and validity of research (Israel, Schulz, Parker and Becker 1998:180). At the same time, this approach requires methodological flexibility, in view of community research partners' expertise, proclivity, availability and a range of other factors. In this study, the exploratory sequential mixed methods design (see Creswell and Plano Clark 2011:86; Ziegler and Kang, Chapter 4, this volume) was employed to develop *ILEC* in the first phase, and then to validate and refine it in the remaining two phases. The first phase consisted of qualitative data collection and needs analysis, which resulted in the creation of a sample test. In the remaining two phases, mainly quantitative, and some qualitative data was obtained for the purposes of test validation and test refinement.

The goal of this chapter is to show how a CBPR approach and a mixed methods research design were used to develop a test of English for Specific purposes.

Community-based participatory research: Definition and principles

A traditional approach to research typically comprises the researcher and the research participant(s). The researcher approaches research participants with pre-determined hypotheses, research questions, goals and methodology. Therefore, the role of research participants is typically limited to provision of information. In contrast, the CBPR approach is more collaborative in nature, which results in the blurring of distinctions between the researcher and the researched. In CBPR, non-academic researchers who are members of a community, and academic researchers external to the community, work together and 'contribute their expertise to enhance the understanding of a given phenomenon and to integrate the knowledge gained with action to benefit the community involved' (Israel et al 1998:173). A community is a socially constructed unit of identity, with 'common interests and a commitment to meeting shared needs' (Israel et al 1998:178). CBPR involves a long-term commitment between the partners and an establishment of mechanisms of sustainability, so that the partnership may continue beyond the initial study. Table 1 provides an overview of the key features which distinguish CBPR from a traditional approach to research.

The features and principles of CBPR are seen to lie on a continuum, given that the community partners' interest to participate in every research stage, the available time, funding and expertise vary across projects (Israel, Parker,

Table 1 Traditional research versus community-based participatory research approach (Adapted from: Horowitz, Robinson and Seifer 2013, Palinkas and Soydan 2012 and Strand et al 2003)

	Traditional research	Community-based participatory research
Goal of research	Advance knowledge	Betterment of community (e.g. improving the well-being of the community and empowering it via research training)
Source of research question	Theoretical work	Community-identified problem
Designer of research	Trained researcher	Trained researcher and community
Role of researcher	Outside expert	Collaborator, learner
Role of community	Subject of study	Collaborator, learner; CBPR identifies and builds on the strengths and resources within the community
Relationship of researcher to participants	Short-term, task-oriented, detached	Long-term, multifaceted, connected
Value of research	Acceptance by peers (e.g. publications in academic journals)	Contributions to community change
Ownership of data	Academic researcher	Community
Dissemination of findings	To academic audiences	Researchers and community partners disseminate findings to academics, research participants, relevant communities and decision makers
Sustainability of relationship between researcher and community	Contact ends with a research project	Sustainability built from inception; partnership continued beyond the initial project to implement recommendations, to effect a social change, solve a community problem and evaluate outcomes and processes

Rowe, Salvatore, Minkler, López, Butz, Mosley, Coates, Lambert, Potito, Brenner, Rivera, Romero, Thompson, Coronado and Halstead 2005). At one end of the continuum, community partners and research partners external to the community actively engage in all, or most, aspects of the research process, from the problem definition and research questions to the application of recommendations. At the other end, at the very least, 'the community must be fully involved in the first phase of the project – identifying the research needs and questions – and in the final phase, where the results are disseminated and implemented' (Strand et al 2003:11).

CBPR has been widely adopted in public healthcare (Horowitz et al 2013, Israel et al 2005, Roussel, Fan and Fulmer 2002, Minkler and Wallerstein 2003), as well as education and the social sciences (Puma, Bennett, Cutforth, Tombari and Stein 2009, Strand et al 2003, Oakes and Rogers 2006, Weinberg 2003). Within those disciplines, social, environmental, political and/or economic factors contributing to a health-related or a socio-economic issue are investigated with the aim of introducing social or community change (Israel et al 1998, Puma et al 2009).

The CBPR approach is underused in language assessment despite its great potential – particularly in the area of English for Specific Purposes (ESP). ESP tests assess language ability in a discipline-/profession-specific context. They are characterised by three interrelated features: a focus on authenticity (the real-life quality of texts and tasks), specificity (each discipline/profession has a specific linguistic core, e.g. profession-specific terminology) and specific-purpose language ability combining content knowledge and language knowledge (Douglas 2000). In view of this, the development of ESP tests should be, ideally, both theory and data driven, as well as collaborative. A theoretical basis ensures that the underlying test construct is congruent with the current understanding of the general language ability, while empirical grounding allows the identification of the specific features and uses of English in the given contexts so that ESP tests could meet the language needs of specific professional or academic groups. Collaboration is necessary, given that applied linguists/language test developers are typically not experts in other disciplines, and that mismatches have been frequently attested between applied linguists' and domain experts' intuitions on the needs of ESP learners (see Long 2005:27). Therefore, it is only natural – even though rare – that language test and syllabus developers would form a research *partnership* with content specialists who are members of the relevant professional community for which a test, or a course, is being designed.

Within CBPR, 'methodological flexibility is essential' as methodology is determined not only by the purpose of the study, but also by the context, interests and capabilities of the community (Israel et al 1998:189) and also by 'what information is needed to contribute to social change effort' (Strand et al 2003:78). In some available CBPR studies, only a single method of data collection and analysis was used – quantitative or qualitative (see Farquhar and Wing (2003) for an example of a predominantly quantitative and a predominantly qualitative study in public health research), but there seems to be a greater focus on qualitative research (Israel et al 1998, Palinkas and Soydan (2012:160)). In some other studies, sources were triangulated (see Strand et al (2003:78) and Israel et al (1998) for an overview), and quantitative and qualitative data was collected, analysed and discussed in a mixed methods design (Ivankova 2015, Puma et al 2009).

CBPR and mixed methods are compatible, given their common features. Within both, qualitative and quantitative data is collected and analysed. Ivankova (2015) further highlights that both are aimed at providing comprehensive information: the former provides comprehensive solutions to practical problems, while the latter provides comprehensive answers to research questions. In addition, both are cyclical in nature, with clearly defined study phases. Both also combine insiders' and outsiders' perspectives: in CBPR, this combination is achieved through collaboration between insiders (community – internal researchers) and outsiders (external researchers), while mixed methods researchers combine insider and outsider perspectives through different strands of their study: the quantitative strand requires the researcher to take on an observer (outsider) role for the collection of numeric data, while the qualitative strand requires the same researcher to explore the perspectives of insiders in a system or an organisation (see Ivankova (2015) for further discussion). The value of mixed methods design in community-based participatory research is recognised primarily because it provides 'a sound methodological framework ... due to its ability to produce conclusions about the research issue that are more rigorous and more consistent' (Ivankova 2015:58).

The evolving role of content specialists in ESP

ESP tests are often derived from an analysis of language use and needs in specific workplace or academic settings (i.e. needs analysis). During this initial stage in the development of a test or a syllabus (an outline of topics to be covered in a course), content specialists have typically been research subjects within the bounds of a traditional 'researcher-researched' relationship. Only recently has there been evidence of a more intrinsic involvement of content specialists in ESP test development (see Table 2).

In the 1970s and the early 1980s, content specialists were not even consulted. Traditional needs analyses were either based on a research of representative corpora or applied linguists' intuitions (Long 2005, Robinson 1991, Widdowson 1983). The former were criticised for being too atomistic and divorced from real-life language use, resulting in lists of specific vocabulary and syntactic units, rather than indicating 'the kind of activity learners will have to be involved in when using language for their particular purposes'

Table 2 The role of content specialists in EAP/ESP test development

Timeline	The role of content specialists	Research approach	Test/Study
Pre-1983	None	Traditional	ELTS/Carroll (1981)
1983–1990s	Research subjects/informants in needs analysis and/or provision of feedback on sample tasks	Traditional	TEEP/Weir (1983) ELTS/Carroll (1981) OET/McNamara (1996) Test for Teachers of Italian/Elder (1993) The Eurocontrol Standard Test in English for Trainee Air Traffic Controllers/Teasdale (1996) TOEFL Test of Written English/ETS (2004)
1993	Commission language assessment specialists to develop a test Research subjects in needs analysis and provision of feedback on sample tasks and test structure Broadly influence the development of assessment criteria (i.e. request inclusion of non-linguistic criteria besides the linguistic ones) Collaborate with language assessment specialists to identify assessment criteria and provide performance descriptors	Traditional, with elements of CBPR	The Japanese Test for Tour Guides/Brown (1993)
2000s	Initiate test development project; recruit a core development team consisting of domain experts (air traffic controllers) and language assessment specialists Collaborate with language assessment specialists in initial test development (test specifications, item writing, piloting, test revisions) Ensure test validation by external language assessment specialists Disseminate the outcome with language assessment specialists to the aviation industry Ensure test sustainability via examiner and marker training and creating new teams of item writers	CBPR	ELPAC Test for Air Traffic Controllers/ Enright (2005)
	Collaborate with language assessment specialists in the development of test specifications and a sample test: joint decisions	CBPR	ILEC/Corkill and Robinson (2006) ICFE/Ingham and Thighe (2006)

Table 2 (continued)

Timeline	The role of content specialists	Research approach	Test/Study
2000s	on test focus, content and research questions; lead on needs analysis; jointly work on item writing and test specifications; contribute to data collection Collaborate with language assessment specialists beyond the initial test development (e.g. in ongoing task vetting, dissemination and marketing)		
	Initiate the test development project and recruit a task force consisting of domain experts and language assessment specialists Unilaterally decide on general test design principles (e.g. skills coverage, test content, language) without consulting language assessment specialists Collaborate with language assessment specialists in needs analysis based on content specialists' intuitions Collaborate with language assessment specialists during test development (item writing, piloting), standard setting, training and standardisation of oral examiners	Elements of CBPR	FCAA Test of Aviation English/ Huhta (2009)

(Widdowson 1983:33). The latter were criticised for a thorough lack of empiricism, neglect of a major source of information (content experts), as well as for limited coverage in ESP syllabus design (Long 2005) and ESP test development (Clapham 1981, Criper 1981, Skehan 1984).

The revised English Language Testing Service (ELTS), introduced in 1980, was seen to be a product of such tradition. The test was criticised for being based on applied linguists' intuitions of what hypothetical and prototypical test takers would be required to do in each of the several academic disciplines (Clapham 1981, Criper 1981). Carroll (1981) explained that time constraints steered test developers away from observing what students do during their courses and guided them towards a less generalisable and a more subjective, case-study approach to determining the needs of students in different academic disciplines. So, test developers focused 'the collection and interpretation of data on a real, or at least, a putative individual so as to counteract the natural but dangerous tendency to overgeneralise about communicative needs' (Carroll 1981:71). Some test developers on the team may have had a background which bridged the applied linguistics and the content specialist world, e.g. 'the Business Studies specification involved two staff members one of whom had published a course in Business English, the other had a degree in Commerce and had lectured in Economics and Accountancy to adults . . . The Medical profile was prepared by a staff member with considerable experience in teaching a University Medical English course and who had close family connections in Medicine' (Carroll 1981:69). However, the needs analysis that informed revisions to ELTS was very far from the comprehensiveness, objectivity and rigour of those which informed ESP tests to come.

In the domain of ESP syllabus design, the focus of ESP needs analysts gradually shifted from the product (e.g. taxonomies of linguistic items) to the task and the process, i.e. workplace or academic tasks and the processes and strategies students employ when engaged in their tasks (Long 2005, Robinson 1991). This shift was accompanied by a growing reliance on content specialists as research subjects or informants. In the domain of ESP assessment, the empirical void of the early 1980s began filling up with needs analyses which fed into the development of the Test of English for Educational Purposes (TEEP; Weir 1983). Using Munby's taxonomy of language skills and sub-skills as a basis for data collection instruments, Weir (1983) devised questionnaires and carried out observations in the university and college setting in the UK. This methodology provided rich and empirically grounded findings, shedding light on study demands of overseas students in the UK, the frequency of activities and the difficulties such activities presented.

A few years after TEEP was developed, a re-designed test of English for overseas-trained health professionals – the Occupational English Test (OET) – was launched in Australia in 1987. A range of expert informants with a background in healthcare had been consulted and directly observed in their workplace activities in order to ensure the relevance of OET to the healthcare context in terms of content, language, task format, language ability and skills. As a result, key tasks in the healthcare sector and their essential features were identified (McNamara 1996:100).

All the above instances of test development are examples of a traditional approach within which content specialists acted only as sources of information. Their role was more significant in the development of the Japanese Test for Tour Guides (Brown 1993), as the initiative was part of an industry-driven accreditation scheme for tour guides. Language assessment specialists were commissioned by content specialists to develop the test and assessment criteria. The content specialists' requirement was that the ability to interact properly with a client be assessed along with language proficiency. The needs analysis and test development stages were fairly traditional in that they were carried out by language assessment specialists, who observed content specialists at work or interviewed industry representatives, reviewed literature and designed the tasks themselves. However, assessment criteria and performance descriptors were a product of true collaboration between language assessment specialists and tour guides who teamed up for a period of two weeks. There is no indication that the collaboration continued beyond the initial project, and content specialists were indeed referred to as 'informants' rather than partners, but it is clear that there were elements of CBPR in this project: the professional community identified the problem, initiated the project and worked with assessment specialists as collaborators and learners during one stage of the process. The attitude of the assessment specialist who authored the paper is congruent with CBPR as she vehemently argues for collaboration: 'we must not allow ourselves as language testers to . . . make unilateral decisions about how candidates should be tested and what the assessment criteria should be. Rather we must go back to these people [representatives of the industry] and find out how they themselves best consider assessments of performance should be made' (Brown 1993:49).

In the 2000s (see Table 2), examples of test development enterprises that were envisaged as CBPR, and explicitly adhered to many CBPR principles, included the development of *ILEC* and *Cambridge English: Financial* aka the *International Certificate of Financial English (ICFE)*. Cambridge English perceived the need for a cyclical and iterative engagement with legal content specialists in the development of *ILEC*, 'from the first design of the test through to the ongoing production of live test material' (Corkill and Robinson 2006:10). Precisely due to the ESP nature of *ILEC*, bringing together two kinds of expertise was deemed essential for creating a test that would sustainably meet the needs of the legal community, by being 'fit for purpose and accessible to candidates with a range of experience and from different jurisdictions' (Corkill and Robinson 2006:10). The development of *ILEC* is discussed at length in the remaining sections of this chapter.

At about the same time as *ILEC*, another test development project took place – a Test for Air Traffic Controllers (ELPAC) – which could also be considered an example of CBPR in language assessment (see Table 2). Content specialists took a lead on the test development project, but the relationship between content specialists and language assessment specialists was collaborative, extensive and, apparently, long term and iterative. The plan was to extend collaboration to post-test development activities through a series of workshops to train test administrators, markers and examiners and create new teams of item writers (Enright 2005). Another test development project within a related domain, FCAA Test of Aviation English (Huhta 2009), had elements of CBPR: it was initiated by the industry specialists who established a task force consisting of aviation, language and testing experts. The task force worked together on 'intuitive' needs analysis and item writing (see Table 2). There was a sense of commitment to meeting a common goal, sharing expertise and learning from it: 'the aviation experts and testing/language experts learned a lot from each other, and there was a genuine desire to develop a maximally useful and defensible test' (Huhta 2009:26.13). However, certain key decisions about language testing were made unilaterally by the contracting aviation organisation without necessarily having been subject to discussion, and there was no continued collaboration with assessment specialists beyond the initial project.

Next, we turn to a discussion of the development of *ILEC*, a Cambridge English test of English for law students and legal professionals and its development through a CBPR design.

Snapshot of the *ILEC* test development study

Key goals:

- agree on the roles of legal content specialists and language assessment specialists in *ILEC* test development and live test production to build a sustainable relationship
- develop a valid and reliable test which is needed by, and is relevant to, the global legal community.

Approach and design:

- An exploratory sequential mixed methods design (instrument development model) was used within a community-based participatory research approach to test development (this approach also has elements of the 'embedded design', see Ziegler and Kang, Chapter 4, this volume). The design was selected with the goal to explore the language needs of target test users and develop a test that would meet their real-life language needs.
- Research partners: Cambridge English Language Assessment (language assessment specialists) and TransLegal (legal content specialists).
- The community research participants: lawyers from legal firms, departments and associations, lecturers from university law departments, law students and legal English instructors. They were involved in various phases of the project by providing their perceptions of *ILEC* (its relevance, authenticity and breadth of coverage) and taking the test.

Qualitative data collection and analysis:

- Phase 1 (needs analysis) consisted of focus group discussions and the collection of open-ended written comments; key themes were analysed and the language needs of lawyers were identified.

- Phases 2 and 3 (viability and trial studies): data was collected through perception and attitudinal questionnaires; open-ended responses were analysed for key themes to inform modifications to the test.
- Post-launch *ILEC* test construction/production: expert judgements of language assessment specialists (during the item writing, test editing, and test construction stages) and legal content specialists (during the vetting of legal content and language) inform decisions on item revision and test construction.

Quantitative data collection and analysis:

- Phases 2 and 3 (viability and trial studies):
  - Perception and attitudinal questionnaires; frequency counts and percentages were used to analyse fixed-choice questionnaire responses and investigate the authenticity and appropriateness of *ILEC* for the target candidature.
  - *ILEC* test administered in Phase 3; Classical Test Theory (CTT) and Item Response Theory (IRT) statistics were used to analyse test responses and determine test reliability and other statistical properties at item and task level.
- Post-launch *ILEC* test construction/production: pretest and live test data is analysed using CTT and IRT to produce item and task-level statistics, which inform expert judgement and feed into further stages of test construction.

Integration

An outcome of one phase fed directly into the next phase (see Figure 1). In the first phase, qualitative needs analysis research resulted in a sample test of *ILEC*. This test and questionnaires were used in the second phase to investigate the perceived validity of the test and its market viability. As a result, the test was refined. The refined test was administered to a sample of test takers in the third, and final, phase along with another set of questionnaires, to determine its validity and statistical properties. A further test refinement was informed by the findings of the third phase.

ILEC test development

Research goals

The key goal of *ILEC* test development was to create a valid and reliable test which is needed by, and is relevant to, the global legal community. Therefore,

Figure 1 An overview of the main phases in the development of ILEC

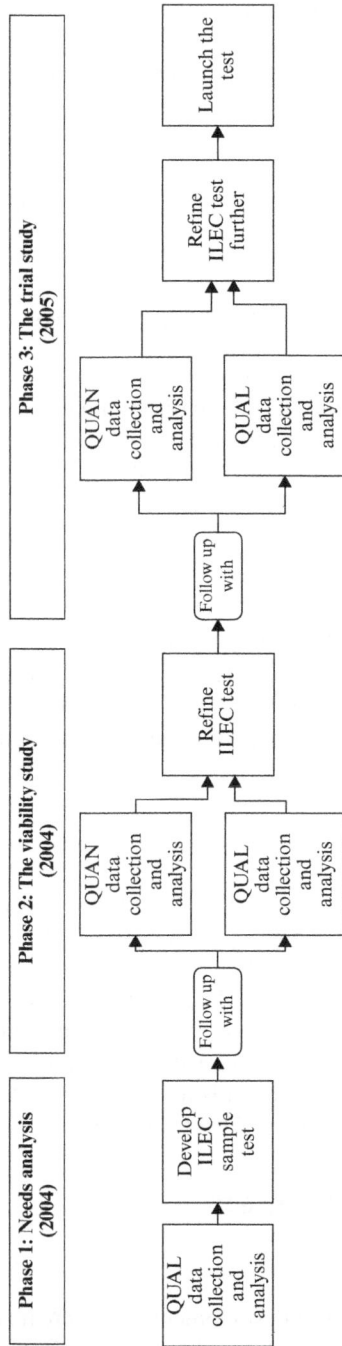

it was necessary to design a test which reflects the authentic use of language in the legal domain and ensure that test tasks possess the features which place similar requirements on test takers as real-life tasks in the same domain. This is congruent with a socio-cognitive approach to language assessment (see Weir (2005) and Figure 1 in Saville, Chapter 2, this volume). The ultimate aim was to achieve a positive impact on test takers and other test users. As stated by Saville (see 'Construct definition and validation – A socio-cognitive approach' in Chapter 2, this volume), test impact has become a central consideration for test providers. Saville specifically stresses the importance of impact by design which requires ensuring from the outset – from the initial test design stage – that an examination can have positive effects and consequences on its users. The initial test design and development stage, which is the focus of this chapter, corresponds to the first two steps in the Operational assessment cycle (see Figure 2 in Chapter 2, this volume).

Given the collaborative nature of the project, another goal was to define the roles of legal content specialists and language assessment specialists in *ILEC* test development and live test production in order to build a sustainable long-term relationship.

Research partners and research participants

Research partners

Cambridge English Language Assessment is an organisation with long-standing expertise in all aspects of language assessment: test development, item writing, live test production and research and validation. The community research partner of Cambridge English Language Assessment was TransLegal, an international firm of 'lawyer-linguists'. Their staff are former practising lawyers, many of whom have taught at university level. They are specialists in the European, UK and US jurisdictions, providing legal translations, instructions and training in legal English. With an apparent sensitivity to language-related issues, and bridging professional and academic legal worlds in their ranks, TransLegal was seen to be a suitable partner in the development of a language test tailored to legal settings. The firm was founded in Stockholm, Sweden in 1989, but has extended its reach ever since, with offices in Frankfurt, Paris, Oslo and Madrid. This was beneficial as it facilitated a wide geographical coverage for the purposes of test development research.

Research participants

As some aspects of research informing *ILEC* test development had strong elements of the traditional approach, there were also 'traditional' research participants whose function was to provide information (e.g. opinions on the new test) rather than collaboratively shape *ILEC* test development.

Since *ILEC* is intended for law students and legal professionals, research participants were drawn from academia and law firms, in collaboration with TransLegal. They were legal professionals, lecturers in law, law students and legal English instructors. Besides being varied by type of workplace and levels of legal content knowledge, the research participants were also geographically diverse. Europe had the highest representation, with more limited coverage of non-European countries (Brazil, China and Indonesia). More specific information on different groups of research participants in each phase is provided in the following sections: Phase 1: Needs analysis and sample test design, Phase 2: The viability study, and Phase 3: The trial study.

The conception of the *ILEC* test development project is discussed next, with a focus on discussions related to test construct as well as decisions on the roles of research partners.

Project conception: Test construct and the roles of research partners

Two overarching questions, with associated sub-questions, formed part of the project conception, and guided *ILEC* test development:

1. What should be tested in *ILEC*? Should *ILEC* be a test of language in a legal context or a test of language and legal knowledge?
   - How can language and legal knowledge be separated to make *ILEC* a language test only?
   - Which aspects of language ability should be tested?
2. What are the roles of legal content specialists and language assessment specialists in *ILEC* test development and live test production?

The involvement of legal content specialists and language assessment specialists on *ILEC* test development formed the foundation for a fruitful collaboration. The need for a test of English for legal candidature had been identified independently by both partners to be. Through their work with lawyers, government employees involved in legal issues, trainees and law students, TransLegal perceived the need for a test of legal English, which is consistent with CBPR principles (see Table 1). They approached Cambridge English Language Assessment and initial discussions revealed that the latter had already been interested in such an examination.

Partners with different expertise inevitably have different perspectives and priorities, which became evident during discussions on what *ILEC* should test and why. Initially, TransLegal thought that the examination should primarily test legal vocabulary in different areas of law (e.g. banking and finance law, corporate law). The reason for this was that the majority of those taught by TransLegal staff were particularly interested in legal vocabulary which they sometimes found difficult to interpret. The view of Cambridge English

Language Assessment was that the coverage of the exam should be much broader, to include the assessment of all major language skills (reading, listening, speaking and writing), besides the knowledge of vocabulary and (lexico-)grammar. The rationale for the wider and more balanced coverage was two-fold:

- the inferences derived from test performance would be generalisable to a non-test situation
- the test would be a language test, rather than a test of legal knowledge, which a vocabulary test only would have had a high risk of becoming.

Since both partners wanted a test of language ability rather than legal knowledge, the discussion was resolved by a joint decision that *ILEC* should test all four language skills as well as Use of English (the knowledge of vocabulary and grammar). The understanding was that the future collaborative work on test development would ensure the creation of items/tasks where the content is specific to the legal profession, but where performance can be rated on the basis of language ability only. So, for example, listening comprehension questions would test 'understanding through language rather than fine points of technical expertise' (Whitehead 2003:11), and a similar principle would apply to papers testing productive skills (Speaking and Writing). This was also important in view of the fact that examiners would be language (assessment) specialists, rather than lawyers. Teasing out language ability from content knowledge is a subtle (and sometimes impossible) task, especially in view of the fact that one of the features distinguishing ESP tests from General English tests is specific purpose language ability, which combines language knowledge and content knowledge (see 'Community-based participatory research: Definition and principles'). Given the complexities of navigating through these waters, the collaborative work of legal and language assessment specialists was certainly a necessary aspect of the project.

Another related point of consideration was the level of content specificity. It was deemed that making *ILEC* highly specific would introduce numerous issues. Firstly, legal content knowledge would most likely have a strong effect on language performance (Clapham 1996). Consequently, separate test versions would need to be created for different specialisms and different legal jurisdictions, so that candidates would not be disadvantaged. This would be very resource intensive and impractical. Moreover, if *ILEC* were highly specific, it would be difficult to determine whether inadequate performance on the test was due to inadequate language ability or inadequate background knowledge. Secondly, item writing would be wrought with difficulties. Highly specific texts may not be (fully) understandable by language specialist item writers which could make item writing difficult or, unreliable. This would require TransLegal to make all the judgments on the quality of texts and items and heavily reduce the role of language specialists' expertise and the benefits of this expertise in the construction of a *language* test. In view of the above issues, it was jointly decided that the level of specificity should be such that *ILEC* would be accessible to lawyers with different specialisms, law students and language specialist item writers who would be able to select appropriate texts and write adequate items, which would then be vetted by legal content specialists for legal language, content and jurisdiction neutrality.

The next step was to define the roles of the two research partners in the test development process and beyond. Since authenticity and specificity are key features of ESP tests (see 'Community-based participatory research: Definition and principles' and 'The evolving role of content specialists in ESP'), it was envisaged that, during test development, TransLegal would carry out a needs analysis, provide authentic materials and vet tasks for their legal language, content and international accessibility (see Table 3). TransLegal also initially contributed to item writing, after some basic

Table 3 The role of the legal community research partner in test development and beyond

Time period	Stage	Activity
2003–2005	Phase 1: Needs analysis and sample test design	Needs analysis, e.g. what lawyers read, write, listen to, etc. Advice on test content, e.g. areas of the law that the test should cover, types of legal documentation and context in the test Advice on test design, e.g. task types and timing Advice on sources (e.g. books, journals, websites) Provision of item writing materials (e.g. task scenarios, topics, Writing test tasks, legal correspondence, etc.) Vetting the texts selected by Cambridge English Language Assessment item writers – for the appropriateness of language and content Vetting items written or modified by Cambridge English Language Assessment item writers – for authenticity, international accessibility
2003–2006	Phase 2 and Phase 3: Viability and trial studies	Contribute to data collection by providing research participants in questionnaire design for the viability study Vet changes made to the test by Cambridge English Language Assessment, as a result of the viability and trial studies
2006 onwards	Post launch	Continued advice on sources, where necessary Continued provision of item writing materials, where necessary Initial vetting of the legal content of texts selected by Cambridge English Language Assessment item writers Vetting of the legal content of items written by Cambridge English Language Assessment item writers Marketing

training by Cambridge English Language Assessment. The intention was that their role in item writing would diminish as Cambridge English Language Assessment item writers become more experienced in sourcing legal materials and writing tasks for *ILEC*. This happened in due course, thanks to TransLegal's needs analysis and the training they provided on the areas of law to cover or avoid, types of scenarios, legal topics, tasks, etc.

In view of language assessment expertise, it was agreed that Cambridge English Language Assessment would play a key role in item writing, editing, pretesting, analysis, banking of test items and question paper construction. After the launch of *ILEC* in 2006, TransLegal would continue to provide the necessary legal expertise during item editing, proofing and task vetting. Given their networks, TransLegal would also help provide access to decision makers in order to facilitate the recognition of *ILEC* by law schools and legal organisations.

It is evident from the above discussion that the two research partners complemented each other well. In line with CBPR principles (see Table 1), their collaboration was envisaged to underlie, and did indeed underlie, all aspects of the project. Discussion and agreement on a range of test development issues and the relevance of different types of expertise guided decisions on when the two partners would work together on the same aspect of the *ILEC* test development process (e.g. initial item writing, provision of test materials) and when one or the other would take a lead (e.g. TransLegal in needs analysis, Cambridge English Language Assessment in test construction). Consistent with a CBPR approach (see Table 1), both partners learned from each other in the process.

Research design

The mixed methods design employed in this study was exploratory sequential, which is well suited to developing instruments (Creswell and Plano Clark 2011:86, Creswell and Zhou, Chapter 3, this volume, Ziegler and Kang, Chapter 4, this volume). In this case, the instrument was a language test. Figure 2 represents all the steps within this design.

Since it was necessary to learn about language use and the linguistic needs of lawyers without preconceptions that a quantitative data collection technique would entail (see Phase 1: Needs analysis and sample test design for discussion), the first phase was a qualitative, exploratory needs analysis. Therefore, in Phase 1 of the study, qualitative data on lawyers' language use and needs in a legal workplace was obtained via focus groups. As a result, an *ILEC* sample test and test specifications were developed in 2004 (see 'Phase 1: Needs analysis and sample test design'). In Phase 2, the sample test was presented to the key test users. Their views on the suitability and relevance of the test to lawyers and law students, and the need for such a test, were elicited via questionnaires. The questionnaires provided mostly quantitative and some

Figure 2 A fine-grained overview of ILEC test development (procedures, products, timeline)

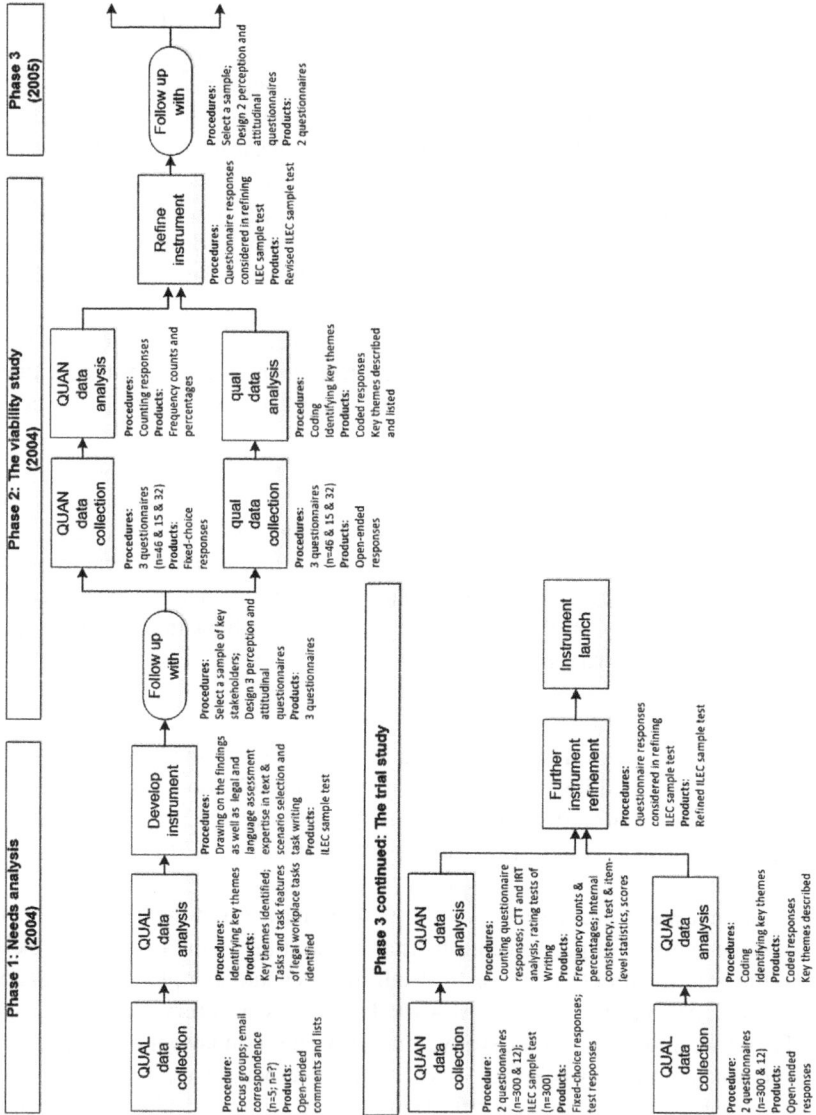

Phase 1: Needs analysis (2004)

QUAL data collection
Procedure:
Focus groups; email correspondence (n=5; n=7)
Products:
Open-ended comments and lists

QUAL data analysis
Procedures:
Identifying key themes
Products:
Key themes identified; Tasks and task features of legal workplace tasks identified

Develop instrument
Procedures:
Drawing on the findings as well as legal and language assessment expertise in text & scenario selection and task writing
Products:
ILEC sample test

Follow up with
Procedures:
Select a sample of key stakeholders; Design 3 perception and attitudinal questionnaires
Products:
3 questionnaires

Phase 2: The viability study (2004)

QUAN data collection
Procedures:
3 questionnaires (n=46 & 15 & 32)
Products:
Fixed-choice responses

QUAN data analysis
Procedures:
Counting responses
Products:
Frequency counts and percentages

qual data collection
Procedures:
3 questionnaires (n=46 & 15 & 32)
Products:
Open-ended responses

qual data analysis
Procedures:
Coding
Identifying key themes
Products:
Coded responses
Key themes described and listed

Refine instrument
Procedures:
Questionnaire responses considered in refining ILEC sample test
Products:
Revised ILEC sample test

Phase 3 (2005)

Follow up with
Procedures:
Select a sample; Design 2 perception and attitudinal questionnaires
Products:
2 questionnaires

Phase 3 continued: The trial study

QUAN data collection
Procedure:
2 questionnaires (n=300 & 12); ILEC sample test (n=300)
Products:
Fixed-choice responses; test responses

QUAN data analysis
Procedures:
Counting questionnaire responses; CTT and IRT analysis; rating tests of Writing
Products:
Frequency counts & percentages; Internal consistency, test & item-level statistics, scores

Further instrument refinement
Procedures:
Questionnaire responses considered in refining ILEC sample test
Products:
Refined ILEC sample test

Instrument launch

QUAL data collection
Procedure:
2 questionnaires (n=300 & 12)
Products:
Open-ended responses

QUAL data analysis
Procedures:
Coding
Identifying key themes
Products:
Coded responses
Key themes described

qualitative data (through open-ended questions) which fed into decisions on test modification (see 'Phase 2: The viability study'). Phase 2 resulted in a refinement of the test, which was subsequently trialled in the third phase (2005). In the third phase, the test and another set of questionnaires were used to collect mostly quantitative and some qualitative data (through open-ended questions) to investigate the validity and reliability of the test as well as the need for any further modifications to the test (see 'Phase 3: The trial study'). Within the overarching exploratory sequential design, a triangulation design – 'validating quantitative data model' – was implemented in the second and third phases. In this design, open-ended items are 'an add-on to a quantitative survey' and they validate and/or expand on the quantitative survey findings (Creswell and Plano Clark 2011:81). However, this component was a secondary part of the design; still the overarching design was exploratory sequential which was adopted to develop a valid and reliable test.

The discussion now moves to the three phases in *ILEC* test development.

Phase 1: Needs analysis and sample test design

The first phase of *ILEC* test development, a needs analysis, was carried out to identify the needs of the legal community in terms of their daily tasks and the types of documents they read and write. This was followed by a design of an *ILEC* sample test (see Figure 2).

The key questions that guided this phase were the following:

- What areas of law should be covered in *ILEC* and why?
- What are the key tasks in the relevant areas of law and what are their features?
- What documents do lawyers read and write?

Legal content specialists from TransLegal with their staff in Stockholm, Frankfurt, Paris, Oslo and Madrid carried out the needs analysis. Following that, Cambridge English language assessment specialists, such as chairs, item writers and subject officers, considered the results of the needs analysis and drew on them, as well as their language assessment expertise, to design a sample test of *ILEC*.

QUALITATIVE data collection and analysis in Phase 1

The needs analysis was entrusted largely to TransLegal. This was done in view of their legal expertise and to avoid the problem that traditional needs analyses suffer from – that of preconceived notions which language (assessment) specialists bring to the analysis of language use, such as the notions on what is salient in tasks in profession/discipline-specific domains outside of their expertise. These notions may or may not be the same as those of content specialists, because a need in needs analysis is a 'value judgment' on a problem, so 'people with different values recognise different needs . . . the person seeing the need and the person experiencing the need may differ' (McKilip 1987:10). Therefore, the goal of the needs analysis was to identify the key tasks, their key features and language skills that are necessary in a legal setting, from the perspective of content specialists. The outcomes of the analysis fed into the design of the *ILEC* sample test in this phase (see Figure 2).

A combination of data collection techniques was employed. The needs analysis started with a focus group of five TransLegal lawyers: two American and one British, Canadian and Swedish respectively. Introspecting and drawing together on their expertise, experience, practice books and the internet, they first identified international commercial law as a subject area appropriate for *ILEC*, since commercial lawyers are the largest single group of lawyers who use English on a daily basis. Subject areas that are not too jurisdiction specific, and hence, not likely to disadvantage international candidates were also recommended (e.g. contract law, sale of goods, remedies). This led to a specification of books and documents that lawyers read and write, what lawyers listen to, and in general – what they do across all four skills (reading, listening, speaking and writing). The main topic areas (e.g. the office/general legal environment and routine, entertainment of clients/relationships with colleagues and clients, travel and conferences), language functions (e.g. justifying decisions or past actions, discussing interests and leisure activities), task purpose, the recipient/audience and level of formality were also listed and categorised. Since nearly all live conversations are protected by attorney–client privilege, observations of lawyers at work were not possible.

Notes were taken during focus group discussions. The notes were analysed for themes and coded by TransLegal research partners; categories and subcategories were identified (e.g. different task features discussed above). Following that, the lists specifying topic areas, language functions, tasks, task purpose, etc. were drafted by the focus group and circulated for comment to TransLegal's offices throughout Europe. TransLegal lawyers from Frankfurt, Paris, Stockholm, Oslo and Madrid provided needs information from their various countries, to ensure that *ILEC* is internationally accessible and appropriate. These comments were reviewed and discussed by the focus group, until agreement was reached on the final drafts.

The outcome of the needs analysis was the identification of the areas of law to cover in *ILEC*, key sources (e.g. books, documents), tasks performed in a legal workplace setting and their features (e.g. topics, text types, language functions, task purpose, the audience). These were presented as lists and tables. Taking into account the findings from the needs analysis, as well as drawing on assessment and psychometric theory and practice, Cambridge English Language Assessment considered the tasks that 'could be authentically simulated in a testing situation in such a way that they could be used to assess language proficiency' in a valid, reliable and practical way (Corkill and Robinson 2006:10). This resulted in the refinement of the lists and tables produced during the needs analysis (e.g. lists of key sources, text types) as the partners were working their way through a sample test design. An account of how a sample test was developed and what challenges were encountered during this process is provided next.

In order to create sample Reading and Listening tasks, the needs analysis was drawn on for the selection of topics, content and text types, as well as a range of scenarios in the case of Listening, in particular. The task of TransLegal was to select texts for the *ILEC* Reading comprehension sample paper. These were then used by Cambridge English Language Assessment to create the Reading comprehension tasks while drawing on key assessment and psychometric principles as well as the reading skills required in the legal context. Listening comprehension tasks were also created by Cambridge English Language Assessment. Both partners reviewed and critiqued each other's materials.

Text selection emerged as a major issue. Even though texts selected by TransLegal were legal in nature, some were not suitable from an assessment perspective. The reasons for this were several:

1. Texts did not lend themselves to the creation of items with good distractors, so that, for example, it was impossible to provide equally appropriate/attractive answer options for 4-option multiple-choice questions consistently.
2. Gapped texts 'need to be a coherent whole, not a series of bits', which was problematic in view of the nature of a vast majority of legal texts provided as they had bullet points and were divided into sub-sections (Harrison 2003).
3. List-like and factual texts would make it difficult 'to produce items that are challenging enough for the level [CEFR B2 and C1], since the items will be largely testing facts rather than ideas' (Harrison 2003).
4. In the case of authentic legal texts, there are limits to how much a text can be edited to ensure its suitability for the target candidature without changing its legal meaning.

A further issue was the specificity of text content. The texts selected by TransLegal were 'highly specialist, dense in technical terms and a kind that practising lawyers would have to read during the course of their work' (Harrison 2003). Language assessment specialists without a legal background struggled to produce a sample paper based on those, and further issues regarding a high level of test specificity were already discussed in 'Project conception: Test construct and the roles of research partners'. On the other hand, TransLegal did not find the texts selected by Cambridge

English Language Assessment to be specific enough as they were accessible to readers without a legal background. The nature, topic and contexts of texts remained an issue and a challenge for a while, and the clash in expectations required that test specificity be revisited and re-negotiated before they could be reshaped in view of language assessment constraints. The constraints were: suitability for a wide range of target candidates; item writers' lack of legal background; and the ability to find 'suitable materials to match test specifications in sufficient quantities consistently'. Eventually, a common understanding on the level of text specificity was reached and both research partners also agreed on Reading and Listening test structure in terms of task types, task order, and number of items.

As far as Speaking and Writing test components are concerned, TransLegal selected scenarios and topics for sample Speaking tasks and created sample Writing tasks, drawing on the findings from the needs analysis. Cambridge English Language Assessment then created sample Speaking tasks following assessment theory and best assessment practice, as well as the findings of the needs analysis in terms of the speaking and writing skills required in the legal environment. Again, the research partners reviewed and critiqued each other's materials. The key considerations were task purpose, the audience (which informed language, content and the level of formality), task type (e.g. a letter to a client, a report to a managing partner, a proposal) and interaction type in Speaking (e.g. a monologue, an interview with an examiner, a discussion with another test taker). The main challenge was creating tasks that were suitable both for law students who have not worked in a legal environment and legal professionals. These considerations informed task design, so that some tasks allowed a choice between two or three options (some more technical and some less so), while those without options were written in such a way as to be accessible both to law students and law professionals.

In line with CBPR principles, the sample test design was the result of a dialogue between TransLegal and Cambridge English Language Assessment and an agreement on test structure, content, test focus and task format. The findings from the needs analysis, language assessment theory, psychometric theory and best assessment practice informed sample test design.

Phase 2: The viability study

In the second phase of *ILEC* test development, the goals were to determine if *ILEC* was needed by the global legal community and also to gauge the key stakeholders' (i.e. test users') perceptions of the *ILEC* sample test.

Three research questions guided the viability study:

- Is there a need within the global legal community for an internationally recognised method of assessing English language skills?
- Is there a need for *ILEC*?

- Is *ILEC* perceived as valid by the key stakeholders (i.e. test users) in terms of authenticity, targeted proficiency levels, and the appropriateness of timing?

At the data collection stage, the two research partners, TransLegal and Cambridge English Language Assessment, collaborated by identifying and contacting potential research participants and by co-designing the questionnaires. Cambridge English Language Assessment analysed the data and wrote a report.

The research participants who were identified as 'suitably qualified to offer an opinion' (Corkill and Robinson 2006:11) were contacted. However, the role of the global legal community was that of a traditional research participant – as questionnaire respondents, they were sources of information for researchers. They represented a range of jurisdictions which were based on common law and civil law (Corkill and Robinson 2006:11) and they were pooled from a variety of countries. This diversity was necessary to ensure the appropriateness of *ILEC*, and gauge the need for it across jurisdictions and countries. The participants are listed below:

- 34 legal organisations (e.g. law firms, legal departments in multinational firms, international lawyer and Bar associations and governments, e.g. Supreme Courts) in China, Czech Republic, Denmark, France, Germany, Greece, Italy, Spain, Sweden and the UK
- 12 university law faculties in Belgium, China, France, Germany, Italy, Latvia, Netherlands and Spain
- 15 legal English instructors from Brazil, France, Germany, Indonesia, Ireland, Italy, Russia and Spain
- 32 test takers (law students and legal professionals).

QUANTITATIVE and qualitative data collection and analysis in Phase 2

In Phase 2 (see Figure 2), the sample *ILEC* test was presented to research participants from the legal community to obtain feedback on test viability (in terms of the potential of future usage), the relevance of test tasks and their content, test structure, timing, and the proposed proficiency levels. The feedback was obtained via three questionnaires: one for practising lawyers and lecturers in law, one for legal English tutors and one for test takers who took the sample test. The questionnaires predominantly contained fixed-choice questions which required selecting the level of agreement on a 5-point scale, 5 corresponding to strong agreement and 1 to strong disagreement. Respondents were also given the choice of 'not applicable'. Therefore, the questionnaire data was mostly quantitative, but some was qualitative, having been obtained via open-ended questions.

The quantitative data was analysed through frequency counts and percentages to arrive at findings on the perceived validity of *ILEC* and confirm the market need for *ILEC*. A majority of respondents confirmed that there was a need within the global legal community for an internationally recognised method of assessing English language skills and that their organisation would recognise *ILEC* as reliable evidence of advanced legal English skills. Their view on the relevance of *ILEC* test tasks and content was very positive with at least 75% of respondents in each group agreeing that the test tasks and the language skills tested were authentic and appropriate in a test of legal English (Chamberlain and Robinson 2004).

Open-ended responses were analysed for key themes to expand on the quantitative survey findings. Some of them fed into a refinement to the test design. Some others were considered and rejected. For example, there were suggestions that the test could be 'sectorial', with different versions for each area of law. However, this would have reduced the practicality of the examination and it would have introduced issues associated with differences in legal jurisdictions, as well as, possibly, the problem of choice among alternatives. The latter was an issue for ELTS which had several subject-specific modules for prospective students, with some having a difficulty identifying the most appropriate module (Criper and Davies 1988).

Phase 3: The trial study

In Phase 3 (see Figure 2), the modified version of *ILEC* was trialled by Cambridge English Language Assessment. The aim was to re-examine the authenticity of the modified *ILEC* examination, investigate the psychometric properties of the test and arrive at suggestions for any further modifications. A test of *ILEC* was administered to test takers, which was followed up with questionnaires eliciting feedback on the test from test takers, legal English instructors and Cambridge English language examiners. Quantitative data about validity and reliability of the test was obtained through the test of *ILEC* and the questionnaires. Qualitative data about the validity of the test was obtained through several open-ended questions in the same questionnaire and also through shadowing the test takers during the test.

The key questions explored in this phase were the following:

- Is *ILEC* perceived as valid by the key stakeholders, in terms of authenticity, skills coverage, clarity of instructions, timing and task weighting?
- Is *ILEC* a reliable test?
- Does *ILEC* differentiate across CEFR levels?

A total of 300 test takers sat the *ILEC* test and completed a feedback questionnaire. The test takers were law students and legal professionals with the following first languages: French (41%), Italian (8%), German (7%), Chinese, Czech, Polish, Romanian, Spanish and Swedish (all below 5% each). In addition, 12 legal English instructors completed the feedback questionnaire, thus providing their views on the test. Finally, several examiners who marked writing and speaking performances provided their views on the clarity of task instructions in their questionnaire responses.

The test

All four components of *ILEC*, Reading, Listening, Speaking and Writing, were administered to test takers. The Reading and Listening test data was analysed using CTT and IRT to examine the statistical performance of the test and its items, as well as test reliability. SPSS analysis produced descriptive statistics on Speaking and Writing test results.

The quantitative findings revealed that the *ILEC* trial test was reliable, as seen in the high Cronbach's alpha values for the Reading and Listening tests (0.93 and 0.88 respectively, out of 1.0). The reliability of individual test scores was also adequate, the standard error of measurement (SEM) being 3.2 for Reading and 2.2 for Listening. The conclusion was that the majority of candidates would achieve an appropriate grade (e.g. below B1, B1, C1 or above) and that the cut-off scores at the bands were appropriate (Thighe 2005).

Item facility and discrimination were also calculated to check on the performance of items and tasks. It was determined that all Reading and Listening items and tasks discriminate adequately between low-performing and high-performing candidates and it was also shown that most tasks had an appropriate level of facility, but the facility of some was too high or too low (Thighe 2005).

The correlation between test parts within Reading and Listening, respectively, was adequate. All parts correlated moderately or strongly with each other (0.43–0.74 in Reading and 0.47–0.62 in Listening; Thighe 2005). This indicated that there was an acceptable overlap between test parts in terms of their assessment focus and that they test the same broad underlying construct.

Questionnaire feedback: Test takers and Legal English instructors

The quantitative questionnaire data consisted of responses to fixed-choice questions. Research participants were asked to respond to statements by indicating their level of agreement on a 5-point scale. This data was analysed through frequency counts and percentages.

The questionnaire feedback on the authenticity of the test was largely positive and consistent with the findings of the viability study from the previous phase. Most trial candidates (legal professionals and law students) and legal English tutors agreed or strongly agreed that all components of the *ILEC* examination were authentic, containing topics, texts and language likely to be encountered in a legal setting.

Qualitative data was obtained through a few open-ended questions in the questionnaires and through shadowing of the trial candidates. Open-ended responses were analysed for key themes, which showed that the *ILEC* examination was authentic and relevant to the target candidature. The qualitative questionnaire findings, along with shadowing, also revealed that the timing of the examination components and task weighting was adequate.

Questionnaire feedback: Cambridge English Language Assessment examiners

The examiners provided qualitative feedback on the clarity of task instructions, drawing on the instructions themselves and test takers' performances. The instructions were generally found to be clear. However, they noticed that in the test of Writing, a majority of candidates wrote 'a general answer to a vague reader' regardless of the task instructions and that some of them had 'borrowed' considerable chunks of text from task instructions and incorporated them in their responses. The former had implications for communications to stakeholders (e.g. tips for teachers and test takers) and the latter resulted in revisions to task rubrics.

As a result of the trial, some minor changes were made to test processes and systems such as the collection of candidate information and the anchoring process (a statistical procedure for item banking purposes) as well as to task instructions. In general, the trial indicated that *ILEC* was a valid and reliable test of legal English, differentiating well between candidates at C1, B2 and below B2 levels of English language ability, according to the CEFR. The outcome of the last phase was the launch of *ILEC* in May 2006.

Post-launch: *ILEC* test production phase

The main focus of the chapter has been the test development phase. Once a test has been designed, trialled and finalised, the live test production phase begins with test launch (see Saville, Chapter 2, this volume for an overview of the operational assessment cycle). Live *ILEC* test production is the responsibility of Cambridge English Language Assessment, but the collaboration with legal content specialists continues. A team with expertise in English language teaching and assessment, consisting of a chair and item writers, creates tasks and ensures that their topics, content and language are appropriate and in line with test specifications and item writer guidelines. Tasks pass through several cycles managed by an Assessment Manager, from pre-editing and editing, through pretesting and pretest review, to live test construction. The expert judgement of legal content specialists is solicited before pre-editing and editing, when a panel of jurisdiction specialists consisting of Swedish, UK, US, German, French and Spanish legal experts vet the legal content, language and jurisdiction neutrality of *ILEC* question papers. They make a judgement on text/task accessibility to all target candidates regardless of work experience and jurisdiction, the authenticity of scenarios and dialogues, the appropriate use of legal terminology and nuances in legal content before and after text edits.

The qualitative judgement of language assessment and legal content specialists informs item writing and editing stages, while item- and task-level statistics obtained from pretesting and live test sessions inform the judgement of assessment specialists on rejecting, reviewing or accepting items and tasks, and feed into further stages of live test construction.

Integration

The integration of qualitative and quantitative data and findings in this mixed methods project occurred through a linking of outcomes from each research phase: the outcome of the first phase – a sample *ILEC* test – fed into the viability and test validation research carried out in the second phase. The outcome of the second phase (i.e. a refined *ILEC* test) was used in the third phase for more thorough test validation research. This resulted in the launch of *ILEC* in 2006.

In the first, qualitative phase, test developers drew on the products of needs analysis, i.e. lists and tables detailing tasks, task features and language skills lawyers use, as well as on the judgement and knowledge of language assessment specialists to design a sample test. This ensured the authenticity, relevance and validity of the test, as well as its psychometric soundness. The predominantly quantitative phases that followed allowed the testing of the instrument and its further refinement. In Phase 2, the sample test was shown to be authentic and appropriate for the target candidature; in Phase 3, the authenticity and appropriateness of the refined test was confirmed and it was established that the test had good psychometric properties. All the phases in this mixed methods design, in their chain-like formation, contributed to the development of a test that is tailored to the specific needs of its target users, besides being valid and reliable. Together, they introduced the '"value-added" element' discussed by Creswell and Zhou (Chapter 3, this volume). If *ILEC* had been developed simply by drawing on the qualitative findings of the needs analysis only, a likely risk would have been the lack of test reliability. On the other hand, if the quantitative aspect (e.g. statistical properties of a test) was the only consideration in *ILEC* test development, the test may have lacked validity and may also not have been specific and relevant to the legal profession. In all likelihood, either scenario would have engendered a negative impact on test users.

Conclusions

The CBPR approach has only recently begun to emerge in language assessment (see 'The evolving role of content specialists in ESP'). It is, however, a necessary approach to ESP test development since ESP tests are, by definition, derived from specific contexts of language use (Douglas 2000), with which language assessment specialists may be quite unfamiliar. The partnership between legal content specialists and language assessment specialists has certainly been essential in the development of *ILEC*, to ensure that the test better meets the real-life language needs of test users. The use of the CBPR approach in this test development project is summarised in Table 4.

A key advantage of the CBPR approach is the bringing together of different kinds of expertise. This increases the relevance of findings and is more likely to result in a valid and reliable language test which could positively impact on test users. The approach provides a platform for different voices and perspectives, and crucially, it allows language assessment specialists to

Table 4 The CBPR approach in ILEC test development

Phase	Participants	Actions performed
Phase 1: Needs analysis, test specifications and sample test	TransLegal TransLegal and Cambridge English Language Assessment	Language needs analysis (QUAL) Develop test specifications Design a sample test
Phase 2: The viability study	TransLegal and Cambridge English Language Assessment Law professionals and law students Cambridge English Language Assessment	Recruit research participants (law professionals and law students) Design a questionnaire Provide questionnaire feedback on the sample test (QUANT and qual) Analyse questionnaire feedback (the integration of QUANT and qual) Refine the test
Phase 3: The trial study	Cambridge English Language Assessment Law professionals and law students	Design a questionnaire Administer the revised test Analyse test data (QUANT) Analyse questionnaire feedback data (QUANT and qual) Integrate all quantitative and qualitative findings Implement minor changes to the test Sit the trial test Provide questionnaire feedback on the trial test (QUANT and qual)
Live test production	Cambridge English Language Assessment TransLegal	Create, analyse, review and approve tasks, and construct a test (integrate QUAL and QUANT) Analyse live data (QUANT) Vet the legal content and language of tasks (QUAL)

view specific domains of language use through the eyes of content specialists. For example, the analysis of lawyers' and law students' language needs carried out by TransLegal avoided the problem of traditional needs analyses: that of 'outsiders' (language specialists) bringing in their own preconceived notions and categories to an analysis of language use domains they know little about (see 'The evolving role of content specialists in ESP' and 'Phase 1: Needs analysis and sample test design'). Drawing on the expertise of language assessment specialists enhanced the 'raw' needs analysis findings to ensure that the test of *ILEC* is reliable and valid, covering all relevant and necessary aspects of language ability.

A further advantage of CBPR in the context of language assessment is broader access to potential test users. Different domains of expertise open doors to different networks and institutions, thus providing a springboard for test trialling, marketing, publicity and test recognition. Nowadays, besides live test production, marketing is another area of collaboration between Cambridge English Language Assessment and TransLegal.

CBPR is also associated with numerous challenges (see Israel at al 1998, Palinkas and Soydan 2012), but the focus here is on those particularly relevant to language assessment. Besides time and resources, one of the challenges is access to content specialists, particularly the ones who 'have a feel for the technical language . . . and [are] open to linguistically-oriented questions' (Selinker 1979:213). Access to content specialists may also be subject to institutional constraints if their involvement in a CBPR project is perceived as irrelevant to the organisation they work for and takes away time from their day job. Also, partnerships with content specialists inevitably introduce differences in perspective, values and priorities, as a result of differences in professional background and experience. These should be addressed through discussion and negotiation if the partnership is to work. Moreover, as a long-term process, CBPR requires iterative and cyclical engagement of the partners. In view of potential differences in perspective and priorities and in view of the length of time that CBPR projects necessitate, it is essential to build a sustainable relationship. This is best done by jointly developing and following CBPR principles and operating norms that 'foster attentive listening . . . inclusiveness . . . identifying and addressing conflicts . . . negotiation, compromise and equality' (Israel et al 1998:185), as well as by jointly defining roles early on, to make the most of different skill sets and to pre-empt sensitivities around the distribution of power and control. Given all the above, the sustainability of a CBPR project and partnership is built on commitment, collaboration, flexibility and clarity. As the partnership between Cambridge English Language Assessment and TransLegal was made sustainable from the start, no major issues were recorded, while discrepancies in perspective and priorities were resolved through discussion and agreement (see 'Project conception: Test construct and the roles of research partners').

Some ESP tests may be developed using an approach which is at the lower end of the CBPR spectrum, or which only has some elements of CBPR (see 'The evolving role of content specialists in ESP'). This brings along further challenges. For example, language assessment specialists may be hired by an organisation to design and trial a test, as part of a task force which also includes content specialists from the said organisation. The hiring organisation may impose certain requirements which are not subject to discussion or change and 'the underlying traditional assumptions in the contracting organisation about what is sufficient for a testing system to work' may pose 'challenges to the development work' and may also be 'likely to affect the way the system will be maintained, reviewed and further developed in the future' (Huhta 2009:26.13).

As far as methodological considerations are concerned, CBPR allows a free choice of relevant methodology, guided by research partners' skill sets, resources, research goals, etc. (see Community-based participatory research: Definition and principles). This freedom requires familiarity with a range of data collection techniques and analyses, which has implications for the expertise and training of either research partner. Methodological versatility is also required for mixed methods research designs, regardless of whether the CBPR approach is adopted or not.

The benefits of employing a mixed methods design (see Moeller, Chapter 1, and Creswell and Zhou, Chapter 3, this volume) overlap with the benefits of adopting the CBPR approach, and integrating different methods and different types of expertise provides a value added element to a research endeavour. Both help arrive at a richer and more reliable picture of the investigated issue by allowing different voices to be heard and to be brought together (see Ivankova (2015) for further discussion). In addition, a combination of qualitative and quantitative research strands provides a broader and deeper understanding of an issue than either strand would on its own. In the case of *ILEC* test development, the adoption of an exploratory sequential mixed methods design allowed a strong empirical grounding of the test. The initial qualitative needs analysis phase produced valuable information for test specifications and sample test development. From then on, the outcomes of one phase fed into the next phase, which formed a link between qualitative and quantitative data and findings in the three phases of test development research (see the study of *ILEC* test development). A challenge of using exploratory sequential mixed method design lies in the time and other resources. In the case of the *ILEC* development project, it took three years to implement all three phases. A further challenge is the skill set: both the qualitative and the quantitative research skills need to be strong in view of the sequential nature of the process; the qualitative phase feeds directly into the creation of an instrument, which is then tested in the quantitative phase.

...

What comes in at one end of the process will heavily determine what comes out at the other end.

In the spirit of CBPR, the partnership between legal content specialists and language assessment specialists continues, informing and guiding the routine live test production process which rests on the qualitative and quantitative strands.

9 Rating scale development: A multistage exploratory sequential design

Evelina Galaczi

Nahal Khabbazbashi

Cambridge English Language Assessment

This chapter exemplifies the application of the exploratory sequential design and discusses its use in the development of scales for assessing second language (L2) speaking. It focuses on:

- The essential features of *scale development* and the natural fit with the *exploratory sequential design*
- *Complex designs* which can be used in large-scale projects
- The different *stages of the process*, starting with the planning stage, and moving on to the development stages which comprise qualitative and quantitative data gathering and analyses
- The evaluation of the study against key *mixed method validity concerns*

Introduction

The project chosen to showcase the application of the exploratory sequential design in second language (L2) assessment focuses on the development of a set of scales for a suite of high-stakes L2 speaking tests. The assessment of speaking requires the systematic assignment of numbers to given speech samples by referring to explicitly defined criteria which describe different levels of performance (Ginther 2012). Rating scales are the instruments used in this evaluation process, and can be either holistic (i.e. providing global overall assessment) or analytic (i.e. providing independent evaluations for a number of assessment criteria, e.g. Grammar, Vocabulary, Organisation, etc.). While the discussion in this chapter is framed within the context of rating scales in speaking assessment, the principles espoused, stages employed and decisions taken during the development process have wider applicability to performance assessment in general.

We will start with a brief discussion of scale development and hope to illustrate the natural fit between the essence of scale development and the methodological possibilities offered by mixed methods research and the exploratory sequential design. We will then describe the studies which were undertaken at each stage of the project and highlight key elements which shaped the scale development process. We will discuss their value and potential in scale development and the steps taken to ensure methodological rigour. Our discussion will also illustrate how the findings and insights from the different stages were used in an integrated and additive manner, which is a key consideration in mixed methods research. In the interest of space and clarity of focus, our discussion will be mostly methodological; a more detailed account of the project and its findings can be found in Galaczi, ffrench, Hubbard and Green (2011).

Scale development and a mixed methods approach

With some phenomena, such as the assessment of L2 proficiency, decisions are made based on a complex web of interaction between a multitude of factors, such as the tasks, the raters, the interviewers and the background characteristics of the interlocutors (McNamara 1996). In such cases the gathering of data from a wide range of perspectives is instrumental in supporting the validity and trustworthiness of the decisions taken. Assessment scales are the product of such a complex process, where learner performance has to be reduced into finite and concrete categories representing the underlying construct.

Two key approaches have typically supported scale development over the past half a century: one is the expert-judgement approach (aptly termed the 'armchair approach' by Fulcher 2003), which is based solely on the expertise and intuition of experts who may be working collectively in a committee or as individuals; the other approach is empirically informed, as shown in the work of Upshur and Turner (1995), Fulcher (1996), Knoch (2009), to name but a few, and can comprise quantitative or qualitative data or both. For example, Fulcher (1996) used discourse analysis and multiple regression in his analysis of fluency features in learner speech in order to generate fluency scale descriptors. While rating scales of the past used to be based entirely on expert judgement, the empirically informed approach to scale construction and validation has now become the norm in the L2 assessment community (Fulcher 2003). A scale development approach grounded both in empirical data and expert judgement is also reflected in the procedures recommended in the influential Common European Framework of Reference for Languages (CEFR, Council of Europe 2001:205), which advocates the complementary use of both qualitative and quantitative methodologies in scale construction and the integration of findings. It advocates, in essence, a mixed methods approach. An empirically grounded mixed methods approach to scale development is also at the heart of a socio-cognitive approach to assessment and the *scoring validity* of a test, as was discussed by Saville, Chapter 2, this volume.

The building of an empirical basis for the development of a set of assessment scales for large-scale high-stakes examinations is a complex undertaking, which requires a multi-dimensional approach in order to produce an instrument of the necessary rigour and validity. A mixed methods approach and its potential to address the task at hand from a range of different complementary perspectives is therefore a suitable methodological choice which also allows for a comprehensive understanding of a phenomenon by building on the strengths of the independent methods and minimising their respective limitations (Sale, Lohfeld and Brazil 2002:50). As Greene, Caracelli and Graham (1989:256) note:

> ... all methods have inherent biases and limitations, so use of only one method to assess a given phenomenon will inevitably yield biased and limited results. However, when two or more methods that have offsetting biases are used to assess a given phenomenon, and the results of these methods converge or corroborate one another, then the validity of inquiry findings is enhanced.

Mixed methods research, however, is not just about convergence of findings (see Ziegler and Kang, Chapter 4, this volume) but it can also help pinpoint (a) cases of divergence which would have otherwise gone unnoticed, and (b) ways of addressing them; for example outliers in quantitative research may simply be removed from analysis, whereas a qualitative outlook invites a more in-depth examination of those cases. The use of different methods could also potentially shed light on possible reasons for divergences and/or could inform further empirical investigations.

The complementarity of methodologies in a mixed methods study lays the ground for a symbiotic relationship where, as Aristotle noted many centuries ago, the whole is greater than the sum of its parts. Similar to the synergy of musical parts in the creation of a song, for example, where the overall effect is more dramatic than the effect of each of the parts played individually, the complementary integration of methods in a mixed methods design provides richer insights into the project at hand.

The premise of compatibility and complementarity in mixed methods research has not always gone unquestioned (see discussions in Chapters 3 and 4, this volume), as seen in the debates in the mixed methods literature about the compatibility of quantitative and qualitative methodologies, aptly referred to as the 'paradigm wars' by Tashakkori and Teddlie (1998:3). The pragmatist approach, which reconciles the use of two different paradigms and advocates the eclectic use of any range of philosophies, methodologies and tools which are suitable to the project at hand, is now widely seen as one of the underlying theoretical paradigms for mixed methods research (Creswell 2014b, see also Creswell and Zhou, Chapter 3, this volume). A pragmatist approach conceptualises qualitative and quantitative viewpoints not as 'competing dualisms' (Onwuegbuzie and Johnson 2006:59) situated in dichotomous opposition, but as potentially complementary elements on a continuum. Such a pragmatist orientation resonates with the purposes of large-scale 'real-world' projects, of which scale development is one example, that are driven by the very practical and powerful imperative to use all available approaches which work. There is, therefore, a natural fitness-for-purpose between mixed methods and scale development.

Scale development and the exploratory sequential design

Empirically based scale development is by its very nature a cyclical iterative process; it moves in a spiral-like manner, with subsequent stages drawing on the findings of previous ones and leading to more in-depth and meaningful insights. Scale development is also a reductionist process; it aims to distil the richness and complexity of learner language to a finite set of assessment categories (e.g. Grammar, Vocabulary) and discrete competency statements within each category. These descriptors, ordered from low to high, ultimately correspond to a single score or set of scores along the proficiency continuum.

One possible starting point in this reductionist process is an empirical investigation into the views of key stakeholders, e.g. teachers, as exemplified in the development of the CEFR (North 2000), where teachers' views and wealth of experience about language proficiency at different levels were used in the generation of a bank of draft descriptors characterising different aspects of language proficiency. Another starting point could be learner performance data, as shown by Fulcher (1996) in his development of a Fluency scale. Whatever the approach adopted, the initial starting point is typically characterised by an inductive exploration stage which allows for the complexity of language performance to be captured in the form of themes, codes, illustrative language or distinguishing linguistic features. This is in line with the constructivist paradigm, which espouses multiple meanings and realities, acknowledges the complexity of views and data and is characterised by inductive interpretative generation of meaning. Findings from this stage can then be reduced to general categories and descriptors, which are embedded in the assessment scales. This subsequent Stage 1 is in line with the reductionist orientation of the postpositivist paradigm, where the intent is typically to reduce ideas into a final product/number/scale/ survey. The nature of scale development, i.e. a progression from an inductive exploratory stage to a deductive measurement stage, finds a suitable match in the exploratory sequential design; an initial inductive qualitative discovery stage, in tune with the constructivist paradigm, followed by a reductionist, generalisable quantitative stage embedded within a postpositivist paradigm. In line with a pragmatist theoretical stance, they are seen as complementary paradigms which contribute to successful accomplishment of the task at hand.

Complex exploratory sequential designs

As noted earlier in this discussion (and also in Chapters 3 and 4, this volume), the exploratory sequential design would typically occur in three stages: 1) qualitative data collection/analysis followed by 2) quantitative data collection/analysis (QUAL➜QUAN), and 3) leading to a final stage which might involve the development of a measurement instrument or a procedure. This basic QUAL➜ QUAN progression, with stages following from one another in a linear fashion, is well suited to smaller-scale empirical endeavours, where the first stage would be exploratory, the second stage would result in instrument development and the third would involve the large-scale quantitative administration of the instrument.

In large-scale projects, such as the one discussed in this chapter, the basic exploratory sequential design may need modifications to ensure fitness-for-purpose with the complex nature of the project. As such, the design could take a multistage character, where the basic 'QUAL➜QUAN' unit is iteratively repeated with some variation. Creswell terms this approach 'multiphase or multistage mixed methods' (2014b:228). A staged approach of this kind carries the overall features of the exploratory sequential design (i.e. very first Stage 1s qualitative and very last Stage 1s quantitative), but there may be nesting of other designs at some of the in-between stages. It is an advanced design where each stage, while independent, is connected to the other stages sequentially. As discussed by Ziegler and Kang, Chapter 4, this volume, this is a practical way to address a large-scale project 'by breaking it into multiple smaller, semiautonomous studies' and is the underlying design in the scale development project discussed here.

We now turn our attention to more detailed descriptions of each stage of the study. In doing so, we hope to not only provide a comprehensive account of what was done but to also draw explicit links between the content of the project and the methodology adopted. We start with a brief discussion of the project considerations, which were at the heart of the planning stage.

Snapshot of the study

Research goal	• Theoretically and empirically supported development of a set of assessment scales for second/foreign language speaking tests
Design	• Advanced multistage scale development mixed methods design
Stages	• QUAL → Convergent QUAN and QUAL → QUAN Stage 1 Stage 2 Stage 3

Qualitative data collection and data analysis	• Stage 1: Conversation Analysis of learner speech
	• Stage 1: Thematic analysis of examiner extended survey comments
	• Stage 2: Verbal Protocol Study of examiner comments while using draft scales
Quantitative data collection and data analysis	• Stage 2: Multi-Facet Rasch Measurement of descriptor performance
	• Stage 3: Multi-Facet Rasch Measurement (MFRM) of rater, scale and assessment criteria performance
Methods level strategies*	• Connecting, building, merging
Interpretation level strategies*	• Data preparation: Reduction, Transformation
	• Data analysis: Comparison
	• Data integration: synthesis of findings at each stage through a matrix containing all flagged up issues/scale descriptors based on all recommendations from the QUAL and QUAN stages
Mixed methods value added	• Meta-inferences based on a range of qualitative and quantitative methodologies and a staged, additive approach
Conclusions	• Operational functioning scale developed

See Ziegler and Kang, Chapter 4, this volume, for a more detailed explanation of these mixed methods research strategies.

Planning stage: Considering complementarity of methods

During the planning stage of the project, methodological tools needed to be critically considered, with careful attention given to their underlying assumptions, strengths and shortcomings. As Sandelowski (2003:329) notes:

> . . . most studies in social and behavioural sciences . . . entail the use of more than one of something (e.g. investigators, participants, sites) for data collection. The mere use of more than one of some research entity in a study does not constitute a mixed methods study.

The aim of method selection in this project was therefore to increase the meaningfulness and validity of results through 'complementarity' (Greene et al 1989:259); methods were therefore chosen not simply as tools with different technical qualities, but as methodologies which can provide data and interpretations tapping into different yet equally important aspects of reality, and which can optimise strengths and minimise limitations in a symbiotic relationship.

As such, the development team decided that during Stage 1 different types of data would be gathered from two key stakeholder groups: 1) examiners, whose views would provide individual perspectives about the scales, and 2) learners, whose speech data would form the basis of the project. Speaking examiners – the primary users of assessment scales in test conditions – have valuable experience and as such, their collective perspectives can usefully feed into decisions about assessment scales. Learner speech data, on the other hand, allows us to look 'inside' speaking tests (van Lier 1989), to gain insights about what learners actually say and to extract features of their speech that can (and need to be) captured in scales and descriptors of their performance. During Stage 2, the methods were once again selected with the aim of complementarity in providing insights from different angles: in one study, the discrete draft descriptors were mapped to levels on the scale, and in another study, the focus was on the examiner experience in using the draft scales. Stage 3, which aimed at finalising the scales, was planned to include quantitative investigations which would allow for generalisable findings.

The robustness of selected methods, the collection and analysis of the qualitative and quantitative data, was also addressed at the planning stage. This is a key consideration and challenge in mixed methods research, since methodological criteria of quality differ based on the empirical paradigm guiding the study. In a positivist paradigm, quantitative studies are typically governed by the scientific requirements of objectivity, systematicity, validity and reliability. Lincoln and Guba (1985), working in an interpretative research paradigm, propose the criteria of credibility, transferability, dependability and confirmability for qualitative enquiries. Adding to the latter, Richards (2009) suggests transparency. Irrespective of the methodological orientations of the underlying studies, every mixed method study should be based on methodological rigour or 'legitimation', a term advanced by Onwuegbuzie and Johnson (2006). At the planning Stage 1 in our project, steps were taken to ensure methodological rigour by specifying quality control criteria for the different studies and addressing validity concerns relevant to the project by drawing on relevant literature in the field (see also Ziegler and Kang, Chapter 4, this volume, for a more comprehensive discussion of validity concerns specific to mixed methods research). For example, the analysis of learner language followed established Conversation Analysis procedures (Atkinson and Heritage (Eds) 1984); the data collection and analysis of raters' verbalised thoughts when using the scales were closely guided by recommendations on carrying out Verbal Protocol investigations (Green 1998); the investigations using Multi-Facet Rasch Measurement ensured that requirements of data connectivity were met that fit statistics fell within acceptable quality control limits (Myford and Wolfe 2003, 2004).

A further consideration at this stage was to have a strategy in place to ensure an *integration* of findings from the different autonomous stages in drawing meta-inferences. This is arguably the most crucial and challenging aspect of a mixed methods study (see Chapters 3 and 4, this volume). Attention has to be paid, therefore, to how to use the information from one Stage 1 in the other, so that the two stages 'are not discrete or just superficially sequential, but build on one another' (Creswell 2014b:226). To support this goal, the group members responsible for the development of the scales first considered each set of findings independently followed by regular discussions and evaluation of findings as a whole group, allowing for ongoing revisions and decisions on the scales based on an integrated consideration of all available findings to date. A graphical display of the project is given in Figure 1.

Stage 1: Setting out empirically based design principles of the assessment scales

Goals for Stage 1: Development of draft scales

The first stage of the project aimed to gather information from a range of sources, including the academic literature and leading experts, speaking examiners, and learner speech, which would then support establishing the key design principles of the scales. The goals were to:

- decide on a definition of the speaking construct, i.e. the components of ability to be measured (e.g. Grammar, Vocabulary, Fluency, Pronunciation, Organisation, etc.)
- decide on the weighting of each component of ability
- decide on features that allowed reliable distinctions in ability across points in the scale
- produce draft competency statements in each assessment category at different proficiency levels.

In order to accomplish these goals the development team had to reconcile two competing demands in scale construction: on the one hand, the need to develop scales which have construct coverage, accurately and comprehensively capture the constructs of interest and are therefore relatively long and detailed, and on the other hand, the need to produce scales which are practical and can be used by examiners in real time and are therefore relatively short and succinct.

Method, data collection and analysis for Stage 1

Two key sources of data fed into this initial stage: learner speech and open-ended survey responses from speaking examiners. The details were as follows:

Figure 1 Graphical display of the research design stages, procedures and products

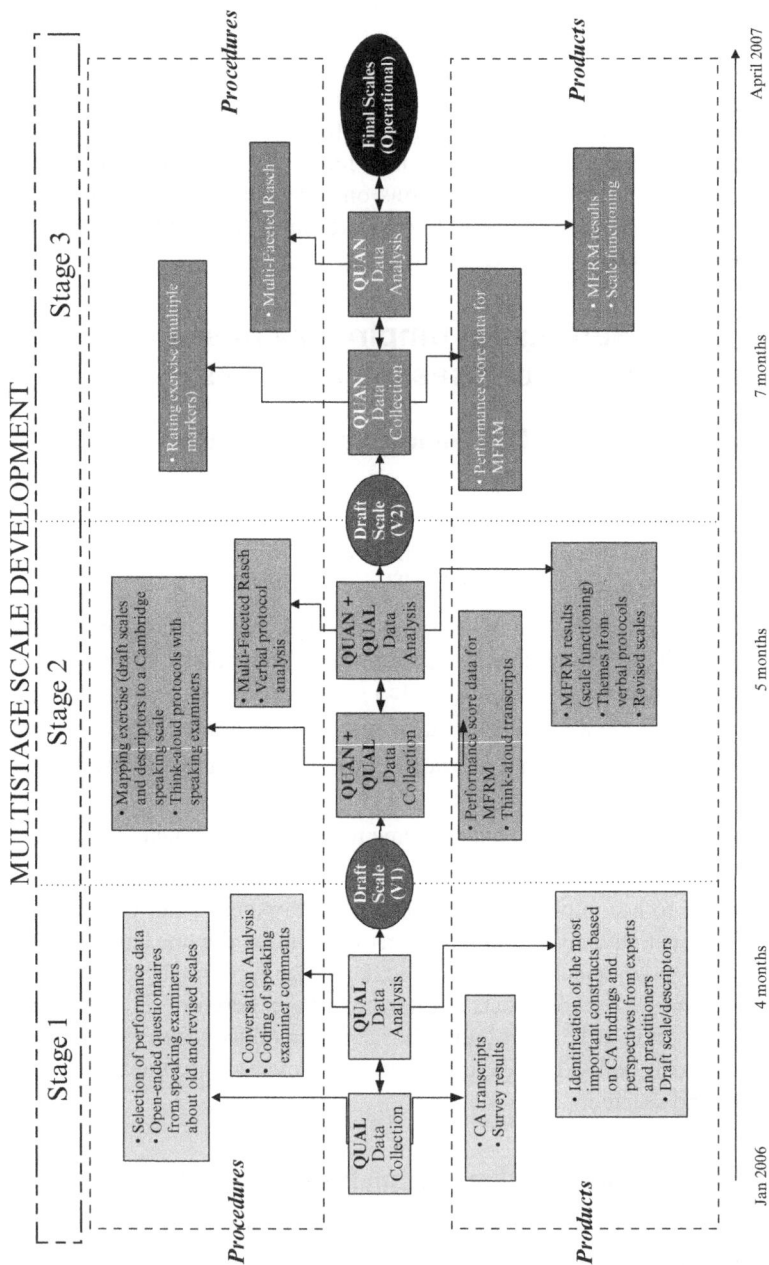

MULTISTAGE SCALE DEVELOPMENT

Stage 1 | Stage 2 | Stage 3

Procedures

Stage 1

QUAL Data Collection

QUAL Data Analysis

• Selection of performance data
• Open-ended questionnaires from speaking examiners about old and revised scales

• Conversation Analysis
• Coding of speaking examiner comments

Draft Scale (V1)

Stage 2

QUAN + QUAL Data Collection

QUAN + QUAL Data Analysis

• Mapping exercise (draft scales and descriptors to a Cambridge speaking scale
• Think-aloud protocols with speaking examiners

• Multi-Faceted Rasch
• Verbal protocol analysis

Draft Scale (V2)

Stage 3

QUAN Data Collection

QUAN Data Analysis

• Rating exercise (multiple markers)

• Multi-Faceted Rasch

Final Scales (Operational)

Products

• CA transcripts
• Survey results

• Identification of the most important constructs based on CA findings and perspectives from experts and practitioners
• Draft scale/descriptors

• Performance score data for MFRM
• Think-aloud transcripts

• MFRM results (scale functioning)
• Themes from verbal protocols
• Revised scales

• Performance score data for MFRM

• MFRM results
• Scale functioning

Jan 2006 | 4 months | 5 months | 7 months | April 2007

216

	Analysis of learner speech (Lazaraton and Davis 2006, 2007)	Speaking examiners' open-ended survey responses (Green 2006)
	QUAL	**QUAL**
Objectives	• To identify discourse features associated with differently ranked performances based on 'thick' description of test performances • To identify salient features of candidate discourse at the CEFR B1, B2 and C1 levels • To review the extent to which such features are captured by the current scales and elicitation procedures	• To explore the opinions of speaking examiners about the use of the 'old' speaking scales used for Cambridge English speaking tests and their ideas about the development of the 'new' scales
Data collection	• 32 speaking test performances of test takers representing a range of L1s and ability levels	• 316 speaking examiners with a range of experience • Open-ended examiner feedback
Data analysis	• Conversation Analysis of micro-level conversational features	• Thematic analysis of extended examiner comments

In the first study focusing on learner speech, the data was chosen from learner speaking test performances used for examiner training and standardisation and was thus reliably marked performances. While this was a qualitative study, sample selection was done systematically and a stratified sample of 32 performances (16 paired speaking tests) covering a range of L1s and proficiency levels (from B1 to C1 on the CEFR) was selected for analysis (Lazaraton and Davis 2006, 2007).

Conversation Analysis was chosen as the preferred methodology (as opposed to, for example, just an analysis of lexico-grammatical features), as it allows investigations to go beyond words and sentences to also consider interactional aspects of speech, which is an important feature of the Cambridge English Speaking exams. Two researchers with expertise in Conversation Analysis (CA) of L2 learner speech transcribed the data using CA transcription conventions (Atkinson and Heritage (Eds) 1984, ten Have 1999), in order to capture features of the interaction such as pausing, turn taking and speech overlap. Initial transcriptions were compared to audio played in real time, and finally to the video. At times the researchers referred to the printed task materials to help understand the words or concepts the learners were trying to convey.

The data analysis in this study was an iterative process, following the 'data exploration strategy' outlined by ten Have (1999) and Lazaraton (2002), in which the researchers scrutinised the transcriptions for relevant and interesting features of the learner talk as they relate to the different assessment categories in the scales. The analysis was carried out independently by the two researchers, and then comments were considered together, as a quality check for inter-coder agreement. Once the transcription notes were discussed and agreed on, the learner performances were arranged from high to low scores, so that patterns within and across a score level could potentially emerge. The key objective was to identify salient features of learner discourse at the CEFR levels of interest, to review the extent to which such features were captured by the 'old' assessment scales (in use at the time of the project), and to subsequently make suggestions for features of learner speech which *should* be included in the new assessment scales.

The data collection, transcription and analysis procedures followed established CA guidelines in order to ensure methodological rigour of the findings (ten Have 1999). They were in line with a qualitative orientation to research and provided an emic perspective and a look 'inside' speaking tests (van Lier 1989).

The second study focusing on examiner perspectives consisted of the collection and analysis of examiner comments about the performance of the scales (in use at the time) as well as their views on potential changes. The data collection involved a questionnaire distributed to speaking examiners worldwide exploring their use of the current assessment scales. Questionnaires were returned from 316 examiners and the responses were used to inform the ongoing development of the new scales. The thematic analysis of the open-ended examiner comments provided a rich set of data and recommendations for features of the new scales.

Results for Stage 1

The two research studies from Stage 1 yielded a set of general recommendations about the scales and specific suggestions about wording of the performance descriptors and assessment categories. Data integration – a key element of mixed methods research – was based on the additive insights from the quantitative and qualitative findings from the studies in this stage, and resulted in decisions about assessment categories in the scale, the number of scale points and the specific wording of the descriptors. To illustrate, findings from the CA analysis pointed to a general need for more precision in the language used in the scales:

> The descriptors for the PET Speaking test rating scale are extremely general and abbreviated. Although the descriptors seem reasonably accurate, they aren't very precise. Precise scores appear to be based upon a set of exemplars, i.e., the training videos, and the examiner training process more generally. The rating scale seems better suited for use as a 'reminder' or mnemonic device for examiners, rather than a catalogue of features that distinguish levels of performance on the PET (Lazaraton and Davis 2007:91).

The analysis also allowed for specific recommendations to be made regarding the wording of the descriptors. For example, regarding the CEFR B1 descriptors for Grammar and Vocabulary, the authors noted:

> Given the degree of inaccuracy we saw at the 3.0 level, it might be useful to extend the description to read: *Shows a good degree of control of simple grammatical forms,* **but errors may obscure meaning**. Similarly, the 5.0 band descriptor might read: *Shows a good degree of control of simple grammatical forms, and attempts some complex grammatical forms,* **although errors may occasionally obscure meaning** (Lazaraton and Davis 2007:34).

Most importantly, there was convergence of findings between the questionnaire data and the analysis of learner talk on some issues relevant for the assessment scales. To take the Interactive Communication assessment criterion as an example, the CA findings indicated that the concept of 'turn-taking' in the scales is too vague, which was a point corroborated by the examiners:

Conversation Analysis

All candidates seem to follow the norms of turn-taking, so this feature does not seem useful for distinguishing performances at the 3.0–5.0 level (Lazaraton and Davis 2006:66).

Examiner survey

Interpreting sensitivity [to turn taking] requires a more subjective assessment. I feel much more comfortable with the objectivity of other [assessment] criteria (Examiner ID 63) (Green 2006:12).

The inclusion of 'hesitation' in the Interactive Communication was noted in the Conversation Analysis and also emerged as a theme in the examiner feedback:

Conversation Analysis

We do feel that there is the potential for a confounding effect between hesitation and the discourse management subcategory, because if a candidate hesitates excessively, coherence may suffer. If hesitation is a feature of relevance to *both* categories, then scores in the two categories are not independent (Lazaraton and Davis 2006:70).

Examiner survey

Hesitation is difficult to decide if it belongs in Interactive Communication or somewhere else, e.g. insufficient vocabulary' (Examiner ID 191) (Green 2006:11).

The results from the examiner questionnaire went beyond learner language and provided insights into a wide range of issues, such as aspects of the scales which examiners found difficult to award scores for, sub-criteria which examiners found most or least difficult to award scores for, or which they find most/least useful. For example, the survey indicated that the main aspects of the scales which cause difficulty for examiners are the 'Range' aspect in the Grammar and Vocabulary scale, the 'Adequacy' aspect in the Discourse Management scale, the 'Turn taking' and 'Hesitation' aspects of the Interactive Communication scale, and 'Stress' and 'Rhythm' in the 'Pronunciation' scale. The examiner feedback also indicated that examiners favoured a splitting up of the single Grammar and Vocabulary assessment category into two at the higher CEFR levels. In the words of one examiner:

> If a candidate has good vocabulary but poor grammar, it's difficult to decide on a score. Candidates' vocabulary resources do vary enormously and with the present scales it is not possible to give enough credit to the candidates with a wide vocabulary [Examiner ID 244, Exam: *BEC Vantage* CEFR B2] (Green 2006:23).

This was, in short, the process which characterised the integration of findings at this initial qualitative Stage 1 in order to produce a set of meta-inferences forming the basis for the next stage.

Decisions made at end of Stage 1

The inductive exploratory approach during this initial qualitative stage allowed issues to be explored in depth from two different perspectives (learner speech and examiner views) and provided an empirical basis for the decisions taken at the end of this stage. These decisions related to general features of the scales, such as: 1) the assessment categories, 2) the sub-categories, 3) exceptions to the general design principles, 4) the weighting applied to each category, and 5) the number of scale points. They also referred to principles about wording of the performance descriptors, as given in the CEFR (Council of Europe 2001).

Stage 2: A componential analysis of elements of the assessment scales

Goals for Stage 2: Investigation of functioning of the draft scales (version 1) and production of revised draft scales (version 2)

The second stage of the project aimed to investigate the functioning of the draft performance descriptors from two perspectives: 1) comparing the *observed* vs *intended* level of each descriptor, and 2) exploring the use of the draft scales by raters in real time (examples of the draft descriptors can be seen in Tables 1 and 2). The aim of the first study was to establish difficulty parameters and MFRM proved useful for this purpose. The second study had a predominantly qualitative approach (with some quantification of codes) and aimed to gather extended feedback from examiners while they were using the draft scales.

The choice of both a quantitative and qualitative methodology at this early stage was felt to be important as the project moved forward from descriptors on paper to their real-time use by examiners. At the same time, it was important to establish the extent to which descriptors were able to reliably distinguish between candidates at different ability levels. This required statistical evidence for the successful functioning of the descriptors which complemented evidence from the more subjective individual perceptions of raters. As we noted earlier, such complementarity of methods is an important characteristic of mixed method research and was a fundamental feature of all stages of the project.

Method, data collection and analysis for Stage 2

The two studies which formed the basis of this stage focused on (1) mapping the draft descriptors against the CEFR (Council of Europe 2001) and the Cambridge English Common Scale (Green 2006), and (2) examiner use of the draft descriptors (Hubbard, Gilbert and Pidcock 2006).

	Mapping of the draft descriptors (Green 2006)	Examiner use of draft descriptors (Hubbard et al 2006)
	QUAN	QUAL
Objectives	• To provide evidence for the validity of draft descriptors by mapping against the Cambridge English and CEFR scales	• To explore the use of the draft descriptors and scales by experienced speaking examiners
Data collection	• 31 examiners and 64 draft descriptors	• 8 examiners and 12 test performances
Data analysis	• MFRM of descriptor 'difficulty'	• Verbal Protocol Analysis

The participants in the mapping study were 31 speaking examiners who represented a cross section of the examiner hierarchy, but with a strong representation of the most senior and experienced members of the examiner cadre. They were divided into four groups and each received a set of 20 of the 64 new descriptors. Each set had eight descriptors which overlapped with other sets in a linked design. This was a practical solution which ensured that examiners were not overwhelmed by 64 descriptors, but also served to meet the requirements of MFRM which necessitates a linking of data through overlapping items.

The examiners, working independently, were asked to indicate which level on the Cambridge English common scale they believed each descriptor represented. The data collection, therefore, included examiner ratings for each descriptor. An MFRM analysis of the ratings was completed using FACETS

(Linacre 2006); this is a robust analysis which takes relative severity of the examiners into account before generating a 'fair average' difficulty measure for each descriptor.

These 'difficulty' estimates of the descriptors were then compared against the intended difficulties by the scale developers. The extent to which examiners displayed consistency in their interpretation of descriptors was also investigated, with results suggesting high degrees of self-consistency. This study was quantitative in orientation, as at this stage it was important to start gathering findings which have generalisability and are based on the views of a group of examiners and on a powerful statistical procedure.

The goal of the second study in Stage 2 was to investigate the comprehensibility and applicability of the scales using verbal protocol analysis and think-aloud procedures as related to the assessment process in real time. Participants in this study were eight examiners, representing all levels of the examiner hierarchy and selected from four different major test taker regions, who assessed a set of recorded test performances at different ability levels using the draft descriptors and verbalised their thoughts during the process. In order to simulate live examining conditions as closely as possible, pausing of the recordings was not allowed. Data on examiner reactions to using the draft scales was also collected through an open-ended questionnaire administered after the marking.

The analysis involved a transcription of the examiner verbal reports which were subsequently coded for key themes. The coding system involved a set of categories: 'Grammar and Vocabulary', 'Discourse Management', 'Pronunciation', 'Interactive Communication', 'Assessment Comment/ Decision', 'Other'. The coding scheme had been piloted in an earlier study (Hubbard et al 2006) and the categories were found to work well in capturing examiner comments relating to the assessment categories, to their assessment decisions and any other comments. A thematic analysis of the extensive examiner comments was also carried out. This study was qualitative in orientation, as it focused on individual experiences when using the scales.

Sampling in both studies in this stage was an important consideration, and similar to the sampling approach during the previous stage, purposive sampling was used, since the study necessitated the use of speaking performances which display a range of abilities and first language backgrounds, with the view of ensuring representation of weak/average/strong learners and different geographic locations. Purposive sampling was also used to select examiners with the aim of achieving representativeness of examiners at different levels of experience and covering a range of positions within the speaking examiner hierarchy.

A further important question at this stage was whether the sample for the qualitative (Stage 1) and quantitative (Stage 2) parts of the project should be the same. Creswell (2014b) cautions against this, since the qualitative sample would typically be much smaller than the quantitative sample, the findings from which need to be generalised to the population. In line with this recommendation, samples were drawn from the same population of examiners and test taker performances, but care was taken to use different individuals who met the selection criteria defined in the stratified sampling framework, e.g. years of experience for examiners, range of L1 and proficiency for test takers.

Results for Stage 2

The findings at this stage included difficulty measures for the perceived CEFR level of each descriptor and extended rater feedback on the usability of the scales and descriptors. The integration of these two sets of findings provided the basis for making any changes to the descriptors. Meta-inferences were drawn from a joint consideration of the mapping of the draft descriptors and the verbal protocol feedback of the examiners, with special attention focused on those descriptors which did not map as expected and/or were flagged by the verbal protocol data.

The quantitative scaling exercise provided evidence of broad agreement between the intended levels of the performance descriptors and the examiner ratings and showed that the descriptors could reliably be separated into seven statistically distinct difficulty levels. The analysis also identified a small number of performance descriptors where the examiner ratings contradicted the intended levels. Table 1 provides an example of the types of findings which were generated and which served as the basis for further decisions. It gives the intended level of the descriptor in column 1 and the empirically observed Rasch difficulty values in ascending order (the 'fair average') in column 3. The Interactive Communication criterion has been chosen as an example.

The findings in Table 1 show that the rank order and clustering of the descriptors and the range of levels covered (from A1 to C2+) were broadly in line with the scale developers' intentions, providing evidence for the validity of the descriptors. Some cases of divergence from the intended levels were also observed (shaded in Table 1). For example, towards the lower end of the scale, 'Maintains and closes simple exchanges' (B1) was rated easier than the two A2 descriptors, indicating that the distinction between 'maintains exchanges' and 'keeps the interaction going' may not be clear-cut, as both appear to refer to the same aspect of interaction, although originally intended to discriminate between different levels of interaction ability. Towards the higher end of the scale, 'Collaborates with (an)other speaker(s) to widen the scope of the interaction' (C2) is placed at the same level as 'Initiates and responds appropriately, linking his/her own contributions to those of (an) other speaker(s)' (C1), again indicating that the distinction between the

Table 1 Interactive Communication draft descriptors and CEFR mapping

Intended level	Descriptor	Fair average
A1	Has considerable difficulty answering questions or responding to descriptors.	1.15
A1	Requires extensive prompting.	1.15
B1	Maintains and closes simple exchanges.	1.76
A2	Answers questions and responds to simple descriptors.	1.92
A2	Engages in the interaction, but occasionally needs additional prompting to keep up the exchange of information.	2.58
B1	Keeps the interaction going with minimal prompting.	3.04
B2	Initiates and responds appropriately.	3.67
B2	Maintains and develops the interaction without support.	3.77
C1	Develops the interaction and/or negotiates an outcome.	3.89
C2	Collaborates with (an)other speaker(s) to widen the scope of the interaction.	4.38
C1	Initiates and responds appropriately, linking his/her own contributions to those of (an)other speaker(s).	4.38
C2	Interacts with ease, linking his/her own contributions to those of (an)other speaker(s).	4.98
C2+	Collaborates with (an)other speaker(s) to develop the interaction fully and effectively.	5.32
C2+	Interacts with ease by skilfully interweaving his/her contributions into the conversation.	6.62

descriptors needed to be made more explicit. Quantitative findings of this sort, which focused on each descriptor in isolation, formed the basis of decisions about further revisions to the descriptors.

The qualitative verbal protocol findings explored the use of the scales as a whole in real-time conditions. In addition to the thematic analysis of rater protocol comments, the verbal protocols were also converted to codes in order to calculate frequency counts of the assessment categories on the scale and their extent of use (Figure 2). The coding and quantification of the examiner verbal reports provided information about the assessment criteria examiners paid attention to and the extent to which there was a balance among the criteria they focused on. For example, Figure 2 indicates the key components in the 'Interactive Communication' assessment category and confirms the decisions taken at the end of Stage 1 to include 'initiating', 'responding' and 'developing the interaction' as key features of this criterion.

The extended examiner comments gathered during this stage of the project provided additional insights about the wording of the descriptors. For example:

'I found that using "control" rather than "accuracy" forced assessments to look at grammatical forms over a number of utterances rather than just focusing on individual mistakes.' (Grammar and Vocabulary)

Figure 2 Verbal protocol codes: Interactive Communication, CEFR B2 level

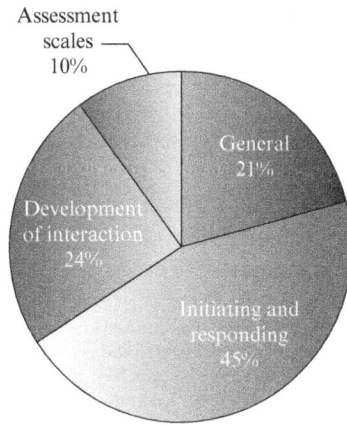

'The removal of "incoherent" and "coherent" and their replacement with notions of "repetition" and "digression" are easier to match to performance.' (Discourse Management)

'A judgment on intelligibility is easier to apply.' (Pronunciation)

'I like the reference in Interactive Communication to "linking contributions to those of other speakers". This is useful and immediately comprehensible.' (Interactive Communication)

The need for greater clarity also emerged as a theme:

'What constitutes "a good degree of control", "limited control"?'
'The "range" aspect was quite difficult to judge.'
'What is meant by "some complex grammatical forms"?'

An important final step during this stage was the *integration* of the quantitative statistical findings and the qualitative verbal protocol findings. This allowed the scale development team to focus attention on specific descriptors and wording choices. The statistical results signalled an issue with the wording of some of the descriptors while the extended examiner feedback provided insights into the cause of some of those issues and how they might be addressed (e.g. through a revision of the wording of the descriptors and/or through examiner training). This was done through a joint display (see Ziegler and Kang, Chapter 4, this volume, for a more in-depth discussion of joint displays), which included the problematic descriptors and compared relevant findings from the examiner verbal protocols and the mapping study.

Decisions made at end of Stage 2

The qualitative and quantitative findings at this stage confirmed that the criteria, sub-criteria and wording of the descriptors were generally appropriate and applicable in real-time assessment. The findings also provided guidelines about further revision. The examples in Table 2 illustrate the changes in wording that the draft descriptors went through during Stages 1 and 2 of the project.

Findings at this stage also led to the development of a supporting Glossary of Terms as a practical aid for all users of the scale, defining and exemplifying some of the terms used in the scales. For example:

Development of the interaction — Actively developing the conversation, e.g. by saying more than the minimum in response to the prompt, or to something the other candidate/interlocutor has said, or by proactively involving the other candidate with a suggestion or question about further developing the topic (e.g. What about bringing a camera for the holiday? Or Why's that?)

Stage 3: Operational analysis

Goals for Stage 3: Investigation of operational functioning of the scales (version 2) and finalisation of the scales

Two quantitative studies formed the final stage of the project and had the overall aim of confirming the appropriate functioning of the scales, assessment criteria and descriptors as a whole prior to their use in rater training/ standardisation and in operational live test conditions. The need to investigate the scales as they would be used in large-scale live conditions was well suited to the adoption of a quantitative methodology and carrying out a marking trial with a large enough number of examiners and test performances to allow for generalisability of the findings.

The studies had dual aims: the first marking trial aimed to gather statistical measures about the performance of the scales and also to allow a

Table 2 Examples of initial and revised draft descriptors for Interactive Communication

CEFR level	Initial draft (version 1)		Draft (version 2)
A2 Band 3	Engages in the interaction, but occasionally needs additional prompting to keep up the exchange of information.	→	Engages in the interaction, but occasionally needs additional prompting and support to keep the interaction going.
A2 Band 1	Has considerable difficulty answering questions or responding to questions.	→	Has considerable difficulty maintaining simple exchanges.

comparison between the 'new' and 'old' scales in order to ensure that the new scales had not changed the standard of the tests they are used with. The aim of the second marking trial was to provide a final check of the functioning of the scales, and additionally to produce benchmarked test performances exemplifying the different levels on the new scales which would directly inform examiner training and standardisation procedures.

Method, data collection and analysis for Stage 3

The two trials at this stage involved gathering of multiple marks on video-recorded tests, and the use of MFRM as the analysis tool. Rasch measurement was once again used because of its value in providing an overall picture of the assessment context and all facets involved e.g. raters, learners, assessment scales and criteria (Linacre 2006, Myford and Wolfe 2003, 2004) and for providing fine-grained statistical information regarding the functionality of the scales that can be used for diagnostic purposes. The data collection in both studies consisted of raters individually assigning marks to video-recorded speaking tests. The participants were speaking examiners with extensive rating experience.

The overall objectives, data collection and analysis features of this stage were as follows:

	Marking trial 1 (Galaczi 2007a) QUAN	Marking trial 2 (Galaczi 2007b) QUAN
Objectives	• To provide statistical evidence of the functioning of the scales in terms of level of learner discrimination, examiner severity/agreement/consistency, assessment criteria separation/consistency, and scale points • To compare the marks awarded using the 'new' scales with the 'old' scales • To provide recommendations for examiner training	• To provide statistical evidence of the functioning of the scales in terms of level of learner discrimination, examiner severity/agreement/consistency, assessment criteria separation/consistency, and scale points • To provide benchmark test performances for examiner standardisation
Data collection	• 12 raters, 32 test performances (full tests and test parts)	• 28 raters, 96 test performances (full tests and test parts)
Data analysis	• MFRM of the performance of the raters, learners and assessment criteria	• MFRM of the performance of the raters, learners and assessment criteria

As a rule of thumb, good practice in rating studies requires that raters are standardised in their interpretation of the scale used. The most effective way to do this is to standardise raters with benchmarked test performances which exemplify the different points on the scales. This was not possible in the first trial, since no benchmarked performances existed yet. The standardisation of the raters was instead accomplished through familiarisation with the scales and the Glossary of Terms. During the second study the examiners were standardised with benchmarked performances which had been produced based on the first marking study. Once again, this is an illustration of how different stages in the exploratory sequential design additively built on one another and how one stage could not have been completed without the pre-ceding one. We also see the importance of rigour in the research design and data collection to ensure validity of the findings (e.g. including a familiarisa-tion stage before the data collection).

The size of the data sets for this stage met the criteria for a quantitative study which needs to have the power of generalisability. A total of 32 speak-ing test performances (some as full tests and others as test parts) were rated in the first study by 12 raters; the performances displayed a range of ability levels, e.g. at the CEFR B2 level, weak, average and strong learners were included. A total of 96 test performances (some as full tests and some as test parts) representing learners at different speaking ability levels were rated by 28 raters in the second study. In both studies each rater gave between 3 and 5 marks per candidate. The analysis was carried out separately for each CEFR level.

The analysis involved calculating descriptive statistics and a Rasch analy-sis (using FACETS, Linacre 2006). The facets were: test taker, examiner and assessment criteria; logit and infit mean square measures were provided for each facet. The analysis focused on:

- Relative rater harshness/leniency, as seen in the logit measure for each rater and the rater separation strata. If harshness/leniency differences between raters proved to be small, this would provide evidence for similar interpretation of the scale by examiners and therefore, the adequate functioning of the scale.

- Rater consistency, as seen in the outfit and infit mean square values. If few raters displayed inconsistency or central tendency (i.e. restricting their scores to the middle of the scale), this would provide evidence for the adequate functioning of the scales.

- Test taker separation, as seen in the test taker separation ratio. A higher separation ratio, i.e. a large spread of test takers, would provide evidence for the ability of the scales to discriminate between test takers at different ability levels.

- Difficulty of the assessment criteria, as seen in the logit measure for each one. If differences in difficulty between the criteria proved to be small (but statistically distinct), this would provide evidence for the equal role played by each criterion in contributing to a final score.

Results for Stage 3

The results from the first study provided measures for the functioning of the assessment criteria and rater severity and consistency. Table 3 provides an example of the type of findings, which informed this stage of the project.

In terms of the discriminatory power of the scales, the findings in Table 3 indicate that the scales adequately separated test takers into different ability levels. The results also indicated that there were different levels of rater harshness/leniency (as seen in the logits spread and separation strata in Table 2). This was an expected finding, since rater variability is an inevitable part of the rating process, even with highly trained raters. Nevertheless, these differences in rater severity fell within acceptable parameters, lending support that raters were interpreting the scales in similar ways and, by extension, that the scales were performing at an acceptable level. The results also generated measures of rater consistency. Rater inconsistency is a cause for concern since it could potentially indicate scales which are not applied consistently and are therefore not reliably used. The small number of inconsistent raters suggested that cases of inconsistency were idiosyncratic, and not indicative of an inherent

Table 3 FACETS measures (from Galaczi et al 2011:231)

	CEFR A2 level	CEFR B1 level	CEFR B2 level	CEFR C1 level	CEFR C2 level
Number of data points used for estimation	252	748	831	832	560
Learner discrimination					
Number of learners	12	24	24	24	12
Spread (logits)	−1.46 to 5.22	−1.73 to 4.35	−1.61 to 3.00	−1.84 to 3.84	−1.50 to 1.77
Separation strata	9.45	10.56	9.21	10.27	12.12
Rater separation and consistency					
Number of raters	11	19	22	22	14
Spread (logits)	−1.39 to 1.89	−.92 to 1.11	−.95 to .76	−.94 to 2.19	−.64 to .59
Separation strata	4.8	4.0	3.7	6.6	4.3
Raters with infit mn. sq. > Mean + S.D.	1 (none critically)	2 (1 critically)	4 (1 critically)	5 (1 critically)	1 (1 critically)
Raters with infit mn. sq. < (Mean − S.D.)	1	1	1	3	2
Assessment criteria separation and consistency					
Spread (logits)	−.51 to .5	−.29 to .36	−.38 to .29	−.16 to .37	−.38 to .26
Criteria with infit mn. sq. > Mean + S.D.	None	None	None	PR* (marginally)	PR (marginally)
Criteria with infit mn. sq. < (Mean − S.D.)	None	None	None	GR** (marginally)	LR*** (marginally)

*PR = Pronunciation **GR = Grammatical resource ***LR = Lexical resource*

issue with the scales. The results further indicated that the assessment categories were similar in difficulty and, as intended, were contributing equally, yet in distinct but statistically significant ways, to the overall assessment.

Decisions made at end of Stage 3

The results at the end of Stage 3 provided justification for the finalisation of the scales and sign-off for operational release.

Conclusion

The aim of this chapter has been to demonstrate the application of a multi-stage exploratory sequential scale development mixed methods design in L2 assessment research. We have shown the natural fit between the scale construction and this particular mixed methods design. Stage 1 of the project cast a broad net in order to tap into examiner perceptions and analysis of speech and generate inductive findings. Stage 2 adopted a narrower focus and looked at individual aspects of the scales, both through a discrete 'clinical' approach, which focused on each descriptor individually, and through an in-depth consideration of examiner experiences when using the draft scale and descriptors in real time. Stage 3 broadened the empirical focus by using a larger sample of examiners and learner performances and by using the scales in their entirety. Each stage drew on the findings of the previous one in an additive fashion. Such an approach, which capitalises on complementary strengths, enables meta-inferences based on integration of findings and seeks to counterbalance methodological shortcomings, provided the final product of the project – the set of assessment scales – with a strong validity argument about their robustness.

We hope to have also demonstrated the necessity for careful consideration of a range of issues at the planning stage, which in turn would support the rigour and systematicity underlying the final outcome or product. Careful planning leads researchers to weigh different possibilities during the multiple stages of data collection and analysis, which ultimately leads to a more rigorous final product.

Every research study needs to be evaluated against criteria of empirical quality and validity. This was discussed conceptually at the beginning of this chapter and it would be fitting at this stage to close by addressing the empirical quality and validity of the mixed methods project discussed here. In Chapter 4, this volume, Ziegler and Kang provide a useful list of concerns for researchers to address regarding the validity of a mixed methods investigation. Their list, even though more suited to basic mixed methods designs and very detailed, will serve here as a useful taxonomy of key validity areas which this project has addressed (Table 4).

Table 4 Validity concerns as addressed in this project

Validity concern	How the research team has addressed the concern
Internal validity: Design quality (Multistage exploratory sequential design)	A constructivist paradigm espousing variable and multiple realities and focusing on individual 'voices' and 'stories' was complemented by a postpositivist paradigm which reduces ideas into a final product/ number/scale/survey.
	Scale development is suited to a progression from an inductive exploratory stage to a deductive measurement stage, which is reflected in the exploratory sequential design. The large-scale nature of the project further necessitated an advanced design which broke the process into semiautonomous stages.
	Established procedures were followed within each stage and study, e.g. Conversation Analysis procedures were applied during the initial exploration of learner language, Verbal Protocol norms were followed during the exploration of examiner views when using the scales, data assumptions about linking were taken into account for the quantitative studies employing Rasch analysis.
Internal validity: Interpretive rigour	Consistency between meta-inferences was observed through the high level of convergence of the findings from the qualitative and quantitative investigations.
	Both qualitative and quantitative findings were integrated additively to form meta-inferences.
	Interpretations, findings and recommendations were discussed within the development team which included members with a range of theoretical and practical knowledge about scale development and the different methodologies employed.
External validity	The samples of learner test performances in each relevant study were selected to represent a range of background variables, such as first language, age, gender, and as such to be representative of the population and to have wider applicability. The use of a large-scale final phase which drew on a varied sample of learners contributed to the generalisability of the assessment scales. The sample of examiners used in the study was selected to be representative of examiners at different levels of the speaking examiner hierarchy, thus supporting the transferability of inferences to the examiner cadre as a whole.
	High transferability to other contexts of assessing speaking ability, since the final product – the scales – is theoretically based, empirically supported and generic in nature.

The amount of effort which was needed for the completion of this project also highlighted some general caveats which need to be noted. The successful completion of the project necessitated a large team with different areas of expertise including qualitative and quantitative research, test development, language learning, scale development, speaking assessment, and last but not least, project management. It is important to note, therefore, that a key limiting factor in the use of this design is the need for a team with a wide range of research expertise. For this reason, the methodological literature consistently identifies this design as a challenging one, since both quantitative and qualitative skills are needed, much more so than in an explanatory sequential design (Creswell 2014b, Hesse-Biber and Johnson 2013). As Creswell and Zhou note in Chapter 3, this volume, 'a large repertoire of research skills' are needed when carrying out an advanced mixed methods design and collaboration between individuals with diverse methodological skills is essential.

A further caveat is the considerable length of time needed for the completion of such complex multistage designs. The project discussed in this chapter covered 16 months, which is a substantial period of time that needs to be factored in during the initial planning stage. Complex projects based on the exploratory sequential design, therefore, have considerable resource implications which are not to be underestimated.

Despite these practical issues, we believe that a multistage exploratory sequential scale development design is exceptionally well suited to scale development projects as its sequence of methods and potential for additive insights leads to a synergetic relationship between the individual parts – a relationship which allows the whole to be more than the sum of the parts.

10 The development of a new Reading task: A mixed methods approach

Mark Elliott

Gad S Lim

Cambridge English Language Assessment

This chapter provides a case study of the use of mixed methods in the revision of an established test and the development of a new Reading task. The aim is to describe the process firstly by which the validity of a well-established test was assessed with respect to a specific context of use and, secondly, by which a threat to validity was addressed by the development and validation of a new task.

This chapter covers the following areas:

- *Construct definition*
- *Task design*
- Aspects of *validity, validation* and mixed methods
- The *test revision process within assessment systems*
- Integrating mixed methods into the *test revision process*

Introduction

The Cambridge English: Advanced revision project

This research project represents part of a larger project, namely the 2015 *Cambridge English: Advanced* revision project. *Cambridge English: Advanced* (UCLES 2012a, 2014), also known as the *Certificate in Advanced English (CAE)*, is primarily targeted at Level C1 of the Common European Framework of Reference for Languages (CEFR, Council of Europe 2001). Level C1 is the second-highest level defined within the CEFR, representing 'an advanced level of competence suitable for more complex work and study tasks' (2001:23); in other words, a C1-level user possesses the requisite level of language proficiency for higher education (university-level) study. With this in mind, among several other high-level goals, one goal of the *Cambridge*

English: Advanced revisions project was to strengthen the validity argument for *Cambridge English: Advanced* as a test which might be used as a measure of language proficiency for the purpose of entry into an English-medium university environment. This objective formed the motivation for the work described in this chapter.

In keeping with the above, each of the existing test components was scrutinised to identify threats to validity, whether in terms of construct under-representation (not adequately testing the full extent of sub-skills and cognitive processes involved in reading) or measurement issues identified by analysis of live performance of tasks. The revision also considered issues such as administration, timing, score aggregation and overall reliability. Since this process necessarily entailed both qualitative work (relating to the cognitive and context validity of the test) and quantitative work (relating to the scoring validity of the test), a mixed methods research design was chosen in order to integrate these two essential, complementary aspects.

This chapter describes the use of a multi-phase parallel convergent mixed methods research design for one part of the test revision process, focusing on a single test component – Reading – and the revisions made to the component in order to strengthen the validity argument for its use as a test of language proficiency for the purpose of entry into an English-medium university environment.

The process of test validation involves the gathering of evidence to demonstrate that a task shows acceptable levels of cognitive, context and scoring validity (Weir 2005). The natures of these three aspects of validity are such that this evidence will inevitably be a mixture of qualitative and quantitative data and that decisions must be based upon a principled evaluation of both types of data; thus a mixed methods approach is indicated as the most appropriate.

The particular mixed methods design chosen for this project was a multiphase parallel convergent design (see Ziegler and Kang, Chapter 4, this volume). After an initial qualitative phase based on a literature review and evaluation of the existing Reading component in order to determine the need (if any) for a new or revised task, the development of the task required an initial, relatively small-scale study to evaluate different options for the new task, followed by a larger-scale study to gather validation evidence for the final chosen task. These phases are described in more detail below.

The use of Cambridge English: Advanced for academic purposes

The main focus of this study is the use of *Cambridge English: Advanced* for academic purposes, and specifically its use as a test of language proficiency for the purpose of entry into an English-medium university environment, as stated above. In order to evaluate the appropriacy of *Cambridge English: Advanced* for this purpose, we should first understand what specific validity claims are being tested here.

Users often refer to tests of 'academic English', or EAP (English for Academic Purposes) tests. While this may be a convenient shorthand, it does risk obscuring what is meant by 'academic English' and, by extension, what is expected of a test of academic English. That being the case, it is worth defining the use domain against which the exam is being evaluated, which is captured by the earlier stated purpose of the exam as an exam of 'language proficiency for the purpose of entry into an English-medium university environment'. Each part of that statement will now be considered in turn.

The test use being considered here is of the test as a measure of *language proficiency* and not as a measure of academic preparedness. What needs to be demonstrated is the extent to which the exam targets language ability at the appropriate level.

The test use being considered here is *entry* into higher education. That is, the intent is not to determine whether or not candidates have full grasp of the specialised conventions of academic discourse they will find in their subject areas. Rather the intent is to see the extent to which they will be able to cope with those underlying language-related study skills which are common across academic disciplines, i.e. basic, generic academic literacy.

University is mentioned without distinguishing between undergraduate and postgraduate study or between different fields of study. This is because research into academic language (Biber, Conrad, Reppen, Byrd and Helt 2002) shows that 'students tend to encounter the same structural linguistic features, regardless of their academic field or level of study' (Jamieson, Eignor, Grabe and Kunnan 2008:83). Research into academic field-specific language assessment also confirms the above finding (Clapham 1996, Weir 1983).

Finally, intended inferences include the ability of candidates to operate within a university *environment*. That is, the interest is not merely in specifically academic activities (e.g. lectures, formal intertextual written assignments) but also in related activities undertaken as part of university life (e.g. study groups, service encounters). This conceptualisation understands that academic success depends on the ability to engage with various participants about a variety of content in various university settings for different purposes using different registers. Other research has conceptualised 'academic' in this way (e.g. Biber et al 2002, Feak, Reinhart and Rohlck 2009, Simpson-Vlach and Leicher 2006, Taylor and Geranpayeh 2011), as have other tests of academic English such as the internet-based TOEFL (Chapelle, Enright and Jamieson 2008, Jamieson, Jones, Kirsch, Mosenthal and Taylor 2000).

In sum, a use domain has been specified which shows the scope and parameters for which the validation argument is being made, and indeed for the design of academic English tests. As can be seen, other tests used for the same purpose have followed similar definitions of the domain.

Having defined the use domain for which the validity argument is being made, it would be good to also specify the scope of that evaluation. Validity has a number of aspects; Weir's (2005) socio-cognitive framework identifies at least five: a cognitive aspect, a contextual aspect, a scoring aspect, a criterion related aspect, and a consequential aspect. It is also worth keeping in mind that validation is a matter of degree and a continuing activity that is never completed as such (Kane 2006, Messick 1989, Saville 2003). New exams are necessarily limited in the extent to which they can be validated as, for example, the consequential aspect cannot yet be properly evaluated, where the test is not yet in live use.

On the other hand, the test being considered in this project is not an entirely new test, but is a revision which retains many features of the earlier test, for which significant validation work has been conducted, covering all aspects of validity (e.g. Buckendahl, Foley and Lim 2011, Geranpayeh 2011, Gosa and Frentiu 2008, Hawkey 2006, Khalifa and Weir 2009, Lim, Geranpayeh, Khalifa and Buckendahl 2013). Validation work was also undertaken in support of the revised test in general (Elliott 2011, Elliott, Lim and Galaczi 2012, Lim 2013, Lim and Vice 2012). That being the case, this paper will focus only on those aspects of validity that are most pertinent to validating this particular use of the test – the cognitive and contextual and scoring aspects, otherwise known as construct validity – and only as they are relevant to this particular use.

With regard to construct parameters, it needs to be said that language exams cannot completely replicate real-world contexts of language use (Field 2013, Ginther and Grant 1996), and this therefore cannot be the goal of testing or a requirement in the validation thereof. But in order to minimise the 'inferential leap' in test validation, tests are often developed to be as similar to those contexts as possible.

Being similar to the real world also facilitates a test's being 'adequately representative' (Field 2013:79) of the construct. The more aspects of a construct that are sampled, the better. It also needs to be said that the correct aspects need to be sampled. That is, if a particular skill involved performing six levels of lower and higher order cognitive operations, coverage of the lower order operations only in the absence of the higher order operations would not be sufficient. On the other hand, performance of the highest order operations typically requires all the levels below it, and an exam that tests this would have a greater claim of construct validity.

With language proficiency for entry into an English language-medium university environment in mind therefore, the *Cambridge English: Advanced* revisions consider the extent to which *Advanced* covers an adequately representative range of *cognitive processes* involved in reading and appropriate contextual parameters, according to the socio-cognitive framework (Weir 2005). Indeed, the *context validity* (2005) of a test, which concerns 'the extent to which the choice of tasks in a test is representative of the larger universe of tasks of which the test is assumed to be a sample' (2005:19), is of equally fundamental importance to the test's cognitive validity. With this in mind, determining the requirements for the target language use (TLU) domain is a critical first step in the development or revision of any test. In the case of *Cambridge English: Advanced*, with its focus as a test of language proficiency for the purpose of entry into an English-medium university environment, the context validity of the *Cambridge English: Advanced* Reading component needed to be appraised to account for of the specific claims of the suitability of the test for drawing inferences related to the TLU domain of Higher Education.

There are naturally many varied TLU domain tasks, considerations of which led to both minor and major changes to components of the revised *Advanced* test format. These changes affected all the test components to a greater or lesser extent. Falling outside the scope of this study were a major change to the Writing component, where a new compulsory essay task was included and a more minor change to the Speaking component, where the collaborative task saw a change to written prompts in order to shift the emphasis onto the evaluation of more abstract concepts which more closely correspond to those the successful candidate might encounter in formal discussion in the TLU domain.

In addition to the context validity and cognitive validity aspects of the test, the *scoring validity* aspects of the test must be considered to ensure that it is reliable and that inferences drawn from test scores are sound.

The development of a new Cambridge English: Advanced Reading task

During the process of appraising the construct coverage of *Cambridge English: Advanced* as a test of language proficiency for the purpose of entry into an English-medium university environment, a validity threat was identified: the construct coverage of the Reading component did not cover the full range of cognitive processing indicated by the cognitive processing model for reading which underpins the Cambridge English suite of exams (Khalifa and Weir 2009).

The study described in this chapter records the process by which the validity threat was identified and the process by which Cambridge English sought to address the threat and build a stronger validity argument for *Cambridge English: Advanced* as a university entrance test.

Research design

Description/discussion of the project phases

Each phase below will be described and discussed in turn.

Phase 1: Identification of need for new task and development of draft task

	Identification of need for new task (embedded within broader exam revision programme)	Outcome of QUAL analysis
	QUAL	QUAL
Objectives	• To identify threats to the validity of inferences drawn from candidate performance on the *CAE* Reading component with respect to the target language use domain of Higher Education • To develop proposed revised and/or new tasks to meet any identified threats to validity	• To operationalise the desired testing focuses within a suitable task type and response format
Data collection	• Literature review of cognitive processing models of reading and expected C1 performance • Review of current *CAE* Reading format (Question papers and Item Writer Guidelines)	• Outcome of previous QUAL phase
Data analysis procedures	• Use socio-cognitive framework, and particularly model of reading outlined in Khalifa and Weir (2009), to identify gaps in the testing focuses of the *CAE* Reading component by comparing the cognitive processing required by *CAE* Reading with performance expectations according to the socio-cognitive framework in relation to C1-level language users • Conduct content analysis of reading texts	• Identification of textual parameters and possible response formats for new task type • Draft item specifications

Outcome: Provisional trial task specifications, preliminary trial tasks.

Phase 2: Trialling and task analysis

	Trialling	Task analysis
	QUAN	QUAL
Objectives	• To provide statistical evidence for the scoring validity of the task items	• To provide preliminary evidence of the functioning of the task

Data collection	• Anchored, timed administration of versions of revised *CAE* Reading component featuring different trial tasks under pretesting conditions	• Trial tasks analysed within socio-cognitive framework using expert judgement
Data analysis procedures	• Classical and Rasch analysis of candidate response data • Timing data	• Content analysis of the cognitive and context validity of the trial task, following the approach of Phase 1

Outcome: Development of final task specifications.

Phase 3: Pretesting

	Pretesting	Textual analysis
	QUAN	QUAN
Objectives	• To provide further statistical evidence for the scoring validity of the task items	• To provide statistical evidence for the appropriacy of the texts with relation to the specified TLU domain, Higher Education (HE)
Data collection	• Standard anchored pretest administration of six tasks	• Coh-Metrix and Lextutor analysis of input texts for six tasks
Data analysis procedures	• Classical and Rasch analysis of candidate response data	• Comparison of textual features of input texts with *IELTS* and undergraduate texts

Outcome: Final live task, validation argument.

Procedures, products, timeline

Figure 1 outlines the procedures used in the study and the products which formed the outcomes of those processes, alongside a timeline of the study. Each phase will be described in turn in detail; the focus will be on how mixed methods were used and what the use of mixed methods brought to the study, rather than a full rigorous analysis of all the data from each phase.

Phase 1: Task design

Goals

• To evaluate the strength of the validity argument for the existing *Advanced* Reading paper format for use within a Higher Education context and identify any threats to validity.

• To produce draft specifications for new/revised task(s) designed to address identified threats to validity.

Figure 1 Multi-phase exploratory sequential design with a nested parallel convergent phase

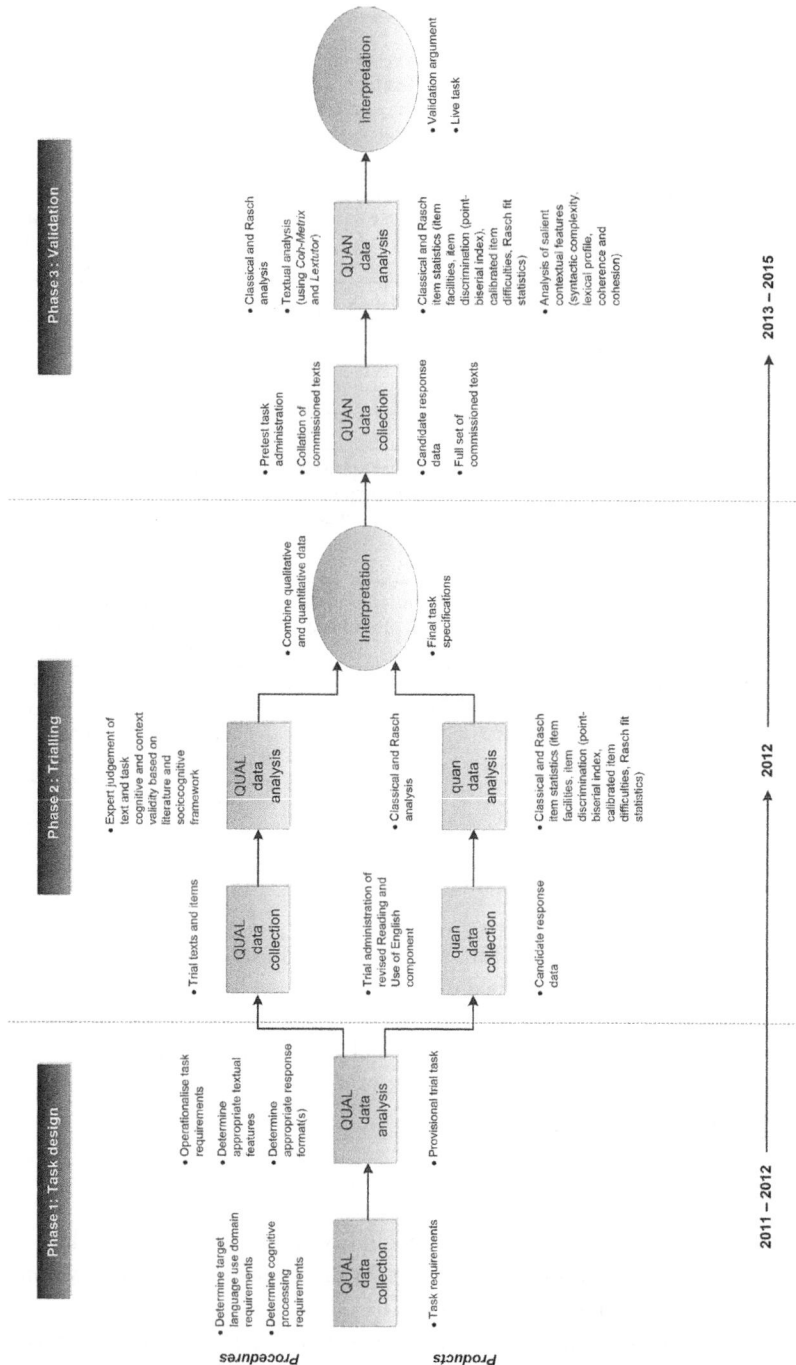

Overview

The first phase of the project involved a review of the current test specifications with respect to the use of the test as an instrument for Higher Education institutions to assess applicants' English levels. This involved a literature review of the requirements for such a test and a critical analysis of *Cambridge English: Advanced* against these requirements. Following this, draft tasks were to be produced to address any validity threats identified by the analysis.

Research questions

Qualitative research questions

1. Are there any significant threats to the validity of inferences drawn from candidate performance on the *Cambridge English: Advanced* Reading component with respect to the target language use domain of Higher Education?

2. What textual features and cognitive processing requirements would need to be incorporated into a revised *Cambridge English: Advanced* Reading task in order to address any threats to validity?

Qualitative data collection

Determining target language use domain requirements

In terms of the TLU domain of Reading within a Higher Education context, one specific demand task of many university-level courses is the ability to assimilate information from various sources for the purpose of producing a critical evaluation of the opinions expressed in the texts. A review of the existing *Advanced* Reading component (UCLES 2012a:7–21) indicates that the first three of the four parts of the test all involve items relating to single texts, while Part 4 includes reading across multiple texts. A close inspection of the items in Part 4, however, indicated that while multiple texts may need to be read in order to answer the items, the reading operations involved in responding required the candidate to focus on each text one by one in isolation, and did not involve the integration of meaning across texts.

Determining cognitive processing requirements

Cambridge English: Advanced Reading was analysed in depth by Khalifa and Weir (2009) using Weir's (2005) socio-cognitive framework in terms of its cognitive validity. This analysis is framed within an eight-level hierarchical cognitive processing model of reading, which does not represent a simple linear process but rather a series of interacting processes which may occur simultaneously (Field 2013:94) and with each higher-level process drawing on lower-level processes as necessary. Not all levels of cognitive processing may be engaged by a particular reading task (whether a test task or a real-world task); the eight levels are outlined briefly below.

- *Word recognition*, the lowest level of cognitive processing, describes 'matching the form of a word in a written text with a mental representation of the orthographic forms of the language' (Khalifa and Weir 2009:47).

- *Lexical access* describes the 'retrieval of a lexical entry from the lexicon, containing stored information about a word's form and its meaning' (Field 2004:151). In other words, a meaning is assigned to the word identified from the reader's lexical store.

- *Syntactic parsing* is the process by which a syntactic structure is imposed on a string of words; the process involves 'not only word order, but also word form (morphology) and structural elements (determiners, prepositions, auxiliary verbs etc.)' (Khalifa and Weir 2009:49).

- *Establishing a propositional meaning* involves taking a parsed sentence and establishing 'a literal interpretation of what is on the page. The reader has to add external knowledge to it to turn it into a message that relates to the context in which it occurred' (Khalifa and Weir 2009:50).

- *Inferencing* involves elaborating the meaning of a proposition by supplying 'details that the [writer] has not felt it necessary to include' (Field 2013:101) due to the assumptions of shared knowledge – as Khalifa and Weir (2009:50) note, 'a text cannot include all the information that is necessary in order to make sense of it'. This process also includes identifying the referents of pronouns and other referring items, and pragmatic evaluative inferences (Khalifa and Weir 2009:51).

- *Building a mental model* involves integrating information into a representation of the text so far and monitoring this representation to ensure that it remains 'consistent, meaningful and relevant' (Field 2004:241).

- *Creating a text-level structure* is the highest level of processing which takes place when reading a single text. Main and supporting ideas must be identified and related in a hierarchical structure, while some information may be discarded if it is not considered relevant (Field 2004:241).

- *Creating an organised representation of several texts*, a higher level of cognitive processing still, does not take place unless information needs to be integrated and reconciled from multiple sources. This represents a greater cognitive challenge since the elements which create coherence and cohesion within a single text are not present across multiple texts, and the arguments presented may be contradictory (Lacroix 1999).

The relationship between these processes, together with the reader knowledge and contextual features which inform each level of processing, is summarised in Figure 2.

Figure 2 A cognitive processing model of reading (Khalifa and Weir 2009:43)

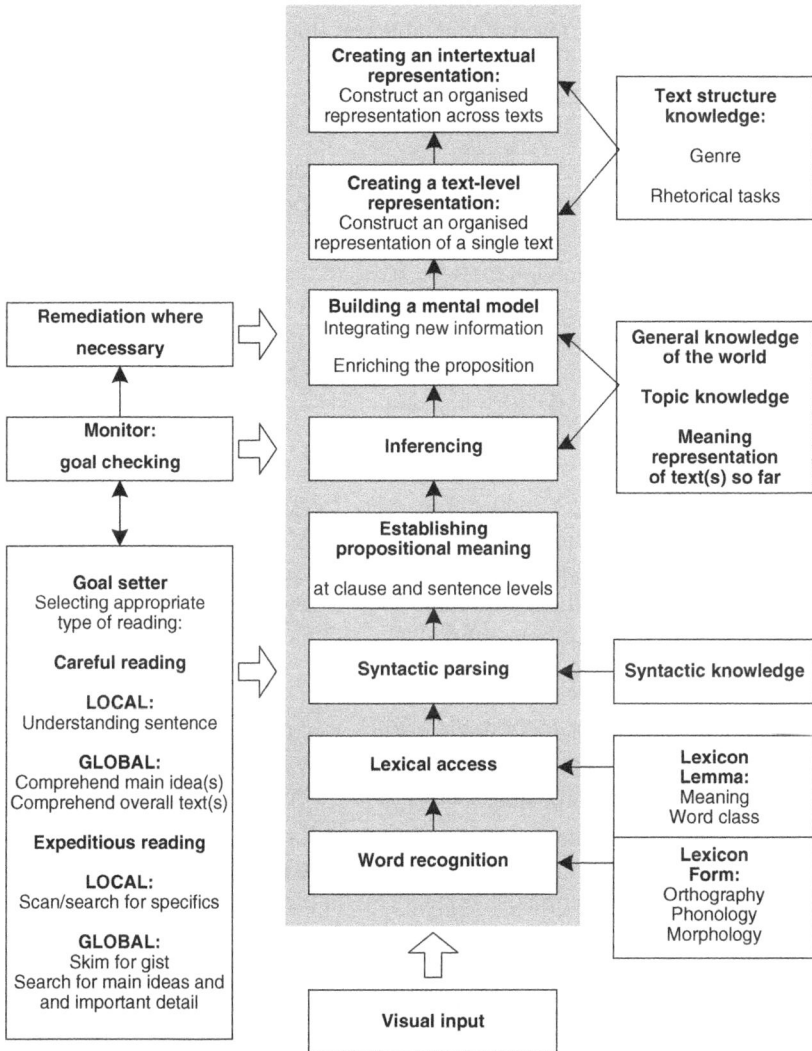

Task requirements

The considerations of cognitive and context validity outlined above indicate that a new task involving the assimilation of information from various texts would strengthen the validity of the *Cambridge English: Advanced* Reading component both in terms of its coverage of the cognitive processes which might be expected of a C1 level user and in terms of its sampling of the universe of tasks successful candidates might be expected to encounter within the target language use domain of HE. The decision was therefore taken to investigate the feasibility of either producing a test task or adapting an existing task to elicit the desired cognitive processes and which parallel the required TLU domain task. Such a task, however, would also need to exhibit an acceptable level of scoring validity:

- it should be possible to generate multiple tasks consisting of items within the required difficulty range for *Cambridge English: Advanced* Reading items
- the items should exhibit acceptable levels of discrimination (as measured by the point-biserial correlation coefficient) and should fit the Rasch model (as measured by the infit mean square statistics).

Qualitative data analysis

Task requirements

A literature review was conducted in order to establish typical features of texts encountered at undergraduate level in an HE context. In conjunction with already established cognitive processing requirements, this provided a blueprint of the theoretical requirements of a new task; what remains is to operationalise these requirements within a concrete task.

Operationalising task requirements

Operationalising the task requirements involves taking the targeted testing focus and producing appropriate texts and items which adequately meet the cognitive and contextual requirements. In this case, the requirements were:

1. Texts which adequately resemble those which the candidates might encounter within the specified target language use domain in terms of complexity and functions; here, there are natural limitations in terms of length of text and specificity of topic, which will be discussed below.
2. Items which require the candidate to engage in discourse representation at the intertextual level; here, the response format is important since it may influence the levels of cognitive processing required (see below).

Determining appropriate textual features

In determining appropriate textual features for the task, it should first be noted that the notion of familiarity with any specific academic genres is problematic since there is considerable variation in genres across different academic fields. In other words it is difficult to infer from the ability to deal with one field's genre that the same holds for another field (Clapham 1996). Since this implies that tests and texts either need to be highly specific to a particular field or not field specific, more general texts which share the higher-level features of academic texts without being written within field-specific registers are indicated. It is worth noting that this same argument led to the move during the development of *IELTS* (a test of academic English) from multiple modules within its predecessor, ELTS, to a single academic module within the then-new *IELTS* (1996).

For these reasons, texts from non-academic sources but which contain the type of abstract argumentation typical of academic texts were selected, for example those found in popular science or literary review magazines.

Determining appropriate response formats

As discussed earlier in this chapter, a critical concern for the new/revised task is that it engages the highest level of cognitive processing of creating an intertextual discourse representation. With this in mind, response format becomes an important consideration since, as Field (2013:133) notes regarding the effect of response format on cognitive processing (for listening tests), 'formats such as MCQ [multiple-choice questions] or gap filling mainly target discrete points of information. There is no requirement on the candidate to recognise the logical links that connect these points, or to build them into a discourse-level information structure'. This corroborates Rupp, Ferne and Choi's (2006:469) assertion that multiple-choice reading items 'focus predominantly on the microstructure representation of a text base rather than the macrostructure of a situation model. As a result, higher-order inferences that may lead to an integrated macrostructure situation model in a non-testing context are often suppressed or are limited to grasping the main idea of a text'. Since the creation of a discourse-level information structure at the level of an individual text is a necessary precondition for the desired testing focus of the creation of an intertextual discourse representation, a response format which does not unduly interfere with higher-level cognitive processing should therefore be chosen – for example, in line with Field (2013) and Rupp et al (2006) above, multiple-choice items provide a variety of potential meanings in the options before the reader engages with a text and therefore interfere with the meaning construction process since the reader becomes engaged in a process of confirming or disconfirming the various potential meanings rather than creating meaning from the text in the way a reader does outside of a testing context.

Among the existing selected response formats used across the *Cambridge English* suite – multiple choice, true/false, right/wrong/doesn't say, multiple matching and gapped text, the first three formats are compromised in the manner described above. Gapped text tasks are designed to primarily focus on textual coherence and cohesion, which also renders the response format unsuitable for the required purpose.

While it would be possible to create a constructed response format task focusing on intertextual discourse representation, such a task would present considerable marking issues in terms of constraining the list of acceptable responses and standardising the marking to ensure consistency and reliability; the high-level, relatively abstract and complex nature of the intertextual discourse representation would rule out short, constrained keys and would be expressible in a wide variety of ways which would prove problematic to manage in terms of a large-scale test.

By a process of elimination, the considerations outlined above left only multiple matching as a potential response format among existing *Cambridge English* test response formats. Khalifa and Weir (2009:85) note that multiple matching is essentially a form of multiple choice; however, the key difference in the context of the required testing focus is that the texts themselves form the options, which means that the issue surrounding the presentation of various meaning representations through the options of a standard multiple-choice question should not arise and the cognitive processing of the text should not be unduly interfered with to the same extent. This format was already present in Part 4 of the *Advanced* Reading component, albeit with a different testing focus, that of 'locating specific information, detail, opinion and attitude' (UCLES 2012a:8). This led to the decision to investigate two potential solutions for:

1. Adapting the existing Advanced Reading Part 4 task to include items focusing on intertextual discourse representation while retaining the existing testing focus for other items.

2. Developing a new multiple-matching task focusing specifically on intertextual discourse representation and separate from the existing Part 4.

With two sets of possible task specifications identified, two experienced item writers were commissioned to produce tasks for trialling.

Phase 2: Trialling

Goals

- To produce trial texts and tasks according to the draft specifications.
- To evaluate the appropriacy of the trial texts and tasks in terms of their cognitive and context validity using expert judgement according to salient criterial features established in the socio-cognitive framework (Khalifa and Weir 2009, Weir 2005).
- To trial the tasks in order to evaluate their scoring validity (Khalifa and Weir 2009, Weir 2005).

Overview

Two tasks were written, edited and trialled using a multi-phase exploratory sequential design. Two alternative formats were used:

Adapted Part 4 task

Two existing Part 4 tasks were adapted and two new items were written for each task by experienced members of the *Cambridge English: Advanced* item-writing team. The existing Part 4 focuses on expeditious reading, requiring the candidate to identify which writer from a selection of four or five short texts, linked by theme, expresses a particular opinion, states a particular fact or narrates a particular experience.

New task

Four evaluative texts on the same theme (for example, reviews of a book) were selected and items written in order to test whether the candidate can identify agreement or disagreement between texts, with the texts themselves forming the four options for the item. The trial items followed two different templates (Elliott, Vidaković and Corrigan 2013):

A. Firstly identify an opinion expressed in one of the texts and then identify which other text shares or contradicts this opinion, or

B. Identify which text differs from the others in terms of an expressed opinion.

In both cases, candidates must select one text only; the item only provides information on the subject of the opinion but not the opinion itself, which the candidate must identify. This last point is important since it prevents the item from interfering unduly with the meaning and discourse representation processes by 'feeding' meaning to the candidate in terms of what opinions are being expressed. In this way, the aim was to elicit the desired cognitive processing of the creation of discourse-level information structures for individual texts, then incorporating the individual discourse representations into an intertextual discourse-level information structure.

Research questions

Qualitative research questions

1. On the basis of expert judgement, to what extent are the trial tasks likely to elicit the desired cognitive processes?

2. On the basis of expert judgement, are the texts in the trial tasks of an appropriate register and complexity in order to draw inferences about performance in the TLU domain of Higher Education?

Quantitative research question

3. Do the items in the trial tasks exhibit scoring properties (item difficulty and discrimination) appropriate for *Advanced* Reading?

Mixed methods question

4. In terms of their cognitive validity (qualitative), contextual validity (qualitative) and scoring validity (quantitative), do the trial tasks meet the requirements to address the validity threats identified in Phase 1?

Qualitative data collection

The data comprised the texts (in the two formats) and their accompanying items, to be analysed separately to evaluate their context validity (the appropriacy of the texts for a university context) and cognitive validity (the appropriacy of the level of cognitive processing engaged by the items). See the Appendix for sample texts and tasks.

Qualitative data analysis

Texts

Content analysis was employed to evaluate the texts in terms of salient criterial features of context validity (Khalifa and Weir 2009, Weir 2005): overall text purpose, style/register, functional resources, lexical resources and grammatical resources. The nature of the texts found in the new and adapted tasks was noticeably different, reflecting the different natures of the tasks for which they were intended. The following conclusions were reached, as described by Elliott et al (2013:2):

> The texts for [the new task] are of a nature consistent with academic texts in terms not only of vocabulary, structures and lexical bundles but also in their expository/argumentative overall text purposes and their detached tone and formal style. This contrasts with the descriptive/narrative, informal texts of a personal nature in the tasks for [the adapted task], which do not contain the lexical or grammatical complexity of their counterparts in [the new task].

> Critically, and as a consequence of the features described above, it is necessary to read across stretches of text in order to locate the answers to the items in New Tasks 1 and 2, whereas the information required to respond to the items in Adapted Tasks 1 and 2 is found locally within individual sentences (and across no more than three sentences), and is more explicitly stated. This means that considerably more higher-level processing is engaged by [the new task], whereas [the adapted task] may only require processing up to the level of individual propositions.

> Since the intention of the task is to focus on high-level processing in academic-type reading, this represents extremely strong construct-based evidence for the appropriacy of the task in New Tasks 1 and 2 over the task in Adapted Tasks 1 and 2, which do not elicit the appropriate levels of cognitive processing or involve dealing with appropriate texts. It should also be noted that the texts in New Tasks 1 and 2 present a high level of face validity, particularly in conjunction with a task which closely resembles types of reading candidates will encounter in real-life university contexts.

In other words, based on the content analysis, it was reasonable to claim regarding the context validity of the task that the new task is broadly 'representative of the larger universe of tasks of which the test is assumed to be a sample' (Weir 2005:19), while it would be difficult to sustain such an argument for the adapted task in that the candidate is not required to demonstrate the appropriate level of cognitive processing on a text resembling those of the TLU domain in terms of functions or complexity.

Tasks

The items within the trialled tasks in both the new and adapted tasks were similar in terms of their focus; all items focused on identifying agreement or disagreement between the texts. There were three distinct item types, however:

1. The first item type took the form 'Which author agrees/disagrees with [Author X] on . . .', going on to give the topic but not the opinion.
2. The second item type took the form 'Which author disagrees with the other authors on . . .', again going on to give the topic but not the opinion.
3. The third item type took the form 'Which two authors agree/disagree on . . .', once again going on to give the topic but not the opinion and with the candidate required to select two texts for two marks.

The first two item types, which appeared in the new task, involve a rather different task: while the first item involves identifying the opinion from one given source to those in the others, the second is essentially an 'odd one out' task. While the former can be argued to resemble a reading task typical of a Higher Education situation, where a student preparing an assignment reads multiple sources on a topic and compares different viewpoints, the second type seems somewhat artificial. Trial New Task 1 contained a mixture of the first and second item types, while Trial New Task 2 contained only the second. Note that the question of the suitability of the items is separate from that of the suitability of the text – a suitable text may have unsuitable items and vice-versa – so need to be considered separately.

The third item type, which appeared in the adapted task, could be considered analogous to the first item type, but with the first text not given and with the candidate therefore needing to identify both relevant texts.

One key difference between the new and adapted tasks was that while the new task was a self-contained whole, featuring only items with a focus on creating an intertextual discourse representation, the adapted task featured such items in combination with items which retained the original task purpose of expeditious reading; this entailed the candidate switching from one type of reading and level of cognitive processing to another quite different level in mid-task. Additionally, there is a risk of item interdependency when the intertextual items follow items focusing on specific information across the texts, which may in some case have relevance to the opinions expressed. Four versions were produced for trialling, with two versions each of the new and adapted tasks.

Quantitative data collection

The four tasks were trialled according to standard Cambridge English Language Assessment pretesting procedures (see Corrigan and Crump (2015) for a discussion of Cambridge English pretesting procedures), which involve administering the tasks under controlled, timed conditions to a sample of candidates ($n \geq 150$ after pruning) from an appropriate mixture of first language groups (no more than one third from a given language group) who are preparing to take the live test, in combination with a set of shared Reading and Use of English tasks which in each case comprised a mock-up of a full Reading and Use of English paper (subject to final decisions on the number of items in each task and the order of tasks). The shared tasks allowed a concurrent Rasch analysis of the trial tasks, and therefore for a robustly anchored comparison of their relative difficulties and their difficulties relative to the shared tasks (see Geranpayeh 2013:242–253 for a discussion of the Cambridge English approach to item analysis and calibration). Standard classical analysis at both item level (facility and point-biserial correlation coefficient) and test level (Cronbach's alpha and standard error of measurement (SEM)) were also generated.

Quantitative data analysis and results

The quantitative statistical analysis provided summary statistics for the four trial test versions (Table 1), mean item difficulty estimates for each test part (Tables 2 and 3), and item-level statistics (Tables 4 and 5).

Table 1 indicates that all the trial test versions exhibited similar, satisfactory overall levels of reliability (Cronbach's alpha > 0.85 for all versions, which is acceptably high). Tables 2 and 3 show that overall version mean difficulties were reasonably similar since most tasks were identical across all four test versions, and only the trial tasks varied in difficulty.

Table 1 Test summary statistics

Version	N	Mean P	Cronbach's alpha	SEM
New Task 1	172	0.518	0.871	3.072
New Task 2	178	0.519	0.853	3.084
Adapted Task 1	216	0.543	0.883	3.024
Adapted Task 2	207	0.539	0.852	3.104

Table 2 Mean difficulty estimates by test part, New Tasks 1 and 2, deviation from target difficulty (scaled logits*)

Test Part	New Task 1	New Task 2
Part 1	0.83	0.83
Part 2	1.86	1.86
Part 3	9.88	9.88
Part 4	−0.57	−0.57
Part 5	2.35	2.35
Part 6†	10.25	7.32
Part 7	−4.22	−4.22
Part 8	−6.02	−6.02
Version Mean	**1.03**	**0.87**

* 9.1 scaled logits = 1 logit
† New task

Table 3 Mean difficulty estimates by test part, Adapted Tasks 1 and 2, deviation from target difficulty (scaled logits*)

Test Part	Adapted Task 1	Adapted Task 2
Part 1	0.83	0.83
Part 2	1.86	1.86
Part 3	9.88	9.88
Part 4	−0.57	−0.57
Part 5	2.35	2.35
Part 6	−4.22	−4.22
Part 7a†	0.92	−0.23
Part 7b†	14.03	4.98
Version Mean	**2.33**	**1.81**

* 9.1 scaled logits = 1 logit
† Part 7a = existing multiple-matching items, Part 7b = new items

The results reported in Tables 4 and 5 indicate that the trial task in New Task 1 did not function acceptably well: two of the three items displayed unacceptably low levels of discrimination (Point-biserial correlation index (PBSI) of 0.04 and 0.18) and the mean difficulty of the three items was high at 10.25 scaled

Table 4 Item difficulty estimates, deviation from target difficulty (scaled logits*)

Task	Item	Difficulty estimate	Mean difficulty
New Task 1 Part 6	1	7.02	10.25
	2	10.01	
	3	13.72	
New Task 2 Part 6	1	7.29	7.32
	2	5.34	
	3	9.33	
Adapted Task 1 Part 7	1+2	21.19	14.03
	3+4	6.86	
Adapted Task 2 Part 7	1+2	1.82	4.98
	3+4	8.13	

* 9.1 scaled logits = 1 logit

Table 5 Item discrimination (point biserial correlation indices): Trial items

Task	Item	Point-biserial correlation index (PBSI)
New Task 1 Part 6	1	0.18
	2	0.04
	3	0.26
New Task 2 Part 6	1	0.31
	2	0.20
	3	0.27
Adapted Task 1 Part 7	1+2	0.33
	3+4	0.53
Adapted Task 2 Part 7	1+2	0.44
	3+4	0.40

logits above the target. Here we should note that a high difficulty on the new items is perhaps to be expected since the candidates, who were all preparing to take *Advanced*, would have been familiar with the existing task types but had not seen the new task type before and would have been unlikely to have undertaken much practice in the type of intertextual reading required on their courses.

The trial task in New Task 2 performed better, with one item displaying low, but not exceptionally low, discrimination (PBSI of 0.20, which is below the target minimum of 0.25 but may be acceptable as a single item in an otherwise well discriminating task – see Geranpayeh (2013) for a discussion of the use of PBSI in relation to test construction). The mean difficulty of the trial items was also high, but the difference from the target of 7.32 scaled logits is less concerning in light of the expected difficulty created by unfamiliarity with the task. The statistics indicate that, as a prototype task in a trial test, the task has performed acceptably well to proceed to further development, where the production of multiple forms and refinements to the crafting of items should produce tasks which acceptably meet the criteria for test construction.

Adapted Task 1 performed worst of all the four versions, with a mean item difficulty of +14.03, which is too high even in light of the unfamiliarity of the task; even taking into account the good discrimination of the items (PBSIs of 0.33 and 0.53), the task could not be considered to have performed acceptably.

Adapted Task 2 performed best of all the tasks in terms of scoring validity, with a mean item difficulty of +4.98, which is acceptable in light of the unfamiliarity of the task; the items also discriminated well (PBSIs of 0.44 and 0.40). This evidence, however, needed to be interpreted within the context of the suitability of the texts, as discussed above.

Interpretation: Mixed methods question

The joint display below summarises the findings of Phase 2 in terms of the acceptability of each task by test version, according to both qualitative (text and task features) and quantitative (psychometric properties) criteria. (See Ziegler and Kang, Chapter 4, and Guetterman and Salamoura, Chapter 7, this volume, for a discussion of joint displays.)

Table 6 Phase 2 joint display

Task	QUAL	QUAN
New Task 1	Text – **YES** (text is of a suitable register and complexity) Task – **NO** (some items represent a somewhat artificial 'odd one out' task)	**NO** – items display poor discrimination, difficulty probably too high
New Task 2	Text – **YES** (text is of a suitable register and complexity) Task – **YES** (items should exhibit acceptable cognitive validity and be of a type of reading applicable to the TLU domain)	**YES** – items generally display acceptable discrimination and difficulty, although high, within acceptable parameters considering the unfamiliarity of the trial task
Adapted Task 1	Text – **NO** (not of a suitable register or complexity, not suitable for eliciting desired cognitive processes or exhibiting acceptable context validity) Task – **YES** (items should exhibit acceptable cognitive validity and be of a type of reading applicable to the TLU domain)	**NO** – difficulty of items too high
Adapted Task 2	Text – **NO** (not of a suitable register or complexity, not suitable for eliciting desired cognitive processes or exhibiting acceptable context validity) Task – **YES** (items should exhibit acceptable cognitive validity and be of a type of reading applicable to the TLU domain)	**YES** – items display acceptable discrimination and difficulty

The only trial version to meet acceptable levels in all three areas was New Task 2, which was selected as the task to proceed with to the next phase of refining item writing specifications and producing multiple versions for pretesting. In particular, it was decided that the adapted task could not be suitable under any circumstances due to textual considerations which rendered the tasks unsuitable in terms of cognitive or context validity. (The Appendix provides an example of New Task 2. It is similar but not identical to the new task, which cannot be published due to confidentiality of live test material.)

Based on New Task 2, the task specifications for item writers were refined utilising the findings of Phase 2. Six further tasks were written based on six different sets of texts in order to provide the first potential set of live test material and, in terms of this study, to provide the basis for the collection of further validation evidence based on a larger data set and more refined task specifications.

Phase 3: Validation

Goals

- To use automated textual analysis to evaluate the task context validity by means of a comparison of criterial indices compared to those in a mini-corpus of core undergraduate texts.
- To evaluate the scoring validity of the same tasks through an analysis of pretesting data.

Overview

Phase 3 represents an in-depth quantitative analysis of a greatly expanded pool of tasks produced for live test use (n=27), considering both their scoring validity in terms of item characteristics and context validity based on automated text analysis, which can usefully generate meaningful results based on the amount of text available at this phase.

Research questions

Quantitative questions

1. Do the items in the trial tasks exhibit appropriate scoring validity (item difficulty and discrimination) appropriate for *Advanced* Reading?
2. In terms of computational cohesion and coherence metrics generated by Coh-Metrix (McNamara, Louwerse, Cai and Graesser 2005), to what extent do the texts in the new/revised tasks exhibit similar

properties to those likely to be encountered in the TLU domain of Higher Education?

Mixed methods question

1. Using the socio-cognitive framework (Weir 2005) as outlined in Phase 1, what evidence is there that the new/revised task exhibits an appropriate level of cognitive validity (qualitative, from Phase 2), context validity (quantitative, from Phase 3) and scoring validity (quantitative, from Phase 2) as a means of addressing the validity threats identified in Phase 1?

Quantitative data collection

Green and colleagues (Green, Weir, Chan, Taylor, Field, Nakatsuhara and Bax 2012) used Coh-Metrix (McNamara et al 2005) to compare pre-revision *Advanced* Reading texts with those found in undergraduate textbooks as well as those in *IELTS*. The textbooks provide a benchmark of authentic texts, whereas *IELTS* provides a benchmark of what might be possible with examination texts. Coh-Metrix is an automated, web-hosted 'computational tool that provides a wide range of language and discourse measures . . . that [users] can use to obtain information about their texts on numerous levels of language' (McNamara, Graesser, McCarthy and Cai 2014:1). It provides a range of quantitative indices which describe a text's lexical, syntactic and text-level (coherence) properties; these indices can be used to quantify a text's difficulty and also to identify features which typify certain text types, or differentiate between two text types in empirical, objective and quantitative terms which can often usefully augment qualitative judgements made by humans.

Following the lead of Green et al (2012), the six *Cambridge English: Advanced* texts were analysed along with a sample of undergraduate texts using the latest version of Coh-Metrix (version 3.0, McNamara et al (2014) and indices were generated for comparison.

Quantitative data analysis and results

Following Green, Ünaldi and Weir's (2010) investigation into the role that quantitative textual analysis tools can play in the selection of reading texts, Green et al (2012) conducted an empirical study into the textual features of texts drawn from *Cambridge English: Advanced* Reading papers and how certain salient metrics compared with those pertaining to a selection of reading texts drawn from *Cambridge English: First* and *Proficiency* Reading papers, *IELTS* Reading papers and, which is of interest to this tudy, the corpora of core undergraduate texts from the University of Bedfordshire (42 extracts from 14 texts) originally assembled in 2005 for an *IELTS* predictive validity study (Green et al 2012). Green et al used the online tools Coh-Metrix 2.0 (McNamara et al 2005) and VocabProfile (Cobb 2003a, 2003b, Heatley, Nation and Coxhead 2002) to establish a set of salient quantitative measures by means of which to compare textual features. Coh-Metrix generates a range of indices relating to lexical, syntactic and text-level features using latent semantic analysis (McNamara et al 2014), while VocabProfile generates indices relating to vocabulary frequency and the proportion of words from the Academic Word List (AWL) (Coxhead 2000) in a text.

Green et al (2012) used the following procedures to determine a salient set of features:

1. Determine a set of criterial indices which show statistically significant differences (p<0.05) across the three levels represented by *Cambridge English: First*, *Advanced* and *Proficiency* according to an independent-samples Kruskal-Wallis Test.

2. Determine which of the selected indices are salient in terms of the cognitive processing model of reading described in Khalifa and Weir (2009) in that they could be related to cognitive processes and exclude the non-salient indices. Seventeen indices were selected by this method.

3. Group the remaining indices into three categories: lexical indices, syntactic indices and text-level representation indices.

See Green, Khalifa and Weir (2013), who provide a detailed account of the index selection process and a guide to the interpretation of each index, and Weir (2013b) for an illustration of using Coh-Matrix in the quantitative analysis of reading passages to investigate context validity from a trace historical perspective.

Once a set of criterial indices which show statistically significant differences was established (phase 1), multiple regression models were computed, which indicated that the lexical indices set provided the best level of prediction of text level (adjusted R2=0.434) (Green et al 2012:29) but that combining all three sets produced considerably better predictive power (adjusted R2=0.583) (2012:32). Six individual indices emerged as key indices in that they were predictive of text level individually (Green et al 2013:34):

- Logical operator incidence score
- Argument Overlap, adjacent, unweighted
- Proportion of content words that overlap between adjacent sentences
- Celex, logarithm, mean for content words (0–6)
- Academic Word List (AWL) words

- Very infrequent (Offlist > 15K) words.

The 17 selected indices were then used to compare the sample of 49 *Cambridge English: Advanced* texts with the 42 undergraduate texts and 42 *IELTS* Reading texts, again using a Kruskal-Wallis analysis to provide a three-way comparison. Green et al (2012:38) concluded that:

> the CAE texts did not reflect the nature of academic text (as represented by the Bedfordshire mini-corpus of undergraduate textbooks) as closely as the IELTS texts. The study suggests that selected automated text analysis tools, if employed at the text selection stage, could help the test developers to more closely match the level of the texts employed in CAE to the demands of the academic texts that prospective students might encounter on entering university.

This conclusion is unsurprising in that Green et al did not differentiate between texts drawn from the four different tasks in the (pre-2015) *Advanced* Reading paper; unlike *IELTS* Reading, which comprises three texts chosen according to similar criteria, *Advanced* texts are more varied: texts for Part 4, for example, which focuses on expeditious reading, are not selected from sources which could be expected to reflect academic texts in their nature. The new intertextual task, however, might be expected to exhibit criterial indices which more closely resemble those of the undergraduate corpus; in order to test these, it was decided to make a two-way comparison between the 27 *Advanced* new intertextual task texts – the full contents of the task bank at the time of this study, totalling 16,009 words (here 'text' should be interpreted as meaning the full text for a task, i.e. all four short texts plus, where relevant, a brief introductory paragraph) and the undergraduate corpus, the results from which were kindly made available by the Centre for Research in English Language Learning and Assessment (CRELLA) at the University of Bedfordshire (42 extracts from 14 texts, totalling 18,484 words).

In order to compare the new texts with the undergraduate corpus, the texts were subjected to Coh-Metrix (McNamara, Louwerse, Cai and Graesser 2012) and VocabProfile (Cobb 2003a, 2003b) analyses; here an issue arose in that the version of Coh-Metrix at the time of writing, Version 3.0, produces a different output which, although it includes a greatly increased number of indices, does not produce all the Coh-Metrix 2.0 indices (at least in directly comparable form). Specifically, the discontinued indices were:

Lexical
Higher level constituents per word
Text-level representation
Concreteness, minimum in sentence for content words

Anaphor reference, adjacent, unweighted
Anaphor reference, all distances

This left 13 indices (five lexical, five syntactic and three text-level representation) for comparison. Descriptive statistics for the indices from the two sets of texts are shown in Table 7.

The data sets were then compared for each index using the 2-tailed Mann-Whitney U test, which is the equivalent of the Kruskal-Wallis test for two data sets (i.e. a non-parametric alternative to a Student's t-test). The results of this analysis are shown in Table 8.

Lexical indices

The Mann-Whitney U test did not indicate any statistically significant differences between the two sets of texts for the following indices:

- Average syllables per word
- Celex, logarithm, mean for content words (0–6)
- Academic Word List (AWL) words
- Very infrequent (Offlist > 15K) words.

The proportion of AWL words is noteworthy here, since Green et al found a significantly and considerably lower proportion of AWL words (1.64%) in the pre-2105 *Advanced* Reading paper texts than in the undergraduate texts, suggesting that the language in the new task is considerably closer to academic texts (9.01% in the new task versus 9.34% in the undergraduate texts). The average number of syllables per word, which contributes to processing difficulty, was also statistically significant in Green et al, although the difference is not as marked (mean 1.66 versus 1.54, compared to 1.72 for the undergraduate texts).

The Mann-Whitney U test indicated statistically significant differences between the two sets of texts for the following index:

Type-token ratio for all content words

Interestingly, this index suggests that the type-token ratio (the proportion of distinct content words in the text – the higher, the greater the source of difficulty) presents more difficulty for the reader in the new *Cambridge English: Advanced* tests than in the undergraduate texts.

In other words, the analysis suggests that the new *Advanced* texts are broadly similar to the undergraduate texts (four out of the five indices do not indicate any statistically significant differences), with no indication that they are less lexically challenging.

Syntactic indices

The Mann-Whitney U test did not indicate any statistically significant differences between the two sets of texts for the following indices:

Table 7 Descriptive statistics for Coh-Metrix and VocabProfile indices, new *Cambridge English: Advanced* intertextual task versus CRELLA undergraduate mini-corpus

Index	Advanced intertextual tasks (n=27)				CRELLA undergraduate mini-corpus (n=42)			
	Min	Max	Mean	SD	Min	Max	Mean	SD
Lexical								
Average syllables per word	1.53	1.82	1.66	0.09	1.46	2.07	1.72	0.14
Type-token ratio for all content words	0.66	0.80	0.73	0.03	0.51	0.9	0.65	0.08
Celex, logarithm, mean for content words (0–6)	2.01	2.37	2.19	0.09	1.79	2.48	2.14	0.15
Academic Word List (AWL) words	3.80%	14.49%	9.01%	2.50%	0.12%	22.22%	9.36%	4.92%
Very infrequent (Offlist >15K) words	0.32%	6.6%	2.76%	1.60%	0.41%	11.62%	3.98%	3.06%
Syntactic								
LSA, Sentence to sentence adjacent mean	0.12	0.34	0.18	0.05	0.11	0.45	0.26	0.08
Average words per sentence	14.92	26.35	20.73	2.57	13.76	30.3	21.47	4.26
Mean number of modifiers per noun-phrase	0.68	1.11	0.87	0.12	0.64	1.24	0.95	0.15
Mean number of words before the main verb of main clause in sentences	2.78	7.39	4.81	1.18	1.86	7.97	4.59	1.39
Sentence syntax similarity, all, across paragraphs	0.05	0.09	0.07	0.01	0.05	0.1	0.07	0.01
Text-level representation								
Argument Overlap, adjacent, unweighted	0.14	0.74	0.39	0.16	0.26	0.9	0.56	0.15
Logical operator incidence score	22.58	59.41	40.60	9.09	20.54	71.43	46.14	11.78
Proportion of content words that overlap between adjacent sentences	0.02	0.09	0.06	0.02	0.04	0.17	0.1	0.03

Table 8 Results of 2-tailed Mann-Whitney U test on Coh-Metrix and VocabProfile indices

Hypothesis	p value	Decision (threshold p<0.05)
Lexical		
Average syllables per word is the same for both sets of texts	0.099	*Retain the null hypothesis*
Type-token ratio for all content words is the same for both sets of texts	0.000	Reject the null hypothesis
Celex, logarithm, mean for content words (0–6) is the same for both sets of texts	0.119	*Retain the null hypothesis*
Academic Word List (AWL) words is the same for both sets of texts	0.373	*Retain the null hypothesis*
Very infrequent (Offlist >15K) words is the same for both sets of texts	0.230	*Retain the null hypothesis*
Syntactic		
LSA, Sentence to sentence adjacent mean is the same for both sets of texts	0.000	Reject the null hypothesis
Average words per sentence is the same for both sets of texts	0.857	*Retain the null hypothesis*
Mean number of modifiers per noun-phrase is the same for both sets of texts	0.016	Reject the null hypothesis
Mean number of words before the main verb of main clause in sentences is the same for both sets of texts	0.267	*Retain the null hypothesis*
Sentence syntax similarity, all, across paragraphs is the same for both sets of texts	0.129	*Retain the null hypothesis*
Text-level representation		
Argument Overlap, adjacent, unweighted is the same for both sets of texts	0.000	Reject the null hypothesis
Logical operator incidence score is the same for both sets of texts	0.063	*Retain the null hypothesis*
Proportion of content words that overlap between adjacent sentences is the same for both sets of texts	0.000	Reject the null hypothesis

- Average words per sentence
- Mean number of words before the main verb of main clause in sentences
- Sentence syntax similarity, all, across paragraphs.

The Mann-Whitney U test indicated statistically significant differences between the two sets of texts for the following indices:

- LSA, Sentence to sentence adjacent mean
- Mean number of modifiers per noun-phrase.

The lower sentence to sentence adjacent mean for the *Advanced* new task texts (mean of 0.18 versus 0.26 for the undergraduate texts) indicates a source of increased difficulty in the *Advanced* texts, while the lower mean number of modifiers per noun-phrase (0.87 versus 0.95 for the undergraduate texts) should facilitate reading and make the text easier. Given that the majority of indices are not statistically significantly different and that the two which are differ in opposite directions by moderate amounts (the differences in both cases are no more than the standard deviation of the undergraduate text scores), the results suggest little difference in syntactic complexity between the two sets of texts.

Text-level representation indices

The Mann-Whitney U test did not indicate any statistically significant differences between the two sets of texts for the following index:

- Logical operator incidence score.

The Mann-Whitney U test indicated statistically significant differences between the two sets of texts for the following indices:

- Argument Overlap, adjacent, unweighted
- Proportion of content words that overlap between adjacent sentences.

In both cases where there are statistically significant differences between the two sets of texts, the higher scores for the undergraduate texts (0.56 versus 0.39 for Argument Overlap, adjacent, unweighted and 0.1 versus 0.06 for Proportion of content words that overlap between adjacent sentences) suggest features which should facilitate reading of the undergraduate texts. This is perhaps unsurprising given that the *Advanced* texts each comprise four separate mini-texts – the point of the task is to focus on incorporating information from different texts into a single discourse representation, which is cognitively challenging precisely due to the lack of coherence and cohesion (plus the possibility of contradictory information in different texts).

Key indices

Four of the key indices which were identified as being individually predictive of text level (Green et al 2013:34) showed no statistically significant differences between the two sets of texts:

- Logical operator incidence score
- Celex, logarithm, mean for content words (0–6)
- Academic Word List (AWL) words
- Very infrequent (Offlist > 15K) words.

The Mann-Whitney U test indicated statistically significant differences between the two sets of texts for the following key indices:

- Argument Overlap, adjacent, unweighted
- Proportion of content words that overlap between adjacent sentences.

As discussed above, both these indices indicate additional sources of difficulty in the *Advanced* texts, which may be due to the fact that each *Advanced* text is comprised of four separate mini-texts; in any case, there is no evidence from the six key indices that the *Advanced* texts are easier than the undergraduate texts.

Textual data: Summary

The Coh-Metrix and VocabProfile indices provide quantitative evidence that the texts in the new intertextual *Advanced* Reading task are broadly similar in terms of complexity to the undergraduate texts: eight of the 13 indices show no statistically significant differences between the two sets, including four of the five lexical indices and three of the five syntactic indices. Of the five indices which did show statistically significant differences, four indicated additional sources of difficulty in the *Advanced* reading texts and only one indicated an additional source of difficulty in the undergraduate reading texts.

There is naturally much variation in the indices from text to text in both sets, as a cursory glance at Table 7 will confirm, and there is of course a considerable difference in the length of complete texts undergraduates are presented with compared to those in the new *Advanced* task, but the results of this empirical analysis suggests that the texts in the two sets possess more similarities than differences, and in particular in terms of key indices. This provides strong evidence to support the context validity of the task in relation to studying in HE.

Interpretation: Mixed methods question

The joint display in Table 9 summarises the findings of Phase 3 in terms of the acceptability of each task by test version, according to both qualitative (cognitive processing) and quantitative (textual features according to Coh-Metrix and psychometric properties of items) criteria. Relevant findings from Phase 2 are also incorporated into the joint display, which can be considered to represent an evidence-based validation argument within the socio-cognitive framework (Weir 2005) for the new task within the context of its stated purpose, focusing on the aspects of cognitive validity, context validity and scoring validity.

The specifications of the new task were finalised and the task was incorporated into the revised *Advanced* Reading component for live administration.

The format of the new task (given in the Appendix) is summarised in the revised *Cambridge English: Advanced Handbook for Teachers*:

> Candidates must read across texts to match a prompt to elements in
> the texts. The prompts require candidates to read across the four texts
> to understand the opinions and attitudes expressed in order to identify

Table 9 Phase 3 joint display

Aspect of validity	QUAL	QUAN
Context validity	The texts are of a nature consistent with academic texts in terms not only of vocabulary, structures and lexical bundles but also in their expository/argumentative overall text purposes and their detached tone and formal style. Critically, and as a consequence of these features, it is necessary to read across stretches of text in order to locate the answers to the items.	Coh-Metrix analysis shows that the texts have scores on key indices which are similar to those from a mini-corpus of core undergraduate texts, suggesting that the reading difficulty of the texts is likely to be similar due to shared lexical, syntactic and text-level features. Texts in the new task are shorter than those encountered in the TLU domain, but this is unavoidable in the context of a test which has practical time constraints.
Scoring validity	n/a	Items perform to an acceptable standard of discrimination and at an appropriate difficulty level for C1 candidates.

agreement and disagreement between the writers. The items only provide information on the subject of the opinion, not the opinion itself: this is for the candidate to identify. Candidates may need to identify an opinion expressed in one of the texts and then identify which other text shares or contradicts this opinion, or they may need to identify which text differs from the other three in terms of an expressed opinion (UCLES 2014:9).

Conclusions

This chapter has described the process by which a new Reading task came to be introduced into the *Cambridge English: Advanced* Reading component and the role played by mixed methods research in this process. The research outlined does not of course represent the entirety of the process, since rather than a piece of 'pure' academic research, the project was a practical project. In such a project, the research element played one, albeit critical, part; however, when developing a task for a standardised international test such as *Advanced*, there were also considerations of practicality, such as the replicability of a task which must be produced in large quantities, as well as of face validity, which cannot be ignored and need to be considered alongside the research evidence. It should further be reiterated that the development of the new Reading task formed only a small part of the broader project of the *Advanced* revisions process (and within the ongoing process of revision of the entire Cambridge English suite of exams), meaning that decisions made regarding the new task needed to be weighed against decisions taken regarding the rest of the Reading component, the balance of *Advanced* across the five components and the relationship between *Advanced* and the rest of the Cambridge English suite. Such considerations of scope and practicality, despite their obvious importance, fall outside the scope of this chapter.

A mixed methods approach provided a robust and rigorous framework within which to conduct the research described in this chapter, facilitating the development of a task while simultaneously producing a validity argument for its intended use within the socio-cognitive framework – in other words, demonstrating its fitness for purpose, as outlined in the joint displays (Tables 6 and 9) showing the analysis of merged data within a convergent design.

While there are many possible research design approaches which could be used for a test revision project, a mixed methods design seems to provide clarity, balance and overall coherence to the process since it forces the test developer to consider the relationships between the phases of the process and the interaction between the qualitative and quantitative aspects *a priori* in an objective manner. The *a priori* approach here needs to be interpreted in terms of each phase – there is a natural evolution since successive phases are dependent on the outcome of earlier ones; for instance, the quantitative textual analysis in Phase 3 was not decided upon at the start of the process but rather later, when it was determined that there were questions around text appropriacy in Phases 1 and 2 which merited empirical investigation. This requisite flexibility in a multiphase design presents certain challenges within the mixed methods paradigm, since any changes required as the research progesses need to be introduced in a way which does not compromise the integrity of the mixed methods design – the QUAL and QUAN aspects still need to dovetail appropriately so that the work remains mixed methods rather than simply the application of both qualitative and quantitative methods in a parallel but non-convergent design.

Validation is not a one-off activity, however; it is an ongoing process and no validity argument can ever be considered to be 'finished'. In this spirit, it is worth considering what further research could be carried out in the future to further strengthen the validity argument detailed here. It is suggested that more data on the cognitive validity of the task could be generated by an appropriate qualitative method, such as verbal think-aloud protocols or retrospective questionnaires carried out with test takers completing the task. This data could provide further evidence of the extent to which the task engages cognitive processing at the level of the creation of an inter-textual representation, which was the original reason the new task was developed.

In conclusion, it seems that a mixed methods approach to research during test development promises a practical and rigorous approach to combining the qualitative and quantitative considerations which must of necessity both contribute to the process.

Appendix
Sample tasks

New task: Texts used

You are going to read four extracts from articles in which academics discuss the contribution the arts (music, painting, literature, etc.) make to society. For questions 1–4, choose from the academics A–D. The academics may be chosen more than once.

Mark your answers on the separate answer sheet.

The Contribution of the Arts to Society

A Lana Esslett

The arts matter because they link society to its past, a people to its inherited store of ideas, images and words; yet the arts challenge those links in order to find ways of exploring new paths and ventures. I remain sceptical of claims that humanity's love of the arts somehow reflects some inherent inclination, fundamental to the human race. However, exposure to and study of the arts does strengthen the individual and fosters independence in the face of the pressures of the mass, the characterless, the undifferentiated. And just as the sciences support the technology sector, the arts stimulate the growth of a creative sector in the economy. Yet, true as this is, it seems to me to miss the point. The value of the arts is not to be defined as if they were just another economic lever to be pulled. The arts can fail every measurable objective set by economists, yet retain their intrinsic value to humanity.

B Seth North

Without a doubt, the arts are at the very centre of society and innate in every human being. My personal, though admittedly controversial, belief is that the benefits to both individuals and society of studying science and technology, in preference to arts subjects, are vastly overrated. It must be said, however, that despite the claims frequently made for the civilising power of the arts, to my mind the obvious question arises: Why are people who are undeniably intolerant and selfish still capable of enjoying poetry or appreciating good music? For me, a more convincing argument in favour of the arts concerns their economic value. Needless to say, discovering how much the arts contribute to society in this way involves gathering a vast amount of data and then evaluating how much this affects the economy as a whole, which is by no means straightforward.

C   Heather Charlton

It goes without saying that end-products of artistic endeavour can be seen as commodities which can be traded and exported, and so add to the wealth of individuals and societies. While this is undeniably a substantial argument in favour of the arts, we should not lose sight of those equally fundamental contributions they make which cannot be easily translated into measurable social and economic value. Anthropologists have never found a society without the arts in one form or another. They have concluded, and I have no reason not to concur, that humanity has a natural aesthetic sense which is biologically determined. It is by the exercise of this sense that we create works of art which symbolise social meanings and over time pass on values which help to give the community its sense of identity, and which contribute enormously to its self-respect.

D   Mike Konecki

Studies have long linked involvement in the arts to increased complexity of thinking and greater self-esteem. Nobody today, and rightly so in my view, would challenge the huge importance of maths and science as core disciplines. Nevertheless, sole emphasis on these in preference to the arts fails to promote the integrated left/right-brain thinking in students that the future increasingly demands, and on which a healthy economy now undoubtedly relies. More significantly, I believe that in an age of dull uniformity, the arts enable each person to express his or her uniqueness. Yet while these benefits are enormous, we participate in the arts because of an instinctive human need for inspiration, delight, joy. The arts are an enlightening and humanising force, encouraging us to come together with people whose beliefs and lives may be different from our own. They encourage us to listen and to celebrate what connects us, instead of retreating behind what drives us apart.

New task: Questions

Which academic . . .

1. has a different view from North regarding the effect of the arts on behaviour towards others?
2. has a different view from Konecki on the value of studying the arts compared to other academic subjects?
3. expresses a different opinion to the others on whether the human species has a genetic predisposition towards the arts?
4. expresses a similar view to Esslett on how the arts relate to demands to conform?

Adapted task: Text

Starting out on your career

Are you a graduate trying to plan out the best career path for yourself? We've asked five careers consultants to give some tips on how to go about it.

Consultant A

A university degree is no guarantee of a job, and job hunting in itself requires a whole set of skills. If you find you are not getting past the first interview, ask yourself what is happening. Is it a failure to communicate or are there some skills you lack? Once you see patterns emerging it will help you decide whether the gaps you have identified can be filled relatively easily. If you cannot work out what the mismatch is, get back to the selection panel with more probing questions, and find out what you need to do to bring yourself up to the level of qualification that would make you more attractive to them: but be careful to make this sound like a genuine request rather than a challenge or complaint.

Consultant B

Do not be too dispirited if you are turned down for a job, but think about the reasons the employers give. They often say it is because others are 'better qualified', but they use the term loosely. Those who made the second interview might have been studying the same subject as you and be of similar ability level, but they had something which made them a closer match to the selector's ideal. That could be experience gained through projects or vacation work, or it might be that they were better at communicating what they could offer. Do not take the comments at face value: think back to the interviews that generated them and make a list of where you think the shortfall in your performance lies. With this sort of analytical approach you will eventually get your foot in the door.

Consultant C

Deciding how long you should stay in your first job is a tough call. Stay too long and future employers may question your drive and ambition. Of course, it depends where you are aiming. There can be advantages in moving sideways rather than up, if you want to gain real depth of knowledge. If you are a graduate, spending five or six years in the same job is not too long provided that you take full advantage of the experience. However, do not use this as an excuse for apathy. Graduates sometimes fail to take ownership of their careers and take the initiative. It is up to you to make the most of what's available within a company, and to monitor your progress in case you need to move on. This applies particularly if you are still not sure where your career path lies.

Consultant D

It is helpful to think through what kind of experience you need to get your dream job and it is not a problem to move around to a certain extent. But in the early stages of your career you need a definite strategy for reaching your goal, so think about that carefully before deciding to move on from your first job. You must cultivate patience to master any role. There is no guarantee that you will get adequate training, and research has shown that if you do not receive proper help in a new role, it can take 18 months to master it.

Consultant E

A prospective employer does not want to see that you have changed jobs every six months with no thread running between them. You need to be able to demonstrate the quality of your experience to a future employer, and too many moves too quickly can be a bad thing. In any company it takes three to six months for a new employee to get up to speed with the structure and the culture of the company. From the company's perspective, they will not receive any return on the investment in your salary until you have been there for 18 months. This is when they begin to get most value from you – you are still fired up and enthusiastic. If you leave after six months it has not been a good investment – and may make other employers wary.

11

Investigating the impact of international assessment: A convergent parallel mixed methods approach

Hanan Khalifa

Coreen Docherty

Cambridge English Language Assessment

In this chapter, we illustrate the application of the convergent parallel design for investigating the impact of international assessments on teaching, learning and assessment practices in a state school system. The chapter focuses on:

- The nature of and issues associated with *impact research* which provide a rationale for using the *convergent parallel design*
- The different stages of the impact project and *the methodological choices* made at each stage to ensure data could be 'mixed'
- The *potential threats* to this design and *how they were mitigated* at each stage of the study
- The *benefits* of using the convergent parallel design for impact research

Introduction

In the field of language testing, impact research aims to understand the effects of assessment on learning and teaching (the micro context) and on educational systems and society in general (the macro context). Although debate about the nature of test impact has a long history (for an overview see Cheng 2014, Wall 2005), it has only been in the last 30 years that empirical research has been conducted to investigate this phenomenon and identify how it operates in practice (Alderson and Hamp-Lyons 1996, Cheng 2004, Hawkey 2006, Wall 2005, Watanabe 1996). A common thread running through impact research to date is that there is no one method that can be used to fully capture the complexity of educational systems and the effect of tests within them or to ensure various stakeholders' true and active participation in an impact study in order to fully capture their views and attitudes. As such, there is growing interest in using a mixed methods research approach when investigating test impact because (a) it enables researchers to have an in-depth understanding of the situational context thus building the knowledge base to better identify possible causes and effects, (b) it enables investigators not only to obtain results but to explain such results in more detail, and (c) it enhances stakeholders' confidence in the findings reported as a result of the triangulation of information derived from multiple data sources.

Although all mixed methods research designs described in Ziegler and Kang, Chapter 4, this volume, are relevant and appropriate for research-ing impact (depending on the aims and stage of the impact research project), in this chapter, we will exemplify the application of the convergent parallel design to a specific mixed methods research study. The study reported here aimed at investigating the impact of international language assessment which was introduced into the Vietnamese educational system as part of a reform initiative. We will first explore the features and issues associated with impact research which will provide a rationale for using mixed methods in general and the convergent parallel design in particular. Then, the remainder of the chapter will focus on the methodological choices that were made when con-ducting the Viet Nam Impact Study, making reference to the key elements of mixed methods research outlined in Sections 1 and 2 of this volume. As the focus of this chapter is on the method rather than the findings, readers are invited to read a full account of the study in Khalifa, Nguyen and Walker (2012).

Investigating impact

Issues

It is accepted in the academic literature that tests have the potential to influ-ence behaviour within the classroom (i.e. the micro context) but also beyond it more generally (i.e. the macro context) in that their introduction may result in stakeholders engaging in behaviours that were not present before the test was introduced (Alderson and Wall 1993, Cheng and Curtis 2004, Saville 2012a, Wall 2000). For example, teacher and learner attitudes towards the language being learned may change in response to a newly introduced exam, while at the same time, parents may modify the type of support they give their children with homework. A snapshot of potential assessment effects on key stakeholders can be seen in Figure 1.

Although test impact is often perceived as a negative phenomenon, the changes associated with the introduction of an exam can be either positive or negative (Bailey 1996, Cheng and Curtis 2004, Messick 1996).

Recognising assessment's potential for positive impact, educational author-ities may introduce international assessment not only to measure achieve-ment against international standards, inform positioning in an increasingly

Figure 1 Overview of assessment effects by stakeholder group

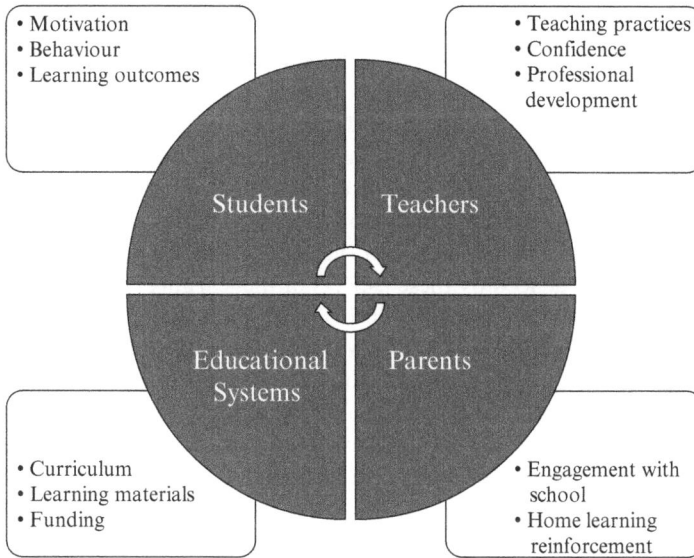

competitive and global market, or provide public accountability but also to indirectly promote desired changes in the educational system in general and in teaching and learning practices in particular (Chambers, Elliott and Jianguo 2012, Eisemon 1990, Heyneman 1987, Shohamy, Donitsa-Schmidt and Ferman 1996, Wall 2005). This is especially common in countries where assessment already has a prominent role in education. As Heyneman (1987) points out, measurement-driven cultures in which teachers already 'teach to the test' may find that it is more efficient to take advantage of this orientation by introducing exams that are designed to promote the teaching and learning practices that are desired rather than trying to change entrenched beliefs and behaviours about teaching. The premise is that a well-designed exam can more rapidly and economically lead to improved instructional quality and consequently better learning outcomes than making system-wide changes such as curriculum reform or improvements to teacher training (Shohamy et al 1996).

The fact that international assessments are used for such a variety of purposes and can potentially influence learning and teaching in a multitude of ways makes test impact a phenomenon that is of great interest to investigate. In addition, as Saville points out in Chapter 2, this volume, part of building a validity argument for an assessment includes determining the effects it has on stakeholders or its consequential validity. By developing a better understanding of the nature of an assessment's influence on learning and different stakeholders, educational authorities and test developers can better support well-intentioned effects and reduce unintended negative consequences of these assessments (Saville 2012b).

Despite agreement that investigating impact is necessary and needed, the process of undertaking this research is challenging because of the complexity of the learning process (Alderson and Wall 1993, Bailey 1996). According to Chapman, Weidman, Cohen and Mercer (2005:526), 'a key characteristic of the educational process is that student learning is influenced by many small factors rather than a few large ones'. Factors such as instructional quality, learner behaviours/attitudes or the curriculum may be influenced by the introduction of assessment but the scope and intensity of the impact may in turn be influenced by these aspects of the learning context (Messick 1996, Watanabe 2004). Hawkey (2006:13) rightly concludes that when investigating impact, one needs to contend with 'a great many independent, intervening and dependent variables', which makes it difficult to tease apart and isolate the different variables in order to systematically measure the influence a test is having on any one aspect of learning and teaching.

The complex nature of test impact and the fact that it operates within a local educational context informs the methodology and methods used to investigate it. This leads us to the topic of our next section.

Methods

Although early attempts were made to measure impact using quantitative methods based on a post-positivist research perspective (Kellaghan, Madaus and Airasian 1982, as cited in Alderson and Wall 1993), there is general dissatisfaction with this approach (Alderson and Wall 1993, Watanabe 2004). Test impact can be affected by context and as such is consistent with the assumptions of a constructivist paradigm. As Messick (1996) notes, a test used in one context may lead to a negative impact whereas in another context its impact may be positive based on the interaction between the qualities of the test and local factors. As a result, researchers have emphasised the need to use qualitative methods such as classroom observation, interviews, focus groups and document reviews which could provide a thorough and in-depth description of the phenomenon of impact (Wall 2000, Watanabe 2004) by recognising that there is not one reality or truth but that meaning is constructed based on the shared experiences of the participants within a particular context (Lincoln and Guba 1994). In fact, the planning stage of impact projects typically starts with a qualitative situational analysis to achieve a better understanding of the educational system and context within which international assessment or an educational initiative is being used. A situational analysis is exploratory in nature and helps in identifying issues and variables that may be having an impact on learning and teaching and is therefore included as an investigation point in the impact research.

Relying solely on qualitative methods, however, is not ideal as there are inherent weaknesses in this approach in terms of prediction and generalisability of the findings beyond the specific research setting (Onwuegbuzie and Johnson 2006), which are often needed for accountability purposes. Impact research tends to have two inter-related aims that Hawkey (2006:3) refers to as the 'formative aspect' which seeks to provide information to improve an initiative, programme and/or test and the 'summative aspect' which is focused on measuring programme outcomes in relation to its goals (i.e. improved language attainment, successful performance in a particular domain (e.g. university, work, etc.)). Educational authorities, parents and employers have a tendency to value the summative aspect which is typically described using quantitative data (i.e. numbers) (Bamberger 2012) because this information allows them to compare performance within and across contexts and can be used for accountability purposes. Although teachers and schools also value the summative aspect of impact research, they recognise that it is through the qualitative strand that the factors associated with positive learning outcomes are identified. This information can then be used to make improvements to the learning environment and potentially lead to better learning outcomes. Therefore, the use of mixed methods for conducting impact research is justified in that neither quantitative nor qualitative methods alone can provide sufficient insight into the phenomenon and the need to address the competing aims (i.e. the formative and summative aspects) of various stakeholder groups cannot adequately be achieved with only one method. A complementary approach, which capitalises on the strengths of each method while offsetting their limitations, is more desirable because this will ultimately lead to more comprehensive findings which will enhance their overall credibility (Bryman 2006a, Creswell and Plano Clark 2011, see also Creswell and Zhou, Chapter 3, this volume).

Having presented an argument for why mixed methods research designs are appropriate and suitable for conducting impact research, the remainder of this section will focus on the use of one of the key mixed methods designs, namely, the convergent parallel design.

Convergent parallel design

As Ziegler and Kang point out in Chapter 4, this volume, the convergent parallel design is characterised by the equal prioritisation of both the quantitative and qualitative data in terms of their role in answering the research question(s) (i.e. QUAN + QUAL). It also entails that both data strands are collected and analysed during the same timeframe of the study with the quantitative and qualitative components being kept independent from each other until the interpretation stage when the data is then mixed.

The strength of this design is that it allows researchers to collect the same and/or complementary data in parallel, creating a snapshot of the phenomenon of interest at one point in time which allows for a richer and deeper understanding of it. It also provides reassurance to users of research results of the comprehensiveness of the findings.

However, despite these benefits, a potential threat to this design is that its successful implementation relies heavily on well-designed, valid and reliable quantitative instruments and credible qualitative data collection procedures. As both data strands are collected within the same timeframe, issues with the instruments or procedures may not come to light until the data analysis stage limiting the researcher's ability to ameliorate the situation after the fact (Creswell and Plano Clark 2011). If not enough care or attention is given to instrument development and data collection procedures, the quality of the data and by extension the credibility of the findings may be limited. Therefore, this design requires researchers who have expertise in both methodological approaches, or a team of individuals with different research expertise to ensure that the instruments, the data collection processes and analysis are done in line with the best practices associated with each method (Creswell and Plano Clark 2011, see also Creswell and Zhou, Chapter 3, this volume). In the following section, we will describe how these potential threats to the data were mitigated when planning and implementing the case study reported below.

Case study: Applying the convergent parallel design to impact research

As mentioned earlier, the context in which an initiative or examination operates can determine the nature of the impact; therefore, we will begin by describing the macro context within which the case study took place.

The context

The research study took place in Viet Nam in one of its largest metropolitan areas, Ho Chi Minh City or Saigon as some Vietnamese prefer to refer to it. Viet Nam embarked on a comprehensive reform initiative several decades ago with the main goal of becoming a modern industrialised society by 2020 (World Bank 2011). The Vietnamese government recognises the important role education plays in achieving this aim as the quality of the workforce is linked to the quality of the education system. Consequently, the government has increased their support for education by earmarking a large proportion of their budget to it. In 2008, 20% of the national budget was assigned to education compared to only 7% in 1986 (World Bank 2011).

As part of the 2020 policy goals, improving English language standards was identified as necessary to better prepare young people for the workforce, for studying abroad and for general participation in the global economy (Nunan 2003, ILO/VCCI no date, Vinh 2008). The first step undertaken by the Ministry of Education and Training (MOET) in Viet Nam was launching its national foreign languages project 2020 which included the setting of target English language standards for key grades based on the Common European Framework of Reference for Languages (CEFR, Council of Europe 2001). These targets are: A1 level at the end of primary school, A2 by the end of junior high school, and B1 at the end of senior high school (Government document 1400/QĐ-TTg (NB the basis for choice of target level was an armchair-based decision)). These are ambitious goals as primary schools in Viet Nam typically operate on a half-day basis due to high demand and limited capacity. Learners generally study 25 periods per week with class periods lasting only about 40–45 minutes. Normally, two class groups share one classroom, alternating morning and afternoon shifts. This means that English provision can consist of as few as one or two lessons per week.

Although MOET sets the national regulations and strategies regarding curriculum, teaching and assessment, the provincial and district Departments of Education and Training (DOET) play a central role in enacting these strategies. This decentralised approach allowed DOET in Ho Chi Minh City (HCM) to initiate an Intensive English Programme (IEP) beginning in 1998–1999 in state-funded primary schools, which included eight additional English lessons a week. These supplementary lessons were accomplished by offering full-day schooling. The IEP was implemented not only to improve English language standards to meet the national strategic objectives set out by MOET but also out of a sense of social responsibility. Until the introduction of the IEP, only children from financially able families had the opportunity to improve their English language proficiency by attending private language centres. It is hoped that the IEP will reduce inequalities in learning outcomes associated with socio-economic class by improving access to education. The provision of full-day schools is a welcome first step towards this aim as the World Bank (2011) has found that it is positively associated with student outcomes.

In response to the IEP's popularity and a desire to measure the programme's effectiveness, HCM DOET introduced mandatory international assessment beginning in the 2010–2011 academic year. DOET required a fair and reliable measure to determine student pathways within the programme due to the high demand on the IEP. In addition, after a decade since its introduction, there was a need to benchmark learner language levels to determine the extent to which the targets set by MOET were being achieved. The *Cambridge English: Young Learners* exams which consist of a suite of three exams: *Starters*, *Movers* and *Flyers* set to measure ability at below A1, A1 and A2 CEFR levels respectively were chosen. Each exam tests all four language skills (i.e. reading, writing, speaking and listening) and is based on a communicative construct of language ability. These tests are specifically designed for young learners in that they introduce children to everyday written and spoken English in a fun and motivating way. All learners receive a certificate which indicates the number of shields awarded (maximum five per skill) and there is no pass or fail result, which is in line with the motivating purpose of the test; that is, all children taking the test should feel that they have achieved something (see UCLES (2012b) for more information on the *Young Learners* exams).

Thus, two years into the introduction of the *Cambridge English: Starters* exam, Cambridge English Language Assessment initiated an impact study in collaboration with DOET in HCM to look at the effect of this decision. The purpose of this study was to gain insight into stakeholder perceptions of and attitudes towards both the introduction of international language assessment and the IEP and to identify any changes in behaviour associated with these initiatives. The findings would then be used to inform DOET of factors associated with effective language learning and teaching as well as areas which may warrant further attention or are in need of improvement.

Research questions investigated

In light of the context described above and the introduction of international English language assessment into the IEP, the impact research study investigated the effect of HCM DOET's strategic decision to increase English language provision through the IEP and to ensure the quality of the provision through the use of international assessment, i.e. *Cambridge English: Young Learners* examinations. Impact was investigated at the micro level, i.e. learning and teaching, and at the macro level, i.e. policy and systems. The following research questions (RQs) in a multi-level convergent parallel design were formulated.

RQ1: What was the intended and unintended impact of this strategic decision at the micro and macro levels as revealed from interviews with policy makers, from focus groups with policy implementers and from focus groups with students?

RQ2: What was the intended and unintended impact of this strategic decision at the micro and macro levels as revealed from surveys completed by parents and teachers and from students' assessment data?

RQ3: How do the intended/unintended impacts of this strategic decision at the micro and macro levels compare among various stakeholder groups (i.e. students, teachers, parents, policy makers, policy implementers)?

As Figure 2 shows, a convergent parallel design was used which involved collecting the quantitative and qualitative data within the same timeframe but analysing it independently (Creswell and Plano Clark 2011, see also Ziegler and Kang, Chapter 4, this volume). The data was only combined at the interpretation stage when results from the qualitative strand were compared

Figure 2 Convergent parallel design procedural diagram (adapted from Creswell and Plano Clark 2011:118)

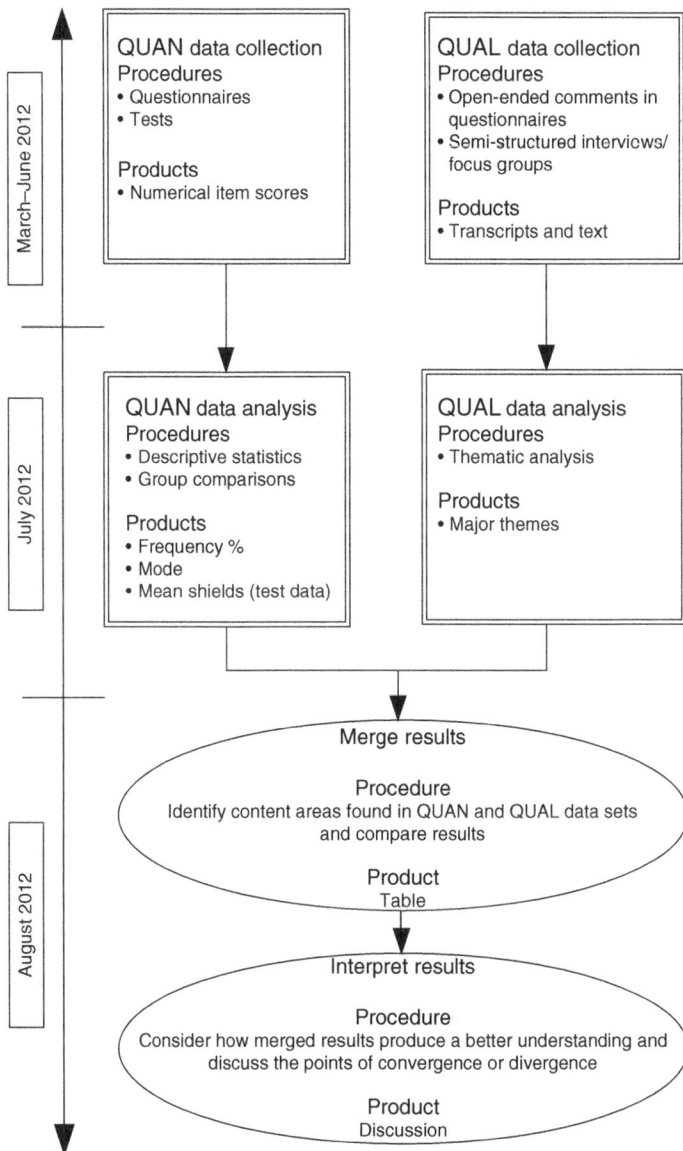

to those from the quantitative strand, discussed accordingly and areas of convergence were highlighted while explanation was provided for areas of divergence. This design was most useful for this particular study because it was important to collect the data during the assessment period so that the researchers could take advantage of the fact that stakeholder perceptions of the examination would be fresh in their mind. That is, stakeholders would not need to activate their long-term memory, which is prone to error (Leeuw 2008), to recall their attitude to or experience of the assessment.

Research participants

Research participants were policy planners at a national and regional level, policy implementers at a district and school level, classroom teachers, students and parents. The inclusion of different stakeholder groups is based on the understanding that tests can have antithetical effects on them in that something viewed as positive by one group may be perceived as negative by another (Green and Hawkey 2005). Also, as Cheng (2014) points out, there is a tendency for impact research to primarily focus on the teacher so there is a lack of research targeted at understanding how learners and parents engage with assessment. This research project hoped to address this shortcoming in the literature. Therefore, including as many different stakeholder groups as possible in the sample was deemed to be desirable to ensure that findings were comprehensive and captured the potentially competing views of each group. The range of participants identified as decision makers or implementers who were included in the sample added an extra dimension to the research because this helped in building up a better understanding of how users at different levels of influence within the same system perceived and responded to the initiative (see Table 1 for an overview of the stakeholder groups who participated in the study).

Another consideration when selecting the sample was the initiative's goal of reducing inequality in educational provision. As such, the sample needed to include schools representing urban, rural and remote districts. HCM is comprised of 24 geographical regions covering an area of 2,095 km^2 extending up to Củ Chi District (19 km from the Cambodian border) and down to Cần Giờ on the South China Sea. The distance from the northernmost point (Phú Mỹ Hưng Commune, Củ Chi District) to the southernmost one (Long Hòa Commune, Cần Gi District) is 102 km, and from the easternmost point (Long Bình ward, District Nine) to the westernmost one (Bình Chánh Commune, Bình Chánh District) is 47 km. With such a large area to cover, it was necessary to restrict the sample to one school per region, which amounted to 24 schools in total. This was achieved using a stratified random sample. Once schools were randomly selected from each location, classes within these schools were randomly selected. As can be seen in Table 1, the participants in the qualitative strand represented a smaller subset of the sample

Table 1 Overview of participants

Participants	QUAN	QUAL
Schools (primary)	59 schools (Questionnaires) 194 schools (Test data)	24 schools (Interviews and focus groups)
Parents of Grade 2 learners	2,683 parents (Questionnaires)	555 (Open-ended comments from questionnaire)
Teachers of Grade 2 learners	113 teachers (Questionnaires)	73 (Open-ended comments from teacher questionnaire) Comments from 65 teachers (Interviews)
Learners (Grade 2)	Learner test score data	Comments from 206 learners (24 focus groups)
Focal persons such as regional policy planners, and policy implementers at district and school level e.g. district heads, school principals and vice-principals and heads of English		Comments from 50 focal persons (Interviews)

selected for the quantitative strand (except for the parents). This was a pragmatic decision based on factors related to the resources needed to collect and analyse the qualitative data and justified by the fact that the smaller sample was representative of the locations of interest and, therefore, would not limit the researchers' ability to identify unequal provision and make inferences which are 'transferable' beyond the sample (Teddlie and Tashakkori 2003). The choice to include the same participants from the quantitative strand in the qualitative strand was based on the desire to use the qualitative data not only to corroborate the quantitative findings but also to inform and clarify the interpretations being made (Greene, Caracelli and Graham 1989). In this study, the teachers received additional training and were well aware of the project aims which Bamberger (2012) points out could prime participants to respond to statements in a questionnaire in accordance with these aims rather than their own views. In this situation, the qualitative component of the research can be used to verify that the teachers' questionnaire responses are an accurate representation of their perceptions. The interviews with teachers can also provide insight into the reasons behind certain questionnaire responses thus building a more in-depth understanding of the situation, which will lead to more credible interpretations.

Research instruments

The strength of an analysis in any research project will depend on the quality of the data collected. Creswell and Plano Clark (2011:171) point out that in mixed methods research, the researcher needs to engage in a 'persuasive' data collection approach for the qualitative strand and a 'rigorous' approach for the quantitative one. The first step in achieving this is to systematically develop the instruments, taking into consideration best practice and the expectations of the associated research communities (Onwuegbuzie and Johnson 2006). As mentioned previously, when using the convergent parallel design (see Ziegler and Kang, Chapter 4, this volume), the choice of instruments and the procedures followed has added significance. This is because a risk associated with data being collected concurrently by a team of researchers is that unexpected findings or limitations of the instruments may not come to light until the analysis stage, after large amounts of data have already been collected (Creswell and Plano Clark 2011). It can be difficult to investigate unexpected information further or go back to the sample population to collect additional data for practical reasons, particularly for impact studies such as this when the data collection period is near the end of the school year just before learners and teachers go off on vacation for several months. Therefore, it is crucial that the instruments are developed rigorously to ensure the data collected is of a high quality and addresses the research questions to reduce, as much as possible, the chance that key constructs are missing or not fully represented as there may not be an opportunity to rectify this problem during/after the collection phase. One way this is achieved, and the approach taken for this research, is to develop a conceptual framework for the study which takes into account existing knowledge on impact and factors that have already been identified in the literature and other studies (e.g. ESLC (European Survey on Language Competences), PIRLS (Progress in International Reading Literacy Study), TALIS (Teaching and Learning International Survey)) as contributing to effective language learning and teaching while also incorporating factors that are associated with the context of language education in Viet Nam.

In the Viet Nam Impact Study, the quantitative and qualitative data was prioritised equally in that both data strands were necessary to fully answer the research questions. The qualitative strand not only allowed the researchers to better understand the teachers' and policy implementers' views but ensured that the voices of an important stakeholder group, the primary-school children, were heard. The quantitative phase allowed the researchers to evaluate the programme as a whole in order to make evidence-based recommendations. In the next section, we will discuss the rationale for using either a quantitative or qualitative data strand for each stakeholder group, the development of the instruments and the actions taken to ensure the data collected was valid, reliable and useful.

Quantitative instruments

The tools used to collect the quantitative data for this study were questionnaires and the *Cambridge English: Starters* exam.

Attitudinal and perception questionnaires were developed for teachers and parents to investigate the main constructs of interest. Questionnaires were selected as the instrument because they are useful for collecting data from large numbers of people in a consistent and structured way, which leads to results that allow for inferences to be more readily made (Larsen-Freeman and Long 1991). The use of questionnaires was grounded in a post-positivist philosophy that values controlled, outcome-oriented approaches that lead to reliable data that can be generalised beyond the sample.

Creswell and Plano Clark (2011:172) emphasise the need for the quantitative strand to be based on '"rigorous" quantitative procedures' to ensure that any inferences made from the data are credible. The process of developing the questionnaires began with the identification of relevant constructs or themes for the target participants. The academic literature on topics such as parental influences on learning, assessment for learning and effective teaching practices (see Black, Harrison, Lee, Marshall and Wiliam 2010, Campbell, Kyriakides, Muijs and Robinson 2004, Carless 2005, Day, Sammons, Kington, and Regan 2008, Hoover-Dempsey and Sandler 1995, Wang, Haertel and Walberg 1990), the Cambridge English Impact Toolkit and the conceptual frameworks from other educational surveys (e.g. ESLC, PIRLS, TALIS) provided a useful starting point in identifying relevant constructs (see Khalifa et al (2012) for more information). A key consideration during the design process was to ensure that the teacher and parent questionnaires contained common, overlapping constructs in order to facilitate the combining of data from different stakeholder groups at the interpretation stage (Figure 3). The construct selection process involved several rounds of review and consultation to ensure that the ones included in the study were clearly linked to the research questions and the researchers were not including constructs that although may be of interest, had little direct relevance to the aims of this particular study (e.g. home resources). An additional criterion used for not including certain constructs was based on the efficacy of questionnaires for investigating the topic. Certain abstract

Figure 3 Questionnaire constructs overview

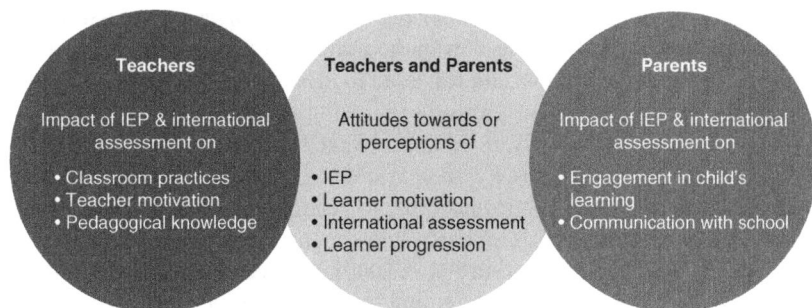

Teachers	Teachers and Parents	Parents
Impact of IEP & international assessment on	Attitudes towards or perceptions of	Impact of IEP & international assessment on
• Classroom practices • Teacher motivation • Pedagogical knowledge	• IEP • Learner motivation • International assessment • Learner progression	• Engagement in child's learning • Communication with school

constructs are much more easily investigated using qualitative instruments than quantitative ones because they can be challenging to capture unambiguously and fully in a questionnaire. That is not to say that abstract concepts cannot be included in questionnaires; on the contrary whole questionnaires have been designed around complex concepts such as self-efficacy, motivation, etc., but in order to do this successfully it is necessary to unpick the concept into its component dimensions. There is a danger inherent in this process, however, of underrepresenting the concept or misrepresenting it. In addition, constructs that require a series of statements to fully capture all aspects and dimensions of it usually add to the length of the instrument. Long questionnaires can negatively affect the response rate because respondents drop out or do not attempt the questionnaire, resulting in missing data (Leeuw 2008). Missing data or a low response rate has implications for the type of analysis that can be done and the validity and reliability of the data. A mixed methods approach helps in overcoming this weakness associated with questionnaires, as the abstract concepts of interest can be more efficiently and effectively investigated using qualitative tools that allow for interaction between the researcher and the participant in order to explore the concepts fully.

Statements to be included in the questionnaires, which represent the underlying constructs, were selected from the Cambridge English Questionnaire Item Bank which contains Likert items used and validated in previous impact studies. Response options for each item indicate respondents' level of agreement using a 4-point scale from 'strongly agree' to 'strongly disagree'. As part of the validation process, the questionnaires were reviewed by two different groups: first by specialists in questionnaire design and secondly by educationalists familiar with the Vietnamese context. Amendments were made in light of feedback from both groups. The parent questionnaire was then translated into Vietnamese and the translation was verified by native speakers of Vietnamese (NB backwards and forwards translation was used). The teacher questionnaire was not translated as the language ability of the teachers in the programme was considered sufficient to complete the survey in English. Both questionnaires were trialled on a small sample of teachers and parents who were not part of the main research sample.

Exam score data from the *Cambridge English: Starters* test sessions in consecutive years 2010 and 2011 was the main source of quantitative data collected from learners. This data was used to investigate learner progression and the effectiveness of the programme in raising standards.

A questionnaire was not deemed appropriate for the learners in this study because of their young age (i.e. 7–8 year olds). It is generally accepted that children under the age of 8 are not able to reliably respond to a questionnaire because they are still at an early stage of their linguistic and cognitive development (Borgers, Leeuw and Hox 2000). Consequently, an alternative method was needed to investigate young learners' attitudes and perceptions in a reliable and valid way, which could be easily compared to the data collected from teachers and parents. Using a mixed methods research design resolved this issue by allowing the inclusion of a qualitative strand (e.g. focus groups), which is the focus of the next section, and thus ensuring that the views of a key stakeholder group were not excluded from the study.

Qualitative instruments

The qualitative data was collected from semi-structured interviews, focus groups and open-ended question fields within the teacher and parent questionnaires. As mentioned previously, an aim of impact research is to be able to provide a rich description of stakeholder behaviour, attitudes and perceptions which may/may not have changed in response to an initiative such as the introduction of an examination. Cheng (2014) points out, however, that individual stakeholders will construct their own perception of a test's impact based on how it serves their purposes. This entails a detailed understanding of the context in which the initiative operates, what policy/decision makers hope to achieve through its introduction and how the implementers view the decision and act in response to it. The contextual information and identification of intended impacts is the basis on which the programme is evaluated and as such the data collected should be as rich as possible. For this reason and the smaller number of participants in the focal person group, a qualitative instrument in the form of a semi-structured interview protocol was chosen rather than a questionnaire. Semi-structured interviews allow interviewees an opportunity to explain their understanding of the context from their own perspective. This is in line with a constructivist philosophy that recognises that meaning is co-constructed and assumes a relativist ontological position (Lincoln and Guba 1994). Ministry policy makers, district heads, school principals and head teachers are all decision makers within the same educational system but the types of decisions they make will depend on their position; for example, strategic decisions about long-term goals of the educational system will be made at the highest levels whereas day-to-day decisions will be made at the lower levels. The contexts in which these decision makers operate will define the way they understand the initiative and respond to it.

The semi-structured interview protocol was designed to investigate the context of learning, teaching and assessment, interviewees' attitudes towards the initiative and what, if any, changes they have seen in response to it. The interview protocol contained a list of topics and general questions to guide the interviewer through the process but these prompts were not meant to limit the interviewer's freedom to explore topics further with the participants or go beyond them if other topics emerge as significant (Hoepfl 1997). Again, there was a deliberate attempt to include constructs that overlap to some extent with those selected for the questionnaires to facilitate the integration of the data collected from all stakeholder groups.

Learner attitudes and perceptions about learning, teaching and assessment were investigated using a focus group protocol. This method was chosen over one-to-one interviews in order to collect data from a larger sample of learners in a shorter timeframe. Interviews by their very nature are time-consuming both at the collection and analysis stages, which often results in a small sample being selected for practical reasons; however, the robustness of the findings and the extent to which they can be generalised to the larger population will depend on the representativeness of the sample (Onwuegbuzie and Johnson 2006). Because an aim of the study was to understand the impact of the programme and the test on learners, it was felt that it was necessary to ensure that the sample included a range of learners from each geographical location and a balance of genders. Focus groups allowed the researchers to achieve this.

The focus group protocols were developed following a similar procedure to the semi-structured interview protocols. Key topics were identified that could help in answering the research questions. These topics tapped into the same constructs contained within the teacher and parent questionnaires:

- their attitude towards the Intensive English Programme (IEP)
- their motivation to learn English
- the use of English in the classroom
- their attitudes towards the *Cambridge English: Starters* exam
- their perceptions of their English language ability/progression.

The number of questions included on the focus group protocol was carefully controlled because of the age of the participants. Research shows that 20-minute sessions (without a break) are optimal for participants between the ages of 7 and 11 and that longer sessions can be tiring for the participants, which can affect the quality of their responses (Morgan, Gibbs, Maxwell and Britten 2002).

In addition to the interviews and focus groups, another source of qualitative data came from the last question in the parent and teacher questionnaires. This question consisted of an open field, which gave participants an opportunity to leave additional comments. The purpose of this comment box was to allow participants to raise any issues or make comments about aspects of the programme or the examinations which were not covered in the questionnaire.

Designing instruments for integration

Both the quantitative and qualitative instruments were carefully designed to contain parallel questions (Creswell and Plano Clark 2011) in order to elicit information on the same constructs and enhance the robustness of the findings by providing the basis for which researchers could identify convergent or divergent views. The data from the three sources (i.e. teacher, parents and learners) could then also be analysed in relation to the policy makers' views in terms of whether the initiative is achieving the desired impact. This approach to instrument design also facilitates the drawing of 'meta-inferences', which Ziegler and Kang point out in Chapter 4, this volume, is a key benefit of mixing methods. That is, the researchers have explicitly built in 'points of interface' where the two data strands can be integrated. Table 2 provides a visual representation of the constructs investigated by stakeholder groups to show the extent of the overlap across the different stakeholder groups and the instruments used to collect this data.

Table 2 Overview of constructs investigated by data strand

Key topics of interest	QUAN	QUAL
Learner progression	• Learner test data • Parent questionnaire • Teacher questionnaire	• Learner focus groups • Focal person interviews
Programme effectiveness	• Learner test data • Parent questionnaire • Teacher questionnaire	• Learner focus groups • Focal person interviews
Learner motivation	• Parent questionnaire • Teacher questionnaire	• Learner focus groups • Focal person interviews
Perceptions of IEP including the intended/unintended impact	• Parent questionnaire • Teacher questionnaire	• Learner focus groups • Focal person interviews
Attitudes towards assessment in general and towards Cambridge English: Young Learners exams	• Parent questionnaire • Teacher questionnaire	• Learner focus groups • Focal person interviews
Classroom practices	• Parent questionnaire • Teacher questionnaire	• Learner focus groups • Focal person interviews
Teacher motivation	• Teacher questionnaire	• Focal person interviews
Changes in decision making		• Focal person interviews

Data collection

Patton (2002:14) points out that in quantitative research the quality of the research is very much dependent on robust instrument development whereas in qualitative research, quality is dependent on the researcher because they are 'the instrument'. As such, this section will describe the data collection procedures, which have particular relevance for the qualitative strand.

The field researchers (n=2) made appointments to visit each of the schools in the sample with the help of HCM DOET to collect all the data. When the researchers arrived at the school, they left copies of questionnaires for the school to distribute to teachers and parents. Each questionnaire came with information about the study purpose and the use of the data. Parents and teachers were asked to complete them and return them to the school.

Completed questionnaires were then returned to the Cambridge English regional office for coding and data entry.

While the researchers were at the school they also conducted the interviews and focus groups. At the beginning of the interviews and focus groups, the study purpose and use of the data was explained to the participants and they were given the option to opt out of the research. The interviews were conducted in both English and Vietnamese by a trained moderator with the support of a research assistant who also took field notes. The focus group facilitator was experienced in conducting research with children and was able to develop rapport with them by following established best practice (Capello 2005). A research assistant was also present during the focus groups to provide support and to take field notes. The interviews and focus groups were audio recorded with participants' consent. Ethical guidelines from the University of Cambridge, the British Association for Applied Linguistics and the British Educational Research Association were followed during all data collection and data analysis phases of this project.

Data analysis

The questionnaire data was analysed first separately for each stakeholder group by calculating the frequency or percentage of responses in each category (i.e. strongly agree – strongly disagree) and the mode. In addition to descriptive statistics, a chi-square test of independence was computed using SPSS software for each item to determine whether there was any relationship or association between response patterns and the variables of interest (i.e. for teachers: ELT experience, academic/teaching qualifications, location of school, grade; for parents: academic qualifications, socio-economic status, location of school). Once the individual questionnaire analyses were done, common questions across questionnaires were compared; for example, in both questionnaires there was a statement about whether or not learners enjoy learning English. The common statements were analysed again using cross-tabulations. These procedures allowed the researchers to identify where there was a significant difference in responses both within and across the two stakeholder groups.

Unlike quantitative analysis techniques, approaches to analysing qualitative data are less standardised and rule governed (Miles and Huberman 1994). That does not mean that rigour is not necessary but that the quality of qualitative research is judged using different criteria than those used for quantitative research. Lincoln and Guba (1985) for instance equate the notion of reliability, which is used in quantitative research to evaluate quality, to the criterion of dependability for qualitative research. Hoepfl (1997) emphasises that dependability is built up through the techniques used by the researchers and by emphasising transparency in terms of explicitly stating the processes involved in the research in addition to the products. In the Viet Nam Impact Study, the interview transcripts, focus group notes and open-ended questionnaire responses were analysed using an inductive approach to thematic analysis. According to Braun and Clarke (2006), thematic analysis involves the identification of patterns in qualitative data sets. The process includes first becoming familiar with the data by transcribing or reading through it while taking notes and then coding the data in a systematic way such as with different colours. Once the data has been coded, then themes can be identified. Finally the themes are independently verified in order to ensure that the analysis is rigorous. The themes with the most frequent responses were identified for each construct, which formed the products of the analysis. This step of identifying the number of responses could be viewed as an example of 'quantitizing qualitative data' or data transformation (Creswell and Plano Clark 2011:216, see Ziegler and Kang, Chapter 4, this volume). However, as Sandelowski (2008:309) notes, 'such counting is inherent to the process of extracting meaning from verbal data'. Without such counting, it would not be possible to identify trends in the data and organise it for interpretation. The intention was not to prioritise certain themes over others but to acknowledge the predominance of certain ideas in the data.

The reliability of the quantitative instruments was also investigated with a particular focus on the internal consistency of the instruments. This step provides additional information about the quality of the instruments, which in turn has implications for the quality and reliability of the data. Cronbach's alpha was calculated for the teacher and parent questionnaires (see Table 3). This measurement reports the extent to which the statements in the questionnaires are measuring the same construct and a value higher than 0.70 is considered acceptable for questionnaires. The reliability measures for the *Cambridge English: Starters* exam in 2010 are presented in Table 3 by component. These measures are typical of the exam. For high-stakes tests, a Cronbach's alpha of 0.80 or higher is usually considered acceptable; however, the *Cambridge English: Starters* exam is not designed as a high-stakes test, but rather it is meant to motivate young learners by providing them with tasks that are fun, engaging and achievable. In order to ensure that the test is valid for its purpose and has a positive impact on learning, the reliability of the test is lower than that for other Cambridge English exams.

Table 3 Reliability measures

Instruments	Cronbach's alpha
Teacher questionnaire	0.96
Parent questionnaire	0.96
Cambridge English: Starters – Listening	0.76
Cambridge English: Starters – Reading and Writing	0.83

Integration of data sets

The steps taken during the data analysis phase set the stage for combining and interpreting the data. As previously mentioned, the instruments were developed to include the same constructs, which allowed the data to be compared more easily (see Table 2). The process of combining the data to prepare for interpretation was done in a systematic fashion in that the data related to each construct was grouped together but separated by stakeholder in a joint display (see Table 4 for an example, and Guetterman and Salamoura, Chapter 7, this volume). In order to answer the first and second research questions, the data was interpreted for each construct by stakeholder group and to answer the third research question, the data was interpreted across stakeholder groups. The latter process involved identifying areas of convergence and divergence in the data. When divergence was identified, the researchers used contextual knowledge, the literature and/or other aspects of the data to determine either an explanation for the inconsistency, a recommendation to possibly reduce this divergence or a plan to further investigate the issue. For example, parents reported that they did not feel they had received adequate information about the exam, yet a number of principals and heads of English mentioned meeting parents face-to-face to explain the exams to them. This contradictory finding could be explained by the fact that the parent sample was much larger than the focal group sample so the information provided to parents may not have been consistent across all schools or comprehensive enough. In similar studies, this issue is quite persistent in that parents typically do not feel that they know enough about their child's language programme or the assessment practices at their child's school even when there is evidence of school efforts to provide this information (Ashton, Salamoura and Diaz 2012, Chambers et al 2012, Salamoura, Hamilton and Octor 2012). This suggests that the dissemination plan does need to be improved by ensuring that information is being provided in a consistent manner across schools but also that information is disseminated using a variety of different channels (e.g. face-to-face, by mail, by email, etc.) on a regular basis.

Presenting the findings

Once the data was combined and interpreted, the findings were presented by construct in Khalifa et al (2012) in order to highlight both the convergence and divergence found. The findings were also presented to teachers and Ministry officials in Viet Nam in a series of presentations to ensure that the formative aspects of the research fed back to the participants. By and large, the authors found that the exams had a positive impact on teaching and learning with the different stakeholders agreeing that the exams motivated the learners and learning, they promoted a more communicative

Table 4 Example joint display for one construct by stakeholder group

Investigation point: Attitudes towards Cambridge English: Young Learners exams and Cambridge English: Starters in particular

	Learners	Teachers	Parents	Focal persons
General attitude to exam (i.e. like / dislike / motivation)	• **Fun element**: 'The test is interesting, I can match, colour and write the words', 'it is fun taking the test, we all like colouring, matching and moving the picture' (semi-outskirts district), 'Speaking is fun because it has lots of pictures' (central district) • **Test practice**: 'I can learn by heart 34 over 36 questions for *Starters* Speaking' (outskirt district) • **Oral examiner effect**: 'The oral examiners are kind, sweet and always smile', 'I like the speaking part. When I say something right, she said very good' (semi-outskirt district)	• 95% agree – They are pleased Cambridge English exams were introduced into IEP • 86% agree – Students like the Cambridge English exams • 82% agree – Students like receiving an international certificate • 95% agree – The topics on the exams are interesting – 'I find the Cambridge English test interesting. It makes me excited in my English teaching. The students like doing the test so much, they are confident when they speak English through colourful pictures'	• 20% agree – My child dislikes the test • 93% agree – They are pleased Cambridge English tests were introduced into IEP • 87% agree – My child likes getting an international certificate	• Exams as motivational tools that support learning – 'It is a motivation for parents and students in IEP to have more focus on learning English. Also it sets the standard for the school to have plans to develop outstanding students and to support students who do not get average number of shields' • Cambridge English exams provide an external reference and quality assurance badge for efforts made by school and teaching staff – 'Nothing is fairer because it is international, independent and professional institution which gives the assessment and results reflect on what we have done on teaching and learning English'

289

Table 4 (continued)

Investigation point: Attitudes towards Cambridge English: Young Learners exams and Cambridge English: Starters in particular

	Learners	Teachers	Parents	Focal persons
Exam as a source of anxiety	• **Test anxiety:** 'I am not afraid of taking the test' (outskirt district), 'the test doesn't scare me because the teacher prepared me well' (semi-outskirt district), 'the test centre is so big. It is a lot bigger than my school. That scares me a lot' (central district)	• 83% agree – Students worry about taking the Cambridge English exams • 18% worry about students taking exams at a young age	• 20% agree – My child worries about taking the test • 41% agree – The Cambridge English tests will bring additional work and pressure to their children – 'The English programme at school includes so many things: the intensive programme, *Starters*, Cambridge, . . . that it sometimes leads parents to confusion as they lack information of the efficiency of study'	• 'The students seem not afraid of taking the test. They get more chances to speak English'
Appropriacy of exam (i.e. difficulty)	• **Test difficulty:** 'The test is as easy as a piece of cake', 'listening to spelling and write the name down is difficult but I can do it very well' (semi-outskirts district), 'the test has a lot of difficult words', 'I like the writing part just because I can think of the word by myself' (central district)	• 74% agree – The tests are at the right level for their students (Grade 2) – 'Cambridge English test is rather difficult for Grade 2 students' • 63% agree – students can perform well on the tests		

- Some teachers report that parents ask them about the exam in terms of if their child can 'pass' or what the child needs to do to 'pass'

- 78% agree – The school has given them enough information about the exams. However a number of comments contradict this:
  – 'The school should provide more information about the *Starters* exam so that students can prepare for this exam as well as to achieve the best result'
  – 'We have not received any information on English in schools'

- Most schools report organising teacher–parent conferences to explain more about using the exams to assess students

Convergence:
- positive attitudes towards Cambridge English exams by all stakeholders
- all stakeholders are pleased with the introduction of the exams
- exams are seen as motivational and support learning by identifying strengths and weaknesses.

Divergence:
- parents and teachers are concerned that the tests cause anxiety but learners do not seem to report this
- parents do not feel they have received enough information about exams but schools report having face-to-face meetings with parents about the exams
- some teachers are concerned that the exam is too difficult for Grade 2 students but students do not indicate that they feel the exam is too difficult, and exam data suggests the test is not too difficult for these learners.

teaching methodology and the adoption of *Assessment for Learning* principles (Assessment Reform Group 2002). There was, however, some divergence found in the data as well as some unexpected findings. One area in which there were differences in opinion related to the perceived level of the test. Teachers raised concerns that the test was too difficult for their learners; however, when looking at the test data and learner responses in the focus groups, it was clear that this view was unsupported. The learners expressed positive views towards the test and its difficulty. They perceived it as achievable; as one learner stated: 'the test is as easy as a piece of cake' and even those who did point out that there were difficult aspects to it, emphasised the fact that they felt they were capable of doing well on it: 'listening to spelling and write the name down is difficult but I can do it very well'. The students' views are further supported when one looks at the test data. The average number of shields achieved by these learners indicated that the test was not too difficult for them. What was most interesting is that when the test data from the IEP learners was compared to the test data from the rest of Viet Nam, which is made up of learners who are studying privately in addition to lessons at school, these learners' performance was comparable. By using a mixed methods design the researchers were able to identify a misconception held by teachers and present the evidence to them during the dissemination phase of the project. It is hoped that this helped teachers recognise that they may be underestimating their learners' abilities, which could push teachers to re-evaluate the difficulty level of their lessons and possibly lead to more challenging lessons and improved outcomes.

The research project also provided the evidence to change a newly introduced policy, which could have resulted in negative test impact. Because of the high demands on the programme, DOET had decided that only students who achieved an average of 10 shields (out of a possible 15 shields available) in the *Cambridge English: Young Learners* examinations could continue in the IEP. This decision changed the stakes of the test. As mentioned earlier, the *Cambridge English: Young Learners* examinations are designed to be motivational and fun (i.e. a low-stakes purpose) and were not intended to be used for gate-keeping purposes (i.e. a high-stakes purpose). Through the process of conducting this study, the researchers were able to discuss this point with DOET and demonstrate the motivational aspect of these exams through the learners' comments. As a result, DOET waived this condition, further demonstrating the importance of not only conducting impact research but also putting the findings into practice, which includes reporting them to a wide audience that includes those in decision-making roles.

Another issue that was raised in the study which could not be answered and is in need of further study is the fact that 77% of the parents surveyed sent their children to private language schools. This is somewhat surprising because one of the aims of the IEP is to reduce inequality in provision, which would ideally reduce the need to seek lessons outside school. Despite the increased number of English lessons per week, it would appear that parents are not fully satisfied with the programme. The next phase of the study will attempt to find out whether this situation is still the case, and if it is, the reasons why parents send their children to lessons outside school.

Benefits of the convergent parallel design for impact research

The convergent parallel design is an appropriate mixed methods approach for investigating test impact. In the Viet Nam Impact study, this design was particularly relevant because it had an 'additive effect' (as discussed by Ziegler and Kang, Chapter 4, this volume, and as further illustrated by the case studies in Section 3 of this volume). That is, the findings were strengthened in that neither the quantitative nor qualitative methodology would have provided enough insight into the phenomenon of interest. This is especially important for research that involves children, whose views and perceptions are not easily captured using instruments such as questionnaires. Providing these stakeholders an opportunity to express their views and personal experiences in focus groups highlighted the powerful effect English in general and Cambridge English exams specifically have on their lives. Had the researchers relied solely on quantitative instruments, it may not have been possible to include these learners' perspective. Similarly, including the quantitative element allowed the researchers to engage with large numbers of parents, a stakeholder group which is under-researched.

Despite the benefits of this design, there are also some challenges that need to be mitigated. Because the main feature of this design is the collection of both the quantitative and qualitative data at the same time, careful planning at each stage was critical to the successful completion of this study. A risk associated with this design in particular is that the quality of data can be endangered if the field researchers are not properly trained or do not follow data collection protocols carefully as there is usually not an opportunity to rectify these problems in subsequent data collections stages. Therefore, taking the time to hold training sessions and having regular catch-ups with the field researchers to track their progress was essential. This can be time consuming for the research team who are under pressure to collect the data in a short period of time. Related to this is the fact that this research took place in a country quite far from where the primary researchers were located, making it difficult for them to have full oversight over the data collection process in country. Having a local team of field researchers, however, had its advantages as they were able to gain access to 24 schools in a relatively short period of time because of their familiarity with the local educational context. Had the field researchers not been able to visit all geographical regions, it would not have been possible to investigate the issue of inequality of provision. Full representation of schools from each geographical region was also achieved through the support of DOET as a local partner. Had the project team not had access to local researchers or the support of DOET, this particular research design may not have been viable as the risk to the quality of the data may have been too high.

It should not be underestimated how important project management is to research studies of this scale that involve a team of researchers who are being managed both locally and in the field from a distance. Coordinating the team to ensure that each member understands their role and responsibilities in terms of both the processes and products of their work is crucial to the success of impact research that employs the convergent parallel design because the data is collected in one phase. One of the lessons learned is the need to find better ways of maintaining management commitment to time and resources required to effectively implement a mixed method approach and to defend these from administrative pressures to cut budgets and time. In hindsight, more briefings in management meetings, short reports or short videos could have been used as awareness-raising tools during the implementation of the study. Similarly, ensuring management has a clear understanding of the research design from the outset and why the use of a mixed methods approach is preferable to either a qualitative or quantitative approach on its own may further strengthen project support.

Conclusion

The way in which an international assessment may influence learning and teaching may change over time, which is why it is recommended that impact research is conducted as part of an iterative process, as also noted by Saville (Chapter 2, this volume) in his discussion of the cyclical process of test development and validation. In line with this position, the case study reported above is considered Phase 1 of a multi-phase study aimed at measuring the impact of this initiative at regular intervals in the future. An iterative process of researching impact means that considerable attention was given to ensure that the research questions and research design were appropriate not only for the current phase of the research but also for future phases. That is, the data/findings from this phase will feed into the next one by informing instrument development and acting as a reference point to measure future findings against.

It is hoped that the case study presented in this chapter demonstrated the benefits of using the convergent parallel design in investigating test impact. This methodology is particularly relevant for this type of research because of the complex nature of educational systems and the need to draw context-specific interpretations to account for a multi-faceted phenomenon. The different philosophical perspectives attached to the quantitative and qualitative data strands (as discussed by Creswell and Zhou, Chapter 3, this volume) allowed for the collection of data that was robust, rigorous and credible. The quantitative approaches based in postpositivism improved the generalisability of the findings and will allow for this data to be compared to future cohorts and also to cohorts in other countries. The qualitative strand grounded in constructivism improved the interpretations of the overall findings because it allowed the researchers to better understand participants' realities in terms of the effect of the tests on them, but more importantly allowed researchers to collect the views from a key stakeholder group – the young learners.

Section 4
From ideas to action

12 Ideas to action: A framework for the design and implementation of a mixed methods study

Andrew Hustad
University of Nebraska–Lincoln
Sarah McElwee
Cambridge English Language Assessment

This chapter presents a series of practical considerations to encourage researchers to scrutinise their use of, and approach to, mixed methods research. With a focus on applied research supporting validation within language assessment systems, key questions are presented to guide a range of issues from the early phases of understanding theoretical worldviews to later concerns such as presenting mixed methods results in the most appropriate way. Maximising the value of the data collected through a mixed methods approach underlines each step. Topics highlighted in this chapter include:

- Ten *fundamental questions* to shape a mixed methods study
- *Key ideas* that affect the *design and implementation* of mixed methods research
- *Real-world examples* from Cambridge English Language Assessment projects and *central considerations* when conducting applied mixed methods studies
- Practical steps to *navigate issues* such as identifying skills gaps and ethical considerations

The final chapter of this volume presents a practical outline for researchers who would like to utilise a mixed methods approach in their own research. The intended approach is interactive and by distilling key concepts from earlier chapters it will assist readers in considering how they can begin to approach their research ideas and in actively getting their research underway. Section 1 of this volume addressed the overarching issues of the evolution of approaches to language assessment and the application of mixed methods research to support assessment. The first section also examined the language assessment system from the perspective of the test provider. The established processes and procedures of Cambridge English Language Assessment form the basis of this discussion of mixed methods, focusing both on the definition and validation of test constructs and the operational cycle through which language tests are produced. The second section opened with a detailed exposition of the history and philosophical underpinnings of the mixed methods tradition, as well as a brief overview of mixed methods designs. This was followed by an in-depth discussion of the critical components of mixed methods research, particularly as they apply to language assessment. In Section 3 of this volume, the practical application of mixed methods, and their power in language assessment research and development was presented through case studies from Cambridge English Language Assessment demonstrating the breadth of research activities involved in the validation and operational cycle of language testing as outlined by Saville in Chapter 2, this volume. To conclude this volume on mixed methods and language assessment, it will now prove helpful to distil this information into a concise framework for application to future projects.

The purpose of this chapter is to provide a practical summary of critical issues that mixed methods researchers and project coordinators should consider in order to conduct a rigorous and effective study. These issues will be illustrated by elements of each of the chapters presenting case studies in Section 3, which focused on an applied project in Cambridge English Language Assessment contributing to the development, revision, or validation of a Cambridge English exam. Vidaković and Robinson (Chapter 8, this volume) outlined the benefits of adopting a community-based participatory approach to developing tests of English for Specific purposes, highlighting both the importance of input from key stakeholders in understanding the market and future test takers, and the synergies that can be achieved bringing together expertise from different aspects of the stakeholder community – in this case legal content experts and language assessment specialists. Galaczi and Khabbazbashi (Chapter 9, this volume) showcased a multi-phase exploratory sequential design to develop new rating scales for high-stakes L2 speaking tests. This chapter described practical modifications to the basic exploratory sequential approach when dealing with complex applied language assessment projects. Elliott and Lim (Chapter 10, this volume) described a multi-phase parallel convergent design used to develop a new Reading task for the *Cambridge English: Advanced* examination. The impact of the mixed methods approach was described at each of the critical points of task design, trialling, selection of the most appropriate task and its ultimate validation as part of the revised exam. Finally, Khalifa and Docherty (Chapter 11, this volume) explored the benefits of taking a mixed methods approach to test impact and provided an immensely practical perspective on instrument design, data collection and integration of findings when working with a range of stakeholders who bring a wide variety of perspectives to the language learning context.

This chapter has been organised around 10 key points that demand the attention of the aspiring mixed methods researcher, divided by theme into three sections: overarching issues and ideas in developing mixed methods studies; mixed methods research questions and designs; and collection, analysis and presentation of mixed methods data (Table 1 provides an overview of the chapter structure).

Each of the 10 points begins with a central question that can be applied to the reader's current project. These questions are phrased directly to the reader/researcher to encourage reflection. The reader is encouraged to engage with each question in depth and take comprehensive notes that will lay the foundation for the study as it develops. Next, a key idea that supports the value and importance of the central questions is outlined. Consideration of how this key idea informs the goals of the intended mixed methods study will strengthen its conception. Additionally, to illustrate how this approach will facilitate a move into mixed methods research for language assessment, relevant examples from the Cambridge English Language Assessment case studies are discussed. Final practical steps to bolster the researcher's toolkit and signpost their thinking are suggested.

This chapter has been positioned as an opportunity for the researcher to engage in a textual dialogue, or self-check, with the central issues covered in the previous chapters. It is also a useful practical partner to Guetterman and Salamoura's discussion of the application of mixed methods to test validation (Chapter 7, this volume). While it may indeed be useful to read the chapter straight through, it will undoubtedly prove more valuable to allow yourself time to pause and consider how each point holds the potential to inform the overall goals for your current research agenda and language assessment projects. As you consider each issue discussed in the chapter, it is strongly encouraged to record your own ideas and thoughts as they evolve, review the basic tenets of mixed methods research (as discussed in Chapters 3 and 4, this volume), and reflect upon the overarching purpose of the study you plan to conduct. Clearly, the sections of this chapter are inextricably tied to one another and the divisions between them are in a certain sense artificial;

Table 1 Themes, ideas and structural overview of Chapter 12

Overarching issues and ideas in developing mixed methods studies	Mixed methods research questions and designs	Collection, analysis and presentation of mixed methods data
1. Research skills and collaboration	3. Central issues for investigation	7. Methodological issues
2. Worldviews and theoretical approaches	4. Nature of research questions	8. Maximising the value of each strand
	5. Rationale for using mixed methods	9. Bringing the strands together
	6. Designs and diagrams	10. Presentation of results

however, as the previous chapters have demonstrated, conducting a rigorous mixed methods study is a substantial endeavour and there is value in considering the key components, while concurrently seeking to keep the larger goals of the study in mind.

Overarching issues and ideas in developing mixed methods research

1. Research skills and collaboration

Question: Do you possess the research skills to conduct a mixed methods study? In other words, are you competent in not only qualitative and quantitative research methods, but in the details of mixed methods as well? If not, how will you ensure the study is conducted with a high degree of rigour?

Key idea: Conducting mixed methods research requires a high level of competence in both qualitative and quantitative research approaches. In the context of language assessment, Saville discussed (Chapter 2, this volume) the socio-cognitive approach to the validation of language tests (Weir 2005), outlining the variety of research evidence, drawing on quantitative and qualitative approaches that are needed to produce a rounded validation argument for a test. Additionally, mixed methods itself represents an additional layer of knowledge that can only be acquired through training and experience. It may prove more helpful to develop a partnership with a fellow researcher who possesses a complementary skill set. Creswell asserted the intrinsic value of teamwork when conducting mixed methods studies, noting: 'The collaboration on teams represents good team interactions, and it requires individuals to openly share their different methodological orientations under the guidance of a leader with diverse research skills' (2014a:42). Therefore, our suggestion when deciding how and why to conduct a potential mixed methods study is to consider carefully the following checklist.

1. Do I possess the necessary skills in both qualitative and quantitative approaches to research?
   - If so, do I also understand the complexities of mixed methods and how the qualitative and quantitative strands can be integrated in substantial ways to provide deeper insight into the research questions?
   - If not, do I know colleagues who would be available to provide specialised knowledge to augment my own areas of research expertise?

2. Upon determining individuals who can support my mixed methods study, can I identify and describe the roles each researcher will assume to maximise the goals of the study?

3. Are there potential areas of tension (e.g. different expectations of the final outcome) that might exist with regard to the research of each involved party? If so, how might this be addressed prior to beginning the collaboration?

Examples: The Cambridge English studies provide a number of examples where the value of research partners and the different strengths that they can bring to a project is evident. Vidaković and Robinson's chapter on community-based participatory approaches is particularly strong in this regard. It was recognised that to develop a test of English in legal contexts, input from linguists and language assessments experts alone would not be sufficient to create a test that was fair and reliable with good face validity. Investing in finding the partner who had the best fit with the project's vision and goals (in this case a firm of international legal content specialists with experience of translation and sensitivity to issues of linguistics) ensured the project could be delivered appropriately and increased its credibility in the market. The specialist knowledge of the research partner was a critical driver in the success of this project and allowed for clear allocation of research roles. It was determined that the community-based partner was better placed to understand the likely requirements of stakeholders in the legal domain than were non-specialist assessment professionals. Therefore to capitalise on that expertise, the research partner undertook the needs analysis for the development of the new test. They also contributed to the sourcing of authentic materials as well as vetting items.

Despite the successful partnership, Vidaković and Robinson give a pertinent example of where tensions can arise, as the creation of sample materials for the new test highlighted different expectations around the specificity of the proposed tests and the trade-off between the authenticity of test materials and their suitability to deliver robust and valid measurement. The resolution was through an open negotiation and revisiting of the test concept, to reach a common understanding with which both partners were comfortable. The impact of the community-based participatory design influenced this negotiation, as Vidaković and Robinson remark that the project required 'iterative and cyclical engagement with the partners' over an extended period of time. Inevitably, not all potential areas of tension will be evident at the outset and building a mutually beneficial and sustainable relationship is important. If partners can have similar levels of input in defining roles and responsibilities at the outset, the relevant strengths and skills of each team can be maximised, and a clear roadmap for progress can limit later dissatisfaction over perceived control or power within the project.

Practical steps:

1. Spend time becoming familiar with the fundamentals of the mixed methods approach, using previous chapters in this volume and other comprehensive, in-depth books.
2. Reflect and self-assess your strengths and weaknesses with regard to both quantitative and qualitative research. Where could you improve?
3. Seek out opportunities to develop skills in both quantitative and qualitative data collection and analysis, for example through courses, seminars, discussions with colleagues, or mentoring.
4. Identify potential partners who are able to complement your skill set and establish a research team that is well equipped to employ a rigorous mixed methods approach.

---

2.   Worldviews and theoretical approaches

Question: Consider how your worldview might affect your approach to mixed methods research. How will you account for this in designing and conducting your study? What theory or theories might be employed?

Key idea: Regardless of the degree of objectivity an individual may purport to employ when conducting research, it is essential to bear in mind that every researcher brings a particular worldview to their research. Throughout the course of study design and implementation, the members of the research team must seek to remain cognizant of how their own beliefs might influence the overall process. Moeller (Chapter 1, this volume) highlighted the generally accepted notion of adopting a pragmatic lens when conducting mixed methods research. As noted by Tashakkori and Teddlie, the power of mixed methods is its 'replacement of the either–or from the paradigm debates with continua that describe a range of options from across the methodological spectrum' (2010b:10). In practice, this either–or dichotomy is most easily observed in the methods and tools utilised for data collection and analysis; however, the differences between qualitative and quantitative research as observed from a larger, overarching perspective are clearly more related to issues of worldview. To conduct a mixed methods study does not demand a researcher jettison their worldview(s) completely; rather, as Creswell (2014a:29) described, it asks the researcher to adopt an underlying philosophy (such as pragmatism, critical realism, or dialectical pluralism) that informs both approaches to data collection and analysis. In recent writings on mixed methods, multiple worldviews informing mixed methods are embraced.

1. Consider the worldview you generally hold with regard to your research practices. How do you envision your worldview affecting your approach to the proposed study?
2. Does your worldview naturally integrate with the mixed methods approach to research?
   - If not, how do you propose to address this issue in order to fully realise the potential of mixed methods research?
3. What theories will underpin your study? How will you incorporate these theories into the overarching mixed methods framework?
4. Have you considered the worldviews of your collaborators and other members of your research team?
   - If differences exist, how will you develop a unified vision among the research team to guide the current study?

Examples: The chapters on the Cambridge English projects give somewhat less explicit consideration to the paradigm or worldview of analysis than other aspects of the research process, perhaps as a consequence of the applied nature of these pieces of work and their fit in the operational cycles of the development of tests or validation arguments. However, Guetterman and Salamoura (Chapter 7, this volume) discuss Cambridge English Language Assessment's *Principles of Good Practice* (Cambridge English 2013) as an example of a philosophical foundation that underpins Cambridge English research, and the projects in each of the four Cambridge English chapters build on the Cambridge *Principles* in their approach to test validation. Galaczi and Khabbazbashi (Chapter 9, this volume) also explicitly discuss the theoretical orientation of their work, with the adoption of a pragmatist worldview in the scale-development project they present. The underlying theoretical worldview remains an important consideration as outlined in Creswell and Plano-Clark's (2011) discussion of four main worldviews that shape research. The postpositivist worldview is most frequently associated with quantitative empirical, and hypothesis-driven research and suggests a singular reality which we must aspire to define. On the other hand, constructivist worldviews are aligned with the notion of multiple realities generated from individuals' interpretation of situations or phenomena and are linked to qualitative approaches to research. The participatory worldview puts participants central to every stage of the research and espouses collaboration and the negotiation of values and findings. Finally, pragmatism is the worldview which is often thought to most closely align with mixed methods, in which it advocates a co-existence of singular and multiple realities and that the epistemological basis for the research is the pursuit of 'what works' to best address the research question. Linked to this is the perspective of critical realism, which accepts the existence of a real world that exists independently of our perceptions, theories and constructions, while acknowledging that understanding the world is driven by our own perspectives and experiences.

Mixed methods studies therefore can adopt a dialectical stance, allowing the application of multiple worldviews. Creswell and Plano Clark (2011) also stress that, rather than a researcher imposing a particular worldview on a piece of research, so too the particular research method can drive the application of a particular worldview – quantitative elements are linked to postpositivism and constructivism is more likely to underpin qualitative work. Therefore, the onus on the researcher is not just to reflect upon their own worldview, but to consider the connection between the mixed methods research design and the potential need to utilise a distinct worldview based on the different stages of the study.

Practical steps:
1. Take time to consider your worldview and reflect upon how it relates to the overarching concepts inherent to mixed methods.
2. Carefully consider the theoretical approach that will help frame your study and seek out existing examples of mixed method studies that are similar in nature.
3. Actively discuss the role of worldview with your research team and identify potential issues that might arise during the course of the investigation.

Mixed methods research questions and design

3. Central issues for investigation

Question: What are the central issues, ideas, and/or concepts you would like to investigate?

Key idea: Although mixed methods research allows questions to emerge over time, it is essential for a study to be initially grounded in a central problem. When considering the central purpose of a study, Creswell (2014b) encouraged the researcher to focus on 'what *needs* to be done', rather than what already exists or is being done. Considering language assessment specifically, Saville (Chapter 2, this volume) noted that a critical issue is 'the management of the integrated processes that are needed to ensure that an assessment system meets the needs of the intended test takers and other test users, and can account for appropriate uses of language tests in educational and social contexts'. Saville distilled this issue into *the what* and *the how* of language assessment, i.e. 1) construct validation and definition, and 2) the operational cycle within assessment systems. To assist the reader in determining how mixed methods can assist a language assessment investigation, we offer the following points of consideration:

1. What are the constructs you hope to better understand, in terms of both validation and definition, through your research?
2. What are the characteristics of the language learners whom you propose will benefit from the goals of this study (e.g. age, proficiency level, context, other socio-cultural factors)?
3. How does this study build on previous studies in language assessment and/or build on the existent knowledge base in language assessment?
4. Where does this study fit within the operational cycle of language assessment? What impact does this have on the central issues, and in turn how might it affect the research design and questions?
5. What are potential avenues for further investigation that might arise from this study?

Examples: Elliott and Lim's chapter on the development of a new Reading task for the *Cambridge English: Advanced* exam provides a useful context to consider some of the issues outlined above. Creating a rounded validation argument for a test has many strands of work that may take place over an extended period of time (for example, it may be some time before data to assess consequential validity can be gathered). In keeping with Creswell (2014b) and Saville (2012a), validating the task type for this revision centred on the aspects of the socio-cognitive framework (Weir 2005) discussed in Saville (Chapter 2, this volume) that are most pertinent operationally: cognitive, contextual, and scoring validity. The model of continual improvement described by Saville (see Figure 1, Chapter 2, this volume) specifically integrates the role of test revisions in the cycle.

Elliott and Lim also showed in this study the identification of a potential gap in the validation evidence for this assessment, which posed a threat to test validity – namely the absence of a task to test candidates' ability to assimilate information from multiple texts to create an organised representation, which is identified as a higher order reading skill (Khalifa and Weir 2009). Thus, the development of the new Reading task builds on the existing knowledge base, and demonstrates the value of established theoretical frameworks as a way to underpin further research. The construct under investigation in their study was reading proficiency in the context of English for Academic Purposes – 'language proficiency for the purpose of entry into an English-medium university environment', which in turn helps to define the characteristics of the likely language learners taking this exam.

Practical steps:

1. Ensure you are sufficiently familiar with the most recent work done in the area of interest.
2. Consider how you can build upon the existing literature to add something new to the field.
3. Think about how the research will contribute evidence for the validation of specific language tests. What issues related to the stage of the operational assessment cycle does this research address?
4. Identify the characteristics of the population you plan to study and determine how this study addresses a gap either in the validity argument of a specific test which poses a threat, or in the broader research literature in the field.

---

4. Nature of the research questions

Question: Are the questions you seek to answer primarily qualitative or quantitative? Both? What questions do you hope to address through the use of mixed methods? Which question(s) specifically address the use of mixed methods and what does this question uniquely add to the study?

Key idea: Saville (Chapter 2, this volume) discussed the interaction of the socio-cognitive approach to construct definition and test validation (Weir 2005) with the operational testing process from test design to results reporting. The complexity of this system, and the breadth of aspects of test validity to be considered, implies that different approaches to data collection might be beneficial. Although your research idea may initially seem to lend itself to either a qualitative or quantitative approach, the comprehensive nature of mixed methods research allows for many questions to benefit substantially from the incorporation of both types of data. It is essential to not only understand the distinction between qualitative and quantitative research questions, but to fully conceptualise the purpose of your study through the use of a mixed methods research question. Ziegler and Kang (Chapter 4, this volume) pointed to Creswell's position on the value of a mixed methods research question, reminding us that this question plays a pivotal role in bringing the two distinct strands together in order to gain a deeper and more comprehensive understanding of the overall phenomena. (Creswell 2011, Ziegler and Kang, Chapter 4, this volume). Mixed methods involves both open- and closed-ended research questions, which can be constructed in such a way as to reflect the goals of any particular mixed methods design utilised by a research team. In Chapter 3 of this volume, Creswell and Zhou assert the inherent connection between research questions and design, offering the following example: 'If our project began with a survey (quantitative) followed by qualitative data (an explanatory sequential design), we would order our questions in a way consistent with quantitative first, followed by qualitative, and then mixed methods' (p.46). (For an in-depth discussion of the various mixed methods designs and their connection to research questions, please refer back to Chapter 4, this volume, to review Ziegler and Kang's coverage of mixed methods designs.)

Creswell and Plano Clark's (2011) guidelines for framing research questions emphasise a three-pronged approach, i.e. identify quantitative questions, qualitative questions, and mixed methods questions. When constructing quantitative research questions, the researcher must identify the relevant variables to be measured in the study, consider potential theories that will help explain and/or predict the relationship between the variables, and attend to the word order of the variables to facilitate the reader's understanding of the questions (Creswell 2014b). Qualitative research questions frequently comprise a central question, which is then augmented by a series of sub-questions that allow for the investigation of more specific paths of enquiry. In lieu of the 'why' nature of quantitative research questions, qualitative questions are generally orientated around questions of 'what' and 'how'. The researcher(s) must remain open and flexible with regard to the qualitative research questions, understanding that a shift in focus or direction may guide the study into previously unimagined territory. Creswell (2014b:73) noted the use of exploratory verbs, such as 'describe, understand, and discover', which relate to the central nature of qualitative research.

Once both the quantitative and qualitative research questions have been formulated, the mixed methods researcher must complete one more step to fully conceptualise the intent of the study. The use of a mixed methods methodology is not simply 'asking one more question', but rather reaffirms the very reason for mixed methods' existence. It must push the goals and purpose of the study beyond what is possible with a singular quantitative or qualitative approach. The mixed methods research question is inextricably tied to the overall design of the study (study design will be discussed in more detail below). At this point however, it may be helpful to consider the overall purpose of your study, and research questions specifically, with reference to the questions below.

1. What are the qualitative goals for the study? What do you plan to investigate using qualitative approaches to data collection and analysis?
2. What are the quantitative goals for the study? What do you plan to investigate using quantitative approaches to data collection and analysis?
3. What is your rationale for employing a mixed methods approach? Mixed methods research does not simply entail the separate use of both quantitative and qualitative approaches. To fully realise the power of mixed methods, it is essential to carefully consider and plan how the

two approaches can be integrated to realise a deeper understanding that would not be possible with only one or the other.

4. Having established your rationale for using mixed methods, how will you formulate the connection and integration of the quantitative and qualitative approaches in the form of a mixed methods research question?

Examples: The Cambridge English chapters provide some pertinent examples of studies where the qualitative and quantitative aspects of the research have been fully articulated and the additional benefit of the mixed methods approach is clear. Khalifa and Docherty's impact study (Chapter 11, this volume) focused on the effect of a strategic decision taken at the local government level to increase English language provision through an Intensive English Programme (IEP) in state-funded primary schools. Thus, their quantitative research questions clearly define the scope of their study and the stakeholders involved. Additionally, in accordance with the advice from Hurlbut (Chapter 6, this volume), the order of the questions reflects the design of the study.

- What was the intended and unintended impact of this strategic decision at the micro and macro levels as revealed . . .:
  - (Research Question1) . . . from interviews with policy makers, from focus groups with policy implementers and from focus groups with students?
  - (Research Question 2) . . . from surveys completed by parents and teachers and from students' assessment data?

Further, their qualitative research question then highlights the integration of the qualitative and quantitative data to give a rich picture of effect that the decision had on the various stakeholder groups:

- How does the intended/unintended impact of this strategic decision at the micro and macro levels compare among various stakeholder groups (i.e. students, teachers, parents, policy makers, policy implementers)?

A further example can be found in Elliott and Lim's chapter on the development of a new task type for *Cambridge English: Advanced* describing a multi-phase design that overall contains 10 research questions that emerged as the phases developed (Elliott and Lim, Chapter 10, this volume). Phase 1 identifies a potential threat to the validity of the reading section of the examination and indicates the need for a new task type. Phase 2 then concentrates on the trialling of several new task types and the research questions centre on establishing the construct validity (defined as the cognitive, context and scoring validity) of the new tasks. The Phase 2 questions are clearly laid out as follows:

Qualitative research questions

1. On the basis of expert judgement, to what extent are the trial tasks likely to elicit the desired cognitive processes?
2. On the basis of expert judgement, are the texts in the trial tasks of an appropriate register and complexity in order to draw inferences about performance in the TLU domain of Higher Education?

Quantitative research question

3. Do the items in the trial tasks exhibit scoring properties (item difficulty and discrimination) appropriate for *Cambridge English: Advanced* Reading?

Mixed methods question

4. In terms of their cognitive validity (qualitative), contextual validity (qualitative) and scoring validity (quantitative), do the trial tasks meet the requirements to address the validity threats identified in Phase 1?

These clear questions help to focus and shape the interpretation of data and results. The qualitative questions are open-ended and neutrally phrased, but still explicit in the variables under exploration. Specific measureable outcomes – item difficulty and discrimination – characterise the quantitative research question. Cognitive, contextual and scoring validity are interdependent elements that together allow an overall judgement of the construct validity of a test task to be drawn, and the phrasing of the mixed methods question follows Hurlbut's best practice advice for mixed methods questions in convergent designs. Thus integrating the information from the qualitative and quantitative research questions supported the consideration of these three elements concurrently to build a picture of the various tasks trialled, and then the selection of the most appropriate for inclusion in the revised examination.

Practical steps:

1. The research questions in a mixed methods study are inextricably tied to its purpose and design; therefore, it is critical that you take both of these factors into account when formulating the questions. Chapters 3 and 4 of this volume discuss the issues in depth.
2. Reflect upon your plans for including both qualitative and quantitative strands, consider issues of sequence and priority, and outline your research questions accordingly.
3. Keep in mind the distinction between the 'why' orientation of quantitative questions and the 'what/how' nature of qualitative questions.

> 4. It is essential to include at least one mixed methods question to ensure the rationale and purpose for using mixed methods is explicitly addressed within the context of the research questions.

5. Rationale for using mixed methods

Question: Now that you have reflected on the nature of your research question(s), what is the rationale for using a mixed methods approach?

Key idea: The power of mixed methods stems from the combined force of the quantitative and qualitative strands. If the strands are not connected, the study does not meet the demands of mixed methods research. This, of course, is directly tied to both the preceding section on research questions, as well as the following section on designs and diagrams. Nevertheless, the rationale for utilising a mixed methods approach resides at the centre of the study. To collect both types of data and then simply attach the term mixed methods as an afterthought does not do justice to the evolving field of mixed methods research. When formulating a rationale, Creswell (2014b) encourages the researcher to consider the strengths and weaknesses of both qualitative and quantitative research. While quantitative research has the potential to provide powerful generalisations, qualitative research engages in the pursuit of more in-depth understandings of personal perspectives and how individuals make meaning of their life experiences. As you seek to describe your overall rationale for employing mixed methods, consider the following questions to guide your thoughts:

1. How do you plan to use a quantitative approach in your study? Identify not only how this will strengthen the study, but also the potential weaknesses that would benefit from a qualitative approach.
2. Similarly, how do you plan to use a qualitative approach in your study? Identify not only how this will strengthen the study, but also the potential weaknesses that would benefit from a quantitative approach.
3. Finally, how then do you understand the rationale of your study through the power of mixing the two approaches to arrive at a deeper understanding of the research topic?

Examples: Each of the Cambridge English studies provides a clear rationale for employing mixed methods approaches, and for the particular design that they have used. Galaczi and Khabbazbashi (Chapter 9, this volume) draw attention to the complementarity between the processes involved in scale development and exploratory sequential design that was employed for the project. Khalifa and Docherty (Chapter 11, this volume) also outline a number of ways in which the application of a mixed methods approach extends the scope and validity of the research. In their impact study, the use of qualitative interviews and focus groups supports the investigation of abstract concepts that would otherwise be difficult to tap using questionnaires alone partly because of the additional length they would add. Further, focus groups allowed for the inclusion of young learners – key voices as stakeholders – who might otherwise not manage to complete a questionnaire.

Practical steps:

1. Identify the distinct purpose of both the qualitative and quantitative strands in your research study.
2. Determine how the two strands fit together in a cohesive, logical, and purposeful manner.
3. Frequently revisit the rationale for using mixed methods as the study progresses, and consider potential ways in which it can be augmented or adapted to enhance the study's value.

---

6. Designs and diagrams

Question: What mixed methods design will be used to address your research questions?

Key idea: In Chapter 3 of this volume, Creswell and Zhou posit that the most effective starting point when considering the potential design of a study is to ask yourself the question, 'What is my intent for combining the quantitative and qualitative data?' When the researcher starts with this fundamental question, they must then consider three overarching approaches. One option is for the two research strands to develop alongside each other, eventually allowing the researcher to investigate potential areas for convergence and divergence. Another option assumes a sequential approach in which one strand precedes the other, where the researcher can develop a connection in which the second strand builds upon and develops the insights of the first. The final overarching design idea employs an embedded approach in which a smaller dataset is incorporated within a larger dataset to inform a particular aspect of the study. As you continue to formulate the various components of your study, remember that each of the potential designs serves a distinct purpose and is directly connected to the rationale for conducting the study.

An important aspect of devising, clarifying and communicating the design of your study is in the use of mixed methods diagrams; heuristic diagrams that guide the viewer in understanding how the data is collected, analysed and combined. These diagrams help to 'present and frame research' (Wheeldon and Åhlberg 2012:1), and are efficient ways to summarise and clarify complex processes for a wide range of readers. Specific conventions in notation and layout are followed to standardise how these diagrams are presented. For example, boxes are used to outline steps within a qualitative or quantitative strand, while ovals denote a step where data is combined or connected in some way. The abbreviations *quan* and *qual* are used and displaying these terms in uppercase or lowercase characters indicates a project strand with a higher or lower priority respectively. Drawing mixed methods diagrams of your whole study can be useful, even in the very early planning phases, as it encourages the researcher to think ahead, helps to focus and structure the planning, and may highlight areas of uncertainty that could be addressed early on. Miller and Bustamante (Chapter 5, this volume) provide a detailed and very practical step-by-step guide to drawing such diagrams.

As you develop and refine the questions you seek to address in your study, the mixed methods design that will best support a rigorous investigation of the key questions will emerge:

1. Reflect on the central reason for conducting the study. With this in mind, what mixed methods design will allow you to accomplish your goals?
2. Do you intend to conduct both the quantitative and qualitative strands concurrently? If so, what will be your strategy for investigating how the strands potentially converge and diverge?
3. Do you intend to conduct one of the strands first and then follow with the other strand to gain further insight? Will the goals of your study be best served by beginning with the qualitative or quantitative strand? How would you describe, in explicit terms, your reasons for selecting this sequence?
4. Do you intend to embed a smaller dataset within a larger study? If so, how would you rationalise the need to use this design? In other words, can you explain the added value of embedding the smaller dataset with regard to accomplishing the overarching goals of your study?
5. Can you draw a mixed methods diagram of your intended study? Does attempting to draw the mixed methods diagram highlight any areas of uncertainty with your study (e.g. the timing available for the strands, the type of data that will be generated by the strands or the capacity to integrate)?

Examples: Khalifa and Docherty (Chapter 11, this volume) are explicit in their reasons for choosing a concurrent design in their impact study – it was important to collect data within a particular timeframe when stakeholders had recently engaged with the assessment of interest, to ensure that the salient details were still fresh and recollections not diminished by the passage of time. This was particularly important given that one core group of participants were young children. Further, as time elapses it can be challenging to access key stakeholders and thus using a concurrent design that commenced soon after the assessment likely secured more participants for the research. A second fundamental reason for choosing a concurrent design was the desire to use the same participants in some aspects of the quantitative and qualitative strands to substantiate and clarify certain findings. The practical considerations of the design are also highlighted; in particular that data collection was time-bound – there was no opportunity to revisit questionnaire items that were ambiguous or to follow up with respondents for a second time. The researcher is advised to consider the time available in the project phases and how to budget their resources appropriately to ensure, for example, the quality of the instruments given this restriction. In order to facilitate examining the convergence and divergence of the strands, the stakeholder questionnaires were designed with overlapping qualitative and quantitative strands, and this was mirrored in the semi-structured interviews and focus groups. After data collection, their rigorous analysis using thematic analysis allowed systematic identification of key ideas, and aspects of divergence were addressed using contextual knowledge and other study data to either explain or reduce the apparent divergence, or flag it for future investigation.

In contrast, Galaczi and Khabbazbashi's study (Chapter 9, this volume), a complex multi-phase project, has a clear rationale for taking an exploratory sequential design. As described in their chapter, the development of new assessment scales is an iterative process starting from a broad base and ultimately extracting a set of focused assessment categories. By beginning with a qualitative investigation of learner speech and examiners' comments, a rich set of insights into speaking performance was gleaned and recommendations to address areas of inconsistency derived.

Each of the Cambridge English Language Assessment case study chapters provides a detailed mixed methods diagram of the study. Examining the diagrams alongside the descriptions of the projects will be helpful in understanding how they were constructed and provide concrete examples of how such diagrams represent complex research designs.

Practical steps:

1. Return to the rationale for using mixed methods, which represents the starting point for determining the overarching design that will most effectively serve to address the research questions.
2. Consider the practical constraints of budget, phase of the operational cycle, time available and access to the population involved in the study. While, for example, conducting a sequential mixed methods study may be desirable, it may not align with practical limitations related to participants and resources involved.
3. Be conscious of the role of the qualitative and quantitative strands, but do not lose sight of the interaction that must be established between them.
4. Consider how you can facilitate the reader's understanding of your study through the use of diagrams. Presenting the overall design of the

study using a diagram will assist those who are unfamiliar with mixed methods in following the complexities of a mixed methods study.

5. Try to draw the mixed methods diagram for your study, adding in as much detail as you can. The mixed methods diagram is a tool to reduce the inevitable complexity of detail in your study into a meaningful summary. Visualising your study in this way may help to shape your thinking, identify problems and see new links. You may find that you go through several iterations of the diagram, even in the early phases of your planning, in order to get it right.

Collection, analysis and presentation of mixed methods data

7. Methodological issues

Question: What are the potential methodological/ethical issues that may arise when conducting the study?

Key idea: As with any study, it is important to anticipate potential problems in advance whenever possible. Unexpected issues will often arise; however, deleterious effects can be mitigated through thoughtful consideration prior to beginning the research. Given that mixed methods research involves both quantitative and qualitative approaches, it is clear that the potential issues inherent to each will be present in a mixed methods study as well. A more pertinent topic in this volume is the methodological issues that might arise due to the act of bringing these two strands together in a variety of ways. When using a concurrent design, it is essential to consider if the constructs are parallel. Questions of sample size, the need to systematically merge the two strands, as well as discussing divergent results, are all important methodological concerns that warrant attention. In an explanatory sequential design, it is important to be purposeful in how the quantitative analysis is used to determine the essential 'who, what, and why' of the qualitative strand to maximise its explanatory power. When using an exploratory design, the qualitative strand will serve as the foundation for developing a quantitative instrument; therefore it is essential to have access to the skills and knowledge necessary to create a valid and reliable tool for measurement (Creswell 2014b). The following questions will assist you in identifying potential methodological issues prior to beginning your study, and are an important step in mitigating problems that could inhibit its success.

1. If you are using a convergent design, are both strands aligned such that they can be merged in a meaningful way?

2. If your research questions call for an explanatory research design, is your sample size for the initial quantitative strand substantial enough to yield results that can be further explored through a qualitative approach? Have you considered the potential directions in which the qualitative strand might move based on the quantitative analysis?

3. If you are seeking to conduct an exploratory study, are you confident that your qualitative analysis will yield results that can be transferred into a robust quantitative instrument? Additionally, do you have access to a population that will allow for this instrument to be used?

Examples: The Cambridge English projects touch on the two aspects of methodological issues described in the key idea summary of this section. First of all, there are challenges that arise with either quantitative or qualitative data that are not specifically related to mixed methods. Khalifa and Docherty (Chapter 11, this volume) offer some useful examples of issues that they faced with their data collection. Time was limited, and while this had an impact on their study design, it also meant that they needed to ensure that every aspect of the intended research questions was captured at once as there was no second chance to revisit it. On this basis, project plans needed to incorporate appropriate time for instrument review, translation (both backwards and forwards) and piloting. Particular attention was given to sampling in order to best use available resources. Stratified random sampling was adopted to manage the resources available for data collection while ensuring representativeness of geographical locations which would allow the researchers to identify inequalities of educational provision. While ethical guidelines from a range of professional bodies and the University of Cambridge were followed in every aspect of the study, particular attention was given to the ethical dimensions of the focus groups with young learners. These considerations were not particular to mixed methods but anticipating and planning for them allowed for the collection of high-quality data and supported the integration of the strands. Their chapter describes ways in which best practice was followed in instrument design specifically to support the mixed methods aims of the research.

In their chapter on the community-based participatory research approach, Vidaković and Robinson (Chapter 8, this volume) are honest about the complications encountered in selecting appropriate and authentic texts to form sample tests at the end of their first phase of research, as well as the difficulties of agreeing upon an appropriate level of specificity and authenticity for the test overall. The difficulties stemmed in part from inevitable differences between the partners in professional experience and priorities with regard to testing. Overcoming these obstacles by negotiation with the research partner as per the principles of community-based participatory design ensured the development of a sample test to take forward. A barrier that was perhaps not anticipated at the outset of the study was that access to community participants may be challenging if their project involvement is outside of their usual day jobs, an issue that may become more apparent in long-term extended projects. Their chapter adds extra depth to the considerations of how data should be integrated by encouraging the reader to think in advance about the ways in which working with a partner in a community-based participatory approach can enrich the data that is collected, but also the potential obstacles to be overcome.

Practical steps:

1. During the planning stages of the study, become familiar with issues that could potentially arise with the type of design that will be used.
2. Seek out exemplar studies that can provide insight into how to address these issues effectively to maintain the integrity of the study.
3. Identify individuals and/or textual resources that can offer proven advice on topics outside your area of expertise.

---

8.   Maximising the value of each strand

Question: Looking at the mixed methods design you have planned, what will be the quantitative and qualitative data collection/analysis procedures for the study?

Key idea: Ensure that in looking ahead to the added value of mixed methods you do not sacrifice the quality of work you invest into each of the component qualitative and quantitative strands. When planning data collection and analysis, it is important to return to the central driving force behind your study, the research questions. These questions should directly and succinctly describe the contribution of both the qualitative and quantitative strands. As noted in the earlier section on the nature of the research questions, the qualitative strand typically seeks to address issues of 'what' and 'how', while the quantitative strand focuses on the 'why'.

The contribution each strand will bring to the overall study will clearly depend on the mixed methods design being employed, but the additive power derived from using both research approaches should not overshadow their inherent individual value. Later on, as you write up your study, ensure that each strand is adequately represented. Furthermore, poorly planned quantitative or qualitative strands that result in lower quality data will compromise the potential that could be derived in combining the data, and may ultimately limit the conclusions that can be drawn. The following questions are important to consider as you work to maximise the value of each strand in a mixed methods study.

1. Have you developed research questions for each strand of data collection that will yield meaningful results?

2. Are you confident that the general design, methods for data collection, and analysis procedures for each strand adhere to the widely accepted parameters for rigorous research? If not, what steps can you take to remedy this (for example, by seeking external advice or training, revisiting the study protocol)?

3. Have you scrutinised your research plans for each strand to ensure you understand the type of data that will be generated and any limitations of it (for example if the quantitative strand will generate continuous, ordinal or categorical data)?

4. Can you anticipate any issues that might arise in either strand that could affect the quality of the data collected? What steps could you take to ensure that you can still derive the maximum benefit from the dataset?

Examples: Each of the Cambridge English projects demonstrates a commitment to understanding the value that both quantitative and qualitative strands bring to the mixed methods approach. Vidaković and Robinson's multiphase study of the development of a test of legal English makes clear in the design the value that can be extracted from each strand of data collection. The needs analysis in Phase 1 was driven by a qualitative strand that led to the development of sample papers for Phase 2, where quantitative data was prioritised but qualitative data was also gathered and used to explain and complement the quantitative data. The different types of quantitative data generated – in this case from a feedback questionnaire and from item statistics on performance of the sample test itself, work together to provide a rounded view of the success and challenges of the trial, further backed up by qualitative data.

Galaczi and Khabbazbashi (Chapter 9, this volume) show the importance of ensuring that each aspect receives appropriate treatment. The initial qualitative phase of the exploratory sequential design comprises a Conversation Analysis of 32 learners representing a range of L1s and different CEFR levels of ability. The richness derived from a dataset this size is considerable. In parallel, feedback from 316 examiners was captured through an open-ended questionnaire, again giving a substantial sample for thematic analysis. Phase 2 of the study, which sought to map speaking descriptors against the CEFR and explore their use by examiners, also utilised substantial samples (31 examiners for the quantitative mapping and eight examiners for the qualitative exploration of descriptor use), as well as sophisticated research techniques in Multi-Faceted Rasch analysis and Verbal Protocol Analysis respectively. The groundwork was laid in these initial phases for two sizeable marking trials that established the adequacy and fitness-for-purpose of the final scales in Phase 3. The range of quantitative and qualitative analysis techniques that contributed to the final outcomes of this applied research indicate not only the value placed on every aspect of the project, but also the importance of a diverse set of skills to extract the full meaning from the data collected.

Practical steps:

1. Bearing in mind the mixed methods design in place for your study, carefully consider how you will maintain a high degree of rigour for each individual strand.
2. Identify the appropriate sample size for your qualitative strand, method for data collection (interview, open-ended survey questions, etc.), data coding procedures, and validation methods.
3. Review the quantitative instrument to be used for data collection, the processes for determining the population, and the method of distribution of the instrument. Ensure a member of the research team possesses the skills to analyse the data.

---

9. Bringing the strands together

Question: How will you establish an explicit connection between the quantitative and qualitative strands of your study, which reflects your study's particular mixed methods design?

Key idea: The design of your mixed methods study structures the data collection and the order in which the quantitative and qualitative strands are collected. However, mixed methods research demands that the two strands are connected in a purposeful manner. Separate collection and analysis of each strand does not constitute mixed methods research until they are brought together in a prescribed fashion. The two strands of a mixed methods study can be integrated in a variety of ways, each of which reflects the overarching design. Creswell (2014a) identified four principal integration methods: merging, explaining, building, and embedding. *Merging* is the central process for bringing together the individual analyses of both strands in a convergent study. *Explaining* occurs when the goal is to use a qualitative analysis to further illuminate the results of a quantitative analysis. *Building* begins with a qualitative analysis, which is then employed to construct a quantitative stage. *Embedding* refers to the process in which one strand is incorporated within the larger context of the other strand to strengthen the overall study. Regardless of the type of design used in your study, it is essential to determine an effective method for representing the results of the integration method. To familiarise yourself with the advantages of using a joint display, as well as the different forms they can take, Hurlbut (Chapter 6, this volume) presents examples and a detailed outline. Consider the following questions to facilitate your plans for integrating the strands of your mixed methods study.

1. If you are using a parallel design, can you identify points at which the two data sets converge on similar results that complement each other?

Additionally, are there areas in which the strands diverge? If so, are you able to explain these points in a meaningful way?

2. If you are using an explanatory design, what are the criteria that will guide the qualitative stage? What specific areas of interest emerged from the quantitative analysis that you believe merit further investigation?

3. If you are using an exploratory design, how will the qualitative analysis inform the creation of the quantitative instrument? Are you able to effectively create items and scales that reflect what you discovered in the qualitative stage?

4. If you are using an embedded design, how will you incorporate one of the strands within the larger overarching strand in a way that enhances the overall value of the study?

Examples: Khalifa and Docherty (Chapter 11, this volume) explicitly describe how the convergence of strands in their parallel design was facilitated by the careful construction of their questionnaires. The process of merging the strands illuminated the level of agreement between stakeholders that the language initiative and exams had motivated learners, supported the use of Assessment for Learning principles, and encouraged teaching approaches that were more focused on communication. Equally, the forethought given to the overlap in their quantitative and qualitative approaches allowed divergences to be identified and explained. A key divergence in the data was seen between the concern of teachers that the children's exams were too challenging, and the learners' voices, backed by test data, that showed the tests were within their capabilities. Disseminating this finding based on integration of data and results at the end of the project could encourage educators to reevaluate their conceptions of the learners and reconsider the difficulty level of their lessons.

Practical steps:

1. Revisit both data sets and their respective analyses to refresh your understanding of the material that you seek to integrate.

2. Seek out examples of previous mixed methods studies that have used the same design and examine how the data sets were integrated.

3. Identify other individuals who have experience merging quantitative and qualitative research to discuss effective ways of bringing your data together in a meaningful manner.

4. Distil your results into a joint display that highlights the central ways in which both the qualitative and quantitative strands were brought together using mixed methods.

---

10. Presentation of results

Question: After data collection and analysis is complete, how will you present the results of your study clearly and effectively?

Key idea: Although the field of mixed methods continues to gain more widespread attention, there are still many researchers who have little or no experience in the field. For this reason, you must be able to present your data in a succinct, understandable format that allows all readers to benefit from your findings. A few practical methods for accomplishing this include through the use of diagrams, tables, and joint displays that effectively communicate the distinct benefits of mixed methods. As you work to prepare your study to share with a wider audience, consider the following questions:

1. Who do you believe will be interested in the results of the study and do you know the degree to which they are familiar with mixed methods research?
2. Would you be able to explain the basics of mixed methods, particularly as it pertains to your current study, to an individual who has limited knowledge of the field?
3. How would you justify the methods used in your study to someone who questions the validity and utility of mixed methods? In other words, do your results evidence the added value and deeper understanding that mixed methods strives to achieve?
4. What of type of visuals (for example diagrams, tables, joint displays) do you plan to incorporate to succinctly and effectively present the results of your study?

Examples: The Cambridge English case studies offer a number of examples of how the complexity of mixed methods studies, with their multiple strands, phases, variety of participants and instruments can be presented to readers in a format that is digestible and clear. Vidaković and Robinson (Chapter 8, this volume) provide a helpful example of how a mixed methods study can be effectively presented to a wider audience. The section in their chapter entitled 'Snapshot of the ILEC test development study' directs the reader's attention to the overarching mixed methods framework. Beginning with the research questions, it continues with a concise description of the explanatory approach, noting 'the design was selected with the goal to explore the language needs of target test users and develop a test that would meet their real-life language needs'. Clearly, the overall design is described in much greater detail in the sections that follow; nevertheless, the succinct explanation of the study at the beginning of the article creates an easily understood foundation for readers who are unfamiliar with mixed methods to gain traction as they move forward in the chapter. Later, in their conclusion, a final table (Table 4) summarises the phases of test development and the associated data collection and integration of results, as well as the different participants involved at each stage. Galaczi and Khabbazbashi (Chapter 9, this volume) also began with an explanation and rationale for why mixed methods was an ideal approach to accomplish their research goals. Through reference to Aristotle's notion that 'the whole is greater than the sum of its parts' and the analogy describing mixed methods as the 'synergy of musical parts in the creation of a song', the authors communicate the larger ideas of mixed methods in a creative and inviting manner. Elliott and Lim (Chapter 10, this volume) presented a series of tables that outlined the objectives, data collection methods, and analysis procedures for both the qualitative and quantitative strands. Their concise and logical presentation in the tables provides the reader with a visual guide that can be used to track the entirety of the study in a readily accessible format. Additionally, they followed Hurlbut's advice (Chapter 6, this volume) with regard to the sequence of research questions, which provides yet another opportunity for the reader to gain an understanding of the flow of the study. Their joint display to present the findings of Phase 2 of their study summarises the decisions on whether new tasks show acceptable validity. A range of complex qualitative and quantitative data is presented succinctly and the joint display demonstrates the important role of both strands in arriving at a conclusion on the appropriacy of a given task.

Practical steps:

1. Identify the target audience for your study and consider the degree to which they are familiar with mixed methods research.
2. Consider how to introduce your study, perhaps by giving an overview that acts as a signpost to help the reader orient themselves as they progress in their reading, particularly if the study is complex.
3. Develop a concise explanation of the methods used to conduct the study that can be readily understood by an individual who does not have a background in mixed methods.
4. Develop a 1-page joint display that accurately and efficiently arrays the quantitative and qualitative results.

Moving from ideas to action

In seeking to provide the reader with a practical framework for employing mixed methods in the field of language assessment, this chapter should assist you in thinking about the practicalities of getting your research project underway. The questions, checklists and practical steps can be used to prime your planning and anticipate some of the issues you may meet. The examples from the Cambridge English chapters illustrate the challenges that other researchers have faced in conducting applied research in the field of language assessment and how they have been overcome to yield successful and valuable validation evidence for specific tests, and add to the body of literature on language assessment more broadly.

This chapter now brings to a close a comprehensive volume that will serve as a guide for anyone interested in amplifying the power and scope of their research using mixed methods. The chapters in Section 1 provided insight into the larger issues and factors that have not only connected mixed methods and language assessment in the past and present, but point to the future potential for a more robust and developed relationship. The socio-cognitive model of test validation (Weir 2005) was presented as a framework for considering the evidence needed to ensure a test is fair, valid and practical. Establishing the validation argument for a test means addressing each of the separate but related dimensions in the model, and the opportunity for mixed methods to support the integration of different types of data in pursuit of this aim is clear.

For those who are interested in refreshing or deepening their knowledge of the various components of mixed methods, Section 2 offered in-depth coverage of the most critical concepts necessary for moving forward with a study. Mixed methods foundations, designs and diagrams, and writing up studies are all addressed in detail with specific focus on language assessment and the benefits of mixed methods in test validation comprehensively outlined.

Lastly, Section 3 shows the Cambridge English Language Assessment approach to test development, validation and revision in action. The general overview and exemplar case studies embed the socio-cognitive approach to validation within the operational assessment cycle, and demonstrate how the quality management system described by Saville (Chapter 2, this volume) supports an iterative cycle of continual improvement. These studies can be used not only as points of reference for understanding overarching study designs, but as sources of inspiration demonstrating that mixed methods can be used in powerful ways to increase our understanding of language assessment, as well as the development, revision and validation of tests as part of a complex system.

Together these sections comprise a volume on mixed methods in language assessment that is comprehensive and immensely practical, addressing theoretical and philosophical issues but rooted in the applied models that underlie modern language assessment systems.

References

Åhlberg, M, Åänismaa, P, and Dillon, P (2005) Education for sustainable living: Integrating theory, practice, design, and development, *Scandinavian Journal of Educational Research* 49 (2), 167–186. doi: 10.1080/00313830500048923

Alderson, J C and Banerjee, A (2001) Language testing an assessment (part 1), *Language Teaching* 34 (4), 213–236.

Alderson, J C and Hamp-Lyons, L (1996) TOEFL preparation courses: a study of washback, *Language Testing* 13, 280–297.

Alderson, J C and Wall, D (1993) Does washback exist? *Applied Linguistics* 14 (2), 115–129.

Alderson, J C, Clapham, C and Wall, D (1995) *Language Test Construction and Evaluation*, Cambridge: Cambridge University Press.

Almutairi, A F (2012) *A case study examination of the influence of cultural diversity in the multicultural nursing workforce on the quality of care and patient safety in a Saudi Arabian hospital,* unpublished doctoral dissertation, Queensland University of Technology, Brisbane, Australia.

Ashton, K, Salamoura, A and Diaz, E (2012) The BEDA impact project: a preliminary investigation of a bilingual programme in Spain, *Research Notes* 50, 34–42.

Assessment Reform Group (2002) *Assessment for Learning: 10 Principles*, available online: www.aaia.org.uk/content/uploads/2010/06/Assessment-for-Learning-10-principles.pdf

Association of Language Testers in Europe/Council of Europe (2012) *Manual for Test Development and Examining*, available online: www.coe.int/t/dg4/linguistic/ManualLanguageTest-Alte2011_EN.pdf

Atkinson, J M and Heritage, J (Eds) (1984) *Structures of Social Action: Studies in Conversation Analysis*, Cambridge: Cambridge University Press.

Bachman, L F (1990) *Fundamental Considerations in Language Testing*, Oxford: Oxford University Press.

Bachman, L F and Palmer, A (1996) *Language Testing in Practice*, Oxford: Oxford University Press.

Bachman, L F and Palmer, A (2010) *Language Assessment in Practice*, Oxford, England: Oxford University Press.

Bachman, L F, Davidson, F, Ryan, K and Choi, I-C (1995) *An Investigation into the Comparability of Two Tests of English as a Foreign Language: The Cambridge-TOEFL Comparability Study*, Studies in Language Testing volume 1, Cambridge: UCLES/Cambridge University Press.

Bailey, K M (1996) Working for washback: a review of the washback concept in language testing, *Language Testing* 13, 257–279.

Baker, B A (2012) Individual differences in rater decision making style: an exploratory mixed-methods study, *Language Assessment Quarterly* 9, 225–248.

Bamberger, M (2012) *Introduction to Mixed Methods in Impact Evaluation*, available online: www.interaction.org/sites/default/files/Mixed%20Methods%20in%20Impact%20Evaluation%20(English).pdf

Barkaoui, K (2007) Rating scale impact on EFL essay marking: A mixed methods study, *Assessing Writing* 12, 86–107.

Bateman, B E (2002) Promoting openness toward culture learning: ethnographic interviews for students of Spanish, *The Modern Language Journal* 86, 318–331.

Berg, B L and Lune, H (2012) *Qualitative Research Methods for the Social Sciences* (8th edition), Upper Saddle River: Pearson Education.

Berliner, D C (2002) Educational research: The hardest science of all, *Educational Researcher* 31 (8), 18–20.

Betancourt, T S, Meyers-Ohki, S E, Stevenson, A, Ingabire, C, Kanyanganzi, F, Munyana, M, Mushashi, C, Teta, S, Fayida, I, Cyamatare, F R, Stulac, S and Beardslee, W R (2011) Using mixed-methods research to adapt and evaluate a family strengthening intervention in Rwanda, *AJTS* 2 (1), 32–45.

Biber, D, Conrad, S, Reppen, R, Byrd, R and Helt, M (2002) Speaking and writing in the university: A multidimensional comparison, *TESOL Quarterly* 36 (1), 9–48.

Black, P and William, D (1998) Inside the black box: Raising standards through classroom assessment, *Phi Delta Kappa International* 80 (2), 139–148.

Black, P, Harrison, C, Lee, C, Marshall, B and William, D (2010) *Assessment for Learning, Putting it into Practice*, London: Open University Press.

Borgers, N, Leeuw, E D and Hox, J J (2000) Children as respondents in survey research: Cognitive development and response quality 1, *Bulletin de Méthodologie Sociologique* 66, 60–75.

Braun, V and Clarke, V (2006) Using thematic analysis in psychology, *Qualitative Research in Psychology* 3 (2), 77–101.

Bresciani, S and Eppler, M J (2007) *Usability of diagrams for group knowledge work: Toward an analytic description*, paper presented at the I-KNOW Conference, Graz, Austria.

Brewer, J and Hunter, A (1989) *Multimethod Research: A Synthesis of Styles*, Newbury Park: Sage.

Brown, A (1993) LSP testing: The role of linguistic and real-world criteria, *Melbourne Papers in Language Testing* 2 (2), 35–54.

Bryman, A (1988) *Quantity and Quality in Social Research*, London: Routledge.

Bryman, A (2006a) Integrating quantitative and qualitative research: How is it done? *Qualitative Research* 6 (1), 97–113. doi:10.1177/1468794106058877

Bryman, A (2006b) Paradigm peace and the implications for quality, *International Journal of Social Research Methodology* 9, 111–126.

Buckendahl, C W, Foley, B P and Lim, G S (2011) *Canadian Language Benchmarks Standard Setting – FCE CAE BECV*, Cambridge: Cambridge ESOL internal report.

Busse, V and Williams, M (2010) Why German? Motivation of students studying German at English universities, *Language Learning Journal* 38, 67–85.

Bustamante, C (2014) *Professional development on Web 2.0 for teachers of Spanish: A mixed methods case study*, unpublished doctoral dissertation, University of Nebraska–Lincoln.

Cambridge English (2013) *Principles of Good Practice: Quality Management and Validation in Language Assessment*, Cambridge: UCLES, available online: www.cambridgeenglish.org/images/22695-principles-of-good-practice.pdf

Campbell, D T and Fiske, D W (1959) Convergent and discriminant validation by the multitrait-multimethod matrix, *Psychological Bulletin* 56, 81–105.

Campbell, J, Kyriakides, L, Muijs, D and Robinson, W (2004) *Assessing Teacher Effectiveness: Developing a Differentiated Mode*, Abingdon: Routledge Falmer.

Canale, M and Swain, M (1980) Theoretical bases of communicative approaches to second language teaching and testing, *Applied Linguistics* 1 (1), 1–47.

Capello, M (2005) Photo interviews: eliciting data through conversations with children, *Field Methods* 17 (2), 170–182.

Caracelli, V J and Greene, J C (1993) Data analysis strategies for mixed-method evaluation designs, *Educational Evaluation and Policy Analysis* 15, 195–207.

Carless, D (2005) Prospects for the implementation of assessment for learning, *Assessment in Education: Principles, Policy & Practice* 12 (1), 39–54.

Carroll, B J (1981) Specifications for an English Language Testing Service, in Alderson, J C and Hughes, A (Eds) *ELT documents 111– Issues in Language Testing*, London: The British Council, 66–111.

Chalhoub-Deville, M (2003) Second language interaction: current perspectives and future trends, *Language Testing* 20 (4), 369–383.

Chamberlain, A and Robinson, M (2004) *International Legal English Certificate: Market research report*, Cambridge: Cambridge ESOL internal report.

Chambers, L, Elliott, M and Jianguo, H (2012) The Hebei Impact Project: a study into the impact of Cambridge English exams in the state sector in Hebei province, China, *Research Notes* 50, 20–23.

Chapelle, C A, Enright, M K and Jamieson, J M (2008) *Building a validity argument for the Test of English as a Foreign Language*, New York: Routledge.

Chapman, D W, Weidman, J, Cohen, M and Mercer, M (2005) The search for quality: a five country study of national strategies to improve educational quality in Central Asia, *International Journal of Educational Development* 25, 514–530.

Cheng, L (1997) How does washback influence teaching? Implications for Hong Kong, *Language and Education* 11, 38–54.

Cheng, L (2004) The washback effect of an examination change on teachers' perception towards their classroom teaching, in Cheng, L, Watanabe, Y and Curtis, A (Eds) *Washback in Language Testing: Research Contexts and Methods,* Mahwah: Lawrence Erlbaum, 147–170.

Cheng, L (2014) Consequences, impact and washback, in Kunnan, A J (Ed), *The Companion to Language Assessment Volume 3,* London: Routledge, 1,130–1,145.

Cheng, L and Curtis, A (2004) Washback or backwash: a review of the impact of testing on teaching and learning, in Cheng, L and Watanabe, Y (Eds) *Washback in Language Testing: Research, Contexts and Methods*, New Jersey: Lawrence Erlbaum, 3–17.

Clapham, C M (1981) Reaction to the Carroll paper (1), in Alderson, J C and Hughes, A (Eds) *ELT documents 111– Issues in Language Testing*, London: The British Council, 111–117.

Clapham, C M (1996) *The development of IELTS: A Study of the Effect of Background Knowledge on Reading Comprehension*, Studies in Language Testing volume 4, Cambridge: UCLES/Cambridge University Press.

Clark, C J, Shahrouri, M, Halasa, L, Khalaf, I, Spencer, R and Everson-Rose, S (2012) A mixed methods study of participant reaction to domestic violence research in Jordan, *Journal of Interpersonal Violence* 27 (9), 1,655–1,676. doi:10.1177/0886260511430383

Classen, S, Lopez, E D S, Winter, S, Awadzi, K D, Ferree, N and Garvan, C W

(2007) Population-based health promotion perspective for older driver safety: Conceptual framework to intervention plan, *Clinical Interventions in Aging* 2 (4), 677–693.

Cobb, T (2003a) *Web VocabProfile*, available online: www.lextutor.ca/vp/

Cobb, T (2003b) *Web VocabProfile*, available online: www.lextutor.ca/vp

Coleman, J A, Galaczi, A and Astruc, L (2007) Motivation of UK school pupils towards foreign languages: A large-scale survey at Key Stage 3, *Language Learning Journal* 35 (2), 245–280.

Collins, K M, Onwuegbuzie, A J and Sutton, I L (2006) A model incorporating the rationale and purpose for conducting mixed methods research in special education and beyond, *Learning Disabilities: A Contemporary Journal* 4, 67–100.

Corkill, D and Robinson, M (2006) Using the global legal community in the development of ILEC, *Research Notes* 25, 10–11.

Corrigan, M and Crump, P (2015) Test analysis, *Research Notes* 59, 4–10.

Council of Europe (2001) *Common European Framework of Reference for Languages: Learning, Teaching, Assessment*, Cambridge: Cambridge University Press.

Coxhead, A (2000) A new academic word list, *TESOL Quarterly* 34 (2), 213–238.

Crabtree, B F and Miller, W L (1992) *Doing Qualitative Research*, Thousand Oaks: Sage.

Creswell, J W (1994) *Research Design: Qualitative and Quantitative Approaches*, Thousand Oaks: Sage.

Creswell, J (2009) *Research Design: Qualitative, Quanatitative and Mixed Methods Appoaches* (3rd edition), Los Angeles: Sage.

Creswell, J W (2011) Controversies in mixed methods research, in Denzin, N K and Lincoln, Y S (Eds) *The SAGE Handbook of Qualitative Research*, Thousand Oaks: Sage, 269–283.

Creswell, J W (2012) *Qualitative Inquiry and Research Design: Choose Among Five Approaches*, Thousand Oaks: Sage.

Creswell, J W (2013a) *Qualitative Inquiry and Research Design: Choosing Among Five Approaches* (3rd Edition), Thousand Oaks: Sage.

Creswell, J W (2013b) *Research Design: Qualitative, Quantitative, and Mixed Methods Approaches*, Thousand Oaks: Sage.

Creswell, J W (2014a) *A Concise Introduction to Mixed Methods Research*, Thousand Oaks: Sage.

Creswell, J W (2014b) *Research Design: Qualitative, Quantitative, and Mixed Methods Approaches*, (4th edition), Los Angeles: Sage.

Creswell, J W (2015) *A Concise Introduction to Mixed Methods Research*, Thousand Oaks: Sage.

Creswell, J W and Garrett, A L (2008) The 'movement' of mixed methods research and the role of educators, *South African Journal of Education* 28, 321–333.

Creswell, J W and McCoy, B R (2011) The use of mixed methods thinking in documentary research, in Hesse-Biber, S N (Ed) *The Handbook of Emergent Technologies in Social Research*, New York: Oxford University Press, 453–469.

Creswell, J W and Plano Clark, V L (2011) *Designing and Conducting Mixed Methods Research* (2nd edition), Thousand Oaks, CA: Sage.

Creswell, J W, Plano Clark, V L, Gutmann, M L and Hanson, W E (2003)

Advanced mixed methods research designs, in Tashakkori, A and Teddlie, C (Eds) *Handbook of Mixed Methods in Social and Behavioral Research*, Thousand Oaks: Sage, 209–240.

Creswell, J W, Klassen, A C, Plano Clark, V L and Smith, K C (2011) *Best Practices for Mixed Methods Research in the Health Sciences*, Washington, DC: National Institutes of Health.

Criper, C (1981) Reaction to the Carroll paper (2), in Alderson, J C and Hughes, A (Eds) *ELT documents 111– Issues in Language Testing*, London: The British Council, 117–121.

Criper, C and Davies, A (1988) *ELTS Validation Project Report, Research Report 1(i)*, London: The British Council/UCLES.

Davies, A (2014) Fifty years of language assessment, in Kunnan, A J (Ed), *The Companion to Language Assessment,* Boston: John Wiley & Sons, Inc, 3–21.

Day, C, Sammons, P, Kington, A and Regan, E K (2008) *Effective classroom practice (ECP): A Mixed Method Study of Influences and Outcomes*, Swindon: ESRC.

Dellinger, A B and Leech, N L (2007) Towards a unified validation framework in mixed methods research, *Journal of Mixed Methods Research* 1 (4), 309-332.

Denzin, N K and Lincoln, Y S (Eds) (2011) *The SAGE Handbook of Qualitative Research*, Thousand Oaks: Sage.

Dickinson, W B (2010) Visual displays for mixed methods findings, in Tashakkori, A and Teddlie, C (Eds) *SAGE Handbook of Mixed Methods in Social & Behavioral Research* (2nd edition), Thousand Oaks: Sage, 469–504.

Dillman, D A (2000) *Mail and Internet Surveys: The Tailored Design Method*, Hoboken: John Wiley & Sons.

Douglas, D (2000) *Assessing Languages for Specific Purposes*, Cambridge: Cambridge University Press.

Driscoll, D L, Appiah-Yeboah, A, Salib, P and Rupert, D J (2007) Merging qualitative and quantitative data in mixed methods research: How to and why not, *Ecological and Environmental Anthropology (University of Georgia)* 18, 19–28.

Driscoll D L and Kasztalska A (2013) *Tables, Appendices, Footnotes and Endnotes*, available online: owl.english.purdue.edu/owl/resource/670/05/

Eisemon, T O (1990) Examinations policies to strengthen primary schooling in African countries, *International Journal of Educational Development* 10 (1), 69–82.

Elder, C (1993) *The Proficiency Test for Language Teachers: Italian, Volume 1: Final Report on the Test Development Process,* Melbourne: NLLIA Language Testing Centre, University of Melbourne.

Elder, C, Knoch, U, Barkhuizen, G and von Randow, J (2005) Individual feedback to enhance rater training: Does it work?, *Language Assessment Quarterly: An International Journal* 2 (3), 175–196.

Elliott, M (2011) *FCE and CAE Construct Validation Study (Part 1)*, Cambridge: Cambridge ESOL internal report.

Elliott, M, Lim, G S and Galaczi, E D (2012) *FCE and CAE Construct Validation Study (Part 2)*, Cambridge: Cambridge ESOL internal report.

Elliott, M, Vidaković, I and Corrigan, M (2013) *CAE Reading and Use of English Trial 5 Report*, Cambridge: Cambridge ESOL internal report.

Ellis, R (2003) *Task-based Language Learning and Teaching*, Clarendon Press: Oxford.

Enright, A (2005) *ELPAC: A Test for Air Traffic Controllers to meet ICAO Language Proficiency Requirements*, available online: legacy.icao.int/icao/en/anb/meetings/ials2/Docs/22.Enright.pdf

Eppler, M J (2006) A comparison between concept maps, mind maps, conceptual diagrams, and visual metaphors as complementary tools for knowledge construction and sharing, *Information Visualization* 5, 202–210.

Erfani, S S (2012) A comparative washback study of IELTS and TOEFL iBT on teaching and learning activities in preparation courses in the Iranian context, *English Language Teaching* 5, 185–195.

Erwin, E J, Brotherson, M J and Summers, J A (2011) Understanding qualitative metasynthesis issues and opportunities in early childhood intervention research, *Journal of Early Intervention* 33 (3), 186–200. doi: 10.1177/1053815111425493

ETS (2004) *Test of Written English: Guide* (Fifth edition), available online: www.ets.org/Media/Tests/TOEFL/pdf/tweguid.pdf

Farquhar, S A and Wing, S (2003) Methodological and ethical considerations in community-driven environmental justice research, in Minkler, M and Wallerstein, N (Eds) *Community-Based Participatory Research for Health*, San Francisco: Jossey-Bass, 221–241.

Feak, C B, Reinhart, S M and Rohlck, T N (2009) *Academic Interactions: Communicating on Campus*, Ann Arbor: University of Michigan Press.

Fetters, M D, Curry, L A and Creswell, J W (2013) Achieving integration in mixed methods designs – Principles and practices, *Health Services Research* 48, 2,134–2,156.

Field, J (2004) *Psycholinguistics: The Key Concepts*, London: Routledge.

Field, J (2013) Cognitive validity, in Geranpayeh, A and Taylor, L (Eds) *Examining Listening: Research and Practice in Assessing Second Language Listening*, Studies in Language Testing volume 35, Cambridge: UCLES/Cambridge University Press, 77–151.

Fielding, N G and Fielding, J L (1986) *Linking Data: The Articulation of Qualitative and Quantitative Methods in Social Research*, Beverly Hills: Sage.

Filer, A (1995) Teacher assessment: Social process and social product, *Assessment in Education: Principles, Policy & Practice* 2 (3), 305–334.

Fox, J D (2004) Test decisions over time: tracking validity, *Language Testing* 21, 437–465.

Fox, J D (2009) Moderating top-down policy impact and supporting EAP curricular renewal: Exploring the potential of diagnostic assessment, *Journal of English for Academic Purposes*, 8 (1), 26–42.

Freeman, M H (2004) Crossing the boundaries of time: Merleau-Ponty's phenomenology and cognitive linguistic theories, *Linguagem, Cultura e Cognição: Estudos de Linguística Cognitiva* 2, 643–655.

Fulcher, G (1996) Does thick description lead to smart tests? A data-based approach to rating scale construction, *Language Testing* 13, 208–238.

Fulcher, G (1997) An English language placement test: Issues in reliability and validity, *Language Testing* 14, 113–139.

Fulcher, G (2003) *Testing Second Language Speaking*, London: Longman/Pearson Education.

Galaczi, E D (2007a) *Main Suite and BEC assessment scales revision: Marking trial Dec 2006*, Cambridge: Cambridge English Language Assessment internal report.

Galaczi, E D (2007b) *Main Suite and BEC standardisation videos: Multi-Facet Rasch Analysis*, Cambridge: Cambridge English Language Assessment internal report.

Galaczi, E D (2014) Content analysis, in Kunnan, A J (Ed) *Companion to Language Assessment*, Hoboken: John Wiley and Sons, 1,308–1,322.

Galaczi, E D, ffrench, A, Hubbard, C and Green, A (2011) Developing assessment scales for large-scale speaking tests: A multiple-method approach, *Assessment in Education: Principles, Policy & Practice* 18 (3), 217–237. doi: 10.1080/0969594X.2011.574605

Geranpayeh, A (2011) The impact of online marking on examiners' behaviour, *Research Notes* 43, 15–21.

Geranpayeh, A (2013) Scoring validity, in Geranpayeh, A and Taylor, L (Eds) *Examining Listening: Research and Practice in Assessing Second Language Listening*, Studies in Language Testing volume 35, Cambridge: UCLES/ Cambridge University Press, 242–272.

Geranpayeh, A and Taylor, L (Eds) (2013) *Examining Listening: Research and Practice in Assessing Second Language Listening*, Studies in Language Testing volume 35, Cambridge: UCLES/Cambridge University Press.

Ginther, A (2012) Assessment of speaking, in Chapelle C (Ed) *The Encyclopaedia of Applied Linguistics*, Hoboken: Wiley & Sons, available online: onlinelibrary.wiley.com/doi/10.1002/9781405198431.wbeal0052/pdf

Ginther, A and Grant, L (1996) *A Review of the Academic Needs of Native English-speaking College Students in the United States*, TOEFL Monograph No. 1, Princeton: Educational Testing Service.

Gipps, C (1994) *Beyond Testing: Towards a Theory of Educational Assessment*, London: Falmer Press.

Gosa, C and Frentiu, L (2008) Exploring attitudes: The Romanian Bacalaureat versus CAE, *Research Notes* 34, 31–36.

Green, A (1998) *Verbal Protocol Analysis in Language Testing Research: A Handbook*, Cambridge: Cambridge University Press.

Green, A (2006) *Main Suite Speaking Test Modifications Questionnaire to Oral Examiners*, Cambridge: Cambridge ESOL internal report.

Green, A and Hawkey, R (2005) Test washback and impact: What do they mean and why do they matter? *Modern English Teacher* 13 (4), 66–71.

Green, A, Ünaldi, A and Weir, C J (2010) Empiricism versus connoisseurship: Establishing the appropriacy of texts for testing reading for academic purposes, *Language Testing* 27 (3), 1–21.

Green, A, Weir, C J, Chan, S, Taylor, L, Field, J, Nakatsuhara, F and Bax, S (2012) *Textual features of CAE reading texts: CAE texts compared with reading texts from FCE, CPE, IELTS and with essential undergraduate textbooks*, final project report, University of Bedfordshire.

Green, A, Khalifa, H and Weir, C J (2013) Examining textual features of reading texts – a practical approach, *Research Notes* 52, 24–35.

Greene, J C (2007) *Mixed Methods in Social Inquiry*, San Francisco: John Wiley & Sons.

Greene, J C (2008) Is mixed methods social inquiry a distinctive methodology? *Journal of Mixed Methods Research* 2, 7–22.

Greene, J C, Caracelli, V J and Graham, W F (1989) Toward a conceptual framework for mixed-method evaluation designs, *Educational Evaluation and Policy Analysis* 11 (3), 255–274.

Guest, G (2013) Describing mixed methods research: an alternative to typologies, *Journal of Mixed Methods Research* 7, 141–151.

Gurr, C and Tourlas, K (2000) Formalising the essence of diagrammatic syntax, in Anderson, M, Cheng, P and Haarslev, V (Eds) *Theory and Application of Diagrams: First International Conference, Diagrams*, Berlin: Springer, 483–485.

Haines, C (2011) *Value added by mixed methods research*, doctoral dissertation, University of Nebraska–Lincoln.

Hall, B and Howard, K (2008) A synergistic approach: Conducting mixed methods research with typological and systemic design considerations, *Journal of Mixed Methods Research* 2, 248–269.

Harrison, M (2003) *Report on reading materials provided by TransLegal*, Cambridge: Cambridge ESOL internal report.

Hashemi, M R and Babaii, E (2013) Mixed methods research: toward new research designs in applied linguistics, *Modern Language Journal* 97 (4), 828–852.

Hashimioto, A and Clayton, M (2009) *Visual Design Fundamentals: A Digital Approach* (3rd edition), Boston: Cengage.

Hawkey, R (2006) *Impact Theory and Practice: Studies of the IELTS Test and Progetto Lingue 2000*, Studies in Language Testing volume 24, Cambridge: UCLES/Cambridge University Press.

Heatley, A, Nation, I S P and Coxhead, A (2002) *RANGE and FREQUENCY Programs*, available online: www.victoria.ac.nz/lals/staff/paul-nation.aspx

Hesse-Biber, S and Burke Johnson, R (2013) Coming at things differently: Future directions of posisble engagement with mixed methods research, *Journal of Mixed Methods Research* 7 (2), 103–109.

Heyneman, S P (1987) Uses of examinations in developing countries: selection, research, and education sector management, *International Journal of Educational Development* 7 (4), 251–263.

Hodgkin, S (2008) Telling It all: A story of women's social capital using a mixed methods approach, *Journal of Mixed Methods Research* 2 (4), 296–316.

Hoepfl, M C (1997) Choosing qualitative research: A primer for technology education researchers, *Journal of Technology Education* 9 (1), 47–63.

Hoover-Dempsey, K and Sandler, H M (2005) Parental involvement in children's education: why does it make a difference, *Teachers College Record* 97 (2), 311–331.

Horowitz, C, Robinson, M and Seifer, S (2013) Community-based participatory research from the margin to the mainstream: Are researchers prepared? *Circulation*, available online: circ.ahajournals.org/content/119/19/2633.full. pdf+html

Hoshmand, L T (2003) Can lessons of history and logical analysis ensure progress in psychological science? *Theory and Psychology* 13 (1), 39–44.

Hubbard, C, Gilbert, S and Pidcock, J (2006) Assessment processes in Speaking Tests: A pilot verbal protocol study, *Research Notes* 24, 14–19.

Hughes, A (2003) *Testing for Language Teachers* (2nd edition), Cambridge: Cambridge University Press.

Huhta, A (2009) An analysis of the quality of English testing for aviation purposes in Finland, *Australian Review of Applied Linguistics* 32 (3), 26.1–26.14. doi: 10.2104/aral0926.

Hurlbut S (2013) *Exploring the Process of Becoming a German Major: A Mixed Methods Study*, unpublished manuscript, University of Nebraska–Lincoln.

Igreja, V, Kleijn, W and Richters, A (2006) When the war was over, little changed: Women's posttraumatic suffering after the war in Mozambique, *Journal of Nervous & Mental Disease* 194 (7), 502–509. doi:10.1097/01. nmd.0000228505.36302.a3.

Ihantola, E M and Kihn, L A (2011) Threats to validity and reliability in mixed methods accounting research, *Qualitative Research in Accounting & Management* 8, 39–58.

ILO/VCCI (no date) *Youth Employment in Vietnam: Report of Survey Findings*, available online: www.oit.org/public/english/dialogue/actemp/downloads/projects/youth/vietnam_reportv5.pdf

Inbar-Lourie, O (2010) Language assessment culture, in Shohamy, E and Hornberger, N H (Eds) *Encyclopedia of Language and Education* (2nd edition), Language Testing and Assessment volume 7, New York: Springer Science + Business Media LLC, 285–299.

Ingham, K and Thighe, D (2006) Issues with developing a test in LSP: the International Certificate in Financial English, *Research Notes* 25, 5–10.

Isaacs, T and Trofimovich, P (2012) Deconstructing Comprehensibility: identifying the linguistic influences on listeners' L2 comprehensibility ratings, *Studies in Second Language Acquisition* 34, 475–505.

Israel, B A, Schulz, A J, Parker, E A and Becker, A B (1998) Review of community-based research: Assessing partnership approaches to improve public health, *Annual Review of Public Health* (19), 173–202.

Israel, B A, Parker, E A, Rowe, Z, Salvatore, A, Minkler, M, López, J, Butz, A, Mosley, A, Coates, L, Lambert, G, Potito, P A, Brenner, B, Rivera, M, Romero, H, Thompson, B, Coronado, B and Halstead, S (2005) Community-based participatory research: Lessons learned from the centres for children's environmental health and disease prevention research, *Environmental Health Perspectives* 113 (10), 1,463–1,471.

Ivankova, N V (2015) *Mixed Methods Applications in Action Research: From Methods to Community Action*, Thousand Oaks: Sage.

Ivankova, N V, Creswell, J W and Stick, S L (2006) Using mixed-methods sequential explanatory design: From theory to practice, *Field Methods* 18 (1), 3–20. doi: 10.1177/1525822X05282260

Jacob, E (1987) Qualitative research traditions: A review, *Review of Educational Research* 57, 1–50.

James, D (2001) *Cultures of learning and the learning of cultures*, paper presented at the cultures of learning conference, University of Bristol.

James, S (1997) Drawing inferences: Visual representations in theory and practice, in Molyneaux, B L (Ed) *The Cultural Life of Images: Visual Representation in Archaeology*, New York: Routledge, 22-48.

James, E A, Milenkiewicz, M T and Bucknam, A B (2008) *Participatory Action Research for Educational Leadership: Using Data-Driven Decision Making to Improve Schools*, Los Angeles: Sage.

Jamieson, J M, Jones, S, Kirsch, I, Mosenthal, P and Taylor, C (2000) *TOEFL 2000 Framework: A Working Paper*, TOEFL Monograph No. 16, Princeton: Educational Testing Service.

Jamieson, J M, Eignor, D, Grabe, W and Kunnan, A J (2008) Frameworks for a new TOEFL, in Chapelle, C A, Enright, M K and Jamieson, J M (Eds) *Building a validity argument for the Test of English as a Foreign Language*, New York: Routledge, 55–95.

Jang, E E, Wagner, M and Park, G (2014) Mixed methods research in language testing and assessment, *Annual Review of Applied Linguistics* 34, 123–153.

Jianda, L (2007) Developing a pragmatics test for Chinese EFL learners, *Language Testing* 24, 391–415.

Johnson, R B (2012) Dialectical pluralism and mixed research, *American Behavioral Scientist* 56 (6), 751-754.

John Wiley and Sons (2013) *Author Guidelines for Contributors to the Modern Language Journal,* available online: onlinelibrary.wiley.com/journal/10.1111/ (ISSN)15404781/homepage/ForAuthors.html

Johnson, R B and Onwuegbuzie, A J (2004) Mixed methods research: A research paradigm whose time has come, *Educational Researcher* 33 (7), 14–26.

Johnson, R B Onwuegbuzie, A J and Turner, L A (2007) Toward a definition of mixed methods research, *Journal of Mixed Methods Research* 1 (2), 112–133. doi:10.1177/1558689806298224

Jones, L and Kafetsios, K (2005) Exposure to political violence and psychological well-being in Bosnian adolescents: A mixed method approach, *Clinical Child Psychology and Psychiatry* 10 (2), 157–176. doi:10.1177/1359104505051209

Jones, N and Saville, N (2014) *Learning Oriented Assessment: A Systemic View*, available online: www.iaea.info/documents/paper_371f45f6.pdf

Jones, N and Saville, N (forthcoming 2016) *Learning Oriented Assessment: A Systemic Approach*, Studies in Language Testing volume 45, Cambridge: UCLES/Cambridge University Press.

Kane, M T (2006) Validation, in Brennan, R L (Ed) *Educational Measurement* (4th edition), Washington, DC: American Council on Education/Praeger, 17–64.

Kellaghan, T, Madaus, G F and Airasian, P W (1982) *The Effects of Standardized Testing,* London: Kluwen, Nijholf Publishing.

Kennett, D J, O'Hagan, F T and Cezer, D (2008) Learned resourcefulness and the long-term benefits of a chronic pain management program, *Journal of Mixed Methods Research* 2 (4), 317–339.

Khalifa, H and Weir, C J (2009) *Examining Reading: Research and Practice in Assessing Second Language Reading*, Studies in Language Testing volume 29, Cambridge: UCLES/Cambridge University Press.

Khalifa, H, Nguyen, T and Walker, C (2012) An investigation into the effect of intensive language provision and external assessment in primary education in Ho Chi Minh City, Vietnam, *Research Notes* 50, 8–19.

Kim, Y H (2009) An investigation into native and non-native teachers' judgments of oral English performance: A mixed methods approach, *Language Testing* 26, 187–217.

Kinchin, I M, Streatfield, D and Hay, D B (2010) Using concept mapping to enhance the research interview, *International Journal of Qualitative Methods* 9 (1), 52–68.

Knoch, U (2009) Collaborating with ESP stakeholders in rating scale validation: The case of the ICAO rating scale, *Spaan Fellow Working papers in Second or Foreign Language Assessment* 7, 21–46.

Krashen, S (1982) *Principles and Practice in Second Language Acquisition*, Oxford: Pergamon Press.

Krippendorff, K (2013) *Content Analysis: An Introduction to its Methodology*, Thousand Oaks: Sage.

Kubanyiova, M (2007) *Teacher development in action: An empirically-based model of promoting conceptual change in in-service language teachers in Slovakia,* unpublished doctoral thesis, University of Nottingham.

Kunnan, A J (2008) Large-scale language assessment, in Shohamy, E and Hornberger, N H (Eds) *Encylopedia of Language and Education* (2nd edition), Language Testing and Assessment volume 7, New York: Springer Science + Business Media LLC, 135–155.

Kunnan, A J (2012) Language assessment for immigration and citizenship, in Fulcher, G and Davidson, F (Eds) *The Routledge Handbook of Language Testing*, London: Routledge, 162–177.

Lacroix, N (1999) Macrostructure construction and organisation in the processing of multiple text passages, *Instructional Science* 27, 221–233.

Larsen-Freeman, D and Long, M H (1991) *An Introduction to Second Language Acquisition Research*, New York: Longman.

Lave, J and Wenger, E (1991) *Situated Learning Legitimate Peripheral Participation*, Cambridge: Cambridge University Press.

Lazaraton, A (2002) *A Qualitative Approach to the Validation of Oral Language Tests*, Studies in Language Testing Volume 14, Cambridge: UCLES/ Cambridge University Press.

Lazaraton, A and Davis, L (2006) *An analysis of candidate language output on the PET Speaking test standardisation videos*, Cambridge: Cambridge English Language Assessment internal report.

Lazaraton, A and Davis, L (2007a) *An analysis of candidate language output on the FCE Speaking test standardisation videos*, Cambridge: Cambridge ESOL internal report.

Lazaraton, A and Davis, L (2007b) *An analysis of candidate language output on the PET Speaking test standardisation videos*, Cambridge: Cambridge ESOL internal report.

LeCompte, M D (2009) Trends in research on teaching: An historical and critical overview, in Saha, I J and Dworkin, A G (Eds) *International Handbook of Research on Teachers and Teaching*, New York: Springer Science + Business Media LLC, 25–60.

Lee, Y and Greene, J C (2007) The predictive validity of an ESL placement test: A mixed methods approach, *Journal of Mixed Methods Research* 1 (4), 366–389.

Leeuw, E D (2008) Choosing the method of data collection, in Leeuw, E D, Hox, J J and Dillman, D A (Eds) *International Handbook of Survey Methodology*, New York: Lawrence Erlbaum Associates, 113–135.

Lewin, S, Glenton, C and Oxman, A (2009) Use of qualitative methods alongside randomized controlled trials of complex healthcare interventions: methodological study, *BMJ* 339.

Li S, Marquart J M and Zercher C (2000) Conceptual issues and analytic strategies in mixed-methods studies of preschool inclusion, *Journal of Early Intervention* 23 (2), 116-132.

Lim, G S (2013) *First and Advanced Revised Writing Tasks Trial 3*, Cambridge: Cambridge English internal report.

Lim, G S and Vice, M (2012) *Validating Revised CAE Writing Tasks Trial 1*, Cambridge: Cambridge ESOL internal report.

Lim, G S, Geranpayeh, A, Khalifa, H and Buckendahl, C W (2013) Standard setting to an international reference framework: Implications for theory and practice, *International Journal of Testing* 13 (1), 32–49.

Linacre, M (2006) *Facets Rasch Measurement Computer Program*, Chicago: Winsteps.

Lincoln, Y S and Guba, E G (1985) *Naturalistic Inquiry*, Beverly Hills: Sage.

Lincoln, Y S and Guba, E G (1994) Paradigmatic controversies, contradictions, and emerging confluences, in Denzin, N K and Lincoln, Y S (Eds) *Handbook of Qualitative Research*, Thousand Oaks: Sage, 163–188.

Lincoln, Y S, Lynham, S. A and Guba, E G (2011) Paradigmatic controversies, contradictions, and emerging confluences, revisited, in Denzin, N K and Lincoln, Y S (Eds) *The SAGE Handbook of Qualitative Research*, Los Angeles: Sage, 97-128.

Long, M H (1983) Native speaker/Non-native speaker conversation in the second language classroom, in Clarke, M A and Hanscombe, J (Eds) *On TESOL '82: Pacific Perspectives on Language Learning and Teaching,* Washington, DC: TESOL, 207–225.

Long, M H (2005) Methodological issues in learner needs analysis, in Long, M H (Ed) *Second Language Needs Analysis*, Cambridge: Cambridge University Press, 19–79.

Machin, D (2007) *Introduction to Multimodal Analysis*, London: Bloomsbury.

Magid, M (2009) The L2 motivational self system from a Chinese perspective: A mixed methods study, *Journal of Applied Linguistics* 6 (1), 69–90.

Maxwell, J A (2012) *A Realist Approach for Qualitative Research*, Los Angeles: Sage.

Maxwell, J A (2013) *Qualitative Research Design, An Interactive Approach* (3rd Edition), Thousand Oaks: Sage.

Maxwell, J A and Loomis, D M (2003) Mixed methods design: An alternative approach, *Handbook of Mixed Methods in Social and Behavioral Research* 1, 241–272.

Mayring, P (2007) Introduction: Arguments for mixed methodology, in Mayring, P, Huber, G L, Gurtler, L and Kiegelmann, M (Eds) *Mixed Methodology in Psychological Research*, Rotterdam/Taipei: Sense Publishers, 1–4.

McConney, A, Rudd, A and Ayres, R (2002) Getting to the bottom line: A method for synthesizing findings within mixed-method program evaluations, *American Journal of Evaluation* 23, 121–140.

McKilip, J (1987) *Need Analysis: Tools for the Human Services and Education*, Newbury Park: Sage.

McNamara, D S, Louwerse, M M, Cai, Z and Graesser, A (2005) *Coh-Metrix version 2.0*, Memphis: Department of Psychology, University of Memphis, available online: cohmetrix.com/

McNamara, D S, Louwerse, M M, Cai, Z and Graesser, A (2012) *Coh-Metrix version 3.0*, Memphis: Department of Psychology, University of Memphis, available online: cohmetrix.com/

McNamara, D S, Graesser, A, McCarthy, P M and Cai, Z (2014) *Automated Evaluation of Test and Discourse with Coh-Metrix*, New York: Cambridge University Press.

McNamara, T (1996) *Measuring Second Language Performance*, London/New York: Longman.

McNamara, T and Roever, C (2006) *Language Testing: The Social Dimension*, Oxford: Blackwell Publishing.

Merriam, S B (2009) *Qualitative Research: A Guide to Design and Implementation*, San Francisco: John Wiley & Sons.

Mertens, D M (2009) *Transformative Research and Evaluation*, New York: Guilford Press.

Messick, S (1989) Validity, in Linn, R L (Ed) *Educational Measurement* (3rd Edition), New York: Macmillan, 13–103.

Messick, S (1996) Validity and washback in language testing, *Language Testing* 13, 241–256.

Miles, M B and Huberman, A M (1994) *Qualitative Data Analysis* (2nd edition), Newbury Park: Sage.

Minkler, M and Wallerstein, N (2003) *Community-Based Participatory Research for Health*, San Francisco: Jossey-Bass.

Moeller, A J and Theiler, J (2014) Spoken Spanish language development at the high school level: A mixed methods study, *Foreign Language Annals* 27 (2), 210–229.

Moeller, A J, Theiler, J M and Wu, C (2012) Goal setting and student achievement: A longitudinal study, *The Modern Language Journal* 96, 153–169.

Molyneaux, B L (1997) Introduction: The cultural life of images, in Molyneaux, B L (Ed), *The Cultural life of Images: Visual Representation in Archaeology*, New York, NY: Routledge, 1–10.

Morgan, D L (2007) Paradigms lost and pragmatism regained: methodological implications of combining qualitative and quantitative methods, *Journal of Mixed Methods Research* 1, 48–76.

Morgan, M, Gibbs, S, Maxwell, K and Britten, N (2002) Hearing children's voices: methodological issues conducting focus groups with children aged 7–11 years, *Qualitative Research* 2 (1), 5–20.

Morse, J M (1991) Approaches to qualitative-quantitative methodological triangulation, *Nursing Research* 4, 120–123.

Morse, J M and Niehaus, L (2009) *Mixed Methods Design: Principles and Procedures,* Walnut Creek: Left Coast Press.

Myers, N and Tucker, J (2011) A developmental English proficiency test (ADEPT): A study in the effectiveness of the ADEPT assessment on teacher candidate instructional planning for English language learners, *Journal of International Education Research* 7, 61–72.

Myford, C M and Wolfe, E W (2003) Detecting and measuring rater effects using Multi-Facet Rasch measurement: Part 1, *Journal of Applied Measurement* 4 (4), 386–422.

Myford, C M and Wolfe, E W (2004) Detecting and measuring rater effects using Multi-Facet Rasch measurement: Part 2, *Journal of Applied Measurement* 5 (2), 189–227.

Nastasi, B K, Hitchcock, J, Sarkar, S, Burkholder, G, Varjas, K and Jayasena, A (2007) Mixed methods in intervention research: Theory to adaptation, *Journal of Mixed Methods Research* 1 (2), 164–182. doi:10.1177/1558689806298181

Nastasi, B K, Hitchcock, J H and Brown, L M (2010) An inclusive framework for conceptualizing mixed methods design typologies: Moving toward fully integrated synergistic research methods, in Tashakkori, A and Teddlie, C (Eds) *SAGE Handbook of Mixed Methods in Social & Behavioral Research* (2nd edition), Thousand Oaks: Sage, 305–339.

Norris, J M (2009) Task-based teaching and testing, in Long, M and Doughty, C (Eds) *Handbook of Language Teaching*, Cambridge: Blackwell, 578–594.

North, B (2000) *The Development of a Common Framework Scale of Language Proficiency*, New York: Peter Lang.

Novak, J D and Cañas, A J (2008) *The Theory Underlying Concept Maps and How To Construct and Use Them: Technical Report IHMC CmapTools*, Pensacola: Florida Institute for Human and Machine Cognition.

Nunan, D (2003) The impact of English as a global language on educational policies and practices in the Asia-Pacific region, *TESOL Quarterly* 37 (4), 589–613.

Oakes, J and Rogers, J with Lipton, M (2006) *Learning Power: Organizing for Education and Justice*, New York: Teachers College Press.

O'Cathain, A, Murphy, E and Nicholl, J (2008) Multidisciplinary, interdisciplinary, or dysfunctional? Team working in mixed-methods research, *Qualitative Health Research* 18, 1,574–1,585.

Onwuegbuzie, A J (2012) Putting the MIXED back into quantitative and qualitative research in educational research and beyond: Moving toward the radical middle, *International Journal of Multiple Research Approaches* 6 (3), 192–219.

Onwuegbuzie, A J and Collins, K M (2007) A typology of mixed methods sampling designs in social science research, *The Qualitative Report* 12, 281–316.

Onwuegbuzie, A J and Combs, J P (2010) Emergent data analysis techniques in mixed methods research: a synthesis, in Tashakkori, A and Teddlie, C (Eds) *SAGE Handbook of Mixed Methods in Social & Behavioral Research* (2nd edition), Thousand Oaks: Sage, 241–272.

Onwuegbuzie, A J and Combs, J P (2011) Data analysis in mixed research: A primer, *International Journal of Education* 3, 1–25.

Onwuegbuzie, A J and Dickinson, W B (2008) Mixed methods analysis and information visualization: graphical display for effective communication of research results, *The Qualitative Report* 13, 204–225.

Onwuegbuzie, A J and Johnson, R B (2006) The validity issue in mixed research, *Research in the Schools* 13, 48–63.

Onwuegbuzie, A J and Leech, N L (2004) *Enhancing the interpretation of significant findings: The role of mixed methods research*, paper presented at the annual meeting of the Eastern Educational Research Association, Clearwater, Florida.

Onwuegbuzie, A J and Teddlie, C (2003) A framework for analysing data in mixed methods research, in Tashakkori, A and Teddlie, C (Eds) *SAGE Handbook of Mixed Methods in Social & Behavioral Research* (2nd edition), Thousand Oaks: Sage, 351–383.

Palinkas, L and Soydan, H (2012) *Translation and Implementation of Evidence-Based Practice*, Oxford: Oxford University Press.

Patton, M Q (2002) *Qualitative Evaluation and Research Methods* (3rd edition), Thousand Oaks, CA: Sage.

Perrone, M (2011) The effect of classroom-based assessment and language processing on the second language acquisition of EFL students, *Journal of Adult Education* 40 (1), 20–33.

Plano Clark, V L and Badiee, M (2010) Research questions in mixed methods research, in Tashakkori, A and Teddlie, C (Eds) *SAGE Handbook of Mixed Methods in Social and Behavioral Research* (2nd edition), Thousand Oaks: Sage, 275–304.

Plano Clark, V L, Huddleston-Casas, C A, Churchill, S L, Green, D and Garrett, A L (2008) Mixed methods approaches in family science research, *Journal of Family Issues* 29 (11), 1,543–1,566. doi:10.1177/0192513X08318251.

Plano Clark, V L, Garrett, A L and Leslie-Pelecky, D L (2009) Applying three strategies for integrating quantitative and qualitative databases in a mixed methods study of a nontraditional graduate education program, *Field Methods* 22, 154–174.

Ponterotto, J G, Mathew, J T and Raughley, B (2013) The value of mixed methods designs to social justice research in counseling and psychology, *Journal for Social Action in Counseling and Psychology* 5 (2), 42–68.

Prosser, J (2007) Visual methods and the visual culture of schools, *Visual Studies* 22 (1), 13–30. doi: 10.1080/14725860601167143.

Puma, J, Bennett, L, Cutforth, N, Tombari, C and Stein, P (2009) A case study of a community-based participatory evaluation research (CBPER) project: Reflections on promising practices and shortcomings, *Michigan Journal of Community Service Learning* 15 (2), 34–47.

Purpura, J E (2010) Assessing communicative language ability: Models and their compoenents, in Shohamy, E and Hornberger, N H (Eds) *Encylopedia of Language and Education* (2nd edition), Language Testing and Assessment volume 7, New York: Springer Science + Business Media LLC, 53–68.

Qi, L (2005) Stakeholders' conflicting aims undermine the washback function of a high-stakes test, *Language Testing* 22, 142–173.

Rea-Dickens, P and Gardner, S (2000) Snares and silver bullets: Disentangling the construct of formative assessment, *Language Testing* 12 (2), 215–243.

Richards, K (2009) Trends in qualitative research in language teaching since 2000, *Language Teaching* 42 (2), 147–180.

Robinson, P (1991) *ESP Today: A Practitioner's Guide*, New York: Prentice Hall.

Rosenberg, J P and Yates, P M (2007) Schematic representation of case study research designs, *Journal of Advanced Nursing* 60 (4), 447–452. doi: 10.1111/j.1365-2648.2007.04385.x

Ross, S J (2005) The impact of assessment method on foreign language proficiency growth, *Applied Linguistics* 26 (3), 317–342.

Roussel, A E, Fan, N L and Fulmer, E (2002) *Identifying Characteristics of Successful Researcher/Community-Based Organization Collaboration in the Development of Behavioural Interventions to Prevent HIV Infection*, available online: depts.washington.edu/ccph/pdf_files/Lit%20 Summary_6900-26.pdf

Rupp, A A, Ferne, T and Choi, H (2006) How assessing reading comprehension with multiple-choice questions shapes the construct: a cognitive processing perspective, *Language Testing* 23, 441–474.

Ryan, C (2013) *Language Use in the United States: 2011,* Washington, DC: US Census Bureau.

Saif, S (2006) Aiming for positive washback: a case study of international teaching assistants, *Language Testing* 23, 1–34.

Salamoura, A, Hamilton, M and Octor, V (2012) An initial investigation of the introduction of Cambridge English examinations in Mission laique francaise schools, *Research Notes* 50, 24–31.

Sale, J E M, Lohfeld, L H and Brazil, K (2002) Revisiting the quantitative–qualitative debate: Implications for mixed methods research, *Quality and Quantity* 36, 43–53.

Salomon, G (1991) Transcending the qualitative–quantitative debate: The analytic and systemic approaches to educational research, *Educational Researcher* 20 (6), 10–18.

Sandelowski, M (2003) Tables or tableaux? The challenges of writing and reading mixed methods studies, in Tashakkori, A and Teddlie, C (Eds) *Handbook of*

Mixed Methods in Social and Behavioral Research, Thousand Oaks: Sage, 321–350.

Sandelowski, M (2008) The challenges of writing and reading mixed methods studies, in Plano Clark, V L and Creswell, J W (Eds) *The Mixed Methods Reader*, Thousand Oaks: Sage, 301–336.

Sandelowski, M, Voils, C I and Knafl, G (2009) On quantitizing, *Journal of Mixed Methods Research* 3, 208–222.

Sandoval, J A, Lucero, J, Oetzel, J, Avila, M, Belone, L, Mau, M and Wallerstein, N (2012) Process and outcome constructs for evaluating community-based participatory research projects: a matrix of existing measures, *Health Education Research* 27, 680–690.

Sasaki, M (2004) A multiple-data analysis of the 3.5-year development of EFL student writers, *Language Learning* 54, 525–582.

Saville, N (2003) The process of test development and revision within UCLES EFL, in Weir, C J and Milanovic, M (Eds) *Continuity and Innovation: Revising the Cambridge Proficiency in English Examination 1913–2002*, Studies in Language Testing volume 15, Cambridge: UCLES/Cambridge University Press, 57–120.

Saville, N (2009) *Developing a model for investigating the impact of language assessments within educational contexts by a public examination provider*, unpublished doctoral dissertation, University of Bedfordshire.

Saville, N (2012a) Applying a model for investigating the impact of language assessment within educational contexts: The Cambridge ESOL approach, *Research Notes* 50, 4–8.

Saville, N (2012b) Quality management in test production and administration, in Fulcher, G and Davidson, F (Eds) *The Routledge Handbook of Language Testing*, Abingdon: Routledge, 395–412.

Schifferdecker, K E and Reed, V A (2009) Using mixed methods research in medical education: Basic guidelines for researchers, *Medical Education* 43, 637–644.

Schnotz, W (2002) Commentary: Towards an integrated view of learning from text and visual displays, *Educational Psychology Review* 14 (1), 101–120.

Schulz, K F, Altman, D G and Moher, D (2010) *CONSORT 2010 Statement: Updated guidelines for reporting parallel group randomised trials*, available online: www.bmj.com/content/340/bmj.c332.

Selinker, L (1979) Interlanguage, *International Review of Applied Linguistics* 10, 209–231.

Shaw, S and Weir, C J (2007) *Examining Writing: Research and Practice in Assessing Second Language Writing*, Studies in Language Testing volume 26, Cambridge: UCLES/Cambridge University Press.

Shepard, L A (2000) The role of assessment in a learning culture, *Educational Researcher* 29 (7), 4–14.

Shepard, L A (2005) Linking formative assessment to scaffolding, *Educational Leadership* 63 (3), 66–70.

Shohamy, E (2001) *The Power of Tests*, Harlow: Pearson Education Ltd.

Shohamy, E (2010) Introduction, in Shohamy, E and Hornberger, N H (Eds) *Encyclopedia of Language and Education* (2nd edition), Language Testing and Assessment volume 7, New York: Springer Science + Business Media LLC, xii–xxii.

Shohamy, E, Donitsa-Schmidt, S and Ferman, I (1996) Test impact revisited: washback effect over time, *Language Testing* 13, 298–317.

Sieber, S D (1973) The integration of fieldwork and survey methods, *American Journal of Sociology* 78 (6), 1,335–1,359.

Simpson-Vlach, R C and Leicher, S (2006) *The MICASE handbook*, Ann Arbor: University of Michigan Press.

Skehan, P (1984) Issues in the testing of English for specific purposes, *Language Testing* 1, 202–220.

Skehan, P (1998) *A Cognitive Approach to Language Learning*, Oxford: Oxford University Press.

Smith, M L (1997) Mixing and matching: Methods and models, *New Directions for Evaluation* 74, 73–85.

Solano-Flores, G and Trumbul, E (2003) Examining language in context: The need for new research and practice paradigms in the testing of English language learners, *Educational Researcher* 32 (2), 3–13.

Spolksy, B (1977) *Language Testing: An art or science*, paper presented at the Fourth International Congress of Applied Linguistics, Stuttgart.

Stafford, B M (2007) *Echo Objects: The Cognitive Work of Images*, Chicago: University of Chicago Press.

Stange, K C, Crabtree, B F and Miller, W L (2006) Publishing multi-method research, *Annals of Family Medicine* 4, 292–294.

Stiggins, R J (2002) Assessment crisis: The absence of assessment for learning, *Phi Delta Kappan* 83 (10), 758–765.

Strand, K, Marullo, S, Cutforth, N, Stoecker, R and Donohue, P (2003) *Community-Based Research in Higher Education: Principles and Practices*, San Francisco: Jossey-Bass/John Wiley Periodicals.

Tashakkori, A and Creswell, J W (2007) The new era of mixed methods, *Journal of Mixed Methods Research* 1 (1), 3–7.

Tashakkori, A and Teddlie, C (1998) *Mixed Methodology: Combining Qualitative and Quantitative Approaches*, Thousand Oaks: Sage.

Tashakkori, A and Teddlie, C (Eds) (2003) *Handbook of Mixed Methods in Social and Behavioral Research*, Thousand Oaks: Sage.

Tashakkori, A and Teddlie, C (2008) Quality of inference in mixed methods research: Calling for an integrative framework, in Bergman, M M (Ed) *Advances in Mixed Methods Research: Theories and Applications*, London: Sage, 101–119.

Tashakkori, A and Teddlie, C (Eds) (2010a) *SAGE Handbook of Mixed Methods in Social & Behavioral Research* (2nd edition), Thousand Oaks: Sage.

Tashakkori, A and Teddlie, C (2010b) Putting the human back in 'human research methodology': The researcher in mixed methods research, *Journal of Mixed Methods Research* 4 (4), 271–277.

Taylor, L (Ed) (2011) *Examining Speaking: Research and Practice in Assessing Second Language Speaking*, Studies in Language Testing volume 30, Cambridge: UCLES/Cambridge University Press.

Taylor, L and Geranpayeh, A (2011) Assessing listening for academic purposes: Defining and operationalising the test construct, *Journal of English for Academic Purposes* 10 (2), 89–101.

Teasdale, A (1996) Content validity in tests for well-defined LSP domains: an approach to defining what is to be tested, in Milanovic, M and Saville, N (Eds) *Performance, Testing, Cognition and Assessment: Selected Papers from the 15th Language Testing Research Colloquium, Cambridge and Arnhem*, Studies in Language Testing volume 3, Cambridge: UCLES/Cambridge University Press, 211–230.

Teddlie, C and Tashakkori, A (2003) Major issues and controversies in the use of mixed methods in the social and behavioral sciences, in Tashakkori, A and Teddlie, C (Eds) *Handbook of Mixed Methods in social and Behavioral Research*, Thousand Oaks: Sage, 3–50.

Teddlie, C and Tashakkori, A (2006) A general typology of research designs featuring mixed methods, *Research in the Schools* 13, 12–28.

Teddlie, C and Tashakkori, A (2009) *Foundations of Mixed Methods Research: Integrating Quantitative and Qualitative Approaches in the Social and Behavioral Sciences*, Thousand Oaks: Sage.

Teddlie, C and Tashakkori, A (2012) Common 'core' characteristics of mixed methods research: a review of critical issues and call for greater convergence, *American Behavioral Scientist* 56, 774–788.

ten Have, P (1999) *Doing Conversation Analysis*, London: Sage.

Thighe, D (2005) *ILEC May 2005 Trial Summary Report*, Cambridge: Cambridge ESOL internal document.

Tschirner, E (Ed) (2012) *Aligning Frameworks of Reference in Language Testing*, Tubigen: Stauffenburg Verlag.

Tufte, E R (2001) *The Visual Display of Quantitative Information*, Nuneaton: Graphics Press.

Turner, C E (2014) Mixed methods research, in Kunnan, A J (Ed) *The Companion to Language Assessment* (1st edition), Hoboken: Wiley & Sons, Inc, 1,403–1,417.

Tversky, B (2001) Spatial schemas in depictions, in Gattis, M (Ed) *Spatial Schemas and Abstract Thought*, Massachusetts Institute of Technology, 79–112.

Tversky, B, Zacks, J, Lee, P and Heiser, J (2000) Lines, blobs, crosses, and arrows: Diagrammatic communication with schematic figures, in Anderson, M, Cheng, P and Haarslev, V (Eds) *Theory and Application of Diagrams: First International Conference, Diagrams*, Berlin: Springer, 221–230.

Twinn, S (2003) Status of mixed methods research in nursing, in Tashakkori, A and Teddlie, C (Eds) *Handbook of Mixed Methods in Social and Behavioral Research*, Thousand Oaks: Sage, 541–556.

UCLES (2012a) *Cambridge English: Advanced Handbook for Teachers*, Cambridge: UCLES.

UCLES (2012b) *Cambridge English Young Learners Handbook for Teachers*, Cambridge: UCLES.

UCLES (2014) *Cambridge English: Advanced Handbook for Teachers*, Cambridge: UCLES.

Uiterwijk, H and Vallen, T (2005) Linguistic sources of item bias for second generation immigrants in Dutch tests, *Language Testing* 22, 211–234.

Upshur, J A and Turner, C E (1995) Constructing rating scales for second language tests, *ELT Journal* 49, 3–12.

Upshur, J A and Turner, C E (1999) Systematic effects in the rating of second language speaking ability: Test method and learner discourse, *Language Testing* 16 (1), 82–111.

Van Gorp, K and Deygers, B (2014) Task-based language assessment, in Kunnan, A J (Ed), *The Companion to Language Assessment*, Malden: Wiley Blackwell, 578–593.

van Lier, L (1989) Reeling, writhing, drawling, stretching and fainting in coils: Oral proficiency interviews as conversations, *TESOL Quarterly* 23, 480-508.

Venkatesh, V, Brown, S A and Bala, H (2013) Bridging the qualitative–quantitative divide: Guidelines for conducting mixed methods research in information systems, *MIS Quarterly* 37, 21–54.

VERBI GmbH (2013) *MAXQDA*, available online: www.maxqda.com

Vinh, D Q (2008) *Vietnam Employment Forum: Decent Work, Growth and Integration*, available online: www.ilo.org/wcmsp5/groups/public/---asia/---ro-bangkok/---ilo-hanoi/documents/publication/wcms_144529.pdf

Wall, D (2000) The impact of high-stakes testing on teaching and learning: can this be predicted or controlled? *System* 28, 499–509.

Wall, D (2005) *The Impact of High-stakes Examinations on Classroom Teaching: A Case Study Using Insights from Testing and Innovation Theory*, Studies in Language Testing volume 22, Cambridge: UCLES/Cambridge University Press.

Wang, M, Haertel, G and Walberg, H (1990) What influences learning? A content analysis of review literature, *Journal of Educational Research* 84 , 30–43.

Watanabe, Y (1996) Does grammar translation come from the entrance examination? Preliminary findings from classroom-based research, *Language Testing* 13 (3), 318–333.

Watanabe, Y (2004) Methodology in washback studies, in Cheng, L and Watanabe, Y (Eds) *Washback in Language Testing: Research, contexts and methods*, New Jersey: Lawrence Erlbaum, 19–36.

Weinberg, A S (2003) Negotiating community-based research: A case study of the 'life's work' project, *Michigan Journal of Community Service Learning* 9 (3), 26–35.

Weir, C J (1983) *Identifying the language problems of overseas students in tertiary education in the UK*, unpublished PhD thesis: University of London.

Weir, C J (2005) *Language Testing and Validation: An Evidence-Based Approach*, Basingstoke: Palgrave Macmillan.

Weir, C J (2013a) An overview of the influences on English language testing in the United Kingdom 1913–2012, in Weir, C J, Vidaković, I and Galaczi, E D, *Measured Constructs: A History of Cambridge English Language Examinations 1913–2012*, Studies in Language Testing volume 37, Cambridge: UCLES/Cambridge University Press, 1–120.

Weir, C J (2013b) Case study: A quantitative analysis of the context validity of the CPE reading passages used in translation tasks (1913–88), summary tasks (1930–2010) and comprehension question tasks (1940–2010) in Weir, C J, Vidaković, I and Galaczi, E D, *Measured Constructs: A History of Cambridge English Language Examinations 1913–2012*, Studies in Language Testing volume 37, Cambridge: UCLES/Cambridge University Press, 472–537.

Wesely, P M (2010) Language learning motivation in early adolescents: Using mixed methods research to explore contradiction, *Journal of Mixed Methods Research* 4(4), 295–312. doi: 10.1177/1558689810375816

Wesely, P M (2013) Language learning motivation in early adolescents: using mixed methods research to explore contradiction, *Journal of Mixed Methods Research* 4, 295–312.

Wheeldon, J (2010) Mapping mixed methods research: Methods, measures, and meaning, *Journal of Mixed Methods Research* 4 (2), 87−102. doi: 10.1177/1558689809358755

Wheeldon, J and Åhlberg, M (2012) *Visualizing Social Science Research*, Thousand Oaks: Sage.

Whitehead, R (2003) *Legal English Certificate Test Development: Listening and Speaking Components*, Cambridge: Cambridge ESOL internal document.

Widdowson, H (1983) *Learning Purpose and Language Use*, Oxford: Oxford University Press.

Wigglesworth, G (2008) Task and performance based assessment, in Shohamy, E and Hornberger, N H (Eds) *Encylopedia of Language and Education* (2nd edition), Language Testing and Assessment volume 7, New York: Springer Science + Business Media LLC, 111–122.

Wild, C L and Ramaswamy, R (Eds) (2008) *Improving Testing: Applying Process Tools and Techniques to Assure Quality*, New York: Lawrence Erlbaum Associates.

Williams, M, Burden, R and Lanvers, U (2002) 'French is the language of love and stuff': Student perceptions of issues related to motivation in learning a foreign language, *British Educational Research Journal* 28, 503–528.

Wolf, D, Bixby, J, Glenn, J and Gardner, H (1991) To use their minds well: Investigating new forms of student assessment, *Review of Research in Education* 17, 31–74.

World Bank (2011) *Overview/Policy Report. Vol. 1 of Vietnam – High Quality Education for All by 2020*, Washington, DC: World Bank.

Yin, R K (2014) *Case Study Research: Design and Methods* (5th edition), Thousand Oaks: Sage.

Zhao, C G (2013) Measuring authorial voice strength in L2 argumentative writing: the development and validation of an analytic rubric, *Language Testing* 30, 201–230.

Author index

Lightning Source UK Ltd.
Milton Keynes UK
UKOW06f0457080416

271834UK00010B/341/P